An Ineluctable Political Destiny

Forest C. Sun

An Ineluctable Political Destiny

Communism, Reform, Marketization, and Corruption in Post-Mao China

palgrave
macmillan

Forest C. Sun
Halifax, NS, Canada

ISBN 978-981-99-3145-3 ISBN 978-981-99-3146-0 (eBook)
https://doi.org/10.1007/978-981-99-3146-0

This Palgrave Macmillan imprint is published by the registered company Springer Nature Singapore Pte Ltd.
The registered company address is: 152 Beach Road, #21-01/04 Gateway East, Singapore 189721, Singapore

For my family and my late brother

CONTENTS

Acronyms

CCCPC	Central Committee of the Communist Party of China
CCDI	Central Commission for Discipline Inspection
CCP	Chinese Communist Party
CCTV	China Central Television
CDI	Commission for Discipline Inspection
CGTN	China Global Television Network
CMC	Central Military Commission
CPI	Corruption Perceptions Index, Transparency International
CPIB	Corrupt Practices Investigations Bureau, Singapore
CPLAC	Central Political and Legal Affairs Commission
CPPCC	Chinese People's Political Consultative Conference
CSRC	China Securities Regulatory Commission
CUFWD	Central United Front Work Department
FCPA	Foreign Corrupt Practices Act, U.S.
FDA	Food and Drug Administration
FDI	Foreign Direct Investment
GCB	Global Corruption Barometer
GDP	Gross Domestic Product
HPC	High People's Court
ICAC	Independent Commission Against Corruption, Hong Kong
IPC	Intermediate People's Court
IPO	Initial Public Offering
NCCCP	National Congress of the CCP
NCCPPCC	National Committee of the Chinese People's Political Consultative Conference
NPC	National People's Congress

NPCSC	National People's Congress Standing Committee
PC	Party Committee
PLAC	Political and Legal Affairs Committee
PRC	People's Republic of China
PSC	Politburo Standing Committee
SPC	Supreme People's Court
SPP	Supreme People's Procuratorate
TI	Transparency International
WB	World Bank

List of Chinese Newspaper and Journal Abbreviations

CCTV	China Central Television (Beijing)
CGTN	China Global Television Network (Beijing)
DBCK	Dubao Chankao (Qingdao)
FZRB	Fazhi Ribao (Beijing)
MP	Ming Pao Daily (Hong Kong)
TQSHWZB	Tequ Shenghuo Wenzaibao (Shenzhen)
ZGJJJCB	Zhongguo Jijian Jianchabao (Beijing)
ZJTV	Zhejiang TV (Hangzhou)

List of Tables

CHAPTER 1

Introduction

It has been more than three decades since the People's Republic of China began to implement a series of rapid and radical reform policies and to modernize the country that had been plagued by political struggles, instability, poverty, and backwardness since the early 1980s. Over the years the world has witnessed the rapid rise of China economically, militarily, and politically. China surpassed Japan in 2008 to become the 2nd largest economy in the world by nominal GDP. According to the World Bank, in 2015 China's nominal GDP reached $11 trillion USD, accounting for 14.8 percent of the world's total only after the U.S. (24.3 percent).[1] Until 2015 China had been the world's fastest-growing economy with its annual growth rate averaging almost 9 percent over three decades. Its GDP per capita grew from $312 USD in 1980 to 8068 USD in 2015, an increase of over twenty-five-fold in 35 years. By comparison, the U.S. and Japanese economies grew by a tenth of China's growth pace in the same period. Since the early 1980s China has rapidly become the manufacturing hub of the world and is the largest exporter of goods in the world. With the opening of the state to international trade and investment in the 1980s as advocated by Deng Xiaoping as well as a series of governmental policies and market fundamentals to attract and enhance foreign direct investment (FDI), China's FDI strategy has been a great success. Over

[1] iMarkets, February 24, 2017. http://www.finance.ifeng.com.

F. C. Sun, *An Ineluctable Political Destiny*,
https://doi.org/10.1007/978-981-99-3146-0_1

the three decades, FDI to China has increased by eighty-two-fold from 20.6 billion in 1978 to 1705 billion in 2016.[2]

China's rapid economic growth has accelerated social changes as well and triggered rapid and massive urbanization in the reform years. On one hand, the inflow of foreign direct investment (FDI) created massive employment opportunities in the cities, on the other hand, the government loosened rules restricting where citizens could live and work. Since the early 1980s there have been continuous flows of rural youth into urban centers, who bid farewell to the poverty-stricken home villages and ventured into cities to seek higher income and a better life. From 1978 to 2015, China has seen its urbanization jump from 18 percent to 55.6 percent, more than tripled in less than four decades. The government even perceived accelerated urbanization as a soaring testament to the state's transformation into an urbanized superpower.[3]

Rapid economic development and urbanization have triggered massive flows of people, materials, and goods in the country and stimulated large-scale developments in infrastructure, real estate, transportation, logistics, etc. While rising skylines sprouting in China's large cities have reshaped their sky landscapes forever, massive and large-scale developments of highways, railways, subways, airways, and waterways, as well as telecommunication over the years, have placed China well ahead of many developing nations, maybe developed countries as well, in terms of infrastructure development, city building, transportation efficiency, communication, e-commerce, and energy and resource development. Take China's high-speed railway development as an example; by the end of 2020, China had more than 37,900 km of high-speed rail lines in service, the longest in the world. With a maximum speed of 350 kph on many lines, the high-speed railway network connects all the major mega-city centers in China, providing a fast and efficient alternative to transportation for its 1.4 billion people and its vibrant industrial development.[4] Rapid development and enhancement of transportation and telecommunication have significantly expanded Chinese citizens' access to information and increased their physical mobility. As of 2016, China's

[2] The World Bank, 2017. http://www.data.worldbank.org.

[3] Adam Minter, "Has China Reached Peak Urbanization?" *Bloomberg*, July 18, 2016.

[4] Xinhua News Agency, "Factbox: China's High-Tech Achievements in 13th Five-Year Plan Period," *XINHUA NET*, July 19, 2022. http://www.news.cn/english/2021-11/02/c_1310286160.htm (accessed July 13, 2022).

Internet users accounted for 52.2 percent of the total population, a dramatic increase from 1.8 percent in 2000.[5] Based on data provided by China's Ministry of Industry and Information Technology, China's mobile phone users exceeded 1.3 billion in 2015—nearly everyone in China owns a mobile phone, of whom 29.6 percent are 4G users.[6] The numbers of both Internet and mobile phone users undoubtedly rank China as one of the most connected countries in the world. While innovation and technologies of electronic money payment and cash transfer originated in the West, their applications and utilizations have been further optimized and innovated in today's China. Nowadays Chinese consumers are definitely the most financially connected and technologically abled consumer group in the world in terms of mobile payment methods and money transfer alternatives—using their smartphones they can make almost any payments while shopping either online or in store and transfer money with great ease and efficiency, either between bank accounts or person-to-person. The giants of the banking world such as JPMorgan Chase and Goldman Sachs are starting to publicly acknowledge the innovation and dominance of mobile payment methods originated in China, in particular, Tencent's Tenpay and Alibaba Group's Alipay. In comparison to JPMorgan Chase's annual payment processing of 94 million payments, Tencent, a Chinese technology giant, processed 46 billion payments in five days during the Chinese New Year, equaling to 800 million payments per hour.[7]

More importantly, what has made China so distinguished and prominent in the reform era is its steady rise as a global manufacturing hub. Dubbed "the world's factory", China has now become the largest manufacturer in the world, and its manufacturing sector has ranked No. 1 globally for 11 consecutive years since 2010, producing 28 percent of the global manufacturing output. According to the Ministry of Industry and Information Technology, China now boasts a complete industrial system, with 41 major industrial categories, 207 medium industrial categories,

[5] *Internet Live Stats*, July 2016. http://www.InternetLiveStats.com (accessed July 14, 2022).

[6] He Yini, "China's Mobile Users Hit 1.3 billion in 2015," *China Daily*, January 26, 2016.

[7] Josh Ye, "Big Banks on Notice that they're Losing Ground to China's Fintech Giants," *CNBC*, August 10, 2017. http://www.cnbc.com (accessed December 10, 2020).

and 666 small industrial categories. The proportion of high-tech manufacturing and equipment manufacturing to industrial value-added has been steadily increasing over the recent decade.[8]

In parallel with the development of its advanced manufacturing sector is the rise of China's S&T and innovation. According to the Global Innovation Index by the World Intellectual Property Organization, China's ranking in the index moved up from 29th place in 2015 to 12th in 2021, a significant advancement in a relatively short period. What highlights China's rapid rise in science and technology in recent years include its successful launch of Tianwen-1, China's first Mars probe on the red planet; sending Chinese astronauts via Shenzhou series spacecraft to its Tiangong space station; the launches of the Chang'e-5 and Chang'e-4 probe on the Moon in 2020 and 2018, respectively; the building of a five-hundred-meter Aperture Spherical Radio Telescope (FAST), the world's largest filled-aperture and most sensitive radio telescope; etc. What underpins China's outstanding performance in S&T is its policy and investment in R&D and science and engineering education. China now ranks as the world's number one in producing undergraduates with science and engineering degrees, accounting for almost one-quarter of the global total. In addition, China now has outperformed any other country apart from the U.S. in producing scientific publications and is the world leader in terms of patent applications, making up 40 percent of the global total.[9]

While China has been demonstrating to the international community a huge economic success or miracle over the years and is open-minded and innovative in furthering economic reform and establishing the so-called socialist market system, it has been, however, reluctant to push for reforms in the political realm. Since the early days of the reform, the CCP has been troubled by a series of negative consequences, most of which are unintended from a policy perspective, and social issues. One of them is political and administrative corruption. Concomitant with the implementation of its rapid and radical reform and the beginning of the

[8] Global Times, "China Becomes Major Manufacturing and Cyber Power After Decades of Achievements: MIIT," June 14, 2022. https://www.globaltimes.cn/page/202206/1268083.shtml (accessed July 4, 2022).

[9] Veinhilde Veugelers, "China is the World's New Science and Technology Powerhouse," *Bruegel*, December 21, 2017. https://www.bruegel.org/comment/china-worlds-new-science-and-technology-powerhouse (accessed July 5, 2022).

modernization process in the early 1980s, large-scale bureaucratic corruption began to spread across the Republic. Since then, corruption has been plaguing the CCP leadership and remains one of the major concerns of Chinese citizens. Compared with corruption in the previous periods (i.e., in the Mao era), corruption in the reform era is more bureaucratic in nature and widespread in scale. Public surveys since the 1980s, to a large extent, share alarming similarities in public opinion on corruption and regard corruption as the most serious social problem of the post-Mao era. Corruption, along with other social and economic problems such as inflation and unfair distribution of social wealth, was the primary reason that triggered the political unrest in 1989. Another tide of corruption characterized by cases involving high-ranking officials, huge amounts of grafted public funds, and the moral degeneration of the ethos of the whole society, emerged in the aftermath of Deng Xiaoping's southern tour in early 1992. The purpose of the tour was to further the dynamics and depth of the reform, but, unintentionally once again, it triggered widespread rent-seeking and corruption. Corruption in today's China is no longer confined to officialdom; it has extended to other social spheres and is exerting considerable impact on various aspects of the social and economic life of the citizens.

Corruption in the reform era, in terms of both breadth and depth, is indeed unprecedented in the history of the PRC. Since the 1980s, particularly in the wake of the Tiananmen Movement, the CCP has been initiating and implementing a series of anti-corruption campaigns to fight this politically deadly phenomenon. However, the CCP's anti-corruption campaigns and efforts were knowingly ineffective and, to a large extent, have failed to fundamentally curb and eliminate the phenomenon. Five years after Xi launched his signature corruption crackdown in late 2012, in July 2017, Sun Zhengcai, the youngest member of the Chinese Politburo and the Party boss of Chongqing, was put under house arrest and then was arrested on charges of power abuse and corruption. Sun, a rising political star since the 2000s, was once regarded as a potential candidate to succeed the CCP Party leadership. Sun was preceded by the downfall of quite a few political heavyweights and Party and government leaders between the 1990s and 2010s, including Zhou Yongkang (member of the Politburo Standing Committee and the national chief of the police and judicial system), Bo Xilai (member of the Politburo and Party boss of Chongqing), Chen Xitong (member of the Politburo and Party boss of Beijing), Chen Liangyu (member of the Politburo and Party boss of

Shanghai), Guo boxiong (member of the Politburo, vice chairman of the Central Military Commission), Xu Caihou (member of the Politburo, vice chairman of the Central Military Commission), and dozens of provincial Party chiefs, governors and ministers. Over the years, particularly since the 2000s, there has been a rapid and dramatic rise in corruption committed by political behemoths and high-profile Party and governmental leaders and officials.

Traditionally the CCP, following the perceptions and practices of the Mao era, relies heavily on internal disciplinary measures and political campaigns to fight corruption, coupled with moral and ideological education and enhancement. However, this approach proves to be problematic and ineffective. As the reform deepened in the 1990s and 2000s, particularly since Deng's well-known southern tour in 1992, transition and transformation were inevitably expanded into land, real estate, SOE (state-owned enterprises) restructuring and privatization, banking, as well as securities sectors. As Yan Sun correctly points out, corruption is likely to occur under two sets of circumstances. "One is the presence of opportunity, such as the extensive role of the government as a regulator, allocator, producer, and employer; the weakening of institutional and legal sanctions; and the prevalence of regulatory loopholes and legal ambiguities. The other is the presence of motivation, such as confusion over changing values; weakness of moral sanctions; relative impoverishment; and a lack of alternative access to self-enrichment."[10] It is obvious that all conditions or determinants, both politically, institutionally, and individually, are present in China's economic reform and social transformation process. Corrupt activities and practices have spread across the bureaucracy so widely and deeply that ordinary Chinese citizens have grown increasingly skeptical of and concerned about the integrity of the government and the ethics and honesty of governmental officials. According to a report by BBC, the CCP's corruption watchdog—the Central Commission for Discipline Inspection—announced in December 2016 that since 2013 more than one million officials had been caught and punished for corruption, ranging from low-ranking officials to top central ministers, as well as individuals of the business and media establishments. Today, various platforms of social media such as Weibo and WeChat have become popular forums for ordinary citizens to communicate and disseminate

[10] Yan Sun, *Corruption and Market in Contemporary China* (Ithaca, NY: Cornell University Press, 2004), 4.

information and grievances, expose corruption, criticize governmental non-performance and wrongdoing, and reveal corrupt and unethical behavior and conduct in important social spheres such as health care, education, environment, food, and drug safety, etc. One popular folk saying vividly describes the scope and intensity of corruption in government: "If the Party executes every official for corruption, it will overdo a little; but if the Party executes every other official for corruption, it cannot go wrong." The outbreak of SARS in 2003 caused devastating consequences both domestically and internationally, but the epidemic inspired political humor among Chinese people to satirize bureaucratic corruption: "Lavish dinner and wining, the Party cannot cure it, SARS did it. Public-funded sightseeing, the Party cannot cure it, SARS did it. A sea of documents and meetings, the Party cannot cure it, SARS did it. Deceiving those above and cheating those below, the Party cannot cure it, SARS did it. Frequenting prostitutes, the Party cannot cure it, SARS did it."[11] A recent widely circulated folk saying among social media compares the income-generating potential among the graduates of the top Chinese universities and jokingly and ironically puts the Central Party School, the CCP's training institute for high-ranking Party officials, on top of the most prestigious universities in China, such as Tsinghua University, Beijing University, the People's University, Fudan University, and so on. The saying goes on to describe that being a provincial or city Party boss is perceived to be the most prestigious and affluent occupation that would enable the officeholders to amass immense wealth in no time.

The dominance and monopoly of the Party and government in legislation and regulation, resource allocation, land distribution, and infrastructure and development always function as a strong inducement or enabler for rampant rent-seeking and corruption in the bureaucracy. As more sectors have been put on the state's drawing board for reforming, restructuring, and market mechanism integration, more loopholes, procedural ambiguities, and hence more lucrative opportunities and incentives emerged for power abuse and power-money collusion and exchange. As reform and restructuring in land and development, SOE, banking, stock exchange, and securities further deepen, the breadth and depth of bribery, embezzlement, illegal acquisition and misappropriation of state assets, as well as stock and securities frauds, have elevated to a new high and the

[11] Ibid., 2.

value and size of the funds involved in corrupt and criminal activities have reached an alarming and unprecedented extent and scope since 1949. Amassing tremendous wealth overnight through corruption and collusions in land and real estate, infrastructure, finance, and securities was no longer an illusion or daydream. As per Western scholars, reform era China may have presented the rarest opportunities to amass a quick fortune in human history. Fairy tales of fortune-making abound, vividly describing how unlawful businessmen, with the help of their colluders or partners in government, rapidly became extremely rich in the reform era. In sharp contrast, however, tens of millions of laid-off workers of the state-owned enterprises and their families became impoverished as SOEs proceeded to the restructuring and privatization phase. It is the increasingly widened income distribution gap and unfairness in social justice in Chinese society that have aroused widespread skepticism and concerns over the reform itself as well as bitter grievances and public anger toward bureaucratic and business corruption. According to a report by the Beijing University Institute of Social Science Survey in 2014, the income disparity that has been increasingly broadening since the 1990s started to show a clear trend toward polarization and one percent of China's population control one-third of the country's wealth. China's Gini Coefficients, a widely used economic inequality indicator, had grown sharply over the past two decades. In 1994, the Gini coefficient for family net worth was around 0.45, whereas by 2012 the coefficient had risen to a shockingly 0.73. It is known that societies with a Gini coefficient of over 0.4 tend to be vulnerable to increased risks of widespread social unrest.[12] Corruption is obviously a crucial contributing factor to the state's rapidly worsening income inequality and growing public discontent toward the regime in reform China.

The new century has witnessed a dramatic increase in the size or value of bribery, embezzlement, and public funds misappropriation. While big cases entailing dozens of millions of yuan may subject corrupt officials to the death penalty or life imprisonment in the 1980s and 1990s, corrupt cases involving hundreds of millions of yuan are no longer uncommon in the new century. In contrast to the severity of the punishment in the early period, senior Party chiefs and high-ranking government officials implicated in major cases are often sentenced to life imprisonment rather than

[12] Jonathan Kaiman, "China gets richer but more unequal," *The Guardian*, July 28, 2014.

capital punishment. As the CCP and Chinese scholars acknowledge, while the returns for being corrupt have increased dramatically in the new phase of the reform, the risk and cost of being corrupt have actually diminished. This may constitute an ongoing challenge for the Party's anti-corruption institutions and control efforts. A study reveals that in the latter half of the 1990s, the economic loss caused by corruption in the form of welfare and benefits may account for 13.2–16.8 percent of GDP.[13]

Widespread corruption has been exerting devastating influence over the society and, as a result, the social ethos, moral standards, and norms of Chinese culture have deteriorated to an unprecedented low level in the post-Mao era. As the income distribution gap increasingly broadens, people who have been economically left behind tend to play catchup by deploying all means, licit or illicit. As a popular adage goes, no official will choose to be clean if they are provided with venal opportunities. This saying, to a large extent, vividly describes not only the mentality and psychology of the bureaucrats but also the average people in almost every walk of life. Unethical, immoral, and even unlawful behavior, means, and practices in seeking gains and profits have become new normal, and as a popular proverb puts it, nowadays there is hardly any "clean soil" left for honesty and integrity. It may not be an overstatement that the Chinese social moral and ethos are currently in a state of crisis, due largely to rampant corruption, severe social wealth inequality, and other social injustice. In the early years of the reform, sectors responsible for the provision of public goods and social services such as housing, electricity, communication, health, education, etc. used their monopoly positions to generate excessive profits through manipulation, extortion, and graft. The often-voracious behavior of the companies has led to various utilities being dubbed "tigers", such as "housing tiger", "electricity tiger" and so on, referring to the way the personnel took advantage of their monopolistic authority to make questionable and corrupt money.[14] The traditional and deep-rooted respect for teachers in Chinese culture is now being thrown into turmoil by seemingly widespread questionable and unethical conduct and practices in the education system as headmasters and teachers seek to make extra income by extorting cash gifts from

[13] Hu Angang, cited in "Corruption Wiped Out 13 percent to 16 percent of China's GDP, Researcher Says," by Peter Wonacott, *Wall Street Journal*, March 8, 2001.

[14] He Qinglian, "On Systemic Corruption in China and its Influence," 2011, 8.

parents, forceful student enrollments for school-run cram schools, and other questionable practices. In comparison, however, it is the degenerated occupational ethics and the utmost profit-seeking behavior and practices in the health sector that has the most degrading and damaging impact on society. Surgeons soliciting or accepting cash or gifts prior to operations, doctors prescribing expensive and unnecessary medicine for kickbacks from pharmaceutical companies, and patients required to take unnecessary check-ups to maximize usage of hospitals' medical instruments and equipment, to name just a few, are common practices in today's hospitals. Lack of occupational ethics and widespread corruption in the healthcare system are destroying people's trust in and respect for medical professionals and the system, and unsurprisingly, cases of clashes between patients and medical professionals, bloodsheds in hospitals, and even murders of medical staff have been on the rise in recent years. As He bitterly points out, in today's China "rarely in civilized societies do occupational ethics sink to such a terrible status."[15]

It may be of diverse opinions to assess and pinpoint the exact stage and scope of corruption in reform China, given its broadly based penetration and presence in various spheres of the state, economy, and social life. Andrew Wedeman asserts that as China's reform advances to new stages, corruption changes form and shape as well, "becoming less based on plunder and more based on the buying and selling of public authority". While perceiving the nature of corruption in China as predatory, like corruption in Equatorial Guinea and Somalia, Wedeman argues that corruption in the post-Mao era was "more parasitic than predatory in the sense that it fed off the growing economy rather than on the economy's vitals". In other words, the damage caused by corruption may be less detrimental to the Chinese economy than to other transition economies, given the strong impetus of an ever-expanding economy in the reform era. However, what is perceived to be the long-lasting effect of corruption is its contribution to the formation of an informal corrupt culture. Rampant corruption forms fertile ground and "breeds a culture of corruption in which corruption becomes informally and quasi-acceptable" in a regime or society and it can "swamp a regime's ability to resist" and control. Once the tipping point is passed, corruption may explode "at exponential

[15] Ibid., 9.

rates as the odds of detection rapidly diminish."[16] As shall be presented and discussed in later chapters, corruption in China may have not reached the level or status of "endemic", but it seems at least to be in the mode of "epidemic".

1.1 Definition of Corruption

The term "corruption" means different things in different societies. Even in the same society, its implications vary in different historical periods. Like many other terms of social sciences, the term "corruption" enjoys no universally accepted definitions. As K. Gibbons points out, "definitions of political corruption have become so numerous as to permit their classification into types".[17] The major difficulties of defining corruption lie in the fact that the concept is so elusive and subject to so many different explanations across cultures and time periods that "a definition incorporating all of the perceptual and normative subtleties is probably unattainable."[18] Some writers even explore the subject in detail without defining it. Robert J. Williams is right when he points out that "the search for the true definition of corruption is, like the pursuit of the Holy Grail, endless, exhausting and ultimately futile".[19] In spite of all the ambiguities and troublesomeness of defining corruption, nevertheless, we still need a serviceable definition that would provide a theoretical framework in which the analysis of the Chinese issues can be conducted.

As this study is formulated to examine and analyze official corruption in a specific transitory society, the definition of corruption, therefore, should be conceptualized to adequately address various dimensions of the phenomenon that both the state and the society condemn as corrupt. The working definition tends to be broad enough to incorporate both abuses of public power and deviations from official standards, prescribed

[16] Andrew Wedeman, *Double Paradox: Rapid Growth and Rising Corruption in China* (Ithaca, NY: Cornell University Press, 2012), 141.

[17] Kenneth M. Gibbons, "Toward an Attitudinal Definition of Corruption," In Arnold J. Heidenheimer, Michael Johnston and Victor T. LeVine (eds), *Political Corruption: A Handbook* (New Brunswick (U.S.A.): Transaction Publishers, 1989), 165.

[18] Michael Johnston, "The Political Consequences of Corruption," *Comparative Politics* (July 1986): 460.

[19] Graeme C. Moodie, "On Political Scandals and Corruption," *Government and Opposition* Vol. 15, No. 2 (1980): 209.

norms, and morality that Chinese society denounces as corruption. This definition would embrace not only the conventional pecuniary patterns of corruption such as illicit power-money exchanges but also non-monetary patterns such as illicit exchanges of power-for-power, nepotism, squandering, privilege-seeking, etc. While some acts may arouse widespread grievances and resentment among the masses, they appear to be "grey" or "white" corruption in terms of official standards. Patronage and nepotism might be two apparent examples in this regard. Incorporation of the concept of deviations from prescribed norms and standards in the working definition would enable the study to conceptualize and analyze official corruption in this specific context more accurately. Thus, this study perceives corruption as bureaucratic behavior and acts that deviate from the duties of public office and the prescribed norms of a given society for personal and cliquish gains.

1.2 Explanations of Corruption

There are various approaches to the analysis of corruption in various academic disciplines, and these approaches probe into various geneses and causes of the phenomenon and explore respective remedies for the problem. As in any other society, corruption in China is a very complex phenomenon, and a variety of factors can be attributed to its genesis. There exist various approaches to the study of corruption, each of which explores a particular dimension of the issue and provides specific explanations of the phenomenon. Many political scientists examine a political system and its processes and argue that the genesis of corruption is in fact embedded in political institutions and economic structures. There exist strong correlations between specific political institutions and the presence and prevalence of deviations and corruption. In particular, socialist regimes with weak institutions are more prone to deviance, corruption, and graft. As the state takes on economic reform and modernization, it can easily trigger surging corruption in the process.[20]

Of particular relevance to surging corruption in China's reform era is Huntington's well-known theory of modernization and corruption. Huntington views corruption as a product or consequence of state modernization. While some cultures may be more prone to corruption

[20] Xiaobo Lu, *Cadre and Corruption: The Organizational Involution of the Chinese Communist Party* (Stanford, CA: Stanford University Press, 2000), 14–16.

than others, but in most cultures, corruption tends to escalate when the states start to intensify their modernization process. Huntington argues that three conditions resulting from the modernization process can cause corruption in a society. First, modernization involves a change in the basic norms and values in a society. New norms, standards, and criteria in a modernizing society regarding "what is right and wrong lead to a condemnation of at least some traditional behavior patterns as corrupt". In addition, the modernization of a bureaucracy and society requires recognition of the distinction and difference between public responsibility and private interest. Such distinctions would label some practices under the traditional value system as nepotism and corruption. Secondly, modernization creates new sources of wealth and power, which, to a large extent, induce corruption. Corruption helps assimilate new groups with resources into the political sphere and facilitates connections between people with power and people who control wealth and resources. The former trade political power for money, whereas the latter is money for political power. Thirdly, modernization causes corruption through "the expansion of government authority and the multiplication of the activities subjected to government regulation". These include not only laws and regulations governing industry, trade, finance, customs, and taxes, but also those regulating popular and profitable operations and occupations such as gambling, liquor, and even prostitution. Heavy governmental intervention and regulation in a modernizing society tend to subject these sectors and industries to rent-seeking and corruption. Corruption resulting from the expansion of governmental regulation may function as "one way of surmounting traditional laws or bureaucratic regulation which hamper economic expansion".[21]

The economic approach to corruption might have been the widely accepted methodology among China scholars. Originating in economics in the 1970s and early 1980s, the school studies the theory of "rent-seeking" and probes the economic aspect of corruption. Rent-seeking is derived from the economic concept of "rent"—earnings in excess of all relevant costs; in a non-economics term it may refer to monopoly profits. Rent-seeking is aimed to acquire access to or control over opportunities

[21] Samuel P. Huntington, *Political Order in Changing Societies* (New Haven, Conn.: Yale University Press, 1968), 492–500.

for earning rent.[22] China scholars apply this perspective to corruption in the reform era. They argue that corruption in this period is, in reality, an activity of "rent-seeking"—individuals "rent" public power at lower cost in the hope of maximizing their personal gain. Chinese officials are both "rent-generators" and "rent-seekers" because they "both generate rent opportunities for others and seek such opportunities to benefit themselves by virtue of a monopoly". In the Chinese context, rent-seeking, to a large extent, refers to "the behavior by government officials or agencies of seeking illicit profits through a monopoly over critical resources or regulatory power".[23]

Tradition and culture constitute another popular approach to the explanation of corruption among scholars in political science, sociology, and economics. The sociocultural approach holds that corruption is inevitable in certain states as it constitutes part of the culture and society, and developing nations are in general more prone to corruption than the developed states as the underlying traditional cultures tend to be the principal genesis of corruption. There is no exception in the case of China as the traditional Chinese culture is often faulted for widespread nepotism, bribery, and corruption in the reform era. As will be illustrated in later chapters, cases and empirical evidence abound in the study of China to support and substantiate arguments and assertions held by the cultural approach. Derived from a culture that has been traditionally valuing family, kinship, and friendship norms and ethos, guanxi networks were (and maybe still are) being broadly utilized by citizens, entrepreneurs, and officials alike to generate reciprocal benefits, both material and non-material such as nepotism, to each other. While concerned with a long-lasting culture of corruption that had emerged in the feudal society in ancient China, critics blame the CCP for its failure to transform such a culture. It is suggested that the Party needs to replace the current value system with a new, stable, and well-articulated moral system to effectively curb corruption in the Party and the society.

China scholars also seek an internal and organizational approach to probing official corruption in the Communist regime. Rather than attributing official corruption to China's market transition and economic

[22] Jacqueline Coolidge and Susan Rose-Ackerman, "High-Level Rent Seeking and Corruption in African Regimes: Theory and Cases," *World Bank*, 1995.

[23] Lu, *Cadre and Corruption: The Organizational Involution of the Chinese Communist Party*, 12–13.

liberalization, in his book *Cadre and Corruption*, Xiaobo Lu probes official corruption in a broader social and political context in which corruption occurs. Lu argues that "organization involution" is the underlying cause of rising corruption in the PRC since the CCP came to power in 1949. Corruption in the PRC under its communist regime emerged as the regime embarked on an evolutionary trajectory in the early years of the republic. Lu attributes official deviance, including corruption, to the CCP's failure to adapt itself to a changing environment in the post-revolutionary period that has weakened the organization's (regime) capability to maintain committed, coherent, and deployable cadres since 1949. The CCP, as an organization, has failed to transform itself through rationalization and bureaucratization that characterize a Weberian model of modern bureaucracy. Instead of blaming corruption as a malaise of a transitional society, which occurs when an imperfect market dictates the behavior of officials with redistributive power, Lu perceives official deviance and corruption as an outcome of choices made by cadres acting within certain structurally formulated confines that are perceived and judged by the organization (regime) as deviant and aberrant. As the regime started to depoliticize and modernize the administrative apparatus in the reform era, "official deviance, which has always been present, became qualitatively more perverse and quantitatively more pervasive". Party officials often failed to put the interest of the regime above those of the more intimate circles, and corruption, under the circumstances, became a routine phenomenon.[24] In the era of economic reform and market transition, in which cadre corruption became more pervasive, serious, and regime-threatening, reform itself, nonetheless, is not perceived by the author as the fundamental cause of corruption.

Some scholars within China hold similar arguments and blame the regime's political structure and power system or arrangements as the root cause of corruption in general. As cited in Sun, Wu Jinglian, a prominent economist in China, frequently faults the "intervention and destruction of economic activities by bureaucratic power." Academics and analysts of the neoliberal school are firm believers in the axiom that "power corrupts and absolute power corrupts absolutely". They, as a school, hold the excessive Party-state power and power abuse as the fundamental cause of corruption and other major problems in the economy and society. The

[24] Lu, *Cadre and Corruption*, 228–233.

Party-state power has permeated all spheres of the polity and society and exerts tremendous influence over and impact on the economy and the life of the citizens. Reduction and elimination of corruption, according to the thought, call for the restriction and reduction of the government power itself. As a remedy, they propose a reduction of governmental control and intervention in the economy and the establishment of a market mechanism, with measures including SOE privatization, protection of property rights, promotion of nonstate enterprises, etc.[25] Others warn of the dangers of the collusions between the state agents and businesses and organized crime at a time of sharply rising income inequalities, and worry that market transition coupled with rampant corruption would lead to economic retardation, distortion, bubbles, and social unrest. Corruption has become a "predatory aspect" of China's reform and the undisciplined state apparatus haunted by corruption is hampering fair competition in China and impeding the reform.[26]

Still others perceive corruption as unintended consequences of the CCP's intended policies. Ting Gong argues that corruption, instead of stemming from certain cultures or social structures, is in reality a "product in generative process". More particularly, in the process of restructuring the society and the economy in the immediate aftermath of the takeover of the state power, the CCP's purposive policies have resulted in various policy contradictions and dilemmas that have in turn led to official corruption. In the reform era, for instance, while the Party intended to revitalize the economy by granting local governments and enterprises more autonomy and decision-making power and replacing the central planning system with a market mechanism, a wide range of power abuses and rampant official speculation had occurred as unintended outcomes of these reform policies. From the perspective of policy outcomes, "human knowledgeability is always bounded by unconscious or unintended consequences of action" in spite of mankind's ability to observe their behavior and actions, and structures of societies are "producible and reformable rather than being given". Corruption control,

[25] Sun, *Corruption and Market in Contemporary China*, 10.

[26] Dali L. Yang, *Remaking the Chinese Leviathan: Market Transition and the Politics of Governance in China* (Stanford, CA: Stanford University Press, 2004), 12.

as argued by this approach, is in fact a question of unintended policy outcomes prevention and correction.[27]

The principal–agent model perceives corruption as illegal and voluntary transactions between two parties (the agent and the customer) with a detrimental effect on a third party, i.e., the principal. A corrupt agent intentionally abuses power delegated by his principal and deviates from his commitment to the principal in an attempt to benefit himself from illegal transactions that hurt the principal's interest.[28] In the public domain, it involves government officials (agents), government (principal) and the electorate, the ultimate principal, and citizens/businessmen (customers). Corruption, in this sense, entails two essential elements: an illegal voluntary transaction between the agent and the customer, and the unfaithfulness to the principal. Based on the principal–agent theory and framework derived from institutional economics, Jiangnan Zhu proposes a different explanation to official corruption in reform China. Zhu argues that given the current Chinese political system, political culture, hierarchy, and governance framework and procedures, career advancement potential or the "promotion likelihood" for an official, under certain circumstances, can induce corruption. Provincial and local administrators, according to Zhu, are agents of the central government and simultaneously principals of their subordinates at lower levels in the bureaucratic hierarchy. Fast rise or promotion in the multi-layered hierarchy serves as a strong incentive for middle-level officials to perform or to buy off superiors at higher levels or to use both means depending on one's "promotion likelihood" and other factors. Determining factors for officials' career advancement and promotion generally include an official's age, education level, local performance and achievements (mainly economic and GDP targets), and personal connections with superiors at higher levels in the hierarchy. It is suggested that officials with a mediocre likelihood of further promotion have an obvious tendency or motivation to engage in corrupt activities. Comparatively, they are worse off than the rising stars as the high performers often have some distinct advantages that others do not have; on the other hand, they are better off than the laggards as the low performers' chances for further promotion are nil.

[27] Ting Gong, *The Politics of Corruption in Contemporary China: An Analysis of Policy Outcomes* (Westport: Praeger Publishers, 1994), 121–132; 149–162.

[28] Osvaldo H. Schenone, "An Economic Approach to Corruption," Universidad de San Andres, 2002.

The mediocre performers would bet on all means including corruption to come up with more advantages and to cultivate more personal connections, possibly through bribes, to facilitate and secure a promotion.[29] There has been a growing trend of buying and selling public offices in the Chinese officialdom in the reform era and this phenomenon is justifiably an attributing factor to the tendency.

In contrast to the views and arguments of neoliberal scholars, the CCP leadership and the so-called New Left scholars in China trace the genesis of corruption from other sources. Scholars of the school fault the weakening of state institutions and capacity for widespread corruption since the reform, and criticize the central government's "blind faith" and zeal in a market system and mechanism, especially after 1992, for the deterioration of state authority and loss of control over local governments. Some scholars in the New Right camp, however, also acknowledge the obvious causal linkages between deteriorating institutions and surging corruption in the reform era. While many studies of Chinese corruption attribute the problem to structural causes or factors such as institutions and policies, a few recent studies link increasing corrupt practices such as abuses in state enterprise reform, managerial corruption and labor protests, and other deviations to the intensified implementation of reform policies in the post-1992 period.[30]

The CCP regime holds a quite different perspective on the genesis of corruption. The CCP leadership mainly takes an ideological approach to tackling the problem. According to this approach, corruption, first of all, is the moral degeneration of individual officials; and then ideological contamination in general and a bourgeois decadent ideology in particular is perceived to be another major cause. In their view, capitalist mentality and lifestyle are in fact synonyms of corruption. Therefore, "the corrosive capitalist ideologies and values" have often been blamed in both Mao's era and the reform period for corroding the Party members and cadres. This approach also relies one-sidedly on countermeasures that are ideologically oriented to combat corruption. The CCP leadership often requires leading cadres to "conscientiously enhance their personal moral and ideological standards" in order to effectively resist the corrosive influence of

[29] Jiangnan Zhu, "Officials' Promotion Likelihood and Regional Variation of Corruption in China," A Ph.D. Dissertation, Northwestern University, December 2008.

[30] Sun, *Corruption and Market in Contemporary China*, 7–9.

bourgeois ideology. Political movements and ideological education are therefore important means to accomplish this end. Due to its overemphasis on ideological and moral factors and negligence of the systemic defects inherent in the political system and the economic structure, this approach has failed to reveal the root causes of corruption and hence seems ineffective and incapable of eradicating bureaucratic corruption.

Does corruption in China, like corruption in other developing nations as Huntington predicts, correlate with the process of modernization and market transition? Are China's political system and institutions, like other communist regimes, the root causes of the persistent and pervasive corruption particularly in the new regime? Is the Chinese culture particularly prone to corruption? How can we effectively curb bureaucratic corruption under the circumstance of the deepened economic reform? Is Xi' Jinping's signature corruption crackdown able to eradicate the problem and is it endurable in the long run? The questions to be raised here may be endless. It seems perplexing that in China there has been limited systematic research ever conducted on this subject, although everybody is talking about and denouncing corruption. According to Jean-Louis Rocca, "analyses so far often only reveal various cases of corruption and conclude by commenting on the retrograde aspect of the Chinese state". These articles seem to be "too static—not considering the historical and cultural dimensions of politics—and too superficial— just concentrating on anecdotal aspects of corruption".[31] Although Rocca's assessment may seem somewhat outdated, his view may still be relevant to the mainstream approach of state propaganda on the subject. Since the official or orthodox diagnosis of the phenomenon, though ambiguous and even misleading, might have predetermined the theoretical framework of the research on the subject, there still exist some degree of political risks that go along with research on corruption if one digs too deep into the subject. This may prevent scholars and observers within China from tracing sources and seeking answers that may point the direction toward the political system and institutions of the state.

[31] Jean-Louis Rocca, "Corruption and its Shadow: An Anthropological View of Corruption in China," *The China Quarterly* No. 130 (1992).

1.3 Study Approach and Structure

While acknowledging the relevance of other perspectives to the analysis of corruption, this study takes a holistic approach to tracing the sources and to determining the genesis of official corruption in modern China. Among various theories and perspectives on the origin of the degradation, the study mainly focuses on the structural/institutional approach to the scrutiny of malfeasance. Structuralism is a broad concept that concerns "concepts of societies, institutions, and social groups of various kinds where these entities are viewed as sui generis wholes, irreducible to their parts", and is embodied in several different approaches to corruption.[32] Unlike the modernization approach that views corruption as a by-product of the social and economic development of a society at certain stages and focuses on external, or socioeconomic, structural—the main approach adopted by this study—explores genesis of corruption through systemic and institutional attributes, i.e., internal, or organizational, structures. It holds that certain political systems and bureaucratic structures are more prone to corruption due to some inherent structural defects. In other words, the root causes of corruption lie in these systems and structures themselves, and the incidence and level of corruption might have been predetermined by attributes and characteristics inherent in these organizational structures. Kenneth Jowitt views corruption in communist states as "innate in a state structure built along Leninist organizational lines". He further points out that three factors contribute to corruption in communist regimes: (1) the existence of "a composite of heroic, status, and secular orientation"; (2) institutional emphasis on some components that associate with bureaucratic hierarchy such as privilege, power, and status; and (3) lack of a sense of "public domain" that minimizes the state's "commitment to society".[33] Jowitt's analysis is correct but lacks comprehensiveness. He has failed to answer the question of where and how these structural characteristics have been generated and to reveal more crucial systemic factors conducive to bureaucratic corruption in communist states.

This study is based on a multi-causal model that seeks to substantiate the institutional and structural approaches to corruption by providing

[32] Gong, *The Politics of Corruption in Contemporary China*, 27.

[33] Stephen K. Ma, "Reform Corruption: A Discussion on China's Current Development," *Pacific Affairs* Vol. 62, No. 1 (Spring 1989): 43–44.

a comprehensive analysis of official corruption in post-Mao China. It argues that, though a variety of factors attribute to the genesis and spread of corruption especially in the reform era, the root causes of the issue lie in China's social system and political and economic structures. The main argument of this study is threefold: (1) China's public ownership of the means of production under the communist regime and the traditional political culture have predetermined the nature, potential scope, and the persistence of certain corrupt practices; (2) the political system and the bureaucratic structure vest party officials with excessive discretionary power on one hand, on the other hand, the economic reform and a series of unsophisticated reform policies and programs rendered them abundant opportunities and incentives for power abuse for personal gain; and (3) the lack of an effective power-constraining mechanism and the absence of a democratic supervisory system—a crucial component of a system of checks and balances in a political regime—aimed to countervail and balance the increasingly decentralized economic power at local level in changing conditions have made the bureaucracy more susceptible to corruption. Moreover, what has compounded the dilemma is the "partial reform trap" that the Party-state is currently stuck in. The conflict between an increasingly liberated economy and a virtually untouched political institution can be traced to the geneses of new problems and challenges and therefore warrants systemic reconfiguration of institutions and governance to emancipate the regime from the trap. When boiling down to corruption control, the same argument holds—systemic corruption calls for systemic institutions and solutions rather than one-sidedly and heavy reliance on enforcement and punishment.

This study also probes the traditional and cultural domain of the phenomenon in an effort to contribute to and substantiate the socio-cultural approach to the explanation of corruption. As illustrated in numerous cases of corruption in reform China, traditional norms and values as well as cultural attributes prove to act as powerful, though not dominant, contributing factors that are conducive to corruption. With the adoption of the Western governance and managerial frameworks and gradual commercialization of patron–client relationships, the influence of traditional norms and the utility of "guanxi" networks seem to be fading and retreating in the post-Mao era. However, as characteristic attributes of corruption in both imperial and modern China, traditional and cultural norms and beliefs prove to have long-lasting influence over the venal behavior and acts of officialdoms across dynasties and regimes.

This book is divided into nine chapters. Chapters 2 and 3 provide an overview of China's economic reform since the Deng era. The economic reform and openness of the country to the rest of the world since 1978 have injected vitality into the economy; however, rampant corruption, on the other hand, has been plaguing the CCP leadership since then. Highlights of the reform include its origin, policies, programs, processes, performance, and achievements, as well as challenges, gaps, and disparities. These two chapters also serve as a backgrounder for the genesis of official corruption in the reform era, laying out the background and contexts in which official corruption emerges, evolves, develops, and spreads. Chapter 3 introduces the common patterns and manifestations of irregularities, corrupt acts, and economic crimes in reform China. The two chapters intend to convey how reform policies and malfunctioning of the government induce incentives for rent-seeking and loopholes of policy formulation and implementation create opportunities for power abuse and corruption. Chapters 4 and 5 are the main body of this study, addressing and discussing corruption in Party apparatus, governments, judiciary and law enforcement. Contents are organized into three parts—bureaucratic corruption, regulatory corruption, and corruption in the judiciary and law enforcement. While pinning down the patterns, actors, loci, and distribution of various malfeasances throughout the course of the economic reform, these two chapters seek to distinguish themselves from the methodologies of other studies by classifying corruption into detailed categories and sub-categories, accompanied by abundant cases and examples of the irregularities and offenses, most of which were major corruption cases that had caught nationwide attention. A major advantage of the approach is to illustrate the breadth, loci, as well as inducements of corruption, originating from either political institutions, economic structures, or sociocultural norms and contexts and also to offer insights into why and how these malfeasances are derived from the defective and distorted institutions and governance of socialist China in the reform era. A portion of Chapter 5 is dedicated to the probe of the linkages and influence between traditional Chinese norms and values and the patterns and ethos of corruption in the Chinese bureaucracy and society at large in the modern day. Chapter 6 discusses irregularities and misconduct characterized by a socialist state in transition like China, such as organizational corruption, squandering of public funds, buying and selling public offices, etc. Chapter 7 discusses the impact and consequences of official corruption, as well as an overview of the CCP's efforts and countermeasures to curb and stamp out the problem in the reform era. Chapter 8 strives to trace the sources and geneses of corruption in reform China through various perspectives and explanations. It takes a holistic approach to the problem but focuses on structural and institutional factors that underpin the root causes of official corruption in socialist China. The final chapter concludes the study. It narrows down to the most fundamental factors that would catalyze systemic changes in China's institutions for sustained corruption control and prevention. While being skeptical of the effectiveness and endurability of Xi's anti-corruption campaign in the long run, the author endeavors to explore various options and measures that may have policy implications in helping make necessary changes to the current strategies and institutions of corruption control and prevention.

CHAPTER 2

The Economic Reform

2.1 Economic Reform

The Historical Context and Rationale of Reform

The Cultural Revolution concluded with Mao's death in September 1976 and the downfall of the "Gang of Four" headed by Mao's wife Jiang Qing in October the same year. The disastrous effects of the Revolution, by 1976, had impacted Chinese citizens from every walk of life. The political disorder and social turmoil resulting from the Revolution had paralyzed the legal system, distorted culture and education, harmed administrative efficiency, held back the development of science and technology, etc. More importantly, however, the Great Leap Forward (GLF), the movement of People's Communes and the Cultural Revolution had jointly brought the economy to the verge of collapse. In a peaceful international environment that favored political stability and economic development, half of the world had been devoting themselves to innovate, develop and even revolutionize their sciences and technologies, industries, and economies by taking advantage of a new round of scientific and technological innovations, whereas the People's Republic of China, however, had come to an almost complete standstill in innovation and economic development during the same period. In this sense, the Chinese, under Mao's rule and the influence of his continuous mass-mobilization political campaigns and radical production movements, had been left well behind the rest of the world economically and technologically, and the nation

F. C. Sun, *An Ineluctable Political Destiny*,
https://doi.org/10.1007/978-981-99-3146-0_2

had lost two decades in terms of time and opportunities to innovate and develop its economy in parallel with the neighboring "Four Asian Dragons" and the developed nations. From an international perspective, these two decades witnessed rapid innovation and development in information technology, atomic energy technology, biotechnology, and space technology in the U.S., Western Europe, Japan, and the Soviet Union. In 1957, the GDP of China, Japan, and the U.S. were $36.9 billion (USD), $30.8 billion (USD), and $440.5 billion (USD) respectively, and Japan's figure accounted for only 83 percent of China's GDP. However, till 1978, while China's GDP rose to $122.3 billion (USD), the U.S. and Japan's GDP had increased to $2112.3 billion (USD) and $973.9 billion (USD), respectively; Japan had obviously made a great stride in economic growth with its economic aggregate in 1978 reached almost eight times that of China. Over the same 20-year period, Japan's annual GDP growth averaged 8.5 percent during 1955–1960, 9.8 percent during 1960–1965 and 11.8 percent during 1965–1970. Between 1955 and 1970, Japan's GDP grew more than sevenfold and overtook Germany in 1968 to become the world's second-largest economy after the U.S. China's GDP growth rates in the 1960s, however, averaged merely 0.2 percent. With respect to the neighboring countries and regions, for example, the economic aggregate of South Korea in early 1950 was comparable to that of Shandong province, China; till the 1980s, however, South Korea began to rise as an emerging economic power in the Asia–Pacific Region with its GDP grown several times that of Shandong. In 1977, Hong Kong's total imports and exports amounted to $19.6 billion (USD), whereas the Chinese figure for the same year was only $14.8 billion (USD). This seemed to be extremely disproportionate when taking into account Hong Kong's city status, its population base, and its limited economic capacity.[1]

The Republic then was stricken with extreme backwardness and impoverishments with the annual income of peasants averaged only 62.8 yuan (an equivalent of about 8 US dollars). It was estimated that the economic loss resulted from the 10-year Cultural Revolution amounted to half a trillion yuan (RMB); to put it in perspective, half a trillion yuan equaled to 80 percent of the state's total infrastructure investment over the three decades since 1949, and exceeded the total national fixed assets for

[1] Author unknown, "The Historical Background of the Reform and Opening-Up" (in Chinese). http://www.wenku.baidu.com/view, September 17, 2017, 4.

the same period.[2] Of the ten-year duration of the Cultural Revolution, economic growth had been negative for three years. Over the 20-year period between 1957 and 1976, salary growth overall had been negative with the average annual salaries of the public sector dropping from 624 yuan in 1957 to 575 yuan in 1976, a decline of 7.9 percent. A rationing system had been put in place by the government until the end of the Cultural Revolution, regulating the rationing of various essential consumer goods such as grains, meat, cooking oil, sugar, cloth, etc. The living condition of urban residents was generally appalling. According to data from the Ministry of Construction drawn from a survey of 182 large and medium-sized cities in 1978, the per capita housing area in urban centers averaged 3.6 square meters. 6.89 million households or 35 percent of the total households in these cities were basically homeless or households that did not have shelters. Housing condition in Shanghai was even worse. According to Shanghai housing data in 1984, there were 44,000 cases in which two households had to share one room, and a cohort of over 260,000 residents had a per capita housing area of less than two square meters.[3]

Apart from the economic hardship and damages to the superstructures, a considerable number of people had suffered a great deal both physically and psychologically from this political calamity. According to statistics, 2.9 million people were prosecuted for politically oriented "crimes" during the period, among whom many were imprisoned, killed or sent into internal exile.[4] Another source indicates that among the 12 million cadres nationwide prior to the Cultural Revolution, 2.3 million or 19.2 percent of the total were wrongfully investigated and charged during the Cultural Revolution. The most victimized group were senior officials at and above the deputy minister or deputy provincial governor level, and officials who were investigated and prosecuted accounted for a surprisingly high ratio of 75 percent. During the campaign, numerous people were tortured and humiliated at struggle meetings, some of whom even committed suicide to free themselves from these psychological insults. Deaths resulting from

[2] Author unknown, "A Review of the Historical Background and the Great Significance of the Reform and Opening-Up in Contemporary China" (in Chinese). http://www.wenku.baidu.com/view, 1–2.

[3] Author unknown, "The Historical Background of the Reform and Opening-Up" (in Chinese). http://www.wenku.baidu.com/view, September 17, 2017, 2.

[4] Gong, 109.

prosecution and torture were in the range of over 60,000 during the Revolution.[5] Grievances, complaints and anger permeated all over the state at the later stage of the Revolution:

> the intellectuals were angered at the persecution they have suffered at the hands of the radicals; young people resented Mao's betrayal of the Red Guard movement; workers were tired of stagnant levels of consumption and crowded living conditions. All were weary of continuous mass movements and ideological indoctrination, and dismayed by the intense factionalism that still plagued the leadership of the Party after ten years of Cultural Revolution.[6]

The harms to education, science, and technology, and culture were particularly severe. The traditional national university entrance examinations, an important talents selection institution to guarantee supply of quality students for universities and colleges, were put on hold during the Cultural Revolution, which resulted in a long-lasting and severe shortage of talent that was essential and critical for development and advancement in science and technology, industry, agriculture, and the socioeconomic spheres. The consequences to the state's science and technology sector were disastrous. A large number of scientists were wrongfully struggled and prosecuted, which dealt a detrimental blow to the capacity of the science and technology sector. Among the 171 senior scientists of the Chinese Academy of Sciences in Beijing, 131 of them were investigated or designated as the objects of down with. 229 scientists in the Chinese Academy of Sciences system nationwide died as a result of prosecution and humiliation.[7] The turmoil in education led to large-scale school closures and caused a rise in illiteracy rate for the period. A census in 1982 revealed that illiteracy and semi-illiteracy in China were in the range of 230 million, accounting for almost one fourth of the national population. Over the 20 years between 1958 and 1978, social development in China had been

[5] Author unknown, "The Historical Background of the Reform and Opening-Up" (in Chinese). http://www.wenku.baidu.com/view, September 17, 2017, 1.

[6] Harding H, *China's Second Revolution: Reform After Mao* (Washington, D.C.: The Brookings Institution, 1987), 37.

[7] Author unknown, "The Historical Background of Reform and Opening-Up", 2.

stagnant and the quality of life basically remained unimproved.[8] In short, the pre-reform China was facing political, economic, and ideological hardships and huge pressures for change both domestically and internationally, and remained extremely uncompetitive on numerous fronts on the world stage.

A variety of factors attributed to the reform in the immediate aftermath of Mao's era. The fundamental drive for reform was the aforementioned internal political and economic situations. The new Party leadership was impelled to take sweeping initiatives to pull the country out of the crises, promote economic growth, and restore political and social order so as to assure the survival and legitimacy of the CCP. The international environment also exerted considerable pressure on the Party-state. As discussed previously, in sharp contrast to the stagnation of the Chinese economy and the backwardness of the society, the so-called "Four Asian Little Dragons"—South Korea, Singapore, Hong Kong, and Taiwan—had made great strides in economic growth and had significantly enhanced the quality of life of their citizens. The success of its east Asian neighbors propelled the Chinese leadership in a desperate move to seek drastic changes that would warrant its political survival and economic growth. On the other hand, China's relatively independent status in the socialist camp, in contrast to the Eastern European socialist bloc, allowed it to undertake reform without worries about the reaction of other socialist nations. Under these circumstances, Harding suggests that "the reforms later undertaken by Deng Xiaoping were inevitable "given both the internal difficulties and external conditions".[9]

Reform—Models, Policies, Stages, and Processes

The economic failure since the mid-1950s was largely attributable to rigid political control and extensive Party interference in economic affairs, and political priorities such as "class and class struggle" had overridden economic objectives since the Anti-Rightist movement. In addition, the flawed system of planned economy modeled after the Soviet economic system proved to be against the law of market and canons of economics,

[8] Author unknown, "A Review of the Historical Background and the Great Significance of the Reform and Opening-Up in Contemporary China", 2–3.

[9] Harding, 39.

and had resulted in significant economic inefficiency, low productivity, and severe shortage of consumer goods and supplies, and widespread low morale and disincentive for production among workers in urban enterprises and farmers in People's Communes in the pre-reform era. There existed a general consensus among the elites in the wake of the Cultural Revolution that dramatic turnarounds in both politics and economy must be carried out to steer the country out of the disastrous situation. In December 1978, under the guidance of Deng Xiaoping, the Third Plenum of the Eleventh Central Committee terminated the erroneous political line of "continuous revolution under the proletarian dictatorship", and formally declared the shift of the focus of the Party's work from class struggle toward the goal of building socialism through the Four Modernizations. Since the Third Plenum the basic state policies of "reform" and "opening-up" had been gradually evolved and firmly established, and this policy has been guiding the nation to evolve from a poor and backward country to the second-largest economy in the world since 1978. Reform, mainly economic reform, after a period of experimentation and implementation, was further consolidated and designated to replace the highly concentrated planned economy system in Mao's era with the so-called socialist market economy system. The policy of "opening-up" was formulated to steer China out of isolation, and to boost exchanges with the outside world in the areas of trade, economic affairs, science and technology, management and governance, etc. In a broader sense, opening-up also means internal openness in the domestic market. As economic reform phased in, government began to gradually loosen up its grip on industry and commerce, in particular the state enterprises, to allow private businesses to play an increasingly important role in the economy of the state. Privatization of state enterprises, for example, opened up opportunities for citizens and private enterprises to participate in the operation and management of economic entities in economic sectors that had been traditionally dominated by the state.

China's mode of reform and its trajectory of economic development since 1978 differ in various dimensions from those of the former Soviet Union and the Eastern European bloc nations. The former Soviet Union and its Eastern European bloc took a "big bang" approach to reform and aimed to make comprehensive, radical, and speedy changes in the political, economic, and social systems of the state. Russia began with reform in the political sphere which was followed by large-scale privatization of its state enterprises; in the meantime, dramatic economic and social reforms were also underway. Its policy framework for political and economic reform known as "Perestroika" is mainly a top-down approach. China, however, adopted a more incremental approach to reform with a clear focus on its economic system and the market economy. The Chinese reform started with initiatives to decollectivize the agriculture sector and to incentivize peasants to increase agricultural production by granting them greater control of land and farming planning. The success of economic reform in rural China was considered a precedent to inspire privatization and reform in other dimensions of the economy. Overall, this is a bottom-up approach characterized by experimentation and incrementality, a determining factor that has contributed to the success of China's economic transition over the succeeding years. While economic reform proceeded on an incremental basis with prudence and caution, reformative measures in the social and political spheres were initiated to facilitate the implementation of the economic reform.

Over the course of the reform for the past three decades, political reform, seemingly sensitive and elusive under the Communist regime in the wake of the Tiananmen Movement in 1989, had also been put on the agenda and began to evolve slowly as economic reform proceeded. Political reform, in this sense, presumably has various dimensions such as promoting democracy, legal reform, separating enterprises from government, downsizing and streamlining government apparatus, transforming government functions and innovating administrative modes, improving the supervisory system, and maintaining stability and unity. Reform in the social domain is aimed to establish and improve the institutions and systems of social security, healthcare, education, housing, etc.

The initial phase of the reform formally began with the introduction of the Production Responsibility System (PRS) in agriculture in 1978, the purpose of which was to replace collective farming (communes) with household farming (the household responsibility system). Under this system, land was contracted out to individual households; after fulfilling the contracts, peasants had the right to dispose of their excess grain and to engage in nonagricultural pursuits.[10] Implementation of the PRS brought about prompt and positive results in rural China, and by 1985 agricultural production had increased by 25 percent. Also diversified and developed

[10] Thomas B. Gold, "Under Private Business and China's Reforms," In Richard Baum (ed), *Reform and Reaction in Post-Mao China: The Road to Tiananmen* (New York: Routledge, Chapman and Hall, Inc., 1991), 85–86.

was the sideline production in rural areas. The economic reform in the agricultural sector led to not only self-sufficiency in grain production and consumption among households in rural China but also surplus production and income to improve their living conditions. The PRS program was completed in 1983, marking a successful transition in agricultural production relations.

The early 1980s witnessed the advent of economic reform in urban centers. With the introduction of a dual-price system to industry, state-owned enterprises were allowed to sell surplus products above the planned or assigned quota, and at the commodities market, by the same token, the dual-price system dictated pricing of the in-plan and the market (above-plan) priced commodities. Also established in the early 1980s was the legitimacy of private businesses. With the creation of a series of Special Economic Zones along the coast or in major urban centers, coupled with streamlined government regulations, favorable policies, and taxation incentives for FDI (foreign direct investment), the period witnessed a dramatic increase in foreign investment in these regions in the form of foreign corporations/subsidiaries and joint-ventures. These Special Economic Zones have gradually evolved into engines of economic growth for the state and directly contributed to the formation and development of clusters of industries in the inland regions.

The period between October 1984 and early 1990s featured a series of programs to reform the urban economic structure. Measures and programs of the sort included enterprise profit retention, granting enterprises more decision-making power for production, marketing, wages, employment, and investment, relaxing price control over a significant number of goods and materials, "tax for profit" aimed at allowing enterprises to keep surplus profits after tax, considerably reducing mandatory planning for production, creating capital and labor markets, separating ownership of SOEs from management by subcontracting out smaller state enterprises to individuals or groups, and establishing a shareholding system for large state enterprises.[11] Statistics show that the number of materials and commodities controlled and distributed by the state dropped sharply in this period, from 256 in 1978 to only 20 in 1985; profits retained by enterprises had increased three times since 1979; as

[11] Nina P. Halpern, "Economic Reform, Social Mobilization, and Democratization in Post-Mao China," In R. Baum (ed), *Reform and Reaction in Post-Mao China: the Road to Tiananmen*, 41–42; Gold, 86.

a result of price relaxing, items with state-set prices constituted only 20 percent of the total in 1986, in comparison to 98 percent eight years earlier.[12] Meanwhile, loosened governmental control and intervention in private enterprises stimulated the development and growth of the private sector. Township-village enterprises, firms nominally owned by local governments but often de facto private ownerships, began to emerge, develop, and eventually became the rivals of the state-owned enterprises in the domestic market. The period also saw the decentralization of the state/central administrative control and the granting of more decision-making power and autonomy to provinces and local authorities to boost economic growth and experiment with ways to privatize the state sector. After Deng's famed southern tour in 1992, economic reform regained momentum after a pause of three years due partly to the Tiananmen Movement in 1989 and partly to the resistance and opposition of the leftist elite led by Chen Yun to the increasingly intensified reform in the 1980s. Growth of the private economy picked up again and privatization of the state sector began to accelerate following Deng's southern tour. As a prelude to deepening reform in the finance sector, the Shanghai Stock Exchange was re-established in November 1990 after a 41-year hiatus since the founding of the new regime in 1949. In short, what all these reform attempts in the 1980s and early 1990s had strived to achieve was to promote enterprise autonomy, expand the private economy, reduce mandatory planning for the production and distribution of resources, and enhance market mechanisms. The Fourteenth Party Congress of October 1992 formally adopted the concept of "China's socialist market economy", affirming a transformative shift from the command economic system to market mechanism in resource allocation and production.

To facilitate and speed up the process of economic reform, other reform measures with respect to organizational innovations were also initiated and carried out in the 1980s. This is considered part of the political reform to augment reforms on the economic fronts. The most far-reaching move toward organizational reform was the separation of the

[12] Dorothy J. Solinger, "Urban Reform and Relational Contracting in Post-Mao China: An Interpretation of the Transition from Plan to Market," *Studies in Comparative Communism* Vol. XXII, No. 2/3 (1989): 177.

Party and government administration as well as the separation of government and enterprises.[13] Government in socialist countries is generally subordinate to the Party committee. The Party Committee usually sets up a variety of departments to oversee their counterparts in government. Concerned about the negative impact of these dual-bureaucracies upon economic reform, the CCP leadership, first of all, abolished those functionally duplicated departments in the Party committee system. Moreover, stipulations were introduced to prohibit leading Party officials from concurrently holding top government posts. In enterprises, Party committees were no longer engaged in the routine work of the management; instead, their major work was confined to political tasks and ideological education. The separation of Party committee and government also induced the separation of government and enterprises. To reduce government's control over and intervention in enterprises' production and operation, the "Manager Responsibility System" (Director Responsibility System) was introduced to enterprises in 1986. The system granted enterprise managers all-round responsibility for production, sales, operation, employment, wage, and benefits.[14] Another important organizational reform attempt was the decentralization of resource allocation, investment, and managerial powers. Initiatives of this sort had significantly enhanced local governments' capacities to regulate and manage the local economy. By 1988, enterprises run by local authorities had accounted for most of the state enterprises whereas the number of the center-owned industrial enterprises dropped dramatically to only 190, in comparison to more than 400,000 in the pre-reform era.[15]

The period of the 1990s and early 2000s was characterized by continuous privatization of the state sector and the deregulation and streamlining of trade. The years 1997 and 1998 witnessed large-scale privatization of the state enterprises, and all state-owned enterprises, except for a limited number of large state monopolies in the sectors of banking, telecommunication, petroleum, railway, etc., were divested and sold to private investors and groups. As a result of the intensified privatization campaign, the number of state-owned enterprises had dropped by

[13] Oiva Laaksonen, *Management in China During and After Mao in Enterprises, Government, and Party* (Berlin: Walter de Gruyter & Co., 1988), 238.

[14] Jan Prybyla, "Adjustment and Reform of the Chinese Economy," In Franz Michael, *China and the Crisis of Marxism-Leninism*, 81.

[15] Gong, 115.

48 percent by 2004. Also impacted by privatization was the sector of the township-village enterprises. Foreign capital, in the form of subsidiaries of foreign corporations and joint-ventures, had been exerting dominant influence over the formation and development of Chinese industries, and foreign investments, to a large extent, have facilitated the transfer and adoption of advanced technologies, managerial models, industry and international standards in Chinese industries. In addition, foreign investment has also contributed to the improvement of the overall quality of manufacturing, in particular in the heavy industry. The dual-pricing system, which had caused widespread speculation and official corruption in the 1980s, was terminated. Also terminated were the enterprises and businesses run by the PLA (People's Liberation Army) through ordered divestment from the central authorities. More importantly, the authorities took initiatives to deregulate and streamline trade by reducing tariffs and eliminating or alleviating trade barriers, and the overall tariff rate consequently decreased from 56 to 15 percent throughout the reform period. In December 2001, China was officially admitted to the World Trade Organization (WTO) after a lengthy process (1986–2001) of negotiations and a series of changes and adjustments to the Chinese economy as required by the WTO. Experiments of the Special Economic Zones (SEZ) created in the 1980s to attract foreign investment and the policies to exempt foreign operations from taxes and regulations for a specified period proved to be a success, and SEZs were further extended to include more coastal cities and major urban centers such as Pudong, Shanghai. By 1993 total SEZ territory had reached 500,000 square kilometers and encompassed 339 cities and counties with a population of 320 million. Foreign Direct Investment (FDI), after being halted briefly in the wake of the 1989 unrest, resumed and reached $160 billion USD in 2004. China's annual FDI attractions had been ranked No.1 among developing countries for years. Furthermore, reform and liberalization of the state financial sector constituted another major event of economic reform in this period. With the accession to the WTO, China opened up its banking, financial services, insurance, and telecommunications sectors to foreign investment. Restrictions on retail, wholesale, and distribution were also terminated. By 2005, the total output of the private sector for the first time had exceeded the 50 percent mark of the national GDP. Deregulation led to the removal of barriers to entry and increased competition in industries and markets and stimulated start-ups and growth of

industrial firms. Between 1980 and 1996 the number of industrial companies/operations in various industries increased from 377,300 to almost 8 million. Also noticeable were the rise and dominance of Chinese operations in several industries in a global setting. In 2005 China overtook Japan to become the second-largest economy in the world.[16]

The period of 2005–2012 saw the continued decline of the state economy in terms of aggregate industrial output. By 2006, the output of the state sector had declined to 31.2 percent of the national total. The basic modern market mechanism and system had been established with the introduction and enaction of relevant laws and regulations, and also established were a production-factor market system, an improved taxation structure, and a modern macroeconomy regulation mechanism. China has become an influential country, both politically and economically, in the world, and it, as one of the permanent members of the United Nations Security Council, has been playing an increasingly influential role in the international politics and global economy.[17] On the other hand, what characterized this period was a reversal of some of the reform policies and practices of the previous regime. Policy turnarounds in the more conservative Hu-Wen regime included halted privatization, increased state investment in mega state corporations—the so-called "national champions"—that have the capacity to compete with giant foreign corporations in international market, etc.; in the social and political domains there emerged "more egalitarian and populist policies" as well as increased subsidies to and control over the health care sector. The Hu-Wen administration's loose monetary policy stimulated large-scale and red-hot real estate development across the country and directly contributed to the formation of property bubbles in large metropolitan regions.[18] This trend has been carrying over into the 2010s; the rapidly rising property prices have become a major deterrent to industry and economic development, and further polarized the unequal distribution of social wealth among various social groups.[19]

[16] http://www.en.wikipedia.org/wiki/chinese_economy_reform.

[17] Guoqiang Tian, "A Review and Outlook on China's Reform and Opening-Up Over the Three Decade" (in Chinese). http://www.wenku.baidu.com/view, 3.

[18] http://www.en.wikipedia.org/wiki/chinese_economy_reform.

[19] Ibid.

The Year 2012 onward marked the rise of the state's new leader Xi Jinping and the resolute implementation of his signature anti-corruption campaign. The Xi regime is marked by a drastic reversal to the traditional CCP ideology and its core norms and guiding principles. In comparison to the Hu-Wen administration, Xi exercises tighter control over the media and public opinion and has been making great efforts to correct the more liberal and pro-Western tendency in ideology, culture, and society that had been evolving with the implementation of the reform and opening-up policy since the1980s. In the economic realm, the Xi-Li administration has also tightened the Party's control over the state-owned and private enterprises, and at least 288 corporations "have revised their corporate charters to allow the CCP greater influence in corporate management, and to reflect the Party line". "This trend also includes Hong Kong listed firms, who have traditionally downplayed their party links, but are now 'redrafting bylaws to formally reestablish party committees that previously existed only at the group level'".[20] To combat the soaring housing prices and to alleviate the potential crisis associated with the real estate bubble, the central authorities and local governments have issued a series of policies and initiated measures since late 2016 to cool the red-hot housing market and to restrict and control price increases. To fundamentally reverse local governments' over-reliance on land sales to generate revenues for the local coffers, relevant long-term mechanisms and policies such as property taxes are now under consideration or in the works. In recent years. due to a variety of internal and external factors such as rising labor cost, shift of foreign investment to lower-cost developing countries for labor-intensive manufacturing operations, fluctuations of international demand for manufactured goods, etc., China has been facing the challenge of over-capacity of various industries and sectors, and downsizing excessive industrial capacity, therefore, has become a priority of the Xi-Li administration.

Internationally, under Xi's leadership, China began to play a more active role in international affairs, and the current period witnesses China's continuous and increasing influence over international geopolitics. What characterizes Xi' ambitious international agenda is his proposal of the Belt and Road Initiative. Unveiled in 2013, the Belt and Road

[20] Ibid.

Initiative (BRI) is an international development strategy aimed at connectivity and cooperation among Eurasian countries. The BRI has two components—the land-based Silk Road Economic Belt and the ocean-going Maritime Silk Road, and its priorities include infrastructure investment, railway and highway construction, real estate development, power grid development, construction materials manufacturing, automobile, and iron and steel manufacturing and production. The membership of the BRI encompasses 60 countries and the cumulative investment over an indefinite timescale is estimated in the range of $4–$8 trillion USD. According to the World Pensions Council (WPC), the BRI "constitutes a natural international extension of the infrastructure-driven economic development framework that has sustained the rapid economic growth of China since the adoption of the Chinese economic reform under Chairman Deng Xiaoping, which could eventually reshape the Eurasian economic continuum, and, more generally, the international economic order".[21] While the promotion and implementation of the BRI facilitates trade among the member countries, the move is also perceived to be China's strategy to migrate its excess capacity in the industrial sector into the BRI partnering countries. Politically, still others assert that the Chinese-led infrastructure development in the BRI member countries is "out of political motivation rather than real demand for infrastructure". The BRI is "a way to extend Chinese influence at the expense of the US, in order to fight the regional leadership in Asia". As most of the funding under the BRI likely comes from the Chinese banks, there are concerns about the Chinese banks' ability and track record to allocate resources efficiently and to control and manage potential financial risks.[22]

Reform—Performance and Achievements

China's economic reform proves to be a success, as evaluated in terms of a multitude of aspects. The following World Bank's report on China's economic and social development in the 1980s may be more illustrative:

> Over the last decade, China's GDP growth rate has averaged 9.5 percent per annum. Investment was high throughout (averaging 31 percent of

[21] http://www.en.wikipedia.org/wiki/one_belt_one_road_initiative.

[22] Ibid.

GDP during the early 1980s and 38 percent of GDP since 1985) and was matched by a strong savings performance, which contained the need for external borrowing. Industrial modernization increased the competitiveness of China's manufactures in the international market and merchandise exports grew from $18.3 billion in 1980 to $52.5 billion in 1989. China's share of international trade rose from 0.97 percent to 1.7 percent during the same period. The average incomes for the 800 million rural population more than doubled and absolute poverty receded nationwide. In 1988, some 13 percent of rural households fell below the poverty line, compared with 17 percent in 1981. Infant and child mortality declined, the rate of population growth was slowed and universal education of five years was achieved.[23]

The updated economic data by the World Bank indicates that China's GDP grew from $149.541 billion (USD) in 1978 to $11.199 trillion (USD) in 2016, an increase of 7.5 times over 38 years. The increase in Total Factor Productivity, an important measure of output not explained by traditionally measured inputs of labor and capital used in production, was remarkable, with productivity accounting for 40.1 percent of the GDP increase. Its per capita incomes grew at 6.6 percent per annum with the average wages rising six-fold between 1978 and 2005. Internationally China is widely viewed as an engine of growth for Asia and the world, and its strong domestic demand and trade deficit with the rest of East Asia is perceived to be an important contributing factor to the revival of the economies of Japan and Southeast Asia. It is suggested that the magnitude of China's economic growth since the inception of the reform may not have been fully illustrated as some of the large sectors of its economy are not counted.[24]

Since the implementation of the Household Responsibility System in the agriculture sector in 1978, agriculture output grew by 8.2 percent per annum, despite a decrease in land use for farming. Enhancement in agricultural productivity enabled the transfer of a large part of the farm workforce to industries and the service sector, while simultaneously increasing agricultural production. Over the years of agriculture reform, China has now become an exporter of food. Continuous transformation

[23] World Bank, *China: Between Plan and Market* (Washington D.C.: The World Bank, 1990); cited in Ting Gong, 111.

[24] http://www.en.wikipedia.org/wiki/chinese_economy_reform.

and development of the industries over the years have granted China dominance in the industries of concrete, steel, ship-building, and textiles; its steel output, for example, quadrupled between 1980 and 2000, and then further increased from 128.5 million tons to 418.8 million tons in the period of 2000–2006, accounting for one-third of the global production. Its textile industry saw an output increase of 18-fold between 1980 and 2005, with its textile exports accounting for 24.1 percent of the world's total for the same period. Growth in the automobile industry seems to be more dramatic with automobile production rising from 139,800 in 1975 to 9.35 million in 2008, representing an increase of almost 67 times over more than two decades. China now is the largest automobile market in the world.

China's trade policy and the increased competitiveness of its industries led to the rapid development of an export sector. To encourage international trade and export, the authorities formulated policies to exempt exporters from paying the Value Added Tax. Trade policies of the sort, coupled with the undervaluation of the currency since 2002, are jointly attributable to the dramatic increase of trade, as measured by percentage of GDP, from under 10 percent of GDP to 64 percent of GDP in recent years. It is suggested, however, that this state policy guided overdeveloped export sector has to some extent distorted the overall structure of the economy, which may, as a result, hinder economic growth in the future. Also noteworthy are the controversy and allegations against China's trade policies and state subsidies to SOEs; as accused by the U.S. and its allies, such practices unfairly boost Chinese SOEs' competitiveness over their trading competitors and distort trade rules and order in the international market.

While the quotation above provides a snapshot of China's reform in the 1980s, quoted below is the World Bank 2017 overview of the People's Republic of China and an outline of its performance and achievements over the course of the reform of more than three decades, seemingly a brief and good summary of this section:

> Since initiating market reforms in 1978, China has shifted from a centrally-planned to a market-based economy and has experienced rapid economic and social development. GDP growth has averaged nearly 10 percent a year — the fastest sustained expansion by a major economy in history — and has lifted more than 800 million people out of poverty. China reached all the Millennium Development Goals (MDGs) by 2015 and made a

major contribution to the achievement of the MDGs globally. Although China's GDP growth has gradually slowed since 2012, it is still impressive by current global standards. With a population of 1.3 billion, China is the second largest economy and is increasingly playing an important and influential role in development and in the global economy. China has been the largest contributor to world growth since the global financial crisis of 2008.[25]

China's successful transition from a planned economy to a socialist market economy and its superior economic performance is attributed to the adoption and implementation of a gradualist and decentralized approach to the reform so that market institutions and mechanisms were able to gradually evolve and develop to the point at which more streamlined replacement of the state planning could take place. As the reform proceeded, a series of transitional institutional arrangements were introduced step by step, which led to the gradual establishment of a functional modern market system. This market system encompasses the system of macroeconomy regulation, the financial market, the labor market, the social security system, the taxation system, the anti-competition system, etc.[26] It is suggested that decentralization of the central power granted provincial and local authorities more autonomy and leeway to innovate and energize local economies. Local governments are generally in a more advantageous position than the central authorities to develop the local economy given their better knowledge and understanding of the localities. They are also financially motivated to boost the local economy and generate more revenues for local coffers through reform. In addition, China's success in the reform era is partly attributable to an institutional transition mode that conforms to the Chinese culture and institutional environment.[27] It is asserted that the economic model of export-led growth as experienced by Japan and the Four Asian Tigers in the 1960s–1980s, to a large extent, has contributed to the rapid development of the Chinese economy. High rates of investment, particularly infrastructure-driven capital investment, as stated by some economists, have contributed to China's superior economic performance. Internal incentives such as promotion and career advancement are cited as another motivation for

[25] http://www.worldbank.org/en/country/china/overview.

[26] Guoqiang Tian, 6.

[27] Ibid., 7.

local officials to attract investments and to boost economic growth as GDP growth rates were generally used as a leading benchmark for the evaluation of performance and achievements of provincial and local leading officials. Still others explain the success of China and other Asian economic powers from a more cultural perspective, arguing that "the Confucian ethic was playing a similar but more spectacular role in the modernization of East Asia than the Protestant ethic played in Europe".[28]

Reform—Gaps, Disparities, and Challenges

The same World Bank overview outlines the gaps, deficiencies, and inadequacies of China's reforms and lays out challenges and opportunities that the state is to overcome and capitalize as the reform continues:

> Yet China remains a developing country (its per capita income is still a fraction of that in advanced countries) and its market reforms are incomplete. According to China's current poverty standard (per capita rural net income of RMB 2300 per year in 2010 constant prices), there were 55 million poor in rural areas in 2015. Rapid economic ascendance has brought on many challenges as well, including high inequality; rapid urbanization; challenges to environmental sustainability; and external imbalances. China also faces demographic pressures related to an aging population and the internal migration of labor.
>
> Significant policy adjustments are required in order for China's growth to be sustainable. Experience shows that transitioning from middle-income to high-income status can be more difficult than moving up from low to middle income. China's 12th Five-Year Plan (2011 – 2015) and the newly approved 13th Five-Year Plan (2016 – 2020) forcefully address these issues. They highlight the development of services and measures to address environmental and social imbalances, setting targets to reduce pollution, to increase energy efficiency, to improve access to education and healthcare, and to expand social protection. The annual growth target in the 12th Five-Year Plan was 7 percent and the growth target in the 13th Five-Year Plan is 6.5 percent, reflecting the rebalancing of the economy and the focus on the quality of growth while still maintaining the objective of achieving a "moderately prosperous society" by 2020.

[28] http://www.en.wikipedia.org/wiki/chinese_economy_reform.

There are various negative consequences caused by the reform that impede the momentum and furtherance of the reform. Large-scale privatization of the state-owned enterprises and official corruption and negligence led to a severe loss of the state assets. As a result of the privatization of the state sector, tens of millions of state sector employees lost their jobs; due to the lack of a sound social security system, a large number of laid-off state employees and their families fell into poverty. Moreover, lack of coordination and poor planning in many localities resulted in repeated imports and introduction of technologies and equipment, and, as a result, newly established enterprises often led to bankruptcies and closures of the existing enterprises, which in turn had given rise to severe waste of the state assets and loss of talents. Excessive exploitation of resources and energy has led to widespread damage and waste to the state assets and resources. Poor planned and irresponsible economic development, to a large extent, have resulted in severe pollution across the country and have brought China's ecosystem to a situation of crisis. Environmental issues and pollution now constitute a major source of public outcry and anger. As economic growth rates in general ranked the top benchmark for the performance assessment of local leaders, there existed strong motivations among localities to falsify economic data such as GDP growth, government revenues, state enterprise revenues, etc., as top performers were often rewarded with promotion and career advancements. This is the so-called GDPism tendency in the era of the reform. Data falsification, in the Chinese context, is classified as a severe corrupt act as falsified economic data impacts and distorts the judgments and decisions of the central authorities.[29]

As the reform deepens, there emerges dramatically widened income inequality among social groups. Inequality in reform China is partly attributable to the loss of state assets and rampant government corruption. If unalleviated, continued increase in inequality of wealth could potentially evolve into social turmoil as the perceived unfair distribution of income in Chinese society has become a main source of social discontent among the middle- and low-income groups. Widespread corruption in government and non-government sectors such as healthcare, education, etc. have eroded people's confidence and trust in the officialdom and is blamed to be the main genesis of the current honesty crisis in

[29] http://www.pit.ifeng.com, January 17, 2018.

society.[30] Given the sensitivity of the political reform in the context of PRC, stagnant reforms in the political arena, to some extent, have become a deterrent to furthering economic reform and social transformation. There still exist widespread political and governmental interventions in economic and social affairs. Corruption, the subject of this book, has intensified in both breadth and depth since the 1990s, and, rather than initiating fundamental changes to the institutions and governance, the regime continues to rely heavily on rectification, punishment, and moral and ideological education and guidance in its fight against the malady.

An overview of the background and context of China's reform in this section is aimed to help readers understand the genesis, patterns, trends, scope, impact, consequences, and gravity of corruption in the reform era, which will be discussed in more detail in the succeeding chapters of this book. As there often exist strong causal linkages between certain reform policies and patterns of corruption, a general understanding of the reform initiatives, policies, and programs at various stages or in various phases of the economic reform helps generate a better understanding of the evolution, development and rampancy of various forms of emerging malpractices and corrupt acts in specific policy contexts or under specific circumstances. More importantly, a better understanding of the approaches, contents, and processes of the reform may also help generate insights into plausible remedies and hopefully more effective measures for the control and prevention of official corruption in socialist China.

[30] Guoqiang Tian, 9.

CHAPTER 3

Official Corruption in the Reform Era

Concomitant with China's economic reform and opening up to the rest of the world since 1978, corruption in the Party officialdom and government has been on the rise. Official corruption in the reform era, in particular since 1992, has grown more entrenched and severe in character and scope. The number of corrupt cases and the dollar amount involved in illicit dealings have surged to an unprecedented level in PRC history. On its course to transition its economic system from a planned economy into a market economy and to reaffirm the Party-state's legitimacy to rule, China has encountered various dilemmas on a large scale as it aggressively pushed for reforming and modernizing its economy and society. While the Party-state has launched a series of anti-corruption campaigns of various scale and intensity over the past several decades, the effectiveness of those corruption-combating efforts was deemed limited or even fruitless. As argued previously, a prerequisite for the formulation and implementation of any effective anti-corruption policies and strategies is a thorough understanding of the underlying incentives and institutions that cause deviations and corruption.

What are the manifestations of malfeasance as well as patterns and characteristics of corruption across various phases of the reform? What characterizes the predators of corruption and their behavior? Where were/are the epicenters of official corruption in the Chinese bureaucracy and hierarchy? What constitutes the most pervasive and most damaging

F. C. Sun, *An Ineluctable Political Destiny*,
https://doi.org/10.1007/978-981-99-3146-0_3

corrupt patterns and acts throughout the reform era? What are the functional effects, if any, as well as detrimental consequences of corruption in reform China? What contributes to the surge of corruption in post-Mao era? Is corruption in the reform era interrelated to and interactive with specific development policies and programs or specific to the stages of the reform and economic development? What are the fundamental issues that underlie the scope and intensity of official corruption as the reform deepens? In this sense, in-depth explorations and analyses in the dimensions of corruption as discussed above need to be conducted to lay a solid foundation on which sound anti-corruption policies and strategies can be formulated and developed.

This chapter begins with an introduction to the deviations and corrupt behavior and acts in the reform era. An evolving trajectory of corruption over the decades based on limited statistics, drawn from both the Chinese supervisory and judicial institutions and academics abroad and within China, will be illustrated. With the introduction of the forms and patterns of corruption, adequate cases of corruption representative of various reform and developmental stages or typical of various reform policies and programs will be provided to demonstrate the correlations between certain reform policies and the resultant abuses of public power and corruption. The sequence of case presentation will be aligned with the phases of the economic reform to better exemplify how bureaucratic corruption originates, spreads, and intensifies throughout the reform era. Presentation, discussion, and analysis of major corruption patterns and types of malfeasances are reinforced with illustrative and representative cases and examples of corruption across various phases and stages of the reform.

Before examining corruption in the reform era in this chapter and the chapters to follow, we'll first of all look into official corruption in the pre-reform era, including the Cultural Revolution, as certain corrupt or illicit behavior and patterns had originated in the 1960s and 1970s and were linked or attributable to various malfeasances and corrupt acts in the early reform period. Unlike corruption in the reform era which has been dominated by bribery, graft, and misappropriation of public funds, corruption in the pre-reform era generally took the form of deviations, privilege-seeking, nepotism, and other minor offenses and seem to be more elusive to define, discipline and prosecute.

3.1 Corruption in the Pre-Reform Era

The elimination of the private economy through the Socialist Transformation Movement in the 1950s had removed the ground where transactive corruption such as bribery generally originates and grows. Radical and continuous political campaigns and mass mobilization in the Mao era had, to a large extent, politically, ideologically, and psychologically constrained and suppressed officials' desire and motivation to seek graft and to commit economic crimes. On the other hand, an overall backward society, poor economy, and widespread impoverishment presented very limited opportunities for cadres to enrich themselves through non-transactive corruption (as the genesis of transactive corruption no longer existed with the nationalization of the state economy) such as embezzlement, misappropriation, etc. Corruption in the pre-reform era was mainly typical of the planned economy and peculiarly Chinese Communist state and society such as "the hoarding and bartering of goods to avoid the consequences of inelasticity and scarcity of supplies", illicit activities for the collective interest of organizations and work units, exploitation of state assets and properties for personal gains, etc. Scholars attribute irregularities and illicit activities of the sort to central planning, public ownership of state resources and assets, shortages of consumer goods and supplies resulting from unbalanced investment in light industry and consumer goods production, and multifunctionality of public organizations such as work units typical of the Chinese political economy and society.[1]

In the poverty-ridden 1960s and 1970s, and even early 1980s, given the absence of the private economy, market, and private property rights, as well as extremely low average family income level, bribery, or more accurately "gift-offering", was in general very limited in occurrence and value. Popular gifts or petty bribes offered then included liquor, meat, cigarettes, clothing material, wool blankets, etc. Different from bribes in the reform era that are normally paid in cash, cash bribe was of little use in the Mao era as there had been a general short supply of consumer goods, and a rationing system was therefore put in place stipulating the distribution of life necessities to ordinary families in the 1960s and 1970s. The universal shortages of consumer goods and supplies as well as the

[1] Yan Sun, 51.

rationing mechanism, on the other hand, had largely alleviated or minimized the occurrence of embezzlement and also limited the amount of grafted public funds involved to hundreds or thousands of yuan.

Other patterns of official deviations and corruption typical of the socialist mode in the pre-reform era included theft or misappropriation of state properties, waste, squandering, housing irregularities, nepotism, negligence, etc. Organizational corruption in the form of accounting irregularities, false reporting, hoarding, squandering, and bribery seemed to be common as well in the pre-reform era as organizations tended to violate state rules and break regulations in the interest of the members of the work units or for the organizations' well-being. Managers in the lower echelons were motivated to misrepresent their needs and performance and to hide their surpluses from their superiors.[2] Obviously, irregularities and corruption in the Mao era had a finite impact on the economy and limited distortion of state policies and social norms. Deviations and malpractices of the sort, in comparison to the scope and severity of official corruption in the reform era, may often fall under the category of what is termed "grey" corruption. Irregularities such as nepotism and "zhou hou men" (through the back door) as discussed below were often more tolerated in traditional Chinese political culture, and many citizens viewed them as inappropriate or deviated rather than corrupt or illegal. This shall be discussed further in the cultural dimension of corruption in later chapters.

"zou hou men" (going through the back door), a socioeconomic phenomenon and widespread practice typical of communist regimes, was perceived and designated by the government as inappropriate or illicit in the pre-reform era. "zou hou men" took off "as an informal response, by both individuals and institutions, to economic problems caused by the failure of the command economic system", mainly shortages of consumer goods and supplies, and it was a common practice for officials and citizens alike to obtain consumer goods in short supply or to make deals through personal connections or "guanxi" networks in the pre-reform period. Purchases and dealings of the sort were usually undertaken on non-open occasions or through "back doors" to avoid public suspicions. People who were able to purchase rationed goods and scarce items through the back door were largely cadres, including high-ranking officials who usually had the privilege to enjoy "special supplies" (te gong) even in

[2] Julia Kwong, *The Political Economy of Corruption in China* (M.E. Sharpe, Inc., 1997), 69–73.

the period of economic hardships. "zou hou men" had become a so widespread phenomenon that it had eventually expanded from the retail sector to almost all walks of life in the pre-reform China. Concerned with its harmful effect on the integrity and legitimacy of the Party and government, the authorities issued a series of official directives to curb "zou hou men" in the 1960s. While the authoritative measures might have restricted the spread of the practice at lower levels in varying degrees, they seemed to be less effective at the higher level as the privileged political elite continued to have access to backdoor supplies and deals. "zou hou men", as a typically informal and deviant means to acquire things or to get things done, continued to exist throughout the period of the Cultural Revolution. It was carried over to the early 1980s and "rose to a new level of intensity" in the early period of the reform.[3]

In the late stage of the Cultural Revolution, cultivation of personal connections (la guanxi) and the utility of "zou hou men" were extended to social, personnel, and political spheres to seek non-material objectives such as favors, considerations, assistance, and support with respect to job placement and transfer, rehabilitation of wrongfully purged officials during various political campaigns, urban residence, and, in the case of youth, admissions to universities and colleges, employment, joining the military, and, for the educated youth who had been sent to the countryside, returning to cities. During the military frenzy in the late 1960s when a career in the military was deemed a top alternative among youth, for example, how to get enlisted often involved widespread irregularities. Due to surging demand and very limited quotas for military enlisting, only those who were children of high-ranking PLA officials or those whose families had powerful guanxi networks had better chance to get in through back door. "Backdoor recruiting" had endured throughout the Cultural Revolution as urban youth were anxious to join the army to avoid being sent to countryside for "re-education by poor and lower-middle peasants", and those, who had already been dispatched to countryside for "re-education", were anxious to find a path to return to city and to seek better career opportunities. The irregularity of military "backdoor recruitment" had become so widespread over time and had triggered such public outrage in society that the central and military

[3] Lu, 130–134.

authorities had to issue official decrees to prohibit the practice, accusing it of seriously jeopardizing "the prestige of our army and internal unity".[4]

A similar malpractice in the 1970s was the "backdoor admission to universities and colleges". The Cultural Revolution demolished the institution of the national university entrance examination, a well-established mechanism and process to select and enroll qualified university students based on candidates' academic merits and potential. The competitive national entrance examination institution was then replaced with a new program of nomination and approval aimed to bring the politically well performed and reliable young workers, peasants, and soldiers to study in universities and colleges. Under the new system, admissions were no longer based on exam scores; rather, it required basic-level work unit nomination and official approval at the higher level. This politically intended and structured new institution and procedure immediately triggered off fierce competition for university admission nominations among youth who had either privileged family backgrounds or personal connections to local officials. Those who may not have direct connections to local officials often motivated their guanxi networks to broker indirect access or connections to the cadres in charge. During 1971–1976, there had been widespread abuses of power across the country to nominate and enroll political elites' children, relatives and acquaintances to universities and colleges through "back doors". Influence peddling, backdoor deals, gift-giving, banqueting, etc., were prevalent in many localities prior to and during the college admission nomination and approval seasons. Again, backdoor deals of the sort had eventually gotten out of hand that the central authorities issued, again, stern circulars to curb the momentum, and many universities and colleges, as instructed by the central government, took measures to scrutinize illicit admissions and enrollments through back doors.[5] For the vast majority of the "educated youth" who were from ordinary families, returning to city through "zhao gong" (employment in state enterprises) was a more feasible career option. However, given the limited hiring quotas allocated to localities, young people and their families still had to resort to various questionable or even illicit tactics or means to win out of the competition for urban

[4] Ibid., 145–146.

[5] Ibid., 147–149.

jobs. Again, like admission to universities and military enlisting, influence through guanxi networks or simply buying the way through various selecting and scrutinizing procedures at various levels were aggressively pursued by the "send-down youths" and their families in order to materialize state enterprise employment opportunities. In many cases, they had to "da dian" (buy off with gifts) enterprise hiring officials who were authorized to allocate quotas and to make hiring decisions, local officials who were to make nominations, and even doctors in local hospitals who conducted and oversaw the medical examination process.

The ability of attaining consumer goods in short supply or getting things done through the back door ("zou hou men") was one aspect of the official privileges; there were, however, other forms or manifestations of official privileges in an era that was characterized by rigidity of political control, radicalness of ideology, backwardness in economy and impoverishment in society. Official corruption and deviations then were typical of a "socialist mode of corruption", which "encompassed more subtle usurpation of power for private purposes such as official privileges", in contrast to "the capitalist mode of corruption" that mainly takes the form of bribery and embezzlement as seen in the period of the Three and Five-Anti Movement in the early 1950s and the reform era since the 1980s. Similar to what characterizes official privileges in the Eastern Communist bloc, access to controlled, restricted, or short-supplied "neibu" (internal) items was in general part of the privileges enjoyed by high-ranking officials, which largely "typified the status orientation of the regime". Only those who were privileged or well-connected had the prerogative of watching "neibu" or internal movies, reading "internally circulated" (neibu faxing) books or materials, attaining "internally sold" (neibu xiaoshou) special supplies (te gong), and their children or relatives being entitled for or had access to "internal hiring" (neibu zhaoshou).[6] Official privileges had become so pervasive in society in the 1970s that they caused widespread public discontent and impaired to some extent the legitimacy of the regime.

[6] Ibid., 141–144.

Acceleration of Corruption in the Reform Era

By their own account, what a senior researcher at the Central Commission for Discipline Inspection (CCDI), the Party's leading anti-corruption agency, described in the late 1990s seems to be more indictive of the breadth, depth, and trends of corruption in the reform era, which I cited below as part of the introduction to this section:

> Not only is corruption widespread in the economic spheres of finance, securities, real estate, land leasing, and construction, but it also has emerged and is growing in politics, culture, and all aspects of social life – in the party, government, and (nonpolitical) organization. A second trend is more collaborative corruption and corruption at high levels of authority. Cases tend to involve more people, some cases as many as tens or even hundreds of individuals. More cases involve close collaboration and bigger amounts of money, rising to the billions (of yuan). More cases involve leading officials at and above the division level of administration. Cases involving middle-ranking and high-ranking officials have tripled in the past few years. A third trend, surfacing despite the major anticorruption effort by the party and government in recent years and some abatement of some sorts of corruption, is the continued growth of corruption overall. Crimes continued to be committed in great numbers. More than 50 percent of cases investigated in a year are crimes committed in that year. The number of cases involving big sums (da an) and senior officials (yao an) rises yearly. Improper conduct is repeatedly prohibited, only to reappear in new forms. The spread of corruption to executive departments of the party and government and departments responsible for law enforcement and discipline becomes more serious by the day.[7]

Both structural and non-structural corruption abound in reform China. Non-structural corruption includes embezzlement, bribery, extortion, etc., and can be distinctively classified as "illegal" or "criminal". Structural corruption is more derived from the political system and economic structures; in the context of post-communist China, "rent-seeking", for example, is perceived as more structural in nature as it apparently results from the government's systemic intervention in and control over

[7] Cited in Melanie Manion, *Corruption by Design: Building Clean Government in Mainland China and Hong Kong* (Harvard University Press, 2004), 84.

economic and social affairs. Structural corruption is therefore "difficult to root out without a change of the broader system".[8]

The following sections examine patterns of corruption, both structural and non-structural, as well as their evolution and development throughout various phases of the reform. Cases and examples of corruption shall be provided at various stages of the reform to project a formative trend of corruption that has increasingly involved more senior or even top-level officials with ever-increasing sizes of graft and collusive dealings. As types of corruption are grouped into various categories for analysis and discussion, an in-depth look into the manifestations of corruption typical of the malfeasances in reform China shall be conducted as well.

3.2 Patterns of Corruption and Economic Crimes

Alan Liu, based on his research on 275 Chinese media reports from 1977 to 1980, identified sixteen types of corrupt acts. These malpractices encompassed embezzlement, bribes or extortion, appropriation of public goods, illegitimate feasting, housing irregularity, illegal trade of public goods, hiring irregularity, sexual abuse of women, illegal imprisonment and torture, obstruction of justice, reprisal against informers, cheating on school examinations, false models, feudal rites, irregularity in residence permits, and irregularity in Party membership. Apart from some common forms such as graft and embezzlement, according to Liu, others such as misuse of public equipment, illegal trade, and housing irregularity were frequent among socialist states. Still, others such as banqueting at public expense, feudal rites, illegal imprisonment, and torture, however, bore typical characteristics of Chinese political culture under the socialist conditions.[9] Some of the patterns of irregularities and corruption as reported in Liu's article are obvious an continuation or extension of malpractices from the Mao era such as misappropriation of public goods, housing irregularities, illicit trade of public goods, hiring irregularities, etc. However, a surge in the number and value of cases of economic corruption and crime in the early years of the reform preluded an all-out pandemic of political and social malaise throughout the decades of the reform era.

[8] Ibid.

[9] Alan P.L. Liu, "The Politics of Corruption in the People's Republic of China," *The American Political Science Review* Vol. 77 (March 1983): 603.

The Chinese judicial authorities define and classify a variety of official corrupt and criminal behavior and act in the economic sphere as "public office related crimes" (zhi wu fan zui). As the reform proceeds and deepens since 1978, concurrent with specific reform policies and programs launched in various phases of the reform, new forms of malfeasances and corruption have emerged, suffused, intensified, and eventually become pervasive. Consequently, as countermeasures, the authorities have been frequently updating and amending the Criminal Law of the People's Republic of China since the advent of the reform in an effort to crack down on new offenses of "zhi wu fan zui" and to accommodate various changes in the economic chapter of the criminal code. Following is a list of the public-office-related economic crimes (zhi wu fan zui) specified in the criminal code:

Embezzlement

The behavior and act that public officeholder, by taking advantage of the influence and convenience derived from the public power, embezzle, steal, defraud, or use other means to illegally appropriate or possess public funds or properties. This definition also encompasses agents entrusted by the government, state enterprises, public institutions, and people's organizations to manage and operate state-owned assets and properties.

The threshold for criminal prosecution of embezzlement is 30,000 yuan and above in public funds or properties misappropriated by individuals. A criminal case can be established, however, if the embezzled amount is between 10,000 and 30,000 yuan that involves specially designated public funds for disaster relief, emergency, flood control, poverty alleviation, epidemic prevention, emigration, welfare, and other funds and properties. In addition, it also applies to cases that involve odious means or behavior in embezzling public funds that may be less than the threshold value.

Decentralization of decision-making power and managerial autonomy for SOE executives have unleashed a surge in cases of embezzlement of public funds and state assets in the reform era. Diverse patterns and acts of embezzlement in the post-Mao era encompass: (1) embezzlement of state funds through contract fraud facilitated by collusive deal-making and concealment with unscrupulous private enterprises and businessmen; (2) embezzlement through payment fraud via private agents to conceal the illicit procedures of the purchase payments or a portion of the funds misappropriated; (3) theft through fraudulent receipts for seemingly legitimate purchases and expenditures; (4) embezzlement through fictitious and fraudulent overstatements of expenses such as fabricated employee roster, bonus payments, and business expenses, or concealment or understatements of other incomes, savings and pay deductions; (5) embezzlement of state assets through unauthorized and illicit transfers of SOE funds and assets.

Bribery

The behavior and act that public officeholders extort or illegally accept bribes; in return, they render favors or facilitate bribers to seek illicit profits or gains. This encompasses kickbacks, commissions, and service charges that public officials accept or extort via illicit business dealings in violation of state laws and regulations.

The threshold for criminal prosecution of bribery is 30,000 yuan and above in bribes extorted or accepted by individuals. A criminal case can be established, however, if the bribed amount is between 10,000 and 30,000 yuan that has caused a significant loss in state or social interest as a result of the illicit acts or involves forcible extortion or other abominable behavior or conduct.

Bribery is obviously the most prevalent form of corruption and crime in the reform era, and its rise at an exponential rate in both scope and intensity since 1992 has provoked serious concerns among top leaders and ordinary citizens alike. People perceive bribery as a universal brokerage mechanism of illicit deal-making between unscrupulous businessmen and corrupt state officials or corrupt patrons and clients in officialdom for a broad range of undertakings, from as large as infrastructure projects, land acquisition, real estate development, mining rights and permits to as trivial as employment, promotion, and job transfer. Bribery is blamed for continuous and intensifying public discontent and resentment against the political and economic elites as the broadly held public presumption or belief asserts that both strata have managed to accumulate astonishing wealth through illicit reciprocal means such as bribery at the expense of the state. While cash deal remains the dominant pattern of bribery transactions, new forms of this venal malfeasance have surfaced in the reform era that seems to be more indirect, implicit, concealed, and illusive. These encompass commission payments, salaries, and bonuses through fictitious firm employee or consultant payrolls, kickbacks in the name of loans, purchases, and reimbursements with IOU slips and sale receipts attached, product trials, special occasion gifts for holidays, weddings and funerals, as well as newly emerged fashions such as the departure of officials' children for university or overseas studies.[10]

The sub-categories and patterns of bribery in reform China are enclosed to demonstrate the paradigms, actors, loci, nature, scope, and intensity of the corruption and criminal offenses in the reform era. Offenders are not limited to individuals but also include organizations or work units as marketization of the state economy and privatization of the state sector, to a certain extent, have forced many state-owned enterprises to join their counterparts in the private sector to offer payoffs, commissions, and kickbacks in exchange for arbitrary decisions, favors or inside information to win public contracts, capital, land and land use rights, business loans, markets, etc.

Bribe-Offering

The behavior and act that an individual bribes a public official in exchange for illicit personal interest or gains. This includes the provision of kickbacks, commissions, and service charges of various forms to public officeholders in violation of state policies and stipulations.

The threshold for criminal prosecution of bribe-offering is 30,000 yuan and above in value or between 10,000 and 30,000 yuan if the offense entails the following behavior and acts: (1) offering bribes to seek illicit interest or gains; (2) offering bribes to more than three persons; (3) offering bribes to Party/state leading officials, judicial personnel and officials, and administrative law enforcement officials; (4) the offense has resulted in severe loss of state or social interests.

Bribery Brokerage

The offense involves bribery brokerage to public officials. The thresholds for criminal prosecution of bribery brokerage to individuals or organizations are different depending on the value of the bribes arranged. It is 20,000 yuan and above in value if bribery is brokered to an individual or 200,000 yuan and above in value if an organization is involved. However, criminal cases can also be established for offenses that involve less than the threshold amounts in both scenarios if the offenses entail one of the

[10] Sun, 28–29.

following acts: (1) The purpose of the offense is to facilitate the briber to seek and obtain illicit interest or gains; (2) Broker bribery to more than three individuals or organizations or the offenses have been committed more than three times; (3) The targets of the offense are Party/state leading officials, judicial personnel and officials, and administrative law enforcement officials; (4) The offenses have resulted in severe loss of state or social interests.

There has been a surge in malfeasance and corruption committed by work units and organizations that opt to violate state rules and regulations in pursuit of benefits and gains to the organizations and their employees. Certain forms of organizational corruption and their pervasiveness are obviously attributable to certain reform policies and programs and these phenomena will be explored and discussed in more detail in succeeding chapters. As stipulated in the criminal code, there are specific articles regulating definitions, measurements, and penalties of organization corruption.

Acceptance of bribes by Organizations

The illicit behavior and acts that government, SOEs, public institutions, and people's organizations extort and accept bribes in exchange for favors and arbitrary decision-making that facilitate bribers to attain illicit personal gains at the expense of the state. Bribes under the circumstances encompass cash, kickbacks, commissions, service charges, etc. This clause, however, does not apply to non-state organizations such as collective economic organizations, domestic-foreign joint ventures and co-ops, foreign-owned enterprises, and private businesses.

The threshold for criminal prosecution of acceptance of bribes by an organization is 100,000 yuan and above in value or less than 100,000 yuan but the offenses involve forcible extortion and other odious conduct or result in significant loss of the state or social interests. As the malfeasances are generally carried out on purpose and have been authorized by the decision-making body of the organization, executives and other personnel of the organization who are directly responsible or liable for the offense shall be prosecuted.

Bribe Offering by Organizations

The subject of the offense of bribe-offering is an organization, and its behavior and acts are similar to those of an individual briber, i.e., rendering bribes in return for illicit interest or gains for the work unit or organization. The malpractice includes the provision of kickbacks, commissions, and service charges in violation of state policies and stipulations.

The definition of organization under this circumstance applies to not only state corporations, state enterprises, public institutions, and people's organizations, but also non-state organizations such as collective economic organizations, domestic-foreign joint ventures and co-ops, foreign-owned enterprises, and private businesses.

The threshold for criminal prosecution of bribe-offering by organizations is 200,000 yuan and above in value or between 100,000 and 200,000 yuan if the offense entails the following acts: (1) offering bribes in exchange for illicit interest or gains; (2) bribing more than three persons; (3) buying off Party/state leading officials, judicial personnel and officials, and administrative law enforcement officials; (4) The offense has resulted in severe loss of state or social interests. Bribes under the circumstance include not only monetary forms but also non-monetary forms such as provision of domestic or international sightseeing or similar benefits. Similar to penalties for bribe-taking by organizations, executives and other personnel of the organization who are directly responsible or liable for the offense shall be prosecuted.

Offering Bribes to Organizations

The venal behavior and act that an individual or business renders bribes to government departments and agencies, SOEs, public institutions, and people's organizations in exchange for illicit personal interest or gains. The offense includes provision of kickbacks, commissions, and service charges to government agencies and state organizations in violation of state laws and regulations. Offenders in this sense encompass both individuals and organizations. Similar to punishment for organizational offenders in other economic crimes, a fine shall be imposed on the organization, and its executives and other personnel who are directly responsible or liable for the transgression shall be prosecuted.

The threshold for criminal prosecution of rendering bribes to organizations is 100,000 yuan and above in value for individuals and 200,000 yuan and above for organizational offenders. However, criminal cases can also be established for offenses that involve less than 100,000 yuan for individual transgressions and between 100,000 and 200,000 yuan for organizational transgressions if the offenses entail the following acts: (1) offering bribes in exchange for illicit interest or gains; (2) bribing more than three organizations; (3) bribing Party and government agencies, judicial institutions, and administrative law enforcement agencies; (4) The offenses have resulted in severe loss of state or social interests.

Misappropriation of Public Funds

The corrupt behavior and act that a public official misappropriates public funds in an attempt to engage in or facilitates illicit or for-profit economic activities for personal gains or misappropriates a relatively large amount of public funds for personal use but has failed to return it to the state in excess of three months. Government officials who misappropriate the specifically designated public funds for disaster relief, emergency, flood control, poverty alleviation, epidemic prevention, emigration, and social welfare are subject to harsher punishments.

The thresholds for criminal prosecution of misappropriation of public funds are various depending on the amounts and uses of the misappropriated funds as well as the nature and behavior of the offenses. For example, a criminal case may be established if the misappropriated funds in the amount of 30,000 yuan and above are used for for-profit activities or the grafter has failed to return the funds to the state in excess of three months; if public funds are misappropriated for illicit uses, the threshold amount for a criminal charge is 15,000 yuan and above.

Like embezzlement, misappropriation of public funds in the pre-reform era were largely minor offenses involving small amounts for personal or family needs. As the transition from a socialist state to a market economy proceeds, coupled with increasing laxity of ideological control and strengthened managerial autonomy for managers of state firms, misappropriation of public funds has grown in both occurrence and intensity; in some extreme cases, public funds misappropriated even amounted to hundreds of million yuan. Diverted funds are in general used for profit-seeking or speculative undertakings such as business investment or operations, stock and securities trading, repayments for urgent debts, or illicit or illegal operations and activities such as smuggling, drug trafficking, manufacturing of fake and inferior goods, etc.[11]

[11] Classifications of public office-related corruption and crimes are based on *The Criminal Law of People's Republic of China* and Dong Keren's book on public-office related crimes. Dong Keren, *Prevention and Warning of Public-Office Related Crimes* (in Chinese) (Xining, Ningxia: Ningxia People's Press, 2010), 11–83.

Illegal Profiteering

The illegitimate act involves profit-generating practices of buying low and selling high and was classified as speculation in Mao's era. It refers to illicit profiteering under the dual-track pricing system in the early years of the reform. The behavior and pattern of speculation or profiteering (tou ji dao ba) are obviously typical of market behavior under the planned economy, and with the phaseout of the dual-track pricing system and the establishment of the market mechanism, the practice of buying low and selling high has become a normal market behavior and a legitimate means of profit-making and business operations. The amendment of the criminal code thus abolished this offense in 1997. It is still included here to provide a historical context in which certain corrupt acts and criminal offenses that were once designated as illicit and illegal shall be discussed in subsequent chapters.

Illicit profiteering was rampant in the early period of the economic reform. While state socialism was transitioning to a market economy, the rigid price control over a considerable number of raw materials and goods under the command economic system was still in effect. This semi-administrative and semi-market mechanism generated a confused pricing system in the second half of the 1980s. There existed three different prices for the same item: the state-planned price, the negotiable price, and the market price. Let alone the "negotiable price" that was closer to market prices in scope, the dual-track pricing system had resulted in fertile ground for rent-seeking and official corruption. Due to the existence of apparent price discrepancies, one could enrich himself simply by selling quotas of some key raw materials and short supplies at the market prices if he was able to gain access to those items at the state-set prices.

The threshold amount for criminal prosecution of illegal profiteering was illicit gains valued at 10,000–200,000 yuan and above for individuals and 300,000–600,000 yuan and above for organizations. Companies affiliated with state departments and agencies mandated with planning and administration of various industries, often dubbed "bureaucratic firms" (guan ban gong si), as well as state enterprises and their employees were often involved in varying degrees in official profiteering (guan dao) and speculation of state-regulated or distributed goods and materials such as key industrial and agricultural inputs, imports and foreign currencies, state-regulated permits such as quotas and authorizing documents for controlled goods, services, contracts, and foreign trade licenses.[12]

Possession of Huge Amount of Assets from Unidentified Sources

The assets or properties possessed by a public officeholder or his/her expenditures are obviously in excess of his/her legitimate incomes. There exist huge variations between the two. The offender is unable to explain and justify the discrepancies and to prove the legitimate sources of the possessions. Under this circumstance, the unjustifiable discrepancies shall be designated as illicit incomes or possessions and be confiscated by the state.

This clause was introduced and enacted by China's national legislature—the Standing Committee of the National People's Congress—in January 1988. This crime is typical of presumption of crime, and the defendant is responsible for proof of the legitimacy of the HUGE gaps or variations. The immensity of discrepancies that cannot be legitimately justified and proved by the accused is one of the conditions that constitute the crime. In general, in the case of state officials and state corporation managers, huge amounts of possessions and assets are usually accumulated through illicit sources such as payoffs, kickbacks, embezzlements, profiteering, etc. The threshold for the prosecution of possession of immense assets from unexplained sources is 300,000 yuan and above in value. However, as the average income level in China has increased significantly over the decades, the conviction of the crime should be case specific to acknowledge the differences in economic development and income levels in various regions across the country.

Concealing Deposits in Foreign Bank Accounts

The behavior and act that a public official, in violation of state laws and regulations, deliberately conceals a large amount of deposits in his or her foreign bank accounts.

As regulated by the authorities, state officials must report to the government about their foreign deposits. Failure to comply with the rule shall result in disciplinary punishment or criminal prosecution depending

[12] Lu, 202–203; Sun, 31–32.

on the amount of the deposits in foreign bank accounts. The threshold for conviction of the offense is foreign bank deposits that are equivalent to RMB 300,000 yuan and above in value.

Partitioning State-Owned Assets without Authorization

The malfeasance that government agencies, SOEs, public institutions, and people's organizations, in the name of the work unit, violate state rules and regulations to unauthorizedly partition and misappropriate public funds in relatively high value or large amount of state-owned assets for the benefits of the members of the organizations. The threshold for the prosecution of the offense is 100,000 yuan in cumulative value. The state executives and other personnel who are directly responsible or liable for the offense shall be charged.

Unsanctioned Partition and Distribution of Confiscated Properties

The illegal act that judicial and administrative law enforcement agencies and institutions, in the name of the work unit, illegally partition and distribute a large amount of confiscated properties to members of the work units. The confiscated properties involved, as stipulated by state rules and regulations, are to be turned over to the state treasure. Confiscated assets and properties, as defined in the provision, include confiscated properties of convicted criminals and offenders as well as fines imposed.

The threshold for the prosecution of the offense is 100,000 yuan and above in value. Executives and other personnel who are directly responsible or liable for the offense shall be charged.

Neglect of Duty

The behavior and act that public officials have failed to carry out their duties, or to perform them correctly and competently, or to act recklessly outside one's duty, and as a consequence, the negligence has resulted in severe losses of public properties and the state and citizens' interests. Public duties under the circumstance encompass duties of supervision, administration, management, enforcement, safety, security, etc.

Conviction of the offense of neglect of duty depends on a variety of factors and resultant consequences caused by the offenses such as human casualties, direct and indirect losses of personal, organizational and state properties, fraudulent purchase of foreign exchanges and illicit evasion of foreign exchanges to specific amounts, consequent shutdown and bankruptcy of corporations and enterprises, severe damage to the reputation of the state or other grave impact on the society, and resultant severe loss of the state and citizens' interests.

Abuse of Authority

The behavior and act that a public official, in violation of state laws and rules, deals with and decides on matters or public affairs that are beyond his/her duty and authority, and has consequently resulted in severe loss of public properties and the state and citizens' interests.

Prosecution for the offense of abuse of authority involves similar violations and conditions as those of neglect of duty, but the threshold numbers and amounts for casualties and loss of personal and public properties are lower than those associated with dereliction of duty. This offense, therefore, is subject to harsher punishment than the wrongdoing of neglect of duty. Under this provision, irregularities and fraudulent practices in violation of proper reporting stipulations and procedures are subject to criminal prosecution.

To cope with and to curb the rise of corruption and criminal offenses in the spheres of administrative law enforcement and judiciary as the reform progressed to new stages, the criminal code has been updated and amended over the years to encompass new provisions and clauses targeting corrupt acts and crimes of high occurrence in taxation, customs, banking, stocks and securities, land and real estate, environment protection, quality supervision and control, etc. In addition, as incidence of judicial corruption began to increase, provisions for various corrupt and criminal behavior and acts in judiciary and law enforcement were enacted and incorporated into the amended criminal code. Listed below are only the titles of the provisions and clauses of relevant offenses without further elaborations.

Irregularities of tax levy exemption or reduction

Taxation officials abuse taxation power to exempt or reduce what should be levied and paid to the state treasure in return for bribes or illicit personal gains. This is one of the offenses of relatively high incidence in administrative law enforcement in the reform era. The offense is subject to criminal prosecution if it has resulted in a cumulative loss of at least

100,000 yuan in state tax revenue or if it involves bribery or other grave behavior even though the cumulative loss of state tax revenue is less than 100,000 yuan.

Irregularities of provision of export tax rebate receipts, bills, and vouchers

Taxation and government officials, in violation of state regulations and policies, render false documents to tax fraudsters to assist them to defraud the state of the export tax rebate claims. This is typical of "corruption with theft". Many convicted cases involve coordinated collusions between local state enterprises and local tax authority and government agencies in a joint attempt to defraud the central/national treasure of tax rebates for illicit local interests and financial gains. The malpractice shall be prosecuted if it has resulted in a cumulative loss of at least 100,000 yuan in state tax revenue or if it involves extortion and acceptance of bribes or other grave behavior even though the cumulative loss of state tax revenue is less than 100,000 yuan.

Illicit approval of requisition and occupation of land

The irregularity that state officials, in violation of state land management regulations and stipulations, illicitly approve requisition and occupation of state or collective lands. Land-related corruption and illicit exchanges occurred as real estate development and construction boom in China had quickly got off the ground since the 1990s. Acquisition of lands and land use rights, by either legitimate or illicit means, has become a lucrative avenue for economic and political elites to amass immense fortunes in no time. In a period in which relatively sophisticated and rigid state land management, acquisition, and bidding regulations and procedures were absent, the local leading Party and government officials, in general, possessed the discretionary power and final say about important land deals. Thus, there existed and still are, to a lesser extent, strong incentives for developers and corrupt state officials to collude in deals of land acquisition and development. Motivated by rent-seeking, state officials often act on behalf of unscrupulous businessmen and land developers to explore various means, either tactful or forceful, to requisite state or collective lands or to grant or sell land use rights to developers at artificially low prices (see definition below). Criminal prosecution of the offense depends on a variety of violations and conditions such as the specific area of land requisitioned, resultant economic loss to a specific amount, consequent impact on production, local residents' well-being, as well as other grave consequences.

Illicit granting of land use rights at artificially low price
The irregularity that state officials, in violation of state land management regulations and stipulations, illicitly grant or sell state or collective land use rights at artificially low price. The offense is subject to conviction if it entails one of the following: (1) illicit sale of land use rights for at least 30 mu of state-owned land at a low price (60% or lower of what is specified as the floor sale price) or free of charge; (2) the resultant loss of state land assets in the amount of 200,000 yuan and above in value or severe impact on the vegetation of the land although the land area involved is less than the specified size; (3) the consequent impact on production, local residents' well-being, as well as other grave consequences.

Irregularities of conniving at smuggling activities
Customs officials, by abuse of authority, collude and connive at smuggling operations and activities in violation of the customs law and regulations. A criminal case can be established if the illicit acts involve one of the following: (1) connivance for criminal smuggling activities; (2) state tariff loss in the amount of 100,000 yuan and above as a result of smuggling collusion and connivance; (3) condoning smuggling acts more than three times or condoning more than three actions of smuggling at one time; and (4) the behavior and act of smuggling collusion and connivance are induced by bribery. Smuggling-related corruption and criminal activities were rampant in the 1980s and 1990s due to a general shortage of consumer goods and key production inputs in the domestic market and significant price discrepancies of certain import goods in the domestic market vs. the international market. Not only individuals and private businesses but also state agencies and state enterprises were involved in the smuggling of a range of consumer and industrial goods and commodities.

Irregularities in performing commercial inspection
Commercial inspection agencies and commercial inspection officials, by abuse of authority and in violation of the import and export commercial inspection rules and regulations, deliberately forge commercial inspection results and documents in exchange for illicit personal or organizational gains or for other illicit purposes or motivations.

Irregularities of conniving at production and sale of fake and inferior goods

State officials of the industry and commerce administration and the quality and technology supervisory authority, in violation of state laws and regulations, collude and connive at production and sale of fake and inferior goods and products. Criminal prosecution of the offense depends on a number of circumstances, including the gravity of the violations and the consequent impact of the act, such as the type and harmfulness of the illegal products (fake drugs, toxic and harmful food, etc.). In most cases, the offense, in general, involves bribery and collusion between unscrupulous businessmen and corrupt officials who are incented to seek illicit gains at the expense of consumers and the state.

Irregularities of approval and registration of corporations and issuance of securities

State officials of the industry and commerce administration and the securities administration, in violation of state rules and regulations, illicitly approve applications for the establishment and registration of corporations and enterprises, or issuance of stocks, debentures, and IPOs, which have consequently led to a severe loss of public properties and state and citizens' interests. The offense is subject to criminal prosecution and conviction if the act has resulted in a direct economic loss of 500,000 yuan and above, severe disruptions to the market, banking and finance order, or grave loss of public properties and the state and citizens' interests.

Irregularities and neglect of duty in environment supervision and protection

Environment protection and supervisory officials' irresponsibility and neglect of duty are often blamed for worsening environment pollution and deterioration of China's ecosystem. While negligence and irresponsibility underlie failures of environmental supervision and enforcement, it often involves deliberate neglect of duty and laxity in supervision and enforcement in exchange for bribes and illicit personal gains.

Irregularities and fraud in recruiting civil servants and students

State officials commit irregularities and fraud in recruitment of public servants and college students in return for illicit interest or gains to their family members and cronies. Illicit acts of the sort include impersonating unqualified candidates (in most cases kin or cronies) as qualified candidates for recruitment or hiring or depriving qualified candidates of employment that they deserve in accordance with hiring policies and procedures. This malpractice, to a large extent, falls under the traditional category of nepotism, and is typical of the Chinese traditional culture and social norms that value and favor traditional reciprocal relationships of kin, crony, and cliquish circles. Deviations and minor nepotism may not be deemed clear-cut corrupt and criminal behavior and offense in traditional sense.

Irregularities, illicit acts and crimes in judiciary and law enforcement

Irregularities, illicit acts and crimes in judiciary and law enforcement are on the rise in the reform era. Illicit behavior, acts, and offenses of relatively high occurrence under the circumstances include abuse of authority or misuse of law in the adjudication of civil, administrative, and economic cases, irregularities in the enforcement of rulings and judgments, irregularities and fraud in commutation and parole, irregularities in handling and turning over cases of serious nature to judicial institutions for criminal prosecution and conviction, etc. Many irregularities and offenses of the sort were bribery induced or committed in return for illicit personal gains and favoritism. Judicial corruption in contemporary China is a complicated phenomenon, which is underlain by a variety of factors such as political, legal, traditional, and cultural, but it is also largely driven by and closely associated with venal incentives for illicit financial gains.

Squandering

A pattern of corruption with Chinese characteristics has been gaining popularity among government agencies, public institutions, and state enterprises since the advent of the reform. Public funds are recklessly lavished and wasted on banquets, fine liquor, gift-giving, sightseeing, etc. for the pleasure and enjoyment of the powerful or for the cultivation of guanxi and favor-buying from officials at higher levels. The malfeasance has become rampant and pervasive with the proliferation of slush funds or secrete small coffers (xiao jin ku) in governments and public organizations, coupled with increased autonomy and flexibility in decision-making on finance and expenditures as well as laxity in supervision and enforcement of financial and accounting rules and stipulations. The malpractices of feasting and lavish spending of public funds on dining and wining across the country had escalated to such an extent that the aggregate expenditures of the sort even constituted 70 percent of the revenues of luxury restaurants and top liquor producers. A more lavish fashion of squandering of public funds involves luxuries such as fancy and spacious offices and office-suites, imported cars, luxury hotel suites, golfing, international sightseeing in the name of observation and study tours, villas and apartment suites for executives, etc. Cases of squandering of public funds in the name of organizations and work units have seldom faced criminal charges; rather, the wrongdoing is largely sanctioned through Party and administrative disciplines.

Selling and Buying Public Offices

It had been a long tradition in imperial China with respect to selling public offices for money or donations, either legitimately under the institution of "juan na" or illegitimately such as illicit trades of money for offices. In the KMT regime, there were similar occurrences mainly in bureaucracies at lower levels. As economic reform gradually marketizes the state's economic sectors and industrial and commercial institutions, it has unintentionally impacted the CCP's integrated and authoritative cadre appointment system and process. As rent-seeking opportunities and incentives inevitably permeated the economic arena as reform deepens, it has also extended to non-economic spheres and turned them into marketplaces. Commercialization of cadre appointments, or in other words, selling official positions or promotions for money, is a deviation and corrupt act that has quickly pervaded the officialdom since the 1990s. The misdeed of "pao guan yao guan" (lobby for promotion or office) and "mai guan mai guan" (buying and selling offices) have quickly evolved into an informal and illegitimate fad for Party-state officials who either seek promotion and career advancement through payoffs to superiors or intend to enrich themselves by selling public offices to subordinates and cronies. Unlike the conventional venal act such as bribery that takes place between businessmen and government officials, this transactive venal misdeed takes place in the officialdom of the state. The phenomenon of selling and buying offices is particularly pervasive in less developed regions where alternatives for enriching oneself and rent-seeking opportunities in government are generally limited. In general, bribe-takers and office-sellers perceive the illicit trade to be relatively safe bets as bribers are often bribees' subordinates and disclosure of the illicit deals would also subject bribers to disciplinary penalties or criminal prosecution depending on the size of the payoffs involved and the nature of the malpractices. Under certain circumstances, the malfeasance is particularly troubling as office-buyers often used their organizations' slush funds or public funds appropriated from other concealed sources to procure promotions or favors from their superiors or high-ranking officials. Revealed and convicted cases indicate that no rank and file in the Party/state bureaucracy are immune to this malfeasance.

Arbitrary Use of Regulatory Power and Illicit Fund Raising

The irregularity entails abuse of regulatory and administrative law enforcement power to impose fines, charges, and fees and illegitimate and illicit disposal of the revenues generated in violation of state accounting rules and procedures to the benefits of the organization and its members. As the planned economy transitioned into a market economy, the role of government started to shift from command and social resource distribution to the functions of regulatory and enforcement of market order. As the so-called irregularity of official profiteering gradually phased out with the elimination of the dual-track pricing system and official monopoly over essential production inputs and short supplies in the mid-1990s, new rent-seeking opportunities and incentives arose as the new functions of the government as market regulator and enforcer took effect. Again, the evolving roles and functions of government in the new economy were soon exploited and distorted for illicit interests of the regulatory and enforcement agencies and organizations. What characterizes the misconduct of the sort are what the central authorities termed "san luan" (the three unruly acts)—illicitly imposed fines (luan fa kuan), illegitimately charged fees (luan shou fei), and forcibly apportioned donations (luan tan pai). Under normal circumstances, "san luan" is not classified as a criminal behavior and act; rather the malpractice is introduced and carried out for seemingly legitimate purposes and procedures such as law and regulation enforcement, economic reform, local economic revitalization, environment protection, etc. The genesis of "san luan" is partially attributable to budgetary pressure on some state agencies as they were forced to raise funds through questionable and illegitimate means to make up for their dwindling state budgetary allocations.

State agencies that often used irregular and arbitrary law enforcement and regulatory power to raise funds from illicitly imposed fines, fees and donations include police, industry and commerce administration, public health, pricing administration, road administration, state land administration, state property administration, industrial standards and quality administration, family planning, financial discipline inspection, etc. Many services that are designated as essential functions of relevant state agencies and should be provided free of charge have been used to extract payments from citizens and enterprises. Fines and fees, in some periods, had accounted for a growing portion of the annual budgets of law enforcement and regulatory agencies. Among over two dozen of tax levies commonly imposed in China, "only a few are solidly grounded in the taxation laws". Another misconduct that has caused widespread public outcry is the imposition of fines and charges through road tolls. Active players of the sort include road administration, tax authority, public health, tobacco and salt administration, and inspections and charges or fines are often carried out and levied in the name of highway safety, prevention of tax evasion, disease control, cigarettes and other regulated goods smuggling, etc. In rural China, for a certain period, the ever-increasing illegitimate charges, levies, forced contributions and fund raising, some of which were arbitrary in nature and forceful by enforcement, had become such a financial burden for peasants that the incidence of tax revolts, violence, suicides, and other turbulences had surged since 1993. A report in 1992 revealed that among the 89,000 fees imposed by state agencies in eleven provinces and cities, 53,000 were "neither legal nor authorized ones"; in addition, 12,000 of the 13,000 imposed penalties "violated local or national regulations".

Irregularities abound in the use of revenues raised through "san luan". Collecting agencies in general would appropriate a portion, or in some cases all the revenues to the benefit of their members without turning the collected funds over to the state treasury. There exist various accounting irregularities to conceal the revenues of the sort to facilitate illicit appropriation among agency members. Illicit use of "small treasury" (xiao jin ku) or secret slush funds was once pervasive among government agencies, state enterprises, and public institutions to hide extra-budgetary and illegitimate incomes. Accounting irregularities and problematic practices that were widely adopted for this purpose include the concealment of receipt records, opening and maintaining bank accounts under personal names, retaining or appropriating extra-budgetary funds, underreporting profits, and retaining or pocketing cash income. It is often common malpractice that state officials and agents use arbitrary power to assess and reduce fines at their discretion in return for bribes.[13]

Moral Decadence

Personal lifestyle, immoral or unethical behavior, and misconduct such as extramarital affairs, sexual harassment, gambling, soliciting prostitutes, pursuing career advancement through fraudulent or immoral means, etc. may be defined by researchers and perceived by the public as scandals or immoral or inappropriate conduct in the West; however, they often fall into the category of corruption in the Chinese context as these behavior and misconduct are in general fall short of the traditional and cultural norms and standards that the culture and society hold for the political elite and high-ranking state officials. Although some of the behavior and deviations, as addressed previously, may not strictly entail abuse of public office for material gain, moral decadence of the sort has been largely intolerant of in traditional Chinese political culture. Of particularly relevance to the subject and context of this book is the fact that some of the personal lifestyles and morally decadent behavior and acts are obvious causal factors and incentives for venal corruption. For example, a corrupt official indulged in gambling has the incentive to graft public funds or extort bribes in order to frequent casinos in Macau. Another example involves the increasingly popular misdeed of sheltering mistresses or concubines among corrupt officials in the reform era. Statistics regarding cadre disciplining and prosecution in recent years reveal that over 95 percent of the disciplined and convicted corrupt officials housed mistresses or concubines. A corrupt official, both voluntarily or involuntarily, may often be compelled to use illicit and venal means to acquire illicit funds to please his mistress, in many cases multiple ones, or to support his secret concubine(s) and their children for the needs of housing, education, and other amenities of quality of life.

[13] Lu, 206–217.

3.3 The Breadth, Depth, and Intensity of Official Corruption

In the early days of the economic reform, prior to the beginning of the urban reform, new patterns of corruption, coupled with existing and traditional forms of corrupt and illicit acts, had risen to a level that timely caught the attention of the central authorities. In a 1982 central directive titled "Resolution on Cracking Down on Serious Criminal Activities in the Economic Arena", the CCP Central Committee and the State Council openly admitted the rise and spread of official corruption as reform commenced:

> There are many ills existing in our economic and political life. What's especially unsettling is the fact that in the last two or three years, activities such as smuggling, embezzlement, bribery, profiteering, and theft of state properties have increased dramatically. In some places, the situation is quite grave. These criminal activities, seriously detrimental to the economy, are often conducted by a few people working in state agencies and other work units in collaboration with criminal elements in society. Sometimes they are done under the guise of serving the state and collectives. Some are even supported by leading officials. The problem is far more serious than in the 1952 Three Anti Campaign.[14]

As the reform proceeded and more reform programs were initiated, new patterns of corruption surfaced accordingly. Throughout the reform process, new reform policies and initiatives and new forms and manifestations of corruption seem to be largely concomitant with each other over their evolutionary courses. This phenomenon had arisen and prevailed throughout various reform stages including price reform, housing reform, administrative reform, as well as more recent fiscal, regulatory, and enterprise reforms. The evolutionary course of bureaucratic corruption, as correctly and vividly described by Lu, "has gradually changed from 'whom one knows' (prebendalism based on guanxi), to 'what one controls' (graft based on one's discretion over resources) and 'how much one pays' (rent-seeking based on market logic)".[15] In the late 1980s, for example, as the government relaxed its price control over a variety of raw materials

[14] Cited in Lu, 191.

[15] Ibid., 191–192.

and short supplies, official profiteering came into existence together with the introduction of the dual-pricing system. When the economic reform deepened both on scale and in-depth since 1992, another tide of the nationwide frenzy of business-engagement rolled back and resulted in more new patterns of corruption. The establishment of the stock market, for instance, had caused a series of stock-related corrupt acts such as stock bribes and "power stocks". The implementation of the refund policy for export increment tax tempted local enterprises and local governments in collusion to defraud the central authorities of large sums of increment tax returns.[16] The list goes on and on ......

Table 3.1 presents statistics on cases of corruption and corrupt senior officials investigated and prosecuted between 1986 and 2021.

Data on official corruption and public-office-related crimes are mainly based on the annual reports of the Supreme People's Procuratorate (SPP) and may not be comprehensive, systemic, and illustrative. There is a lack of systemic data on Party and government officials as well as officials of public institutions and state enterprises who committed minor offenses and are subject to only disciplinary penalties as the Party and governmental supervisory commission and ministry do not normally publicize detailed data on cadre corruption due to its sensitivity and other considerations. By statistics and the Party tradition, officials who are administratively disciplined normally constitute the vast majority of the total number of Party and government officials who have been investigated for corruption and public-office-related crimes. In other words, the true breadth or pervasiveness of official corruption in the reform era should be far more severe than what the annual reports of the Supreme People's Procuratorate convey.

Figure 3.1 is drawn on the statistics of Table 3.1 and illustrates the trajectory of incidence of official corruption and graft in reform China over the past 35 years. Statistics on official corruption before 1986 are not available as the SPP began to separate data on official corruption and public-office-related crimes from other categories of economic crimes and profiteering in 1987. As shown in the chart, official corruption exploded in the 1980s as urban reform began in 1984, and then rapidly rose to an alarming level in the late 1980s. Rampant official corruption and the

[16] *Reform Reference* No. 8 (1996): 32–33.

Table 3.1 Cases filed and high-ranking officials investigated and prosecuted by year

Year	*Cases filed/ investigated*	*County/division level*	*Department/ bureau level*	*Province/ ministry level*
2021	20,754	–	–	–
2020	19,760	–	–	–
2019	24,234	–	–	–
2018	16,902	–	–	–
2013–2017	254,419	15,234	2405	120
2017	46,113	873	348	50
2016	47,650	2882	446	21
2015	54,249	4568	769	41
2014	55,101	4040	589	–
2013	51,306	2871	253	8
2008–2012	218,639	12,193	950	30
2012	47,338	2385	179	5
2011	44,506	2319	198	7
2010	44,085	2529	188	6
2009	41,531	2458	204	8
2008	41,179	2502	181	4
2003–2007	179,696	12,327	930	35
2007	10,961	1896	167	6
2006	40,041	2528	202	6
2005	41,447	2595	196	8
2004	43,757	2751	198	11
2003	43,490	2557	167	4
1998–2002	207,103	12,830 (county and above)	–	–
2002	43,250	3705	–	–
2001	40,195	2670 (county and above)	–	6
2000	45,113	2680 (county and above)	184	7
1999	38,382	2061	136	3
1998	40,162	1714	103	3
1993–1997	387,352	2903	265	7
1996	61,099	2551	143	5
1995	63,953	2262	137	2
1994	60,312	1827	88	–
1993	56,491	1037	64	1
1988–1992	214,318	4451	173	5
1992	27,149	71	69	2

(continued)

Table 3.1 (continued)

Year	*Cases filed/ investigated*	*County/division level*	*Department/ bureau level*	*Province/ ministry level*
1991	46,219	889	34	1
1990	51,373	1188	–	–
1989	58,926	803	70	2
1988	21,100	190	19	–
1987	30,651	1500	–	–
1986	49,557	700	–	–

Source SPP Work Reports 1987–2022

increasingly widened income distribution between the powerful (governmental officials with a discretionary power over resource allocation, wealthy businessmen, etc.) and ordinary people in the 1980s, as pointed out earlier, had caused widespread public outcry and directly attributed to the genesis and intensification of the Tiananmen Movement in June 1989. A swift government crackdown on corruption and economic crimes in the aftermath of the June-4th movement resulted in criminal investigation and prosecution of 156,500 corrupt officials between 1989 and 1991, and the annual average of the three-year period, 52,100 per annum, had more than doubled the 1988 figure of 21,100. In 1992, Deng Xiaoping undertook his famed southern tour and appealed to the CCP leadership for rejuvenation and furtherance of economic reform policies and initiatives. The resultant intensification of the reform on various policy fronts and in various industries and sectors had unsurprisingly led to a proliferation of policy loopholes and rent-seeking opportunities and thus triggered off a dramatic surge in corruption characterized by increasingly large sizes of misappropriations and bribes and soaring incidences of collective and organizational corruption in the 1990s. Over the five-year period between 1993 and 1997, a total of 387,352 cadres were criminally investigated and charged for corruption and economic offenses including embezzlement, bribery, misappropriation of public funds, graft of state properties and assets, neglect of duty, and judiciary corruption. The number of offenders averaged 76,870 per year in this period, which was more than 3.6-fold the 1988 figure. Data from another source indicates that, over the two decades between 1978 and 1998, 2.35 million Party-state officials were disciplined for corruption and economic offenses.[17] Statistically the prosecuted figure peaked in the 1993–1997 period, and then a downward trend started to form and evolve over the succeeding decade.

However, from 2008 onward the number of officials investigated and prosecuted by procuratorates and courts have obviously increased, particularly in the period of 2013–2017, which is largely attributable to the enduring and intense anti-corruption campaign launched by the Xi administration since 2013. By 2017 there had been a 40 percent increase in investigation and prosecution of corrupt cadres in comparison to the 2007 level. As mentioned above, cadre deviations and cases of minor offenses that are subject to only disciplinary penalties generally constitute the vast majority of the cases of official corruption in post-communist China. Economic crime cases involving embezzlement and bribery increased by an annual rate of 22 percent in the period. The latest official data from the Central Commission for Discipline Inspection provides a statistical and in-depth overview of the pervasiveness and gravity of official corruption in the apparatus of the Party and state. Over the five years since late 2012, 1.545 million cases of corruption have been filed and investigated and 1.537 million Party and state officials were disciplined, among whom there were 280 senior officials at the provincial/ministerial level, 8900 senior officials at the prefecture/bureau level, and over 63,000 officials at the county/division level. Over 58,000 officials with criminal offenses have been prosecuted and convicted of corruption and economic crimes in the same period.[18]

Another manifestation of the gravity of official corruption in the reform era is a surge in value of the funds grafted and misappropriated. Embezzlement, acceptance or solicitation of bribes, and misappropriation of public funds constituted 80 percent of all economic crime cases filed for investigation by procurators between 1979 and 2000. This ratio was even higher in "big and major cases" (da an yao an) involving "big sums" (85%) and senior officials (95%) in the 1990s.[19] In the early years of the reform, embezzlement of public funds in the amount of 2000 yuan and above would subject a grafter to criminal prosecution and conviction, and

[17] Huaipeng Chen and Ying Tian, "Further Promoting Party Conduct, Integrity and the Anti-Corruption Campaign" (in Chinese), *Qiu Shi* No. 4 (1999): 24.

[18] CCDI, www.ccdi.gov.cn, November 15, 2017.

[19] Manion, 86–87.

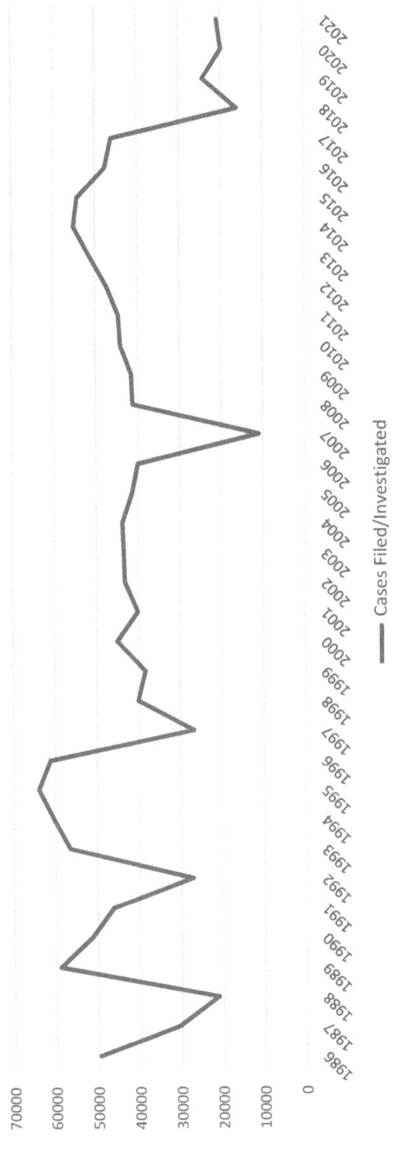

Fig. 3.1 Cases filed/investigated 1986–2021 (*Source* SPP work reports 1987–2022)

cases involving 10,000 yuan and more were classified as "big case". For example, a total of 49,122 big cases involving at least 10,000 yuan and 203 major cases entailing 500,000 yuan and above were filed and investigated between 1988 and 1992. In the succeeding decades, however, major cases involving millions or even hundreds of million yuan are no longer uncommon. During 1998–2002 and in 2005, for instance, major cases involving grafted public funds in the amount of 1 million yuan and above numbered 5541 and 8490, respectively. The number of big cases in the five-year period between 1993 and 1997 had increased by 5.5 times as compared to cases filed between 1983 and 1987. In rare and extreme cases misappropriated state funds even amounted to several billion yuan. The evolutionary course of bribery in the reform era is particularly prominent—from small gifts in the pre-reform era to huge cash and kickback bribes worth millions or even hundreds of million yuan. A convicted bribery case in 2018 reveals that a deputy mayor in Shanxi province took two bribes from unscrupulous businessmen, and each bribe summed to over 200 million yuan! A case study by Guo Yong on cadre corruption draws similar conclusion on an escalating trend of bribe-extraction in the reform period. The study is based on 594 cases investigated and prosecuted between 1978 and 2005. The first cohort contains 68 cases involving senior officials at the provincial/ministerial level and the second cohort includes 526 cases involving officials at the county/division and prefecture/bureau levels. As indicated in the study, solicitation and acceptance of bribes had become the most predominant form of offense among economic crimes during the study period, accounting for 85 percent and 78 percent of all cases of economic offenses in Cohort 2 and Cohort 1, respectively. The rapid surge in the value of grafted state funds and the size of bribes since 1993 had forced the authorities to amend the criminal code in 1997, raising the threshold amounts for "big sum" of embezzlement and bribery to 50,000 yuan and misappropriation of public funds to 100,000 yuan. While inflation was one of the considerations for the adjustment, the dramatic rise in the sum and size of graft and bribery in the period were obviously the decisive considerations and rationale for the amendment.

The proliferation of corruption and ever-increasing criminal cases involving senior officials at the county/department level and above is deemed a valid and effective indicator of the pervasiveness and intensification of official corruption in reform China. Under the influence of the traditional Chinese political culture and norms, leading officials are in general perceived to be the "parental officials" (fu mu guan) in a locality and are symbolic of the legitimacy of the ruling elite and role models of the local citizens. The behavior, ethics, integrity, and rightfulness of the leading officials, to a certain extent, exert positive or negative influence over the officialdom and contribute to the formation of the political culture and ethos in local society. Rampant corruption in the elite, therefore, would most likely conduce to a chain reaction of corruption in officialdom and society, harm the legitimacy of the ruling party, and distort the social norms and ethos in society. Table 3.1 also presents the incidence and evolution of corruption among high-ranking officials over the past three decades. While the period of 1993–1997 saw the largest cohort of government and public officials being investigated and criminally prosecuted, revealed offenses at the county/division level and above remained relatively modest until five years later; in the period of 1998–2002, a total of 12,830 senior officials at the county/division and above levels were investigated and prosecuted, which represents a surge of more than fourfold the figure in the previous five-year period. Incidence of corruption at this level then remained stable in the succeeding decade and started to trend upward with a 19-percent increase in the 2013–2017 period. However, a more dramatic escalation of official corruption occurred at an even higher level; over the same period, cases filed for investigation and prosecution involving senior officials at the prefecture/bureau and provincial/ministerial levels increased by alarmingly 14-fold and 24-fold, respectively. A study by the United Nations surveyed 27 countries with high incidences of bribery, and China ranks No. 1 on the list with its total number of officials prosecuted for venal crimes far outnumbering those of other nations.[20] Again, the revelation and prosecution of an unprecedented number of senior officials particularly at the provincial/ministerial level in recent years is deemed the resultant outcome of Xi's sweeping anti-corruption campaign to hunt "tigers" in the apparatus of the Party and government since 2013.

The spread of corruption from the cohort of low-level officials to top-ranking leaders, from economic administrative departments and agencies to the Party and state apparatus, law enforcement, and the military, to a large extent, manifests the rampancy and seriousness of this political plague in reform China. Since 2000 over 300 Party/state and military

[20] Jiahong He, "An Assessment of the Current Status of Corruption and Public-Office Related Crimes in China" (in Chinese), *Modern Law Science* No. 6, 2014.

leaders, ministers, provincial Party secretaries, and governors as well as other senior officials at the provincial/ministerial level have been prosecuted and convicted of corruption and economic crimes. The top-level cohort includes top Party leaders and members of the politburo as well as leaders of the CPPCC and are listed in Table 3.2.

Another cohort of senior officials notoriously known for a high incidence of corruption and huge sums of bribery and graft are powerful provincial Party secretaries and governors as well as ministers of the central government. Headliners of the sort in recent years are listed in Table 3.3.

Ministers and directors (deputy-minister level) of the central government who were criminally charged and convicted are listed in Table 3.4.

Another cohort of powerful senior officials who are particularly prone to corruption are Party bosses and mayors of the major cities and urban centers such as the capital cities of the provinces and cities that function as the economic and transportation hubs of the regions. In general, a significant number of presidents and vice presidents of the Provincial People's Congress and chairman and vice chairman of the Provincial Political Consultative Conference once served as leading officials of the major cities or regions in the provinces. Although they may be detained in their current positions, it was generally the corrupt acts and criminal offenses they had committed while holding leading positions in major

Table 3.2 Convicted national and sub-national leaders

Name	*Position*
Zhou Yongkang	Member of the Standing Committee of Politburo and Party boss overseeing judiciary and law enforcement
Guo Boxiong	Member of Politburo, Colonel General, Vice Chairman of the Central Military Commission
Xu Caihou	Member of Politburo, Colonel General, Vice Chairman of the Central Military Commission
Sun Zhengcai	Member of Politburo, Party boss of the City of Chongqing
Bo Xilai	Member of Politburo, Party boss of the City of Chongqing
Chen Liangyu	Member of Politburo, Party boss of Shanghai
Ling Jihua	Vice Chairman, the Chinese People's Political Consultative Conference (CPPCC)
Su Rong	Vice Chairman, CPPCC

Table 3.3 Convicted provincial party bosses and governors

Name	*Position*
Su Rong	Former Party boss of Jiangxi province, but was detained in the position of vice chairman of the CPPCC
Bai Enpei	Party boss of Yunnan province
Zhou Benshun	Party boss of Hebei province
Wang Min	Party boss of Liaoning province
Wang Sanyun	Party boss of Gansu province
Cheng Weigao	Party boss of Hebei province
Liu Fangren	Party boss of Guizhou province
Su Shulin	Governor of Fujian province
Li Jiating	Governor of Yunnan province
Zhang Guoguang	Governor of Hubei province
Huang Xingguo	Mayor of Tianjin
Li Chuncheng	Deputy Party boss, Sichuan province
Wei Hong	Governor of Sichuan province (disciplined only)

Table 3.4 Convicted high-ranking officials at ministerial level

Name	*Position*
Jiang Jieming	Minister of State-Owned Assets Supervision and Administration Commission
Liu Zhijun	Minister of Railways
Tian Fengshan	Minister of Land and Resources
Li Liguo	Minister of Civil Affairs
Zheng Youyu	Director of State Drug Administration (executed)
Liu Tienan	Deputy Minister of National Development and Reform Commission and Director of National Energy Bureau
Qiu Xiaohua	Director of the State Statistics Bureau
Wang Baoan	Deputy Minister of Finance and Director of the State Statistics Bureau

cities and regions that had brought them down for convictions or disciplinary punishments. Several Party bosses and mayors of major cities, as listed in Table 3.5, were detained in their current positions and had caught nationwide attention with respect to their corrupt acts and the huge sizes of bribes involved in their cases. It should be noted that leading

Table 3.5 Convicted party bosses and mayors of major cities

Name	*Position*
Wan Qingliang	Party boss of Guangzhou
Xu Zongheng	Mayor of Shenzhen
Liu Zhihua	Deputy Mayor of Beijing
Yang Weize	Party boss of Nanjing
Wang Ming	Party boss of Jinan
Yang Luyu	Mayor of Jinan
Du Shicheng	Party boss of Qingdao
Chen Chuanping	Party boss of Taiyuan
Zhang Tianxing	Party boss of Kunming
Yu Yuanhui	Party boss of Nanning
Mao Xiaobing	Party boss of Xining
Mu Suixin	Mayor of Shenyang
Ji Jianye	Mayor of Nanjing
Li Jia	Party boss of Zhuhai
Chen Xuefeng	Party boss of Luoyang
Lu Ziyue	Mayor of Ningbo
Han Xuejian	Party boss of Daqing
Liao Shaohua	Party boss of Zhunyi

officials of the major cities, namely provincial capitals, are usually ranked at the deputy provincial/ministerial level.

As mentioned previously, reforms in industry and the finance and banking sector induced widespread corruption in the 1990s and 2000s. Genesis of corruption and illicit acts were partly attributable to corrupt senior management of the state-owned corporations and the state-owned banks and financial institutions. Top executives of the largest state monopolies such as Sinopec fell one after another in recent years due to corruption and economic-related charges and convictions. Refer to Table 3.6 for a number of notorious high-profilers in these sectors. Also included in the table are other executives of the state corporations and institutions prosecuted or disciplined in recent years.

The epidemic of official corruption had not only permeated the domains of economic administration, resource control and allocation, goods production and distribution, and the apparatus of the Party and government, but it had also rapidly infiltrated law enforcement and the judiciary system since the advent of the reform. The predominant patterns

Table 3.6 Convicted top executives of state-owned mega corporations

Name	*Position*
Lai Xiaomin	Chairman, China Huarong Asset Management (executed)
Chen Tonghai	President and CEO, Sinopec
Wang Xuebing	Governor, China Construction Bank
Wang Tianpu	CEO, Sinopec
Liao Yongyuan	CEO, Sinopec
Xu Jianyi	President, China FAW Group Corporation
Song Lin	President, China Resources
Chang Xiaobing	President, China Unicom
Zhang Enzhao	Governor, China Construction Bank

of corruption in the fields of law enforcement and judiciary are venal offenses and neglect of duty, and the infection of the domains of justice and administrative law enforcement serves as a strong indicator of the rampancy and gravity of corruption in the state and the society. Motivated by venal interests and illicit personal gains, administrative law enforcement officials in customs, state tax agencies, state administration of industry and commerce, state drug administration, state technology and quality control and supervisory agencies, etc. colluded with unlawful businessmen and smugglers to evade and defraud the state of immense tariff and tax payments, and to flood markets with harmful and bogus drugs and inferior consumer goods and products. It is not uncommon that local police chiefs and officers forge secretive patron–clientele networks with local mafias and act as their "protective umbrellas" (bao hu shan) in exchange for bribes and illicit payoffs. As judicial corruption pervades, judges distort judicial decisions, judgments, sentences, paroles, etc. in return for bribes and illicit interests. As disclosed in the annual reports of the Supreme People's Procuratorate, cases of corruption in administrative law enforcement filed and prosecuted surged almost six-fold from 1993 to 1995 and then doubled the 1995 figure in 2013. Similar to the incidence and trend in administrative law enforcement, revealed cases of judicial corruption more than doubled between 1993 and 1996 and then alleviated in the past two decades.[21] Listed in Table 3.7 are high-ranking

[21] The Supreme People's Procuratorate Work Report 1993–2016, www.spp.gov.cn.

officials in the judiciary and law enforcement who had been investigated and convicted in recent years.

One of the unintended consequences of the economic reform is the widespread corruption in the military. Traditionally the army has been symbolic of revolutionary, loyalty, reliability, integrity, and uprightness since the Mao era. Unfortunately, like other walks of life, the military is not immune to the temptation of money and pleasure, and corruption broke out in the 1980s as the army started to involve itself in profit-driven operations and official profiteering activities. Similar to patterns

Table 3.7 Convicted high-ranking judicial and law enforcement officials

Name	*Position*
Li Dongsheng	Deputy Minister of Public Security
Li Jizhou	Deputy Minister of Public Security
Wang Leyi	Deputy Director, General Administration of Customs
Zheng Youyu	Director, State Drug Administration Bureau (executed)
Xiang Junbo	Chairman, China Insurance Regulatory Commission
Yao Gang	Vice Chairman, China Securities Regulatory Commission
Zhang Lijun	Deputy Minister of Environment Protection
Yang Dongliang	Director, State General Administration of Safety Supervision
Ma Jian	Deputy Minister of State Security
Xi Xiaoming	Vice President of the Supreme People's Court
Huang Songyou	Vice President of the Supreme People's Court
Sun Hongzhi	Deputy Director General, State Administration of Industry and Commerce
Xu Yandong	President, Heilongjiang Provincial High People's Court
Wu Zhenhan	President, Hunan Provincial High People's Court
Tian Fengqi	President, Liaoning Provincial High People's Court
Mai Congkai	President, Guangdong Provincial High People's Court
Xu Qianfei	President, Jiangsu Provincial High People's Court
Chen Xu	Procurator General, Shanghai Municipal People's Procuratorate
Ding Xinfa	Procurator General, Jiangxi Provincial People's Procuratorate
Wu Changshun	Vice Chairman of Tianjin Political Consultative Conference and Director of Tianjin Public Security Bureau
He Ting	Deputy Mayor and Director of Chongqing Public Security Bureau

of corruption and the trajectory of its evolution found in government and the state sector, speculation and official profiteering, extraction of bribes and kickbacks through transactions in land and real estate, procurements of military supplies, infrastructure development, building contracts, as well as embezzlement, constituted the main avenues for the top-level commanders and senior military officials to amass ill-gotten fortunes. In addition, selling and buying offices and promotions had become particularly predominant and rampant in the military officialdom in the reform era. Selling of high-ranking positions generally entails huge sums of bribes as revealed by cases filed and publicized. It is an undisputed fact that the Chinese military has been plagued by omni-directional and rampant corruption for decades. A significant number of top brass and high-ranking military officials have been brought down and prosecuted since Xi became the commander-in-chief. It is believed that generals ranging from colonel generals to major generals investigated and convicted of corruption in recent years are in the range of over 90. Due to the large number of offenders in this cohort, only convicted generals and lieutenant generals are listed in Table 3.8.

An escalation of organizational corruption and collusion cases also manifests the breadth, depth, and complexity of official corruption in the reform era. In the pre-reform era and the early years of economic reform, officials, in general, acted alone in committing corruption and economic crimes. As reform deepened, the organizational forms and dimensions of corruption began to evolve, develop, and has ultimately become a multi-faceted, complex, and relatively sophisticated phenomenon over time. The most noticeable trend is the collectivization and organization of actors and actions in committing corruption and offenses, and since the 1990s there has been an alarming surge in deviations and criminal offenses involving family members, work units, state enterprises, and administrative law enforcement in cases of bribery, embezzlement, misappropriation of state funds, public bribery, squandering, plunder of state assets and properties, and "san luan" (the three unruly acts). Of particularly serious is the outpouring of major and series of cases characterized by huge sums of grafted funds and numerousness of venal officials across organizational charts of government departments and law enforcement agencies. There are various series of cases that involved multiple government agencies and public enterprises at various levels and in various localities and had often implicated a broad range of cadres from low-level to high-ranking at the

Table 3.8 Convicted generals and lieutenant generals

Name	*Position*	*Rank*
Guo Boxiong	Vice Chairman, CMC	General
Xu Caihou	Vice Chairman, CMC	General
Zhang Yang (suicide)	Member of CMC and Director General of the Political Work Department	General
Fang Fenghui	Member of CMC and Chief of Staff of the Joint Staff Department	General
Wang Jianping	Commander of the armed police force	General
Tian Xiusi	Commissar of the Air Force	General
Wang Xibing	President of the PLA National Defense University	General
Wang Shouye	Deputy Commander of the Navy	Lieutenant General
Wang Jiurong	Deputy Commander of the Second Artillery	Lieutenant General Force
Yu Daqing	Deputy Commissar of the Second Artillery	Lieutenant General Force
Gu Junshan	Deputy Director of the General Logistics Department	Lieutenant General
Liu Zheng	Deputy Director of the General Logistics Department	Lieutenant General
Liu Shengjie	Deputy Director of the Logistics Support Department	Lieutenant General
Niu Zhizhong	Deputy Commander of the Armed Police Force	Lieutenant General
Yu Jianwei	Deputy Commissar of the Armed Police Force	Lieutenant General
Fan Changmi	Deputy Commissar of the Nanzhou Military Region	Lieutenant General
Yang Jinshan	Deputy Commander of the Chengdu Military Region	Lieutenant General
Xiao Huaishu	Deputy Commissar of the Nanzhou Military Region	Lieutenant General
Wang Yufa	Commissar of the Air Force of the Guangzhou Military Region	Lieutenant General
Xu Yuanlin	Commissar of the Northern Theater Command Ground Force	Lieutenant General

provincial/ministerial level or even higher. Those corrupt groups are typified by a network of interwoven illicit interests, inside-outside collusion, intra-departmental and inter-departmental coordination, division of labor, conspiracy, as well as extraordinarily high value of grated funds. Under these circumstances, exposure of one case often implicates and reveals other cases and actors throughout the series of cases (wo an). As a matter of fact, many high-ranking officials had become "accidentally" exposed and then were brought down in the course of the investigation of other cases in the series. In some extreme cases, the downfall of a key actor even led to hundreds of government officials in multiple departments, levels, and localities being exposed, investigated, disciplined, or criminally prosecuted.

One form of organizational corruption in the reform era is the so-called "unhealthy tendencies in industries and sectors" (hang ye bu zheng zhi feng). This is not personal behavior and misconduct by individual government officials, but rather, an organizational or "official" behavior to seek illegitimate or illicit incomes by abuse of its administrative or monopolistic power and resources for the interests and benefits of the organization and its members. These unhealthy tendencies have intensified since the 1990s, extending from the sector of public services and utilities to the Party and state apparatus with administrative, regulatory, and enforcement powers, or even to the sectors of health care, education, culture, and media. "san luan", as briefly discussed previously, is the main manifestation of the unhealthy tendencies in this regard. There have been an increasing number of departments and agencies in economic administration, administrative law enforcement, judiciary, public utilities, and services, as well as hospitals, educational institutions, sports, entertainment, and media involved in the malpractice in pursuit of illegitimate incomes to the benefits of the organizations. As mentioned earlier, public services that should be rendered at no or low costs are attached with hefty price tags, and there has been a proliferation of illicitly imposed fees, charges, fines, and compulsory donations that have been "creatively" designed or arbitrarily "justified" in the contexts of their respective service areas and enforcement duties. The illicit proceeds, to a large extent, are illegally retained to either be divided among members of the organization as bonuses or to be used for office and staff residential housing development, vehicle purchase, squandering, and other organizational or staff benefits. The rapid spread of the unhealthy tendencies and irregularities from the public sector and industries to various spheres of society is blamed for the general moral decadence of society and is held accountable in part for the so-called "social corruption". It is asserted that corruption has infiltrated almost every aspect of society and is in the process of evolving into a widely accepted social norm and value in socialist China.

Squandering and feasting at public expense is mocked as corruption with distinctive Chinese characteristics, and its scope and the dollar value involved had once surged to an unprecedented level in the history of the PRC. As mentioned earlier, feasting at public expense often constituted about 70 percent of the revenues of luxury restaurants and top brand liquor producers, and the launch of several anti-corruption crackdowns by the Party/state in recent years had impacted the sector to such an extent that it fell into recession overnight. In fear of the grave consequences of embezzlement and graft, many officials opt to squander and indulge in extravagance paid by public money. In addition to feasting, other forms of squandering and waste include luxury office buildings and renovations/decorations, import vehicles, festivals and celebrations, domestic and international sightseeing in the name of conferences or observation/study tours, golfing, even visiting prostitutes at public expense, etc. It is estimated that annual public expenditures on feasting amount to over 120 billion yuan.[22]

As addressed in *Introduction*, the staggeringly high incidence, rampancy, and persistence of official corruption have set off widespread public backlash and resentment, and by the end of the 1990s it had become the most prominent political and social issue as per consensus of ordinary citizens, scholars, business elite and the CCP officialdom. The subject has remained one of the top focal points in various public surveys in recent decades. According to a nationwide survey by the *Well-Off* ("xiao kang") magazine and Tsinghua University in 2011, corruption ranked fifth among the top ten concerns of the people surveyed after housing prices, inflation, food safety, and healthcare reform. Among the other four public surveys of similar design and scope conducted by the *Well-Off* magazine between 2005 and 2011, corruption was one of the four issues (healthcare reform, food safety, corruption, and social security) that had never been excluded from the top 10 focal points as identified by the public in all the surveys.[23] Other public surveys on social issues concluded with similar findings. For example, a survey conducted by the Academy of Social Sciences of China in 1998 interviewed 2278 city residents in 22 provinces and cities, and "crackdown on corruption"

[22] Fanlin Meng, Baolong Yan and Junxia Li, *Study on Public-Office Related Crimes* (Lanzhou, Gansu: Gansu People's Press, 2013), 31.

[23] Jiahong He, 1.

ranked No. 1 among the top issues as ascertained by the survey participants. Another research carried out by the Horizon Research Consultancy Group in Beijing in 1999 with thousands of participants in 11 cities concluded with similar findings, and corruption was perceived as the most severe issue among all other important social concerns. In the same year, a research group of the Academy of Social Sciences of China interviewed 50 scholars and 103 senior Party/state officials at the prefecture/bureau level, and again, corruption came out on top of the most important social issues as listed by participating experts and senior officials.[24] A survey conducted by the *Far Eastern Economic Review* in Beijing, Shanghai, and Guangzhou in late 1998 involving top-level managers, senior officials, educators, and entrepreneurs pointed to anti-corruption as the most important measure for furthering economic development. The utmost gravity of official corruption was echoed in the Party officialdom as well. A 1998 survey of prefecture/bureau-level officials attending the Central Party School, the top Party training institution in China, concluded with a consensus that curbing and deterring corruption was a decisive strategy to restore public confidence in the Party. The urgency and seriousness of prevalent official corruption were voiced in the national legislature as well. Instead of rubber-stamping meeting agendas and resolutions as they traditionally do, a significant number of NPC deputies (the National People's Congress) opted to vote against or abstain from voting on the work reports of the procurator general of the Supreme People's Procuratorate and the President of the Supreme People's Court in the 1990s and 2000s.[25]

However, public denunciation and a series of anti-corruption campaigns by the Party-state since the 1980s have had limited success in curbing and deterring rampant corruption in government, state corporations, and public institutions. Numerous cases of corruption investigated reveal that a significant number of officials including senior officials committed corruption and economic crimes right in the middle of the corruption crackdowns. In departments and posts where a high incidence of corruption usually occurs, it has been a recurring phenomenon that the

[24] Meng, Yan and Li, *Study on Public-Office Related Crimes*, 17.

[25] Dali L. Yang, *Remaking the Chinese Leviathan: Market Transition and the Politics of Governance in China* (Stanford: Stanford University Press, 2004), 221.

officeholders of those “fat posts” (offices that are able to generate lucrative payoffs) would fall in sequence on corruption-related charges. The fate of the predecessor seems to have no obvious or limited deterrence against the successor’s intent and determination to follow suit in pursuit of rent-seeking. The Second Plenary Session of the Central Commission for Discipline Inspection held in August 1993 was hailed as a landmark event targeting rampant corruption in government and judiciary. However, it was later revealed that 30 percent of the corrupt cases investigated by the commission were ironically committed in 1993, and another 50–70 percent of offenses were perpetrated in the aftermath of the CCDI 2nd Plenary Session.

It seems implausible to assess the true scope and consequences of official corruption in today’s China as there has been a lack of systemic and comprehensive official data on corruption. The central DIC does not release corruption-related data in a national scope on a regular basis, and the randomly released data, which in most cases were timed for propaganda purposes such as the promotion of the agenda of the Party’s National Congress, showing off the results or effectiveness of the Party’s anti-corruption campaigns, etc., generally lacks details and is not systemic in nature. On the government side, the Ministry of Supervision, the counterpart of the CCDI, largely aligns its functions and operations with its superior, the CCDI. Nevertheless, incomplete and unsystematic national data has only become available since 1992. Comparatively, the relatively complete and workable data is provided by the procuratorate. Corruption cases that have been criminally investigated and prosecuted only account for a small percentage of the total offenses, and the vast majority of the violations, which are less serious in extent, are only subject to Party-state disciplinary sanctions. It seems logical to conclude that violators who have not been ensnared and punished should constitute the vast majority of the corrupt cohort in reform China. Given the secretive nature of corruption and, in the context of China, the difficulties to obtain systemic and comprehensive official data on cadre corruption, it is implausible to determine the actual rate of corruption (ARC). The measurement of the revealed rate of corruption (RRC) based on relatively detailed and systemic data provided by the procuratorate serves as a proxy for the ARC. However, as pointed out by Wedeman, RRC measures “the intensity of enforcement” and is based on “case data that are heavily biased toward high-profile cases".[26] There are variables affecting the duration or timing in which a corrupt official commits corruption and eventually gets caught and prosecuted. This further complicates the assessment of the true scope of corruption using limited and unsystematic case data. The previously cited case study by Guo Yong, which is based on 594 cases involving senior officials between the county/division level and the provincial/ministerial level, reveals that the average undetected duration for corrupt officials, in particular officials at the provincial/ministerial level, were getting longer as the reform proceeded to the 1990s and 2000s. For example, the average undetected duration for the second cohort (officials at the county/division and prefecture/bureau levels) extended from 2.19 years in 1980–1988 to 5 years in 1998–2002 whereas the average undetected duration for the first cohort (officials at the provincial/ministerial level) increased from 1.8 years in 1980–1988 to 8 years in 2003–2004. While explanations for this phenomenon are various, one attributes the lengthened undetected duration of corruption to the surge and rampancy of corruption in the 1990s and the weakening of the supervision mechanism for high-ranking officials in the period.[27] Although the study is based on relatively limited sample data and the selection of the samples may not be statistically representative (particularly the first cohort with only 68 cases), the findings and conclusion of the study, however, are able to shed some light on the incidence, distribution, scope, complexity, and gravity of corruption in the transition period. All in all, however, even with limited and non-systemic official data on corruption, it still seems feasible to generate a reasonable understanding of the true scope and severity of bureaucratic corruption in the reform era.

[26] Wedeman, 89.

[27] Yong Guo, 73–75.

CHAPTER 4

Official Corruption in the Post-1992 Period

Deng's famed southern tour in the spring of 1992 opened a new chapter of the reform, and the momentum of the economic reform resumed following Deng's Shenzhen journey. The 14th Party Congress officially endorsed and adopted the concept of socialist market economy, and the Third Plenum of the 14th Congress held in the fall of 1993 passed a number of important resolutions on the direction, scope, and major tasks of the forthcoming reforms in the framework of the socialist market economy. The resolutions encompassed a variety of fundamental policy issues including: (1) transforming the operational mechanism of the state enterprises and establishing a modern enterprise system with various forms of ownership and clearly defined property rights; (2) cultivating and developing a market system and furthering reforms of the price system, financial market, labor market, real estate, etc. (3) transforming the functions of the government and establishing a macroeconomic control and regulation system with reforms in taxation, banking, and investment sectors; (4) establishing a rational personal income distribution system and social security system; (5) fostering the reform of the international trade system and furthering openness to the world economy; and (6) deepening the reforms of the institutions of science and technology and the education system.[1]

[1] http://cpc.people.com.cn/GB/64162/134902/8092314.html.

F. C. Sun, *An Ineluctable Political Destiny*,
https://doi.org/10.1007/978-981-99-3146-0_4

The post-1992 period was marked by intensified reforms on almost all major fronts of the economic sphere, including continuous privatization of the state sector and the deregulation and streamlining of trade. The late 1990s witnessed large-scale privatization of the state enterprises, and all state-owned enterprises, except for a limited number of large state monopolies in the sectors of banking, telecommunication, petroleum, railway, etc., were divested and sold to private investors and groups. Foreign direct investment (FDI) to China increased dramatically, and foreign capital, in the form of subsidiaries of foreign corporations and joint ventures, started to exert a dominant influence over the formation and development of Chinese industries. The dual-pricing system, which had caused widespread speculation and profiteering in the 1980s, was terminated. More importantly, the authorities took initiatives to deregulate and to streamline trade by reducing tariffs and eliminating or alleviating trade barriers to boost export and import. A landmark event for the post-1992 era was China's admission to the World Trade Organization (WTO) in December 2001, a crucial chapter of the state's developmental trajectory that has brought China to what it is today on the world stage. Reform and liberalization of the state financial sector constituted another major event of economic reform in this period. Deregulation led to the removal of barriers to entry and increased competition in industries and markets. Also noteworthy was the establishment of the basic modern market mechanism and system, as well as a modern macroeconomic control and regulation mechanism.

4.1 Deepening of the Reform and Intensification of Official Corruption

While traditional or old-fashioned official deviations and corruption such as "zou hou men", privilege-seeking, nepotism, and graft had endured over time since the founding of the People's Republic of China, as discussed in the previous chapter, new patterns of corruption emerged, evolved, developed, and spread in close alignment with institutions and incentives created and induced by new reform policies and programs. "Incremental reform with new reforms creating new opportunities for corruption as the deepening of reform closed off or reduce opportunities and incentives for earlier forms".[2] In many instances, faulty policy designs and loopholes, unsophistication in policy and program implementation, strong and greedy venal desires and incentives of implementers and enforcers, coupled with weak institutional and supervisory capacity and lack of effective deterrents, both punitive and moral, have more or less attributed to the surge and pervasiveness of official corruption in the reform era.

With the economic reform entering the 1990s, as mentioned earlier, the phenomenon of the dual-track pricing among raw materials and short supplies was no longer noticeable. Nonetheless, other price discrepancies such as loan interest variances, stock price differences, and real estate price discrepancies, etc., still existed, and hence had attributed to the spread of official profiteering and corruption in those areas. What is more critical in this sense was not only the high incidence of corruption in new spheres but also a dramatic surge in cases of corruption that had implicated a growing cohort of high-ranking officials and involved a staggeringly immense amount of grafted funds. Contrary to the beliefs of many Western economists and scholars, the process of transitioning China's planned economy into market economy had triggered an unprecedented level of official corruption in the post-1992 period. Dynamics and interactions between reform policies and patterns of corruption in the new reform era followed similar paradigms as seen in the previous phase of the reform. For example, when the central authorities chose to stimulate the development of targeted sectors and projects through direct public investment, corruption then took on a new format—organizational bribery—aimed at buying off decision-makers in central ministries for their discretionary authority over granting of mega public investment projects and allocation of special or designated state funds.

When privatization and transformation of state enterprises led to the conversion of a sizable number of public firms into shareholding corporations and prompted the rapid development of the so-called stock economy, there immediately occurred an outpouring of corruption linked to the distribution and acquisition of IPOs and stocks, which were in short supply then due to government restrictions and the limited capacity of the stock market in its initial phase. In the land and real estate sector,

[2] Wedeman, 81.

corruption grew wild in both scope and rampancy at various stages of real estate development such as land lease, acquisition of land use rights, planning, zoning, and financing, when the government proceeded to reform its land policy and to consolidate a commercialized housing market in the early 1990s. The central authorities' initiatives and effort to reform the taxation policy and structure were tampered with by widespread tax evasion and tax fraud fueled by collusions between unscrupulous businessmen and corrupt government officials. When the central authorities stepped up reform of international trade and took measures to eliminate or reduce trade barriers, several waves of smuggling activities along China's coastal regions then took place, causing diminished state tax revenues through large-scale tariff evasions. More importantly, the central authorities' initiatives to reform the ownerships of SOEs and to speed up the privatization of state enterprises were met with widespread abuses of the state policies and looting of state assets by colluded SOE managers and their cronies. "Windfall profits in state-owned industrial and commercial enterprises could come either from outright takeover of an existing firm, selling off parts of the company, or, in some cases, stripping the original firm of its assets and selling them piecemeal".[3] Nevertheless, what had exacerbated the spiraling of official corruption in the post-1992 period was the surge of corruption in law enforcement and judiciary, characterized by its scale, pervasiveness, and the levels of the offenders implicated. Although selling and buying offices and squandering of public funds, typical of irregularities in communist regimes, had continued, what distinguished its manifestations and dynamics from the previous ones were the number and ranks of violators and the sizes of the grafts involved.

A review and analysis of high incidence of corruption throughout the new reform era, as mentioned, reveal a causal linkage between the new policies and the legal loopholes they had caused. Ambiguities and loopholes of the sort were largely attributable to the unsophistication of new reform policies and programs, as well as the inexpertness of the policymakers. For example, the interest rate discrepancies between the state banks and the commercial or cooperative banks reflected the continuation of a dual-track pricing system in the finance sector; as a result, there arose rent-seeking incentives and activities through exploitation and profiteering in bank credits if one was able to acquire credits

[3] Wedeman, 112.

from state banks at lower rates and then sell or transfer them to enterprises in need of commercial loans at much higher market rates. The availability or existence of such loopholes had led to widespread irregularities and corruption in the banking sector and had allowed corrupt officials and illicit businessmen to easily capture windfall profits generated from interest rate discrepancies. The construction boom and the real estate frenzy rendered another unprecedented rent-seeking opportunity and caused prevalent corruption in real estate development. Those who had access to discretionary official power for land lease and land use rights acquired low-priced lands and then sold or re-leased them to other developers at hefty rates. Given the high value of real estate development projects, profiteering in land lease and land use rights was extremely profitable in reform China, and almost half of the top-ranked 30 billionaires in 1994 had reportedly accumulated high-value wealth in no time by speculation and profiteering in land deals and transactions.[4] By the same token, bribes and kickbacks rendered to officials in exchange for favors and discretionary decisions on land lease, land use rights, planning, and zoning tended to be sizeable as well, attributing directly to a surge in major bribery cases in the post-1992 period. As mentioned above, the stock market and profiteering in IPOs constituted another area that had been haunted by high incidences of power abuse and corruption. Officials extended favors and assistance in the IPO approval and listing process in return for bribes in the form of company initial offerings or stocks at low or no cost. As IPOs were normally in high demand in the early 1990s due to government control and restrictions on stock issuance, selling shares at hefty market prices could generate staggeringly large profits and enable those who were able to acquire initial offerings free of charge or at very low cost to amass tremendous wealth at a blink of eyes. Ambiguities and loopholes in the reform policies on land and stock market are blamed for the formation and rise of a mostly illicitly enriched wealthy class and a growing inequality of wealth distribution in Chinese society in the reform era. As mentioned, corruption in land/real estate and stock market had caused widespread public outcry and resentment and is held by many citizens as a symbol of failure of the reform design and reform policies.

Comparatively damaging to the reputation and credibility of the policymakers was the outright looting of state assets and properties by

[4] Meng, Yan and Li, *Study on Public-Office Related Crimes*, 37.

colluders in SOEs and their cronies under the guise of SOE reform and transformation. In 1998, the central authorities decided to further SOE reform and transformation by implementing a new policy of "keeping the big and releasing the small" (抓大放小), namely, keeping the large and strategically important SOEs, but selling or privatizing the small and medium-sized state enterprises, most of which were money-losing and beaten-down firms in the new market economy. Given the dearth of a well-planned, comprehensive, and transparent framework and procedures for the transition, this well-intended strategic policy initiative was quickly turned into an extraordinary opportunity by corrupt SOE executives and unscrupulous businessmen to embezzle and loot state assets and properties. An illicit means utilized to steal state assets in a seemingly legitimate way was to artificially under-appraise the value of the state assets that were to be privatized or marketized. Common schemes involved encompassed "siphoning off assets to private savings and profiteering; concealing the real size of a firm's resources, revenues, and credits; inflating firm expenditures and debt burdens to depress the price of a buyout; and excluding land and other elusive assets from appraisal". Other illicit tactics entailed the use of secret accounts to conceal profits earned from covert sources to keep out of sight intended plundering, looting through distribution and acquisition of state corporation shares, and assisting and profiting the cronies' business operations at SOEs' expense.[5]

However, what concerned the central authorities most may be an escalation of corruption in law enforcement and judiciary in the post-1992 period. Nevertheless, this did not arise as a sheer surprise to the elite and the public alike as corruption had gradually spread out to and permeated almost every sphere of the polity, economy, and society. The dominant reasoning and logic held by the vast majority of the citizens that the wealthy have enriched themselves mainly through corruption and illegal means in the reform era underlie and reinforce a general mentality and ethos in Chinese society that motivate people to seek wealth regardless of legitimacy and morality. The concern and fear that they might be left behind as a class of have-nots in the burgeoning market economy may have been attributed to an escalation of irregularities and corruption among officials and personnel in law enforcement and judiciary. Media coverage and numerous cases of corruption involving illicit power-money

[5] Yan Sun, 92–96.

exchanges and large-scale smuggling and tax evasion activities manifested the nature, scope, and gravity of judicial corruption. Well-publicized major and high-profile cases entailing or implicating high-ranking officials and judges were particularly damaging to the image and reputation of a cohort that has been traditionally entrusted with public trust for impartiality and social justice. The continuous downfalls and prosecutions of leading officials of the discipline inspection commissions and anti-graft bureaus on bribery-related charges across the country had stunned the general public and ridiculed the authorities' capability to combat and deter official corruption. Also worrisome as a trend was the rise of what was termed "legislation corruption". Legislation corruption, typical of a form of group corruption, is in general induced by interest groups aimed to enact legislations for the consolidation and protection of their exclusive and monopolistic interests in their respective industries and sectors. Irregularities in legislation were also committed by local governments and local interest groups to enact legislations and regulations to maximize and safeguard local interests, and those local laws and legislations were often in defiance of the central legislations or against the national interests.[6]

Character, Scope, and Tendency of Bribery in the Post-1992 Period

Among the existing and new patterns of irregularities and malfeasances, it is noteworthy that bribery stands out as the most prominent illicit behavior and act in the post-1992 era. It may not be an overstatement to assert that the legitimacy of the ruling party is currently facing gruesome challenges given the widespread and brazen malpractice of bribe extraction in officialdom. Although the economic loss caused by bribery may not be seemingly as grave as that of embezzlement and misappropriation of public funds, the true cost of bribery to the economy and society may top those of all other forms of malfeasance. The severity and impact of bribery in the post-1992 period are manifested in several dimensions. First of all, new patterns of bribery began to emerge, evolve, and spread out in the public sector and in the economy and society at large. These new types or changing patterns of bribery include collective bribery, organizational bribery, and bribery involving family members and kinsmen. Although family colluded corruption and bribery was not a new phenomenon, it

[6] Meng, Yan and Li, *Study on Public-Office Related Crimes*, 41–43.

became rampant with high occurrence and involved the larger amount of illicit funds in the post-1992 period. Secondly, the actors of bribery were no longer limited to officials and businessmen/citizens as typified in Western corruption theories as new actors such as government agencies, public institutions, SOEs, and publicly traded corporations started to come aboard to compete for interests and to materialize collective gains in a less legitimate or illicit way. Furthermore, bribery-induced corruption began to trend from the cohort of low and middle-ranking officials to the circle of high- and even top-level officials, and the sizes of the bribes involved had skyrocketed from generally low dollar figures to staggeringly high values. Type of bribes was no longer limited to cash and goods, and the new reform phase had witnessed a rise of sexual bribes and other favors. Finally, bribery had sadly become a widely accepted tactic, means, or norm to buy favors, services, and personal gains under the table in nongovernment sectors such as healthcare, education, media, entertainment, sports, etc. The deterioration of the ethos of the society and the formation and evolvement of a culture of bribery and collusion pose serious challenges to the modernization of China's economy and the transformation and democratization of its political system and society in the long run. As can be seen in the following chapters, bribery has overtaken embezzlement to become the most prevalent and persistent pattern of corruption that underlay almost all illicit dealings and corrupt acts across all levels of government and economic and societal spheres.

4.2 Bureaucratic Corruption

In this and the next chapter, patterns and manifestations of malfeasance and official corruption in the reform era shall be grouped into three categories: bureaucratic corruption, regulatory corruption, and judicial corruption in line with their loci, geneses, attributes, and consequences. Breakdowns or sub-patterns of the major categories shall be subcategorized to facilitate illustration, comparison, and analysis of various irregularities, corrupt acts, and crimes throughout various phases of the reform. For example, patterns and manifestations of bureaucratic corruption are further categorized into public programs, investments, and services based on the nature, loci, actors, and effects of the corrupt behavior and acts. Chapter 6 discusses regulatory and judicial corruption, as well as corruption induced by culture/heritage. Corrupt and criminal cases and examples that are illustrative and representative of manifestations of official corruption in various phases of the reform are also included in the analysis and discussion of the phenomenon in reform China.

All states, either autocratic or democratic, have the authority to control and administer the distribution of public resources and benefits and the imposition of onerous costs. As the agents entrusted with state administrative and law enforcement powers, public officials in general possess the discretionary power to allocate these resources and benefits or to impose the costs. When a government distributes a benefit or service with a fixed supply that exceeds demand, illicit incentives in the form of bribery may emerge intending to gain a competitive edge over competitors for scarce resources and benefits. "Like a private monopolist, the public servant sets supply below (or raises the payoff above) the officially sanctioned level to increase the economic rents available for division".[7] Dishonest government officials also have the incentive to create situations in which they can demand bribes. For example, they may force those who are qualified for a benefit or service to pay bribes by taking advantage of their monopoly power to create scarcity or red tape or to delay approvals and withhold applications. "In general, the greater the discretion of officials and the fewer the options open to private firms and individuals, the higher the costs of a system that condones corruption even if all who obtain the services are, in fact, qualified".[8] There exists a dilemma that red tape encourages bribery whereas the expectation of bribes reinforces red tape. Corruption harms the state and society in the sense that it not only incurs costs and economic loss to the state but also distorts the purposes and criteria of the distribution of public programs and services.

Generally speaking, payoffs are made in exchange for actions that violate rules. The unqualified may have stronger incentives or higher willingness than the qualified to offer payoffs because they have no legal way to obtain the benefits or services. This constitutes one of the most prominent incentives of rent-seeking in the post-Mao era. Unscrupulous individuals and enterprises who do not qualify for bidding on public contracts or are not entitled to certain benefits and services make illicit

[7] Susan Rose-Ackerman and Bonnie J. Palifka, *Corruption and Government: Causes, Consequences, and Reform* (2nd edition) (Cambridge, UK: Cambridge University Press, 2016), 61–62.

[8] Ibid., 65.

payoffs to get an inside edge in public tenders or to acquire the sought benefits. On the other hand, bribery can not only make the unqualified qualify for entitlements, but also make those who qualify for a government entitlement be judged unqualified for the pure purpose of payoff extortion. While the former occurs mainly at relatively higher levels of the hierarchy in government and SOEs, the latter seems to be more rampant at the lower levels of the officialdom. Low-level corruption, or petty corruption, occurs when the bureaucracy interacts with the public, and "the aggregate quantities involved in petty corruption and the costs to society may be very large".[9] This partly explains the genesis and pervasiveness of the "three arbitraries" (san luan) and their detrimental consequences to the society in the reform era.

Both transactive and non-transactive corruption exist in reform China, and, as mentioned earlier, the transactive forms of corruption such as bribery have seemingly become the most dominant pattern in the new phase of the reform. In its transition from a centrally planned economy to market economy, the state's four-decade-long reform and developmental course may have presented the unprecedented licit and illicit opportunities in the country's history or even in a global setting for both honest and dishonest entrepreneurs and public officials alike to capitalize on. In the context of modern China, it is the political power that prevails over and distributes economic power. In a state that is characterized by "a large government and a small society", rent-seeking opportunities and incentives derived from the immense public ownership of resources and all-inclusive political dominance and control over economic and social affairs abound. Bureaucratic corruption, in this sense, is manifested in the form of both grand corruption that involves state infrastructure, public investments, land and resources, SOE privatization, and widespread abuses of regulatory and enforcement powers by state officials for illicit payoffs.

One of the defining features of the Chinese bureaucratic and political corruption is collusion among elites in the perpetration of malfeasances and corruption. Crony capitalism, as what is conveyed in the study of the post-communist states and societies, refers to an institution or system in which the economic elite, in collusion with political elite, misappropriate or even outright loot state-owned assets and then share the illicit

[9] Ibid., 53.

economic gains with their political cronies. Unlike crony capitalism in non-communist and democratic societies, which is "mostly about rent-seeking and entrenching the power and privileges of the established elites in a relatively stable political environment", crony capitalism in China and the states of the former Soviet bloc is characterized by collusive corruption between capitalists and political power that largely occurred in the process of privatization of state-owned assets and properties. As shall be discussed in subsequent sections, political and economic elites "collude to underprice such assets or seize them for free, either through outright theft or by ostensibly legitimate procedures they can manipulate or control".[10] One of the key contributing factors to the rise of crony capitalism in reform China, as stated earlier, was the decentralization of administrative authority to local elites and the delegation of managerial and decision-making power to SOE executives and managers. What seemed particularly pertinent to the surge of collusive corruption among elites was a delegation of decentralization without a constraining mechanism as lack of enforceable accountabilities often exacerbated corruption at both corporate and local levels.

What differentiates crony capitalism in reform China from that of the former Soviet-bloc states is that misappropriation and looting of state-owned assets by those connected with the ruling elites is a "one-time event" in the latter, whereas "the illicit seizure of such property is an ongoing process in the former" as the Party-state sustains dominant public ownership of state assets and resources.[11] This is particularly the case under the current regime as the state is taking measures to strengthen and expand the role and influence of its state monopolies at the expense of the private sector. With the state continuing to own the dominant immensity of assets and resources in the form of land, minerals, monopolistic SOEs, etc., incentives and proneness to bureaucratic and political corruption will sustain.

[10] Minxin Pei, *China's Crony Capitalism: The Dynamics of Regime Decay* (Cambridge, MA: Harvard University Press, 2016), 15.

[11] Ibid., 20.

Public Programs, Investments, and Services

As discussed, illicit payoffs undermine the goals of a public program or service as corrupt officials tend to allocate public projects or distribute benefits or services to those with the highest willingness to pay rather than those who are either the most qualified or in need of the governmental benefits or services. Indiscriminate rent-seeking and bureaucratic corruption in the delivery and distribution of public programs, investments, and services were once widespread and pervasive throughout various phases of the reform. While bribery and corruption may have to some extent contributed to the leveling of a playing field where disadvantageous entrepreneurs and TVEs were able to gain access to public construction projects, governmental procurements, and bank credits, it had also led to the rise of organizational corruption as many well-qualified state-owned enterprises were forced to make payoffs in order to maintain or reinforce their competitive advantages over their private competitors in a less legitimate way. In this sense, the consequences of reckless rent-seeking and official corruption are particularly detrimental to the state and society as almost all the actors and players across the board were either participating or involved in distorted competition for scarce public programs and benefits.

Public programs and services are seemingly a broad domain encompassing infrastructure projects, public investments, land and resources, privatization of state-owned enterprises, state bank loans and credits, export tax rebate programs, state-allocated goods and supplies, etc. Embezzlement of public funds and squandering are also included in this chapter as both are corrupt and criminal acts that involve either outright plunder of state funds or misspending of public money for personal and organizational benefits and gains. Theft of SOE assets and properties through collusion and abuse of authority in the process of SOE privatization, the most notorious and detrimental manifestation of embezzlement in reform China, will be singled out for probe and discussion. While some patterns of corruption such as bribery, embezzlement, and squandering were sustained throughout the reform era, as pointed out earlier, the breadth and depth of the malpractices had both aggravated in the post-1992 period. While some misdeeds such as official profiteering were typical of wrongdoing in the early phase of the economic reform, mainly a consequence of rent-seeking incentive to the ill-defined dual-track pricing system in the transition of a planned economy to market, most of the malfeasances, particularly those that took place in spheres such as SOE privatization, land and resources, infrastructure, public investments, and bank loans and credits, either arose or spiraled out of control at the advanced stages of the reform.

Official Profiteering

Official profiteering or "官倒" in Chinese is perceived to be a dominant and early pattern of organizational corruption in the mid-1980s and early 1990s. The practice then, by both the stipulation of the reform policy or the legal term, was not illegitimate nor illicit. In response to the state's policies of reform and opening-up as well as the popular slogan or rhetoric of "letting some people get rich first" in the early days of the reform, there emerged a nationwide rush to start businesses and to engage in profit-making activities among individuals and organizations. Under the circumstances the business mania throughout the country escalated unprecedentedly. A proverb vividly described the situation: "900 millions of one billion people are already engaged in trade, and the remaining 100 million are ready to join them (十亿人民九亿商，还有一亿待开张。)". Many Party committees and government agencies at various levels set up their own administrative companies for profit-making operations. Also dashed into the "company frenzy" (公司热) were the military and public institutions encompassing universities, hospitals, and cultural and media establishments. The phenomenon was once so pervasive that the whole bureaucracy from the State Council and central ministries at the top level to local government divisions and branches at the bottom level all setup companies and commercial operations to make money for the benefits and interests of the work units and organizations. According to statistics, by mid-1987 there had been about 360,000 companies, among which 250,000 were involved in the dual-track pricing speculation.[12] Of the 250,000 corporations, many were administrative ones directly run by government agencies and headed by either high-ranking officials or influential retired cadres and children of senior officials. For instance, about 700 such companies belonged to the central ministries and commissions under the State Council, and about

[12] Connie Squires Meaney, "Market reform in a Leninist System: Some Trends in the Distribution of Power, Status, and Money in Urban China," *Studies in Comparative Communism* Vol.XXII, No.2/3 (1989): 212.

47,900 cadres concurrently held positions in both government departments and corporations.[13] Those administrative corporations, dubbed "bureaucratic firms" (官办公司), were officially registered as independent, for-profit business operations under state or collective ownership, and were run by their sponsoring agencies and institutions, either directly or indirectly, to pursue in general non-production, speculative, and profiteering (官倒) commercial activities. Those bureaucratic firms generally had obvious competitive advantages over non-official firms as they were staffed, financed, and supported by their sponsoring agencies with respect to capital, resource, personnel, and equipment. More importantly, they had access to governmental monopolistic power over production input and short supplies allocation and distribution, as well as regulatory and enforcement authority and influence.

The military's engagement in commercial and for-profit activities was largely attributable to central leadership's consideration of prioritizing the limited national financial capacity and resources toward the paramount goal of economic development in the early phase of the economic reform. In other words, the reform policy then provided "the imprimatur for the military establishment's engagement in commercial businesses" to generate revenues to supplement its budget. The mid-1980s and the 1990s consequently saw the proliferation of PLA-affiliated companies and businesses that were widely involved in almost every sphere of the economy, ranging from mining, manufacturing to service. Those military-run companies provided spouses of career military officers with employment opportunities. By 1988 annual income generated by the commercial subsidiaries of the military reached 2 billion yuan. By the early 1990s businesses affiliated with the military had numbered approximately 20,000 with 600,000 civilians employed. A report by *China Daily* in 1999 put the estimated total assets of the businesses operating under the PLA's umbrella in the range of 50 billion yuan, with roughly 5 billion yuan in profits and taxes annually. However, given the military's apparent advantages on several fronts such as state-allocated land, facilities, equipment, vehicles, etc., like their counterparts run by or affiliated with the Party-state apparatus, the military firms were in a comparatively advantageous position to gain an edge on competitors and to rake in "easy" money in no time. For example, the military's privileged access to land,

[13] Gong, *The Politics of Corruption in Contemporary China: An Analysis of Policy Outcomes*, 130–131.

radio frequencies, airports, etc., had largely facilitated the operation and enhanced the profitability of its transport and telecommunication businesses. Another competitive advantage was the tax privileges and legal immunity that many military firms and operations enjoyed due to the armed forces' special status. Like the civilian bureaucratic firms, military bureaucratic firms were also involved in speculative and profiteering activities, capturing rents generated by the dual-track pricing system in the period.[14]

There were three waves of "company frenzy" roaring across the country in the early years of the reform—1985, 1987–1988, and 1992, and, as a result, the number of bureaucratic firms tripled from 300,000 in 1985 to over 900,000 in 1992. Each wave of "company frenzy" was followed by a new round of "rectification of companies" launched by the central authorities. Through their semi-legitimate and illicit operations and acts, those bureaucratic firms were able to seize enormous rents and "transform the public assets and regulatory authority under the command of their sponsoring official agencies into capital for individual and collective gains".[15] Arbitraging and profiteering by taking advantage of the price discrepancies created by the dual-track pricing system remained the main avenue for bureaucratic firms and even state enterprises to make quick windfall profits at the early stage of the economic reform.

As discussed earlier, though the CCP leadership had been emphasizing the key role of the market in economy and had loosened its rigid price control over a considerable number of raw materials and goods, it did not intend to abandon the command economic system completely and was still in control of some factors of production and key raw materials. On the other hand, there existed an obvious shortage of key production inputs and quality consumer goods and supplies in the domestic market. To make things worse, the rapid growth of private and collective enterprises in the 1980s also aggravated the gap between demand and supply in various sectors. The shortages and deficiencies on the supply side, therefore, created rent-seeking opportunities and incentives for government agencies and officials who were authorized to control and allocate key input materials or short supplies. With the introduction of a dual-pricing system to industry, state-owned enterprises were allowed to sell surplus

[14] Dali Yang, 125–130.

[15] Manion, 97–99; Lu, 202–203.

products above the planned or assigned quotas, and in the commodities market, by the same token, the dual-pricing system dictated pricing of the in-plan and the market (above-plan) priced commodities. This semi-administrative and semi-market system had resulted in a confusing price system in the second half of the 1980s. There existed three different prices for the same items: the state-planned price, the negotiable price, and the market price.[16] The dual-track pricing system had nurtured a fertile ground for rent-seeking and official corruption. Due to the existence of apparent price discrepancies, one could enrich himself simply by selling quotas of some materials and short supplies at the market prices if he was able to gain access to those items at the state-set prices. Easy, quick, and potentially extraordinary profits and gains through speculation and profiteering via the dual-track pricing system prompted a proliferation of official profiteering activities nationwide. The previously mentioned proverb for "company frenzy" was timely modified to describe the new phenomenon: "900 million of the 1 billion people are involved in speculation, and the remaining 100 million are looking for opportunities for profiteering" (十亿人民九亿倒, 还有一亿正在找). There had been always a high demand for those state-allocated industrial material inputs and short supplies among the newly emerged township-village enterprises and private operations that had been institutionally shut out of the state allocation and distributary system for controlled materials and supplies. Bribes and kickbacks were therefore generally involved as non-state firms were desperately in search of quotas for inputs of production and short supplies within the plan. Bureaucratic firms and even state-owned factories often profiteered by simply selling the state-priced raw materials for production. It had been a common practice that the same raw materials or short supplies would be sold and resold several times in the process of transaction; as a result, the prices of the finished goods were generally driven up in the speculative process and resulted in soaring inflation. A steel pipe plant in Nanjing, for example, sold its thousands of tons of steel plate obtained at a cheaper price to 31 small factories and received a profit of 1.35 million yuan. Those small factories then resold those items for profits. "The same process went on until after 129 transactions, and the price of the plate was raised from 1,750 to 4,600 yuan per ton". Another case concerned an administrative company

[16] Wojtek Zafanolli, "A Brief Outline of China's Second Economy," *Asian Survey* Vol.XXV, No.7 (July 1985).

involved in official profiteering—Kunming Metallurgical and Economical Technical Resources Development Company in Yunnan province. This company acquired goods in short supply at the state-set prices from its parent company, a governmental resource distributive agency, and then sold those items at higher market prices. In December 1984, just by selling 2458 tons of steel ingots at 650 yuan per ton (the original price was 422 yuan per ton), this company made a profit of 560,000 yuan.[17] Major speculative and profiteering cases often entailed staggeringly large amounts of state funds. One of the high-value profiteering cases for the period concerned Yufeng Industrial Corporation in Fujian province. Led by vice president Du Guozhen, the company had been engaged in a range of speculative and profiteering dealings and activities involving over 190 million yuan in public funds.[18]

In addition to production inputs and short supplies, regulated services and state-controlled quotas were also popular targets for profiteers and favor-seekers. Due to the limited rail transportation capacity in the 1980s and 1990s, competition for rail cargo quotas that were planned, controlled, and allocated by the state railway administrative authority was fierce as profiteering on quotas of the sort often generated extraordinary profits. A case concerning rail cargo quota allocation and profiteering in Zhengzhou, Henan province is illustrative of the malpractice in the 1980s. Three profiteers—a provincial official, a public enterprise manager, and a businessman—colluded to buy off the deputy director of Zhengzhou Railway Bureau and the director of the transportation bureau in the Ministry of Rail Transportation for cargo allocation quotas above the central plan. With the allocated rail cargo quotas, they were able to transport coal by train to other localities for profiteering. In the meantime, the profiteers also bribed "layers of other officials" for their cooperation or took no notice of their illicit activities. By the time they were detained, the profiteers had made a fortune of several million yuan. The case eventually implicated more than fifty officials in the railway transport administration system including fifteen at the bureau level and the deputy railway minister Luo Yunguan.[19] Two years later another deputy

[17] Stephen K. Ma, "Reform Corruption: A Discussion on China's Current Development," *Pacific Affairs* Vol.62, No.1 (Spring 1989): 1045–1046.

[18] http://www.spp.gov.cn/spp/gzbg/200602/t20060222_16380.shtml.

[19] Yan Sun, 56.

minister, Zhang Xintai, was investigated for the same misdeed of allocating rail cargo quotas in return for payoffs. While Zhang was dispatched by the Ministry of Railway to Zhengzhou to investigate the aforementioned profiteering and bribery case in 1989, he returned to Beijing three times to meet with a briber and to take cash bribes. In return, he managed to allocate 50 out-of-plan rail cargo wagon quotas to the briber to facilitate her profiteering on coal transport and sales.[20]

Another phenomenal manifestation of official profiteering in the 1980s was the widespread involvement of top Party and state officials' children in the malpractice. This privileged group, dubbed "the party of princelings", by taking advantage of their parents' influence and political connections, were able to gain access to the state-priced raw materials and short supplies, and hence had amassed enormous fortunes through profiteering. Many high-profile military firms and businesses were led or operated by princelings at the time. The rampant involvement of this privileged group in speculative and profiteering transactions was faulted as one of the major catalysts for the outbreak of the 1989 Tiananmen Movement. Examples abounded concerning the speculative activities of "the party of princelings". The Kanghua corporation in Beijing, for example, in which the son of one of the most powerful state leaders was allegedly "deeply involved", was accused of engaged in official profiteering through buying low and selling high. It was reported that Kanghua once made a profit of 8 million yuan by selling 10,000 color TV sets (then in short supply) at a price that was 800 yuan higher per set than the purchasing price.[21]

Decentralization and the establishment of the Special Economic Zones (SEZ) in coastal regions and cities in the early years of the reform empowered local governments, opened up SEZs for foreign investment, and stimulated the development and growth of the local economies. On the other hand, the same policies created loopholes and incentives among local authorities to manipulate or even abuse those special policies and economic leeway for the interests of the localities. One manifestation of the manipulation and policy abuse was smuggling and profiteering led

[20] *Major and Important Anti-Corruption Cases in the 1990s* (in Chinese) (Beijing: Fangzheng Press, 1998). http://www.shuku.net/novels/baogaowenxue/zgczfbjs/zgczfbjs12.html.

[21] Jae Ho Chung, "The Politics of Prerogatives in Socialism: The Case of Taizidang in China," *Studies in Comparative Communism* Vol.XXIV, No.1 (March 1991): 64.

or condoned by local authorities. The case of large-scale profiteering on import cars in Hainan in 1984 was exemplary of the policy abuse in this regard. In January 1984, the central government decided to open up Hainan Island in Guangdong province, along with other 13 coastal cities, to attract foreign investment and to boost local economies. Came with the decision was a special policy that allowed Hainan to use its foreign currency reserve to import industrial and agricultural inputs and consumer goods in short supply. Attached to the special policy was a proviso that limited the imported inputs and goods to use on the island only; in other words, it would be a violation if the imported goods were shipped out of the island for whatever purposes. The local authorities took the special policy as a profiteering opportunity to import Japanese vehicles, which were then in high demand in the mainland market, and also a potential stimulus to the local economy. In the summer of 1984, an "import car frenzy" started to roar across the island. Eighty-eight out of the 94 government departments and agencies were involved in the business of importing and selling imported cars. Led and influenced by the government agencies, people from almost every trade and occupation were fanatically involved in the import car business, and within six months a total of 872 companies were set up to profiteering in the business. The frenzy had grown so white-hot that almost everyone on the island was in desperate search for "import permits" for profiteering. Unsurprisingly, rent-seeking and official corruption grew rampant in the process of import permit approval and issuance, and equally severe were bribery and collusion involved in the approval of bank loans and credits to fund car importing and transactions.

The island government profiteered in the business by imposing "fine" on vehicle purchases; as long as mainland purchasers paid the "fine" (4000–5000 yuan per car) to the local authorities, they were "officially permitted" to drive or ship the vehicles out of the island. In total, the local government issued 89,000 import permits within 6 months. However, rampant policy abuse and profiteering, as well as widespread corruption involved in the import permitting and vehicle trading process, had eventually enraged the central leadership; as a result, the frenzy came to an abrupt end in late 1984 when the provincial government ordered the island government to stop the illicit trade. The Party chief and other senior officials of the island government were investigated and subsequently disciplined or criminally charged for policy violations and criminal offense.[22]

While bureaucratic firms of government departments and agencies overseeing the distribution of production inputs and short supplies profiteered through price discrepancies between the in-plan price and the market price, administrative firms of regulatory agencies sought economic rents by charging clients hefty fees for approvals, inspections, licenses, permits, etc. For example, instead of conducting construction inspections free of charge as stipulated, a municipal government set up an inspection center (its bureaucratic firm) and started to rake in income by charging clients inspection fees.[23] The municipal department of finance in a major city was authorized to review and approve government procurement under the regulation of "restricted social group procurement"; granting of procurement approvals, as stipulated by the finance department, however, was on condition that applicants must make purchases of merchandises from the bureaucratic firm that was affiliated with the department. Similar practices prevailed in the banking sector as well. A state bank made paid consultation and assessment through a credit consulting firm, its own bureaucratic firm, a prerequisite for clients to apply for and secure bank loans. It was estimated that there were at one time over 700 such credit consulting firms nationwide.[24]

The "company frenzy" and widespread official profiteering in the 1980s proved to have a long-lasting impact on organizational corruption and malfeasances in government, judiciary, and the military in the decades to come. Official profiteering, to a certain extent, was the intervention of political and administrative powers in economy, and for the first time in the PRC history, it acted as a catalyst to convert political capital into economic capital for those who were politically connected. It was bureaucratic commerce and official profiteering that had enabled them to accumulate the original capital to profiteer in more profitable businesses in the 1990s such as land, real estate development, resources, finance, acquisition of state assets, and even smuggling. The rampancy

[22] Xiaobo Wu, *The Surging Thirty Years: Chinese Enterprises 1978–2008* (in Chinese) (Shanghai: Zhongxing Press, 2008). http://www.dubaocankao.com/html/news/shgc/2015/0611/6116.html.

[23] Manion, 99–100.

[24] Lu, 204–205.

and severity of military corruption in later periods were logically correlated to military bureaucratic commerce in the 1980s and 1990s. As shall be discussed later, the armed forces' involvement in profit-making activities was directly attributable to its engagement in smuggling in the South China Sea in the 1990s. As mentioned, bureaucratic commerce had benefited not only privileged and well-connected individuals, but more importantly, it had contributed to the collective interests and benefits of the sponsoring agencies. For example, it provided employment options and opportunities for retired and retained extra-establishment officials as well as the offspring of members of the organizations. The revenues generated in the profiteering process had become an important extra-budgetary and discretionary income source for the collective benefits of the members of the organizations, which were often being divided up as cash bonuses, or being squandered for collective consumptions such as feasting, sightseeing (usually in the name of conferences or observation tours), or residential housing, vehicle and equipment purchase, facility upgrades, etc.

Embezzlement and Misappropriation of Public Funds

Embezzlement and misappropriation of public funds, along with acceptance and extortion of bribes, are the most frequent forms of corruption in reform China, accounting for approximately 80 percent of all cases of corruption. While the two offenses entail similar acts of taking public funds from the public coffer, they differ mainly from intentions and accounting measures for the misappropriated funds. Embezzlement involves intentional misappropriation of public funds by illegal means such as theft, peculation, or defrauding, and the embezzler usually intends to tamper with or eliminate any accounting-related evidence of the misappropriated funds by destroying, altering, or forging bills and accounts, whereas misappropriation entails unauthorized and temporary use of public funds for illicit, speculative, and profit-making activities without any intention to defrauding the funds. In other words, the public official who has misappropriated the funds intends to return the funds in part or in whole after its use in the future. Therefore, misappropriation of public funds generally does not involve elimination of the traces, transactions, or physical evidence of the funds in a public account. Although both behavior and acts are corrupt and serious offenses depending on the amounts involved and the duration of the misappropriation, the nature of the illicit acts and the impact on the state and society are different. When public money embezzled or misappropriated reaches a certain amount, the acts are classified as "economic crimes" and the corrupt actors are usually subject to criminal charges. Those who have been involved in vast amount of peculated public funds are even subject to the death penalty in the Chinese context. In contrast to bribery, which is transactive in nature and generally involves illicit exchanges between public officials and non-state actors such as businessmen, citizens, etc., embezzlement and misappropriation of public funds fall under the category of auto-corruption or non-transactive corruption as they entail in general individual public officials or collusion of officials only and are dire looting of state assets.

Embezzlement and misappropriation of public funds, as discussed earlier, existed in the Mao era, and had increased in both occurrence and scale since the advent of the economic reform. A publicized major case in the early 1980s concerned Wang Shouxin, a female manager and Party secretary of an energy company in Heilongjiang province, who had grafted 530,000 yuan in eight years, and spent part of the misappropriated funds on buying off local influential figures for facilitation, protection, and cover-up of her misdeed. The amount of the embezzled state funds was deemed extraordinarily large as measured by the average income benchmark for the period, and Wang was then labeled as the gravest embezzler in the history of the PRC. Wang received capital punishment.[25] Several years later Wang's embezzlement record was overtaken by another major peculation case in Guangdong province. Pan Qixiong, a procurement agent of the Huaiji County Industrial and Agricultural Trading Company, embezzled over 770,000 yuan in state funds. Wang and Pan both had direct access to monetary transactions and were in a position to abuse authority and to commit accounting irregularities for concealment and fraud. For those who do not have direct access to cash or funds, however, state assets and property under their stewardship often become the targets of looting. For example, Mao Taocheng, a weighman at Shulan County Grain Depot in Jilin province, by taking advantage of the convenience associated with his duty, had managed to defraud the state of grains in

[25] Leslie Holmes, *The End of Communist Power: Anti-Corruption Campaigns and Legitimation Crisis* (New York: Oxford University Press, 1993), 112–113.

the amount of almost 250,000 kilograms in the early 1980s. Ma was prosecuted and received the death penalty in 1984.[26]

As demonstrated in Chapter 3, cases of embezzlement and misappropriation of public funds investigated and prosecuted by procuratorates had increased dramatically in the 1980s. New records of the state funds misappropriated by corrupt officials had been broken consecutively in the mid and late 1980s. For example, Jiang Zhengguo, manager of the finance section of the Wujin County Chemical Fertilizer Plant in Jiangsu province, plundered state funds totaling 1.29 million yuan. Targeted currencies were not limited to RMB; those who were involved in foreign trade and had access to foreign currencies such as USD, Hong Kong dollar, etc., stole foreign currencies from state and company accounts. For example, Lin Xu, an official of Haifeng Trade Company in Fujian province, grafted $170,000 in USD and 3.07 million in RMB from the company accounts, a staggering amount then as per the 1980s standard.

Embezzlement and misappropriation of public funds in the early years of the reform occurred mainly among managers and officials of public enterprises and low-level government officials. Predators at relatively high levels such as the prefecture/bureau level and above seemed to be uncommon. A case of misappropriation of public funds in Shaanxi province in the late 1980s and early 1990s concerned a leading official at the prefecture/bureau level who was entrusted with overseeing the allocation of two provincial special funds. Yang Feng, deputy director of Shaanxi Provincial Economic Commission and member of the Party Group, colluded with his relative, Hu Linri, director of Zichang County Economic Commission, to set up an illegitimate company, Anxi Corporation, in Xi'an City, the capital of Shaanxi province. Hu took the general manager position, and Yang's nephew and son were appointed as the manager and deputy manager of the firm. In addition, Yang's wife and sister-in-law were also "hired" as accountants and cashier. Via a bank account of a provincial institution, Yang Feng misappropriated state funds from the two special funds designated for coal and electricity usage compensation under his control and illicitly transferred the capital to Anxi for business operation and profiteering for profits. Yang basically filled out the fund transfer applications himself and then submitted them

26 *The Supreme People's Procuratorate annual work report (1984)*. http://www.spp.gov.cn/spp/gzbg/201208/t20120820_2488.shtml (accessed January 25, 2020).

to himself for approval. Rules, procedures, due diligence, and supervision regarding funds allocation and approval were outright ignored and violated. Between December 1987 and February 1990, Yang misappropriated state funds nine times totaling 4.427 million yuan. Anxi used some of the misappropriated funds to profiteer in steel and aluminum ingots and to purchase shares in other companies to generate dividends. With Yang Feng being taken into custody in March 1990, Anxi was shutdown and Yang's cronies were investigated for wrongdoing and criminal offenses. Unsurprisingly, a significant portion of the misappropriated state funds was unable to be recovered and had to be written off.[27]

Another embezzlement and profiteering case that had caught nationwide attention and received broad media coverage in the 1990s was more about the status of the predator rather than the amount of public funds the official had grafted. Yan Jianhong, president of Guizhou International Trust and Investment Corporation and deputy director of the provincial planning commission, was a powerful lady in the southwestern province of Guizhou; what had made her even more powerful and influential, however, was her status of the "First Lady", i.e., the wife of the Party chief of Guizhou province. In less than five years, Yan recklessly committed a series of corrupt acts and economic offenses of embezzlement, bribery, and profiteering. As president, she stole public funds and took bribes in collusion with unscrupulous businessmen and her subordinates in the provincial trust and investment corporation; as the deputy director of the provincial planning commission she abused her discretionary power and also the influence of her husband, and together with her son, to aggressively engaged in profiteering in regulated goods and short supplies for windfall profits; as a mother, she was in sheer violation of the Party disciplines and rules to assist and facilitate her son's illicit business dealings and to safeguard his illegitimate interests and gains. Ironically what had motivated Yan, a veteran Party member and high-ranking government official, to recklessly involved in rampant rent-seeking activities was to accumulate sufficient wealth so that she could retire and live with her sons in the U.S. She had reportedly said that she would be willing to give up her job,

[27] Shaanxi Provincial Commission for Discipline Inspection, "Provincial Deputy Director Yang Feng Misappropriated Over 4.4 Million Yuan in Public Funds," in *Major and Important Anti-Corruption Cases in the 1990s*. http://www.shuku.net/novels/baogaowenxue/zgczfbjs/zgczfbjs42.html (accessed July 29, 2020).

Party membership, and even the Chinese citizenship if she could immigrate to the US. Court documents revealed that between 1989 and 1992 Yan had in total embezzled RMB 650,000 yuan and $14,300 USD and misappropriated RMB 2 million yuan and $50,000 USD; collectively she and her accomplices colluded to peculate state funds in the amount of 1.5 million yuan. Yan had also been charged for profiteering and bribery; for example, she made an illicit profit of 400,000 yuan by profiteering in cigarette quotas. Using her official power and the family influence, Yan assisted her eldest son to profiteer in chemical fertilizer, pesticides, coal, and aluminum ingots and had pocketed illicit profits of approximately 1.2 million yuan. Yan was sentenced to death and was executed in 1995.[28]

Unlike high-ranking and influential officials like Yan who oversaw tens or hundreds of million yuan annual budget and had ample rent-seeking opportunities, low-level managers and officials had to take riskier routes for plundering. Conventional illicit tactics for misappropriation of state funds under this circumstance include accounting irregularities, fraudulent claims, fake invoices, false documents, etc. Given the limited sizes, budgets, operations, and commercial or industrial activities of some state-owned SMEs, misappropriation often became detectable if the implicated amount was sensitively large and the accounting irregularities involved were less sophisticated. However, during the company and profiteering frenzy in the 1980s, hundreds of thousands of managers and officials of the state-owned enterprises nationwide, along with their counterparts in large corporations and government agencies, were recklessly engaged in profiteering and graft activities, all rushing through the same route toward their common destination—getting rich quick. Liu Shengwu, a middle-level manager of Ih Yu League Material and Supplies Trading Centre, peculated public funds totaling 3.14 million yuan between 1988 and 1990 by profiteering in goods in short supply such as cars, aluminum ingots, etc. Instead of looting the state by pocketing profits generated through price discrepancies under the dual-track pricing system, Liu simply inflated the purchase prices of those items by submitting fake invoices or committing other accounting irregularities. For example, Liu plundered nearly 1 million yuan in one business transaction entailing the purchase and retail of 30 Jeep Cherokee SUVs by using fake receipts to inflate the purchase price of those vehicles. Using the illicit proceeds, Liu

[28] https://wenku.baidu.com/view/d44129e09b89680203d825da.html.

and his wife purchased luxury residences in Beijing, Shanghai, and Tianjin and had been living a lavish life ever since. Liu's case, reportedly the largest embezzlement case in the history of Inner Mongolia, concluded with Liu being executed in 1993.

In summary, sectors and industries plagued by a high incidence of embezzlement and bribery in the period included banking, construction, grain administration, consumer goods, and production input supplies, as well as materials and equipment supply and distribution. With the reopening of the Chinese stock market in 1990, misappropriation of public funds as interest-free capital for speculative activities such as stock speculation, business capital, and real estate funds had been on the rise. The state finance sector saw a relatively high occurrence of malfeasance as a growing number of state bank officials abused their authority to misappropriate bank funds for personal gain. The illicit act had gone rampant in the 1990s and disclosure of various major cases involving misappropriation of hundreds of million yuan in public funds triggered waves of public uproar in the country. As stated previously, decentralization of decision-making power and implementation of the managerial responsibility system provided SOE managers with increased autonomy and motive to manage and innovate on one hand, on the other hand, it also rendered them opportunities and greater convenience to peculate. The main cohort of predators, like their counterparts in the previous reform period, continued to be low- and middle-level managers, accountants, treasurers, etc., in SOEs and public institutions. While intent, incentives, behavior, and illicit means of plundering remained largely unchanged, what had changed over time were the scope, actors, and sizes of embezzlement and misappropriation. As in the pre-1992 period, the banking industry continued to be one of the sectors with a high incidence of embezzlement and misappropriation, characterized by stunningly high value of misappropriated public funds in tens or even hundreds of million yuan. According to publicized cases, the misappropriated state funds were often used as business capital for businesses run by family members, relatives, and cronies, or were diverted to unauthorized investment or speculation for illicit financial returns. Worst of all, there were even cases involving the diversion of various state specialty funds, such as agricultural procurement, to real estate and construction projects during the development boom of the early 1990s. According to a report by the Agricultural

Bank of China, "over US $1 billion was siphoned out of procurement accounts nationwide for speculative investment, unauthorized loans, or simple embezzlement by local government agencies and officials".[29]

Public Procurement, Investment, and Infrastructure

Not many states—autocratic or democratic, developing or developed—are free from corruption arising from large-scale or high-value public infrastructure projects. While third-world states of autocracy and dictatorship are riddled with corruption in public procurement and infrastructure, highly developed Western democracies such as the U.S., Germany, Italy, etc., are also prone to corruption in capital-intensive public infrastructure and construction projects. Grand corruption in public procurement arises from the incentives of corrupt officials and unscrupulous businessmen as both parties collude to jockey for advantage and divide illicit gains. A complete project bidding cycle is normally comprised of four phases: specification, prebid, bid evaluation, and postbid. According to Rose-Ackerman and Palifka, there are several nodes in the public procurement process in which officials and firms can collude to distort bidding rules and procedures and to appropriate illicit gains at the expense of the state.

> First, firms and officials can select or design projects with lucrative corrupt opportunities even if they are of little social value. ... Firms with political connections or insiders in the procurement process induce officials to underestimate environmental and social impacts or overestimate demand. ... Second, once a project has been proposed, a firm may pay to be included in the list of prequalified bidders and to limit competition. It may also pay for inside information, such as others' bids, that will help it win the contract. ... In the extreme, bribes may induce officials to structure the bidding specifications so that the corrupt firm is the only qualified supplier. ... Once a firm wins the contract it may pay to get inflated prices, to 'extra' (allegedly unanticipated) work, or to skimp on quality. On the other side of the deal, officials may extort extra payments from the firm for subsequent regulatory approvals and other benefits.[30]

[29] Manion, 106–107.

[30] Rose-Ackerman, 104–108.

Corruption distorts decision-making and rationale for the selection and awarding of public procurement and infrastructure projects. Transparency International studies indicate that corruption can raise the costs of procurement by as much as 50 percent. Corruption not only leads to the selection of distorted and inefficient public projects up front but also systemizes the costly and lax project implementation over time. Cost overruns and lower quality infrastructure often serve as the explicit indicators that suggest corruption may be implicated in the project designing, bidding, and awarding process. In many cases, systemic corruption and collusion often factor in the colluders' anticipated illicit gains into the inflated project costs even before the project commences.[31] Through collusion and conspiracy, unlawful bidders and corrupt officials are able to conceal illegal payoffs and create future payoff opportunities over the course of project execution. The detrimental consequences of grand corruption are not limited to the mere scale of public investment and lost revenue to the public coffer. As rent-seeking prospect and potential increasingly shape high-ranking officials' favor and tendency for the selection of public procurement projects, corruption in this sense can influence the structure and composition of a state's macroeconomic formation. For instance, if rents are easier to be extracted from capital investments and input purchases than from labor-intensive projects, influential officials tend to favor capital projects "irrespective of their economic justification". This to a large extent explains why "high levels of corruption are associated with higher levels of public investment as a share of GDP (and lower levels of total investment and FDI)". For similar reasons, corrupt rulers obviously favor public investment over private investment.[32]

Besides its harmful economic consequences, grand corruption in public procurement and infrastructure exerts a negative social impact as it distorts the distribution and time path of net social benefits. Due to various factors and considerations such as the official's venality and insecurity, corrupt officials tend to have a higher discount rate than the populace and they therefore tend to support projects with quick short-term payoffs and costs spread far into the future.[33] Grand corruption arising from rapid and large-scale infrastructure development in reform China proves

[31] Ibid., 97.

[32] Ibid., 101.

[33] Ibid., 102–103.

to be an illustrative case study that reveals the true motives behind the construction hysteria in the reform era. They were partly driven by local government leaders' political ambitions to generate economic growth and achievements for the prospect of promotion and career advancement, and, on the other hand, partly by the political elites' venal incentive to split windfall profits with their colluders. As can be seen below, power abuse, manipulation, collusion, conspiracy, and fraud abound throughout the project bidding process. In many cases, venal political elites often opt investment efficiency and social benefits for illicit personal gain in infrastructure development and public procurement; consequently, "dou fu zha" (inferior quality) projects, repeat constructions, inefficient investment, waste, environmental pollution and damages, etc., had become notorious synonyms of infrastructure development in many localities.

Infrastructure and Construction

Infrastructure and construction have been one of the sectors hard hit by high incidence of bribery and official corruption throughout the reform era. With the construction boom, there arose a nationwide proliferation of construction companies established and owned by individuals and TVEs, many of whom were rural entrepreneurs with insufficient experience and qualifications in the industry. To gain access to construction projects and subcontracting opportunities, those firms in general resorted to bribery to pay for favors and discretionary decisions on project bidding and award. As mentioned earlier, due to policy and procedural loopholes as well as laxity in monitoring and enforcement in the early days of the economic reform, power abuse, collusion, and corruption were widespread and rampant in the procurement process of infrastructure and public construction projects. It may not be an exaggeration to contend that in the infrastructure and construction industry, many private and TVE construction companies had heavily relied on bribery and collusive corruption to gain an advantage over their competitors including well-qualified SOEs to either secure public construction projects or defraud the state by escalating project costs or compromising project quality.

As judged by public opinion, the construction industry was one of the most corrupt industries in reform China as it rendered probably the most lucrative illicit payoffs and kickbacks to venal government officials and SOE executives. In the post-1992 period, bribers were not limited to dishonest private contractors only; as indicated, state-owned construction companies including some large corporations had increasingly resorted to less legitimate means in an attempt to gain a competitive edge over their private counterparts to win large infrastructure projects. As demonstrated in the cases below, public officials at both local and central levels were recklessly involved in collusion with corrupt builders and even SOEs in pursuit of lucrative payoffs at the expense of the state. Wei Shizhong, deputy mayor (prefecture/bureau-level) of the City of Yingtan and also the leading official overseeing municipal planning and infrastructure construction, had long been a prioritized target for builders and contractors to gain access to municipal civil and engineering construction projects. During a two-year period, Wei and his wife either took or extorted bribes and kickbacks from contractors and subordinate municipal civil engineering managers in exchange for favors and discretionary decisions in the project bidding and awarding processes. Wei's fall caught the provincial authorities off guard as Wei had become the highest-ranking official in Jiangxi province who had ever been investigated and prosecuted for corruption by the early 1990s. Another case entails more serious misconduct as the predator both abused his discretionary authority to broker construction loans and also provided bribers with government loan guarantees in return for payoffs. Chen Binggen, director of the municipal housing administration (prefecture/bureau-level) in Shenzhen, Guangdong province, was entrusted with the authority to oversee the construction, marketing, and distribution of welfare housing and subsidized housing in Shenzhen SEZ. Driven by venal incentives, Chen, in violation of state rules and procedures, managed to help his bribers win leasing contracts for the municipal shopping centers and also brokered bank loans for the bribers' real estate projects. To facilitate the approvals of the bank loans he even colluded with the bank managers to provide government loan guarantees in the name of the municipal housing administration in outright defiance of relevant state stipulations and procedures on the provision of government loan guarantees. Chen received capital punishment in 1991 due to the nature and gravity of his criminal offenses.[34]

[34] Cheng Yaowen and Lai Bojin, "The Bribery Case of Shenzhen Housing Administration Director Chen Bingeng," in *Major and Important Anti-Corruption Cases in the 1990s*. http://www.shuku.net/novels/baogaowenxue/zgczfbjs/zgczfbjs23.html (accessed October 8, 2020); Ling Xiang, "The Bribery Case of Wei Shizhong Deputy Mayor of Yingtan City Jiangxi Province," in *Major and Important Anti-Corruption Cases in the*

While the aforementioned two bribery cases entailed only a limited number of actors and construction projects and the bribable amount involved was also limited, large-scale infrastructure and construction projects characterized by high-value capital investment and complicated bidding and contracting processes had become a fertile breeding ground for rampant rent-seeking that in general involved a series of outsized bribes with a large number of venal officials including high-ranking ones. As shall be discussed in subsequent sections, collusive corruption had grown so rampant and pervasive in infrastructure development that in some cases high-ranking officials overseeing highway construction fell one after another on bribery charges from the same post in a given period. Generally speaking, directors of transport departments/bureaus at various levels had become an increasingly high-risk profession for wrongdoing as a disproportionately large number of occupiers of the position had been ensnared for investigation and conviction. For example, between 1995 and 2014 a total of 17 directors of provincial transport departments in 12 provinces were prosecuted and convicted of bribe-taking and corruption. In an extreme case, four directors of the provincial transport department in Henan province were investigated and charged for bribery and corruption in a period of 11 years. What was ironical in this case was that every successor to the position had once vowed to cleanse the legacy of corruption of his predecessor and to lead by example of honesty and integrity.[35]

It had been an informal and implicit rule in the construction industry that kickbacks in the range of 3–10 percent of the project value be rendered to influential officials in exchange for infrastructure and construction contracts. In general, officials with authority over contracting, quality inspection and control, and engineering materials supply were in a more advantageous position to negotiate illicit deals and to extort a higher share of the project profits. As mentioned, the post-1992 period saw a growing number of SOEs that had increasingly turned to illicit means such as organizational bribery to help secure public infrastructure and construction projects. Private businessmen, acted as

1990s. http://www.shuku.net/novels/baogaowenxue/zgczfbjs/zgczfbjs25.html (accessed October 8, 2020).

35 "Seventeen Directors of Provincial Transport Bureaus Have Been Investigated in Nearly Two Decades," *people.cn*, October 17, 2014. http://politics.people.com.cn/n/2014/1017/c1001-25854895.html (accessed November 4, 2020).

middlemen or agents of corrupt officials, often played a pivotal role in the negotiation and brokerage of illicit deals between the two parties. The well-publicized and high-profile bribery and abuse of authority case concerning Liu Zhijun, minister of railway, is exemplary of how high-ranking officials and businessmen collude to loot state funds in the tendering and contracting process of infrastructure and construction projects. When an auditing team of the National Audit Bureau was dispatched to the Ministry of Railway to conduct conventional audit work, the auditors noticed that the SOE contractors including large state-owned corporations had made payoffs in the name of intermediary fees to Ding Yuxin, a private businesswoman, in an effort to win large state railway development and construction projects. What seemed abnormal and absurd was that Ding, with the intervention and facilitation of the railway minister and other powerful ministry officials, was able to help those SOEs to gain an edge in the project bidding process and to eventually ink state railway construction contracts. It was revealed through an investigation that Liu Zhijun and Ding Yuxin had colluded to forge a reciprocal business partnership; while Liu abused his authority to help Ding appropriate windfall profits in the state railway system, Ding, in return, would use the illicit fortune she had acquired under Liu's influence to feed Liu's desires for power, money, and women. Between 2007 and 2010, Ding helped 23 SOEs to win the tendering of 57 railway engineering and construction projects; in return, Ding and her accomplices raked in over 3 billion yuan in "intermediary fees".[36] Grand corruption involving illicit deals in the tendering and awarding of large construction contracts was also a major illicit means for SOE executives to amass rents. Chen Tonghai, CEO of Sinopec (provincial/ministerial level), was prosecuted for bribe-taking totaling almost 200 million yuan between 1999 and 2007; by abusing his discretionary power and influence, Chen had made his ill-gotten fortune by helping his bribers to secure land acquisitions and land use rights, obtain construction contracts, and facilitate their business operations.[37]

The gravest consequence of corruption in infrastructure and public construction is the loss of lives caused by circumvention of building

[36] "'Power Broker' Ding Yuxin Sentenced to 20 Years in Prison," *China News Service*, December 16, 2014. http://www.chinanews.com/fz/2014/12-16/6880681.shtml (accessed September 5, 2020).

[37] http://finance.jrj.com.cn/people/2009/08/0514425701302.shtml.

codes and inferior quality of construction. Those dangerous malpractices are quite common in developing countries and are often greenlighted by corrupt building inspectors and public officials in exchange for illicit payoffs. A 7.9 earthquake in Wenchuan, Sichuan province in May 2008 led to approximately seventy thousand deaths, including fatalities of over 5000 elementary and middle school students. As impacted by the earthquake, "thousands of classrooms collapsed while buildings around them remained intact". The tragedy in Wenchuan was in sharp contrast to the after-effects of earthquakes of similar magnitudes in New Zealand and Chile (one of the least corrupt countries in Latin America) in 2009. While the 8.8 earthquake in Chile caused hundreds of fatalities, the disaster in New Zealand did not lead to any earthquake-related deaths. Angry parents of the dead students in the Wenchuan earthquake protested to accuse builders and school authorities of collusive corruption and bribery and demanded an investigation into concealed illicit deals and criminal offenses in the classroom tendering and construction process. "Despite promises of an inquiry, however, the only related arrests were of parents demanding accountability".[38]

Public Investment

The central authorities' strategic shift from plan allocation of goods and finances toward fiscal stimulation and public investments in targeted sectors and regions in the new reform phase created new rent-seeking opportunities and incentives. The four specifically designated special funds (专项基金) created and administered by the central authorities include poverty relief funds, state bonds for infrastructure construction, hydraulic construction funds, and higher education funds.[39] While the competition for favors and discretionary decisions on the allocation of public investment projects and distribution of special funds triggered a surge in bribery—mainly organizational bribery, administration and allocation of some funds such as poverty relief, agriculture, and rural relocation at the local level also incited misappropriation and plundering of state funds among basic-level government agencies and public organizations.

The Xi-Li administration has been campaigning since 2015 to lift all Chinese citizens above the poverty line by 2020; it turns out, however,

[38] Rose-Ackerman, 71–72.

[39] Yan Sun, 60.

that this campaign proves to be one of the most corruption-plagued crusades in the reform era, especially at the county and village level. A report by the Chinese Academy of Social Sciences revealed that among all the complaints filed to the party's anti-corruption watchdog, more than half of them were related to poverty alleviation funds at the local level. For example, in the first half of 2016 alone, more than 5000 low-level cadres nationwide were prosecuted or disciplined for malfeasances related to poverty alleviation. According to the Central Commission for Discipline Inspection (CCDI), village officials were found to be quite creative in taking a cut from the poverty relief funds allocated from higher offices. In one case, a village official in Guizhou province, one of the most impoverished provinces in China, embezzled 150,000 yuan (US$22,600) from his village's poverty relief funds to run his own business between 2014 and 2016. Another village official in Shaanxi province was caught extorting mandatory "donations" from poor families. All families in the village who had been granted approvals to receive tourism-related small business start-up funds were required to make a donation of 5000 yuan. The 30 families, all living under the national poverty line, received their funds only after they made the extorted payments to the village cadre.[40] However, the nature of the offense and the severity of the consequences, both economic and political, often subject those corrupt low-level officials, dubbed "fly grafters" (蝇贪), to unusually harsh punishments. Zhang Shilong, manager of the welfare office of the civil affairs bureau in Ningyang County, Shandong province, embezzled over 150,000 yuan in poverty relief funds that should have been distributed to the children of over 20 poverty-stricken households as monthly allowances for nine months (600 yuan per family per month). The misappropriated funds were used by Zhang for speculation in stocks and personal consumptions. Zhang was sentenced to ten years and six months in prison, a punishment that seemed to be obviously severe in terms of the total amount misappropriated.[41]

Poverty relief funds in the form of agricultural and housing improvement project funding designated for impoverished localities are often

[40] Jun Mai, "Corrupt Officials Holding Back China's Drive to Eliminate Poverty," *South China Morning Post*, August 29, 2017. https://www.scmp.com/news/china/policies-politics/article/2108613/corrupt-officials-holding-back-chinas-drive-eliminate (accessed August 7, 2020).

[41] http://news.ifeng.com/a/20161023/50143390_0.shtml.

targets of misappropriation and looting. In Huaheng County, a central government-designated ethnic minority impoverished county in Hunan province, several bureau directors and deputy directors colluded to defraud and embezzle state-allocated farmland improvement funding totaling 6.78 million yuan out of the 10 million yuan in funding allocation. Irregularities, bribery, and fraud had been committed throughout the project granting, execution, and inspection processes. Important project documents such as project supervision log and project investment assessment report were either forged or acquired through payoffs. As a result of the multi-staged plundering and embezzlements, the completed portion of the project accounted for only less than 23 percent of what had been planned for a total area of 303 hectares. What seemed ironic and absurd was that such a fraudulent project had not only been able to pass the inspections of the three-level governments (county, prefecture, and province), but had also been rated "good quality" project by the inspection team. The collusive embezzlement and corruption eventually came to light with 24 officials being investigated and prosecuted. Cases like this abound; according to the National Poverty Alleviation Office, a total of 19,500 officials nationwide were disciplined for misappropriation of poverty relief funds in 2016, among whom 1892 officials were criminally investigated and convicted.[42]

Subsistence allowance or income support for urban and rural residents in need is an important social welfare policy and program; however, power abuse and corruption are widespread in program delivery and social aid allowance distribution. One of the common schemes is to enlist unqualified candidates, in general family members and relatives of the officials who oversee program delivery, as recipients of the social welfare benefits. A rampant power abuse and plundering case in this regard, as reported in 2017, was exemplifying the scope and gravity of corruption in program delivery at the county and grassroots levels. The Civil Affairs Bureau of Longchuan County, Yunnan province, the government agency responsible for the delivery of the income support program, was found to have fraudulently enlisted 82 unqualified and ineligible family members and relatives of the bureau officials for the distribution of the monthly subsistence allowances. Among a workforce of 56 officials and staff, 40

[42] "Media Reveals Embezzlements in Poverty-Relief Funds at Basic Level," *fa zhi zhou mo*, July 27, 2017. http://news.ifeng.com/a/20170727/51515987_0.shtml (accessed June 25, 2020).

members or 70 percent of the bureau staff including leading officials were involved or implicated in the corrupt act. Five officials at the bureau level including the director were consequently disciplined and demoted, and two middle-level managers were prosecuted for a criminal offense.[43] With the implementation of the poverty relief and agriculture support and subsidy policies and programs in recent years, the distributed amount of the special funds has increased accordingly and significantly. In Gansu province, a poor province in northwestern China, the annually allocated special funds designated for poverty relief and farming subsidy amounted to over 400 million yuan; in the meantime, cases entailing looting and misappropriation of those special funds have surged correspondingly. In 2013, for example, 599 officials in the province were investigated for violations and criminal offenses in this regard, a 33 percent increase in comparison to the previous year, and the occurrence accounted for 44 percent of the total economic crime cases committed by officials for the year.[44]

The development and construction of the well-known Three Gorges Hydroelectric Project, the largest hydropower station in the world, in the 1990s led to large-scale population migration and relocation of factories and facilities in the affected upstream region of the Yangtze River. Between 1993 and 1999 the authorities allocated 17.68 billion yuan in special migration funds and relocated and resettled 220,000 residents out of the affected area. On the other hand, huge state investment in migration and resettlement programs may have also rendered local officials with a once-in-a-lifetime opportunity for plundering. There had been altogether 138 prosecuted cases since 1993 involving peculation and misappropriation of migration and resettlement funds totaling over 31 million yuan. Huang Faxiang, director of Fengdu County state land bureau, embezzled over 12 million yuan in migration funds by illicitly concealing the funds off the accounts of the bureau and then covertly invested it in his own hotel development project. To facilitate the execution of his thieving scheme, Huang appointed his sister-in-law to be the treasurer of the special migration funds and managed to keep the inflows of the funds allocated out of the bureau's official account. Conspiratorially, Huang intended to blur and eventually eliminate the traces of the

43 http://news.ifeng.com/a/20171122/53488867_0.shtml?_zbs_baidu_news.

44 http://finance.huanqiu.com/roll/2016-03/8746714.html.

transactions as time went by. Huang was sentenced to death and was executed in 2003. Chen Zhilan, Huang's subordinate at the bureau and also Huang's sister-in-law, also misappropriated migration resettlement funds for speculation in stocks. Chen was convicted of fifteen-year imprisonment. A third case concerns a female treasurer in Wanzhou Prefecture Migration Bureau, who was caught on misappropriating state migration funds for mahjong gambling. She was charged and sentenced to fifteen years in prison.[45]

While individuals stole from designated special funds, government agencies misappropriated special funds for extra-budgetary uses such as vehicle purchase, office renovation, even speculation on stocks, etc. A report by the National Audit Bureau revealed that nearly one thousand counties and cities nationwide had ripped off poverty relief funds and funds designated for education to purchase automobiles.[46] It was not uncommon that in small county towns, which were limited in size and were largely within walking distance, officials at the bureau director level and above were often equipped with government vehicles. For example, one county that had been in deficit for a prolonged period had its 84 county governmental agencies each equipped with two cars. One impoverished county in the northeastern region had even purchased over 700 cars by 1989; while being allocated by the central government an annual poverty relief fund of 13.76 million yuan, the county ironically spent 10 million yuan on gas and maintenance of the government fleet on an annual basis. Although widespread plunder and misappropriation of the state-designated special funds often occur at the local level, misuse of state special funds by central ministries and agencies that are supposed to be the administrators and stewards of the designated funds also exists even though it is much less frequent. For example, the Ministry of Water Resources and its subordinate institutions, in a period of four years, had misappropriated 116 million yuan from special funds designated for water conservancy and irrigation, and the diverted funds were used mainly for the benefits and welfare of its staff such as building or purchasing

45 http://t.2web.cn/wfdslsc/jdht/html/?3083.html. http://t.2web.cn/wfdslsc/jdht/html/3087.html.

46 Jean-Louis Rocca, "Corruption and Its Shadow: An Anthropological View of Corruption in China," *The China Quarterly* No.130 (1990): 410.

office space and residential housing, investment, and even speculation on stocks.[47]

In comparison to the incidence and scope of embezzlement and misappropriation of public investment funds, bribery, in particular organizational bribery, constituted the widely employed illicit tactics that firms, both private and state-owned, and even local governments applied in an effort to jockey for large public investment funds and developmental projects administered by central authorities. The emergence and notoriety of the phenomenon of "public bribery" (公贿) in the post-1992 period was partly attributable to the central authority's strategic and structural shift from command economy to market. As discussed previously, many SOEs, in particular SMEs in the non-strategic sectors, with the phasing out of a variety of privileges and advantages under the planned economy, were forced to compete with other SOEs and private enterprises in the marketplace for infrastructure and construction projects, land and real estate, bank credits and loans, government procurements, and marketing. In a bureaucracy and economy that were permeated with corruption and faced with the sad fact that private enterprises in general deployed illicit means such as bribery to gain a competitive edge over rivals in project bidding and contracting process, many SOEs or the restructured or transformed version—shareholding companies—had to resort to bribery as well to compete with their private counterparts for contracts and market shares. Rather than being largely an individual behavior and act, bribery or bribe-offering in the new phase of the reform had become a behavior and illegitimate practice of enterprise or even government. Bribers were no longer limited to individuals and firms as had been the case in the previous phase of the reform, SOEs, public institutions, and even local governments had joined forces or even become the dominant players in organizational bribery. A study of convicted bribery cases in the 2000s revealed that public bribery constituted approximately 60 percent of all bribery cases, and public funds misappropriated for bribe-offering amounted to 65 percent of the total bribe money in the study period.[48] The post-1992 period also witnessed a change of instrumentality and incentives of bribery. "Whereas earlier bribes had served to distort policies already made, now bribes are used to influence the

[47] Meng, Yan and Li, 23–24.

[48] Ibid., 23.

policy-making process by local agencies, firms, and other organizational recipients of public investments". Several popular sayings attested to the means and tactics of organizational bribery. "大跑大项目，小跑小项目，不跑没项目" means "major lobbying wins major projects, minor lobbying wins minor projects, and no lobbying wins no projects".[49] Scarcity of major public projects and special funds at the ministerial level as well as ministerial officials' discretionary power over allocating state funds had led to fierce competition among localities and public institutions and were partly blamed for the surge and rampancy of public bribery in the new reform era. As cited in the case above regarding bribery and corruption in the Ministry of Railway, state-owned construction corporations paid bribes out of public money, via the middleman, to the minister and senior officials overseeing high-speed railway development, a national priority of transport development, to tap into the pool of the priority funds and high-speed railway construction projects.

Public Procurement

Also on the rise were cases entailing collusions between unscrupulous businessmen and corrupt state officials to either sell products or services manufactured or rendered by public enterprises at below-market prices in exchange for payoffs or procure goods, equipment, or services from the colluded private agents at above-market prices for kickbacks. With the rapid growth of the private sector as well as the mushrooming of TVEs, it may be logical to argue that it was corrupt officials' collective venal desires and incentives that may have to some extent objectively assisted or facilitated the private sector's efforts to make inroads in the thriving market economy of reform China, given its overall economic and political disadvantages and vulnerability on various fronts such as capital, technology, expertise and experience, credibility, social status, market access, etc., in its infant stage. As collusive corruption in infrastructure and construction, also a domain of public procurement, has been examined earlier, this section shall look into malfeasances in other sectors. Guan Zhicheng, the Party boss of Beijing Iron and Steel Corporation (the largest subsidiary of the Capital Iron and Steel Corporation), extracted kickbacks and bribes worth over 1.5 million yuan between 1986 and 1990 (a lot of money

[49] Yan Sun, 60–61.

by the income standard then). Steel, the product of the steel corporation, was then a state-regulated good in short supply, and by abusing his discretionary power in allocating steel quotas and approving steel sales Guan had repeatedly demanded cash kickbacks from purchasers in the name of "out-of-plan shipping fee", "price discrepancies", "processing fee", "labor service fee", and "profit sheering". While approving sales of steel wire rods to a steel rolling mill in Hebei province, Guan, first of all, designated the wire rods as agricultural input with its sale price capped at 800 yuan per ton, approximately half of the market value for steel wire rods. Guan then demanded a "price discrepancy compensation" of 400–450 yuan per ton from the buyer and then pocketed all the proceeds. Guan's two young mistresses were also involved in varying degrees in Guan's illicit dealings, and both were convicted as Guan's accomplices. Guan received capital punishment and was executed in the early 1990s.

Buying high for inputs, consumables, and equipment and selling low for finished products and services was another tactic to loot SOE assets and state funds. To facilitate the carryout of the plot, corrupt SOE executives and state officials usually appointed their relatives and cronies to important internal positions such as middle-level managers, procurement officers, accountants, treasurers, etc., and then set up family- or crony-controlled companies as suppliers or agents to sell high to SOEs or buy low from SOEs for profiteering. With internal–external collusion, materials and supplies of low or even inferior quality were often procured by SOEs at above-market prices, whereas SOE products or services were often distributed to those companies at below-market prices to enable them to cash in on the transactions. This was one of the grave consequences of widespread nepotism in the state sector and also an outlet for loss of state assets in reform China. There were numerous cases concerning colluded embezzlement and looting of SOE funds and assets among family members and cronies. For instance, a VP in charge of the import and export portfolio at a SOE, colluded with his wife, the head of the finance department of the SOE, to plunder state funds and assets. The couple, first of all, let their two sons to set up two companies, one in the city and another in Shenzhen, and then, by abusing their discretionary authority, the parent helped their sons' firms to profiteer from business dealings with the SOE through selling high and buying low or other illicit and fraudulent schemes.

The group embezzlement case in the grain industry in Changtu County, Liaoning province serves as a typical case of loss of state assets attributable to official corruption in public procurement. Managers of the state grain depots, as condoned by the director and deputy director of the Grains Administrative Bureau of Changtu County, colluded with the county leading officials' children, relatives, and cronies as well as local criminals to defraud and embezzle state funds and assets by procuring grain storage supplies and equipment at prices ranging from several times to hundreds of times higher than the market prices. The procured materials and equipment were often of inferior quality and even fake products. What was absurd was that some of the supplies were procured in such large quantities that the purchased materials could even last for approximately 70 years. State expenditures on grain storage supplies and equipment, on the other hand, had skyrocketed from 16.9 million yuan in 1990 to 123 million yuan in 1992, an over sevenfold increase in two years. The investigation revealed that abuse of authority and widespread corruption initially started at the top level of the county grain administration in 1988. Led and influenced by a bad role model of the corrupt director of the county grain bureau, grain depot managers, county officials, their children and relatives as well as scrupulous businessmen and unlawful elements in Changtu joined forces to defraud the state by "selling high" to all the grain depots in the county. During a period of two years a total of 1500 people took part in the profiteering and fraudulent schemes. The director's niece reportedly made a profit of 245,000 yuan by selling her uncle's procurement approval notes to speculators. There were cases in which police officers and depot managers colluded to forge procurement receipts and records to defraud the state of payments for goods that had never been purchased. Reportedly, approximately a dozen female speculators even offered sexual favors to the director in exchange for his approval notes of procurement. Among the 412 people who had been directly involved in the case, 54 of them were criminally charged for embezzlement, misappropriation, bribery, dereliction of duty, illicit profiteering, and fraud, and three of them including the grain bureau director were sentenced to death in 1994. Financially, the state incurred a heavy loss of over 68 million yuan as a result of the collective corruption and fraud, and the dollar figure was deemed staggeringly high for an agricultural region in northeastern China in the early 1990s.[50]

[50] http://www.360doc.com/content/14/0429/20/1433596_373297160.shtml.

The following high-profile and well-publicized case concerning the "tycoon" of China's tobacco industry is demonstrative of how executives of state monopolies profiteered from "selling low" of the products SOEs produced in return for kickbacks and illicit gains. Chu Shijiang, dubbed "the king of tobacco of China", was the president of Red Pagoda Group and the CEO of Yuxi Cigarette Factory in Yunnan province in the 1980s and 1990s. After being appointed as the CEO of Yuxi Cigarette Factory in 1979, Chu had transformed this local and little-known plant into a large-scale and modern cigarette manufacturer. It is acclaimed to be the largest cigarette manufacturer in Asia and the fifth largest in the world. The plant was a top contributor to the provincial economy, turning over close to 20 billion yuan in tax and profit payments to the state treasury on an annual basis. Chu was therefore showered with honors, state awards, and titles in recognition of his outstanding work and tremendous contributions to the province and the industry. To consolidate his reform and managerial initiatives, Chu was granted unprecedentedly three-in-one authorities over the production, marketing, and administration of tobacco and cigarette products: CEO of Yuxi Cigarette Factory, General Manager of Yuxi Prefectural Tobacco Company, and director of Yuxi Prefectural Bureau of Tobacco Administration. The "three-in-one" power structure may have undoubtedly assisted Chu to reform and optimize the production, manufacturing, and marketing of tobacco products and to better coordinate various segments of the industry; on the other hand, it also rendered Chu unprecedented opportunities and leeway for rent-seeking. Traditionally, the state maintains its monopoly and control over the production and marketing of tobacco products, given the tobacco industry's high profit margins and its capability to generate sizable income and tax revenues for the state. As the central authorities started to eliminate planned prices on many materials and commodities in the post-1992 period, price control and the dual-pricing mechanism for the tobacco industry had remained untouched. Given the ever-increasing market demand for high-quality cigarette products like the Red Pagoda Mount manufactured by Chu's factory, there existed a lucrative incentive to exploit the price discrepancies between the planned or state-set prices and the market prices for the top-selling cigarette brands. For example, a carton of Red Pagoda Mount plan-priced at 49 yuan could be sold for 100 yuan in market, and incentives to obtain quality cigarettes at the planned prices had to a large extent induced widespread rent-seeking in the industry. Starting in 1991, Chu, the chief accountant, and a VP decided to set up several covert accounts in Hong Kong and Guangdong to receive kickbacks resulted from selling cigarettes at "floating prices". Chu demanded a floating price on top of the planned price ranging between 10 and 20 yuan per carton be paid to those secret accounts, and between 1991 and 1995 total cashflows to those accounts had amounted to over RMB 1 billion yuan and $25 million US dollars. In the meantime, Chu's daughter and wife took or extorted bribes from individuals and companies who were seeking approvals and favors from Chu to purchase top-brand cigarettes at planned prices. An investigation revealed that Chu's daughter had extracted bribes in the sum of RMB 36 million yuan, plus over 1 million Hong Kong dollars and $300,000 USD between 1991 and 1995. In early 1995, after learned that he would be requested to retire, Chu decided to take funds from the concealed accounts to self-compensate for what he called his hard work, outstanding performance, and great contributions to the state that might have been perceivably underpaid for years. The trio, together with the general manager and deputy general manager of a subordinating company, misappropriated $3.55 million US dollars and split it up among themselves. Chu received $1.7 million USD and the funds, at Chu's request, were transferred to his son's overseas account. Chu Shijian was sentenced to life in prison in 1999.[51]

Bank Loans, Credits, and Misappropriation

Sectors and industries plagued by high incidence of bribery and corruption were not limited to land, real estate, infrastructure and construction, public investment, etc., the finance and banking sector was also riddled with rampant irregularities and corruption. Parallel with a dramatic increase in demand for bank loans and credits that had largely resulted from surging economic activities, the reform era, particularly the post-1992 period, saw an escalation in corruption in the banking sector. Fueled by the demand to fund either business expansion or land transactions and real estate development, firms and developers resorted to all possible means, licit and illicit, to either obtain bank loans and credits or misappropriate public funds to get their projects off ground. With escalating

[51] Liu Siyang and Zheng Hongfan, "The Tragedy of the 'King of Tobacco'," *shuku net.* http://www.shuku.net/novels/baogaowenxue/zgczfbjs/zgczfbjs01.html (accessed July 1, 2020).

demand and strong incentives for bank funds, power abuse and rent-seeking activities in the banking sector had surged accordingly. There had always been fierce competition among loan applicants to access and secure scarce state bank funds. Once again, bribery became the widespread illicit means to buy off high-ranking bank executives and low-level branch managers and account managers to access bank credits and to come by business loans. Similar to widespread political intervention in lands, resources, and real estate, Party chiefs and high-ranking officials often defied banking rules, procedures, and due diligence to intervene in business loan decisions on behalf of their bribers and cronies. This was what was dubbed "power loans" in the sector. The rise of high-risk loans and the resultant bad loans in the banking sector were largely attributable to prevalent corruption and illicit exchanges between power and money.

While state bank executives with sufficient discretionary power were able to mishandle bank funds under their stewardship with relative ease due to regulatory and procedural loopholes and laxity in monitoring and supervision, low-level bank managers and account managers often resorted to what were perceived to be reckless and even absurd means to misappropriate bank funds or steal deposits in order to raise loan funds to generate illicit interest income. A misappropriation case in the banking sector is exemplary of the mentality, recklessness, and desperation of the cohort for self-enrichment in the reform era. Liu Huiming, then at the age of 56, was promoted to the sales manager position at the Xi'an Branch of the Agricultural Bank of China in 1988. As what was characterized as "the phenomenon of the age of 59" (五十九岁现象) in the Chinese officialdom, Liu was anxiously and heedlessly seeking opportunities to get rich before his obligatory retirement at the age of sixty. Instead of targeting bank funds, Liu preyed on bank deposits of military-run companies and public enterprises. He defrauded his clients' fixed-term deposits by forgery and other fraudulent means and then transferred the funds to the bank accounts controlled by his son and brother. The misappropriated deposits were mainly used by Liu as high interest business loans to enterprises and businesses in need of capital and credits. For example, Liu, via his brother, once loaned 1 million yuan to a coal distribution company at a monthly rate of 3.5 percent; Liu deducted 210,000 yuan as interest expense upfront and then handed the remaining funds to the borrower. Over a two-year period, Liu had misappropriated a total of 6.15 million yuan. While Liu was preying on bank customers for deposits, he himself was preyed on by illicit businessmen and swindlers as well. By the time Liu was detained, over 800,000 yuan he had lent out as business loans or investments in real estate had been defrauded and had never been retrieved.[52]

In contrast to low-level bank officials like Liu who took on high-risk schemes of stealing or misappropriation, powerful bank executives often deployed relatively low-risk rent-seeking tactics to generate wealth—illicitly trading credits and bank loans for bribes and kickbacks. Gao Senxiang, director of Shenzhen branch, of CITIC Industrial Bank, started to extort kickbacks from loan applicants soon after he was appointed to the branch director position of CITIC. In outright violation of the bank rules and procedures regarding loan application assessment and due diligence, Gao repeatedly directed bank officials and account managers to process and approve loan proposals from companies he had recommended. Between June 1988 and July 1990, Gao raked in lucrative bribes from a dozen businessmen from Hong Kong and mainland China; in exchange he directed and approved a series of business loans and loan guarantees in the amount of RMB 85.8 million yuan, $7 million Hong Kong dollars, $17.5 million USD, and loan guarantee of $9.44 million USD, respectively. It was estimated that the unpaid loans after the due dates had been in the range of over 100 million yuan. During his tenure as the bank branch director, Gao sheltered three mistresses and had been indulging in squandering and extravagance at the expense of the state. Gao was convicted of accepting and extorting bribes and kickbacks totaling $1.48 million Hong Kong dollars and RMB 630,000 yuan, and was sentenced to death.[53] Another scheme involved the misappropriation of bank funds to issue illicit loans aimed to generate interest income for individual or collective gains. Cai Hangang, general manager of the Suzhou branch of the Bank of Communications, and Yang Hesheng, deputy mayor of the City of Suzhou, Jiangsu province, in collusion with middle-level managers of the branch and unscrupulous businessmen and corrupt elements, violated bank rules to misappropriate bank funds totaling 4.1 billion yuan. Those funds were then put into circulation out of the banking system as business loans for the purpose of generating illicit interest discrepancies and

[52] Yue Hongge, "The Liu Huimin Embezzlement Case," *shuku net*. http://www.shuku.net/novels/baogaowenxue/zgczfbjs/zgczfbjs37.html.

[53] *Major and Important Anti-Corruption Cases in the 1990s*. "Gao Senxiang Corruption Case," *shuku net*. http://www.shuku.net/novels/baogaowenxue/zgczfbjs/zgczfbjs11.html (accessed March 1, 2020).

incomes for personal gains. Cai was also involved in bribe-taking and extortion totaling over 1.4 million yuan through irregularities in the approval of bank loans and credits. The insinuation of this case was grave and alarming as it had implicated corrupt acts and criminal offenses of nearly one hundred organizations and institutions across 17 major cities and provinces.[54]

As stated earlier, political interventions in bank loan decisions and issuance were widespread and were often faulted partly for the rise of bad loans and credits in state banks. As shall be detailed in subsequent sections such as *smuggling*, "power loans" had often been appropriated through interventions of political elites to fund their family members and cronies' business operations, capital of construction projects, even smuggling activities. For example, Chen Tongqing, the Party boss of the City of Zhanjiang in Guangdong province, had long been accused of abusing his authority and influence to help his son's smuggling operations and to intervene in law enforcement against his son's illicit business activities. To raise funds to support his son's smuggling of automobiles, copy machines, diesel, and import wine, Chen instructed three deputy mayors to issue a letter of guarantee in the name of the municipal government to help his son acquire a business loan of 40 million Hong Kong dollars from a foreign bank. This act was in outright violation of relevant state regulations and procedures and was deemed an offense of serious nature. When his son's smuggled import cars were seized by a county police department, Chen stepped in to pressure the county Party chief and the director of the municipal public security bureau (the superior of the county police chief) to have the seized cars released. Investigation of the most notorious smuggling operations in reform China led by Lai Changxing, which will be discussed in detail in the section of *smuggling*, revealed that Lai had not only colluded with corrupt officials in the customs and tax agencies in Xiamen to legitimize smuggled goods and to defraud the state of the value-added taxes, but also bribed leading municipal officials and executives of the Xiamen branch of the Bank of Communications of China to issue a total of 25 letters of credits worth $38.41 million USD. The

[54] Meng, Yan and Li, 25. "New Characteristics of Corruption in Banking Sector," *lian zheng liao wang* No.3, 2006. http://news.sina.com.cn/c/2007-01-10/164712001355.shtml.

misappropriated bank funds were used to fund Lai's large-scale smuggling operations on automobiles, petroleum products, and other inputs and goods that had been in short supply in the 1990s.

The irregularity of "power loans" remained one of the major illicit means for rent-seeking among high-ranking officials including those at and above the provincial and ministerial level. As China's reform advanced to a red-hot developmental phase characterized by booming real estate development in the post-1992 period, demand for land, land use rights, developmental approvals, and permits as well as capital had surged accordingly. It seemed to be an adopted pattern or trend that high-ranking officials often rendered developers/bribers "whole-package services" for their development projects; by abusing their power and influence they, first of all, helped developers acquire lands and permits, and then they often proceeded further by aiding developers to secure much-needed capital by pressuring or influencing state bank management over their loan approval decisions. Cheng Kejie, vice chairman of the CPPCC National Committee (top state-level official) and former chairman of Guangxi Autonomous Region (provincial governor), was one of the high-ranking officials who was prosecuted for bribe-taking in the 1990s. By abusing his authority as the governor of the Guangxi Region, Cheng forcefully intervened in a land deal and managed to have the government land reallocated to a real estate developer at a depressed price. Soon after the land acquisition was approved, as requested by the developer, Cheng intervened again to pressure a state bank to provide the developer with a series of business loans totaling 188 million yuan. In return, Cheng and his mistress received cash bribes of over 17 million yuan (RMB) and 8 million Hong Kong dollars. Cheng was convicted and executed in 2000.

As mentioned, one distinct feature of corruption in the banking sector was the stunningly high value of funds misappropriated, often in tens or hundreds of million yuan; in some extreme cases, funds involved may reach billions of yuan. Liang Jianyun, an accountant at a branch of China Construction Bank in Shenzhen, in collusion with his accomplices, had managed to embezzle and misappropriate 19 million Hong Kong dollars and $800,000 USD in bank funds. Wang Xiaodong, a trader of Liaoning Securities Company stationed in Shanghai, misappropriated state funds totaling 40 million yuan to speculate in stocks for personal gains.[55] Huang Zhongtang, a branch deputy director of ICBC in Zhuhai, Guangdong province, was ensnared for misappropriation and embezzlement of state funds in the amount of 128 million yuan in 1996. According to Supreme People's Procuratorate's 1997 annual work report, cases of misappropriation of public funds in excess of 10 million yuan reached 57 in 1996, among which 5 cases involved in excess of 100 million yuan.[56] In the succeeding years, astonishingly high-value cases of embezzlement and misappropriation involving hundreds of millions or even billions of yuan in the banking sector surfaced one after another, some of which even appalled the top leadership and outraged the nation. Another widely media-covered embezzlement case concerns the international extradition of felons from Canada to China for prosecution in the 2000s, and is illustrative of the rampancy and severity of looting in the state banking industry. Gao Shan, a branch manager of the Bank of China in Harbin, the capital of Heilongjiang province, and Li Dongzhe, an unscrupulous local businessman, colluded to lure high-value institutional deposits to Gao's branch with enticements of high interest rates and kickbacks. Since October 2004, Gao and Li had been frequently transferring those deposits, via Li's shell company's bank account, to their accounts in foreign banks. In total, Gao and Li had defrauded over 1 billion yuan in bank deposits of state corporations and institutions. Gao and Li managed to flee to Vancouver, Canada before the felony was uncovered. Gao and Li were extradited back to China in 2012 to face prosecutions.

Laxity of monitoring and supervision of operations and lack of advanced technical infrastructure and expertise in the banking system, to a large extent, were attributable to the surge of major embezzlement and misappropriation cases in the post-1992 era. In addition, sophisticated getaway planning may have encouraged predators to take bold and fearless actions to steal and loot. For instance, Huang Shishan, director of the Bank of Commerce in Zhuzhou, Hunan province, embezzled 700 million yuan in bank funds, and then together with his mistress fled to the Philippines in an attempt to escape punishment. It was in the wake of Huang's flee that had alerted the bank about the missing funds and the felony. In the case of Gao Shan and Li Dongzhe, while Gao was stealing and

[55] *The Supreme People's Procuratorate Annual Work Report.* http://www.spp.gov.cn/spp/gzbg/200602/t20060222_16370.shtml.

[56] *The Supreme People's Procuratorate Annual Work Report (1997).* http://www.spp.gov.cn/spp/gzbg/200602/t20060222_16400.shtml.

secretly transferring funds out of the clients' deposit accounts, he made eight trips to Canada during a period of three years to observe and plan for his hiding place. Gao fled to Canada on December 30, 2004, and the next day his accomplice Li Dongzhe followed along. Again, the missing funds and Gao and Li's criminal acts had remained concealed until the institutional depositors came to the bank branch to withdraw some funds in January 2005.

The embezzlement case of three directors of the Kaiping subbranch of the Bank of China in Guangdong province is probably one of the most publicized cases in the PRC history, given its shockingly immense amount of the misappropriated state funds and the histrionic conspiracy and commission of the crime involved. Xu Chaofan, subbranch director, began to misappropriate bank funds to speculate in foreign exchanges in 1993. In his next move, Xu colluded with deputy director Yu Zhendong and manager Xu Guojun to steal large amount of bank funds through inter-bank lending, and then transferred those funds to Xu's cousin company in Hong Kong, which was de facto under the control of the trio. To conceal the paths and ultimate destination of those transfers, the trio, in collusion with the executives of several large corporations in Kaiping, conspired to issue the funds to the local companies in the name of business loans and then directed the recipient companies to transfer an equivalent amount of funds to Xu's cousin's company in Hong Kong. Another route for illicit fund transfer to their bank accounts in Hong Kong and Macau was through underground banks. After Xu Chaofan was promoted to the position of division director at the provincial branch of Bank of China, Yu Zhendong and then Xu Guojun succeeded the position of director of Kaiping subbranch, which allowed the trio to continue their scheme in tight concealment. In a period of eight years, the triad had stolen hundreds of millions of US dollars in bank funds and had successfully transferred the embezzled funds to personal bank accounts in Hong Kong and overseas. In the meantime, under sophisticated planning, the three crooks and their spouses had crafted out a getaway plan to flee to the U.S. for a hideout. As the first step of the getaway plan, the trio divorced their wives, and then the wives managed to immigrate to the U.S. through fake marriages with naturalized US citizens. The second move entailed the triad's fake marriages too with naturalized American citizens, which opened doors to their permanent residence and citizenship in the U.S. Their scheme remained covert until the Bank of China headquarters began to integrate all its 1040 IT centers across the country into 33 IT regional centers to streamline systemic management and to strengthen monitoring and supervision at the national level. On October 12, 2001, the new integrated system detected a shortfall of $483 million USD within the bank system and then pinpointed the locus of the missing funds to Kaiping, Guangdong. The trio fled to Hong Kong the next day and then flew to the U.S. using fake Hong Kong passports. Again, due to laxity in management and supervision as well as technical and networking deficiencies, their criminal acts and the execution of the getaway plan had remained undetected over the course of eight years. Premiere Zhu Rongji was reportedly furious at the scandal and ordered a thorough investigation and grave punishment to those involved or implicated. In the spring of 2002 a sizable investigation team made of roughly 700 investigators from judicial agencies and the banking system, led and coordinated by the CCDI, was formed and dispatched to Kaiping to conduct investigation.[57] The trial of the case in the U.S. and the international media coverage drew worldwide attention to corruption in China and also raised serious doubts about the capacity and managerial sophistication of China's banking system.

As shall be discussed in subsequent chapters, the Party-state's heavy reliance on punitive measures against graft in its banking industry and other sectors have failed again to deter corruption in the long term. In recent years, even under Xi Jinping's unprecedented clampdown on corruption, theft of state bank funds and bribery have once again spiraled out of control in terms of both scale and magnitude. In 2019, Jiang Xiyun, chairman of Hengfeng Bank, a regional bank based in Yantai, Shandong province, was sentenced to death with a two-year reprieve for embezzlement and bribe-taking. According to the court ruling, Jiang embezzled 754 million yuan (US$108 million) in bank shares; took 60 million yuan (US$8.6 million) in bribes; illicitly issued credit guarantees worth 3.7 billion yuan (US$528 million); and destroyed accounts and records related to 660 million yuan (US$94 million) he had misappropriated. His successor Cai Guohua, former deputy mayor of the city of Yantai, was also ensnared. According to China's influential financial magazine *Caixin*, Cai allegedly squandered bank funds to finance his lavish personal lifestyle, spending roughly 400,000 yuan (US$57,000) per day.

[57] "Principal Offender for the $4-Billion Case of Bank of China in Kaiping Extradited," Xinhua News Agency, September 24, 2015. http://m.jrj.com.cn/news/finance/2015/09/24163419861559.shtml (accessed March 25, 2020).

Cai was handed down the same sentence as his predecessor in 2021. Another similar case involved Yang Chenglin, the former chairman of the Bank of Inner Mongolia, who was convicted in December 2018 for taking more than 300 million yuan (US$43 million) in bribes. Preceding Jiang and Yang was Liu Jinbao, the former chief executive of Bank of China in Hong Kong, and Wang Yi, the former deputy governor of China Development Bank, and both were sentenced to death with a two-year reprieve for embezzlement in 2005 and 2010, respectively. According to recent media reports, several regional banks including Hengfeng and the Bank of Jinzhou had to be bailed out by the state, and corruption and mismanagement were deemed key contributing factors to the bankruptcy of those financial institutions.[58]

Export Tax Rebate

While SOE involvement in tax evasion had diminished over the years partly as a result of state sector reform and SOE transformation and privatization, but collective or organized tax fraud led by SOEs and braced by local governments was on the rise. What seemed preposterous was that outright tax rebate deception was pursued as an alternative for local economic development and was largely ratified by some local authorities. As pointed out by Peter Harris, corporations and factories, driven by various motivations, even "have entered into systematic conspiracies to evade taxes".[59] With the export incremental tax or value-added tax refund policy being carried out in the reform era, cases concerning tax fraud had increased dramatically. While in relatively developed provinces and localities tax fraud largely entailed illegitimate reductions and exemptions of taxes due or inflated tax rebates misappropriated at the expense of the state, tax fraudsters and corrupt tax officials in poor regions would collude to defraud the state of refunds for taxes that had never been paid and on products that had never been manufactured.

Of various types and offenses of tax evasion and tax fraud elaborate deceptions of the value-added tax (VAT) refunds for exported goods

[58] He Huifeng, "Chinese Banker Who Embezzled US$108 Million Handed Suspended Death Sentence," *South China Morning Post*, December 27, 2019. https://www.scmp.com/economy/china-economy/article/3043714/death-sentence-corrupt-banker-china-gets-tough-lending-risks (accessed August 6, 2020).

[59] Peter Harris, "Socialist Graft: The Soviet Union and the People's Republic of China: A Preliminary Survey," *Corruption and Reform* Vol.1 (1986): 27.

may be the most prominent and harmful tax offense in the reform era. The VAT, with a rate of 17 percent, was levied on manufactured goods. However, the government offered exemptions of VAT in the form of VAT refunds if the manufactured goods were exported to the international market. VAT rebate was therefore a tax incentive program aimed to enhance the competitiveness of Chinese goods in the international marketplace. However, the relatively unsophisticated tax structure and administration had subjected the VAT rebate program to widespread abuse and fraud. While VATs were levied by local tax authority, exporters were required to submit claims to the central tax authority for VAT refunds. This structural and administrative loophole resulted from two separate taxation authorities in different localities, to a large extent, had enabled schemers to fabricate local VAT filings, foreign purchase orders, customs documents for exports, and bank documents for foreign currency transactions, all of which were required submissions for the review and approval of VAT rebates by the central authority. Given the complexity of the documentation and the involvement of multiple government agencies and financial institutions, "elaborate and organized efforts were thus needed among several local agencies, sometimes the entire local government: from falsifying sales and tax receipts to fabricating export licenses and others, and from forging customs documents and bank transactions to faking export occurrence".[60] Several publicized VAT rebate fraud cases are exemplifying of the elaboration and coordinated efforts to defraud the central authority of the tax refunds for VATs that had never been filed. In 1992, for example, five enterprises in Xianning city, Hubei province, in collusion with the municipal tax bureau and backed by the mayor, submitted 277 phony invoices and 45 false tax payment bills to deceive the state of tax return worth 12.18 million yuan.[61] Still another case in Ruicang, Jiangxi province, involved a conspiracy between one city and five counties to join forces to defraud the state of even larger amount of VAT refund. The mayor of Ruicang had apparently played a more active role than his counterpart in Xianning in the planning and execution of the scheme and even took the initiative to assign tasks to participating municipal government agencies to assure coordinated execution of the plan. With the support of the local governments, participating firms filed false

[60] Yan Sun, 148–149.

[61] Mingbo Liu, 7.

claims for VAT rebates, backed by 70 phony tax receipts and 304 fraudulent sales receipts provided by government agencies in six localities. The falsified claims entailed over 237 million yuan worth of exported goods and the resultant VAT refund of over 15 million yuan.[62] These two cases serve as a typical scheme of falsifying VAT claims for production that had never taken place and value-added taxes that had never been paid. Tax fraud of the sort is deemed more harmful than tax evasion as it is de facto outright loot of state funds.

As stated above, standardized VAT rebate claims required proofs and documentation of various transactions at various stages of the product manufacturing and exporting process, and an exporter must deal with multiple government agencies and financial institutions throughout the process such as industry and commerce administration, tax authority, customs, banks, foreign currency administration, etc. A successful execution of VAT rebate scheme, therefore, would require division of labor, coordination, managerial sophistication, technical capacity, and most importantly, collaboration with and bracing of government officials in key posts at duty agencies. In general, the following documents were required for the submission of VAT rebate application: (1) Special invoice for value-added tax to prove that goods and supplies have been purchased for manufacturing of the product; (2) Export customs declaration to verify that the manufactured product has been exported to foreign countries; (3) Receipt or money order of foreign currencies to prove that the foreign purchaser has indeed remitted payment for the exported goods; and (4) Special tax payment receipt to show that the required 40 percent tax prepayment has been paid. To satisfy all the requirements and to successfully deceive the state tax authority of the VAT rebates for falsified claims, a de facto professional operation and network integrating schemers who specialized in each of the four stages and the facilitation and support of law enforcement officials were thus required. Fraudsters often bribed key officials in tax bureaus, customs, industry and commerce administration, and state banks for their collaboration and assistance to obtain business permits, tax certificates as well as fake documents for VAT rebate claims. There are cases concerning officials entrusted with the duty of foreign currency administration providing schemers with advice on how to lower operational costs for VAT fraud. Some local tax officials themselves were

62 Yan Sun, 149.

even actively involved in the operation of VAT fraud. Following is another case that reveals how local governments in Fujian participated in schemes in an attempt to either increase local GDP or attain financial gain at the expense of the central authorities. Again, the local governments had not only condoned the wrongdoing but even took the initiative to encourage local enterprises to broaden their revenue sources through illegitimate means. In 1999, a township government in Puning even set up a designated office to facilitate the issuance of fake special VAT invoices. Between January 1999 and July 2000, the VAT Invoice Office of Lihu Township fabricated 429 VAT invoices under the titles of a dozen local firms, and with VAT rebate claims valued at over 300 million yuan, the participating firms and the township government jointly defrauded the state of 22 million yuan in VAT rebate. The malfeasance of tax fraud had grown so overt and rampant in the two localities that the township governments even openly exchanged information and shared best practices in this regard.

The new value-added tax code since 1994 had eliminated the loophole but opened other loopholes for tax abuse and VAT rebate fraud. A centralized taxation system took back various functions and taxation powers from the local authorities and the nationally standardized VAT receipts replaced the local ones to close off the previous loopholes for abuse and illicit exploitation. However, fraud and corruption with respect to falsification of central VAT receipts soon erupted as unlawful firms started to collude with local branches of the National Tax Bureau to illegally acquire VAT receipts for fraudulent claims of VAT rebates. Motivated by similar incentives to swindle state funds for individual and local gains, local firms and local government agencies in some regions were jointly involved in the organized sale of VAT receipts for illicit profits. In some localities, falsification of VAT documents and filing fraudulent rebate claims had even evolved into an illicit industry marked by a division of labor, collaboration, coordination, and even professionalism. The revelation of a major VAT fraud case in eastern Guangdong in 2000 stunned the nation for its nature, scope, the tax rebates defrauded, and the number of suspects and government officials implicated. It started with the dispatch of a large investigation team comprised of investigators from 13 central agencies to the city of Chaoyang and Puning in Guangdong province to investigate rampant VAT rebate falsification activities in the summer of 2000. On September 4, collaborated with local police and administrative law enforcement, the investigation team dispatched over 1200 investigators and officers to inspect hundreds of local enterprises that had been suspected of involvement in VAT rebate fraud. It turned out that 827 out of the 1142 firms inspected were fake enterprises, and many of the so-called registered export companies had neither buildings nor equipment. 98.33 percent of the firms inspected were involved in VAT rebate falsification and tax evasion. In the aftermath of the raid, the investigation team sent out inquiries across the nation to verify the authenticity of over 10,000 VAT receipts and invoices, and over 9000 bills turned out to be fabricated. The final investigation concluded that among 172,000 falsified VAT receipts submitted, 88,000 of them were forgeries. With the involvement of 150 organized groups in the schemes, the total value of fraudulent VAT rebate claims summed up to a staggeringly high figure of 32.3 billion yuan, with the state incurring a loss of 4.2 billion yuan in refund. Widespread tax fraud in the city of Chaoyang and Puning had eventually brought down almost the entire municipal administrative law enforcement and local governments. Government agencies implicated in the scheme included the tax bureau, industry and commerce administration, international trade administration, customs, foreign currency administration, etc. 328 government and law enforcement officials were investigated for bribery, abuse of authority, and dereliction of duty. The Chaoyang-Puning VAT rebate fraud case, reportedly the largest tax fraud in the history of the PRC, concluded in 2001 with 30 offenders sentenced to death and life imprisonment. Many implicated government officials including the local Party chief and the mayor of Puning as well as the directors of Chaoyang and Puning municipal tax bureau received fixed-term imprisonment.[63]

SOE Privatization

Public ownership and abuse of discretionary power are in general faulted for incentives of rent-seeking and the genesis of official corruption in the transition of the former Soviet-bloc socialist states. Privatization, however, can eliminate the underlying fundamentals for rent-seeking and reduce corruption by removing state-owned assets and resources from state control and converting discretionary official actions into private market-driven practices. Empirical experience and evidence indicate that

[63] "The No.1 Case of Tax Fraud in China," *CCTV*, January 12, 2002. http://news.sina.com.cn/c/2002-02-01/465118.html (accessed April 5, 2020). http://www.hangzhou.com.cn/20010825/ca42227.htm.

the privatization process in both the post-communist Eastern European countries and Russia was fraught with rent-seeking opportunities and corruption. While the big-bang approach taken by Russia and other former Soviet-bloc states in transitioning their economic and political systems had induced rampant theft and outright looting of state-owned assets, the political and economic pain proved to be short term and the economic loss incurred seemed to be one time. As China took an incremental approach to the formulation and implementation of its reform policies and initiatives, privatization of its state-owned assets and SOEs had been mainly centered on the small and medium-sized enterprises in non-strategic industries and sectors. Large state-owned monopolies still dominate the state's strategic sectors including finance, energy, defense, transportation, utility, etc., and according to *2022 Fortune Global 500 List*, China has the largest number of companies of any countries represented on the list. Among those that rank top 70 on the Fortune 500 list, there are 19 Chinese state-owned mega corporations.[64] Even though the current Chinese regime is in fact in the process of reversing its reform trajectory and is taking measures to increase the proportion of the state sector in the Chinese economy, given its dominant ownership of public assets and resources, there may exist the latent potential for continued SOE privatization when institutional reforms and systemic changes take place in future.

Illicit transfer of state-owned assets and resources into private hands can occur under various circumstances. First of all, there is a lack or absence of comprehensive and sophisticated framework and methodologies for the assessment of state-owned assets and property, and the tax and regulatory regime that will prevail ex post may also be vaguely or ill-defined. Uncertainties and vagueness of the sort induce incentives for rent-seeking and collusion. Dishonest businessmen may pay to acquire inside information or favorable treatment in the bidding process. A lack of conflict-of-interest laws or lax enforcement of such laws to a large extent induces illicit insider deal-making. Moreover, the assessment process can be readily manipulated by compliant insiders and the assessment results be distorted through collusion and payoffs between SOE executives and corrupt bidders and outside assessors. A profitable SOE with good potential can be marketed as a nonperforming or loss-making entity through

[64] https://en.wikipedia.org/wiki/list_of_largest_chinese_companies.

collusion and manipulation so that it can change hands at a nominal cost. Another concern is the privatized firm's retention of monopoly power that was generally entrenched in a public firm. Given the monopoly rents retained, the privatized firm should be worth more than what it was auctioned for. In addition, the justification and rationale for such privatization also come into question as it is generally with greater ease to monitor and control a public company with monopolistic power than a private monopoly.[65]

While the dominant pattern of corruption in Chinese government may be the extraction of bribes, the public enterprise sector proved to be more prone to embezzlement and plunder in the post-1992 period. What distinguished the corrupt and criminal acts in this period from those of the early years, as discussed earlier, were the extraordinarily high value of public funds and assets plundered and outright partition, transfer, and embezzlement of state assets and property in the process of transformation, reorganization, and privatization of state-owned enterprises. Colluded misappropriation and looting of state assets had evolved into a dominant criminal offense in the SOE sector. This phenomenon was largely attributable to the design and implementation of the new reform policies and programs and may be deemed in part unintended policy consequences. For instance, decentralization of control over state-owned assets with ill-defined ownership rights created an ideal condition for plundering by means of collusion among elites. It is argued that "changes in property rights and administrative decentralization can interact with each other and further facilitate the looting of state-owned property". The combination of these prerequisites and their interaction are contended to be the genesis of crony capitalism in reform China.[66] Generally speaking, collusive corruption in SOEs was mainly perpetrated by senior executives and was most likely to occur in areas of financial management, contract tendering and award, capital-raising, and personnel management. The illicit means that venal SOE executives utilized to seize control of state-owned assets for free or at a nominal cost included self-dealing, asset stripping and theft, and looting through ostensibly legitimate asset transactions.[67]

[65] Rose-Ackerman, 117–118.

[66] Pei, China's *Crony Capitalism*, 49.

[67] Ibid., 163–172.

Although this malfeasance in SOEs falls under the category of embezzlement and misappropriation, given its growing rampancy and the detrimental consequences to the public coffer, wealth distribution, and social justice, loss of state assets caused by plundering and looting of SOE executives and managers is therefore presented and discussed in a separate section below in consideration of the breadth and depth of the subject.

Loss of State Assets—Outright Looting and Embezzlement of State-Owned Assets and Properties

Loss of state assets (国有资产流失) was a popular term in reform China that described the depletion and draining of state-owned assets and property attributable to misappropriation and embezzlement by SOE executives and dishonest businessmen or negligence of duty committed by funders/investors, managers, and operators of SOEs in the process of SOE reorganization, ownership transformation, and privatization. There were various seemingly licit and illicit means to steal and loot state assets, including bankruptcy, enterprise restructuring and transformation, joint venture formation, enterprise mismanagement, exclusion of intangible assets and lands in assessments, and Management Buyout (MBO). Common schemes utilized included the illicit transfer of state funds and assets to private portfolios, concealment of the true size and market value of a SOE's assets, revenues and credits, inflating a SOE's expenditures and debt burdens to depress the price of a buyout, and excluding land and other elusive assets from an appraisal. Still others entailed the use of secret accounts to conceal profits earned from covert sources, looting through distribution and acquisition of state corporation shares, and assisting and profiting cronies' business operations at SOEs' expense.

Li Yaoqi, president of Gang'ao International Group, a large state-owned corporation, amassed an ill-gotten wealth of over 70 million yuan between 1992 and 1997 through various illicit and fraudulent schemes including stock speculation, land profiteering, and embezzlement of SOE funds and assets. In October 1992, Hainan International Trust and Investment Corporation, one of the subsidiaries of Gang'ao International Group, was scheduled to list its IPO on the stock market, and Li, by abusing his authority as the president of the parent company, allocated 8 million initial corporate shares to a "friendly" company in Beijing. In the meantime, Li borrowed 8 million yuan from Hainan International Trust and Investment Corporation in the name of the Beijing office of Gang'ao International Group to enable the "friendly" company to purchase the 8 million corporate shares. On February 28, 1993, Li's "friendly" company sold the 8 million shares to the Group's securities department at the price of 2.85 yuan per share and made a quick windfall profit of 13.32 million yuan after deduction of 8 million yuan in borrowed funds and 440,000 yuan in interest cost from the transaction profit. It turned out that Li's so-called "friendly" company was actually his own shell company that had been set up to conceal illicit transactions and to transfer misappropriated state funds. By the time Li was detained in 1998, the vast majority of the stock sale proceeds had been transferred to a Hong Kong company owned by his wife.

Collective corruption perpetrated by family members and kinsmen had become a common phenomenon in the reform era, and most of the corruption cases of the sort involved spouses, children, siblings, relatives, and close friends. There was no exception with Li's case. In spring 1992, Li decided to purchase land in the suburb of Guangzhou, capital of Guangdong province, to establish a development zone for Gang'ao Group. Instead of going through formal planning and land acquisition process, Li asked his brother, Li Yaosen, and nephew, Li Jianqiang, to search for potential land lot for the proposed development zone. As recommended by Li Jianqiang's mother's brother, Li decided to purchase a stretch of farmland totaling 610 mu (亩, 1 acre equals 6.07 mu) following his field trip of inspection to the locality. The three members of the Li family then colluded to use a series of transactions to inflate the land prices and then resold the land to Gang'ao Group to earn a sizable profit. The plot of looting state funds and assets thus took place: Li Jianqiang's mother's brother purchased the land from the village at a price of 80,000 yuan per mu, and then sold the land under the name of his construction company to Li Jianqiang's private business, Jinxing Company, at a cost of 100,000 yuan per mu; Jinxing vended the land at a much higher price of 150,000 yuan per mu to Li Jianqiang's public company Dongzhan Company in Hong Kong (Dongzhan was a subsidiary of the Gang'ao Group and Li Jianqiang was the general manager of Dongzhan). Dongzhan then handed the land over to its ultimate buyer, Hainan International Trust and Investment Corporation, at a cost of 160,000 yuan per mu. The covert land transactions generated an illicit profit of 70,000 yuan per mu or 49 million yuan in total to the Li family. To assure that the board of directors would approve the land deal, Li Yaoqi directed Li Jianqiang and Li Yaosen to bribe Su Guohua, VP of Hainan International Trust and Investment Corporation overseeing land development, for his cooperation and endorsement. After the land deal was inked, the trio split up the illicit land proceeds, and Su received a luxury Mercedes-Benz sedan, a kickback as promised by Li Jianqiang beforehand.

While land profiteering and stock acquisition and speculation were common schemes employed by SOE executives and managers to misappropriate and steal state assets as what Li Yaoqi did to amass his fortune, arrangements concerning dividend payments to privileged shareholders constituted another scheme of embezzling state assets. Planning and execution of the scheme often required cooperation and collusion of other high-ranking officials in a company. Formation of illicit allies to facilitate stealing and looting of state assets in a more effective and safer mode to a large extent attest to the pervasiveness and rampancy of collective corruption in the post-1992 era. In 1993, Guangdong Tourism and Real Estate Development Corporation decided to withdraw its 25 percent holdings in Ri'an Company, a subsidiary of the Gang'ao Group, and Li Yaoqi and three VPs of Hainan International Trust and Investment Corporation opted to take a loan of 2 million Hong Kong dollars from a Hong Kong company to purchase a portion of the withdrawn shares. Three months later, via Dongzhan Company headed by Li's nephew, Ri'an began to make a series of dividend payments to Li and the three VP shareholders on a regular basis until October 1998 when Li was arrested. It was revealed that rather than making profits, Ri'an had actually been in trouble for some time due to a lack of capital for business operations. However, Ri'an's financial difficulties did not stop Li and his accomplices from misappropriating SOE funds in the name of dividend payments. Li and the three VPs had received 4 dividend payments from Ri'an totaling 3.4 million Hong Kong dollars. Li was convicted of embezzlement, misappropriation of public funds, and plundering of state-owned assets and was sentenced to death in 2002.[68]

A scheme concerning "books out of books" (账外账) to conceal covert incomes was widely utilized by corrupt SOE executives and managers to hide the SOE funds and assets they had misappropriated. This may differ from many so-called "small treasuries" or slush funds as these hidden books and secret incomes were kept outside of an official account of a SOE and were in general known to only a very limited number of

[68] http://t.2web.cn/wfdslsc/jdht/html/?4763.html.

core executives. As these illegitimate or semi-legitimate payments were made generally under the table, it posed significant challenges for conventional auditing methods to detect and uncover the irregularities. In some extreme cases, covert incomes accumulated in these "books out of books" could be staggeringly enormous. For example, as demonstrated in the Chu Shijiang embezzlement case cited previously, Chu, the chief accountant, and a VP of Red Pagoda Group used secret accounts in Hong Kong and Guangdong to receive kickbacks resulted from selling cigarettes at "floating prices". Chu demanded a floating price on top of the planned price ranging between 10 and 20 yuan per carton be paid to those secret accounts, and within four years the trio had extracted over 1 billion yuan and $25 million US dollars into the concealed bank accounts. In 1995, the year that Chu was scheduled to retire, the trio, together with their cronies, secretly embezzled $3.55 million US dollars and divided it up among themselves. Chu received $1.7 million USD.[69]

Acquisition and merger of state-controlled and joint-stock enterprises constituted an opportunity and also a common approach to misappropriating and looting state assets and properties. Looters often colluded to artificially inflate the market value of the to-be-acquired enterprise and then defraud the state of the inflated portion using various accounting irregularities after the acquisition was completed. Liu Zhongshan, director of Sichuan provincial transport department and president of Sichuan Highway Development Corporation (a state-owned enterprise belonging to the provincial transport department), applied this scheme to jointly steal 10 million yuan of state assets with two accomplices. In early 1998, Liu intended to acquire a publicly listed company in order to take Sichuan Highway Development Corporation to the stock market to raise more funds for highway development in Sichuan province. The search for the acquisition candidates was narrowed down to a state-owned listed company, North Sea Merchants Corporation, whose CEO Wang Jin had been acquainted with Liu and the two had known each other well. As the acquisition deal drew to the conclusion after a series of discussions and negotiations, Liu suggested to Wang to artificially inflate the cost of acquisition by 10 million yuan. As various stages of the acquisition must involve legal advice and legal proceedings, the two decided to recruit the corporate lawyer Liu Xirong to the scheme. As planned, Sichuan Highway

[69] Liu Siyang and Zheng Hongfan, "The Tragedy of the 'King of Tobacco'," *shuku.net*. http://www.shuku.net/novels/baogaowenxue/zgczfbjs/zgczfbjs01.html.

Development Corporation successfully acquired North Sea Merchants Corporation at an inflated price, and then the trio conspired to transfer the thieved 10 million yuan into the account of Chengdu Hezhong Investment Management Company, Ltd., a stock trading company held by Liu Zhongshan's son, Wang's secretary, and Liu Xirong's brother. Instead of splitting and taking the cash out of the scheme, Liu, the corporate lawyer, suggested to establish Hezhong Investment so that the 10-million-yuan funds could be put to work in the stock market to generate returns. As agreed, the trio split up the funds in a ratio of 4:3:3 (4 went to Liu Zhongshan), and by the same token the financial returns generated would also be divided up accordingly among the three looters. Liu Zhongshan received a death sentence with a two-year reprieve in 2000.[70]

Another scheme to misappropriate state assets was to manipulate appraisal/assessment of the market value of a participating SOE or/and its private business partners' assets in forming a joint venture or negotiating intended buyout of SOE shares and assets by incumbent SOE managers or private businesses. This normally involved underreporting of a SOE's assets, concealing funds receivables, false declaration of payments for goods that may be retrieved as unrecoverable, and overreporting a private business partner's value of assets to artificially inflate its holdings in a joint venture. One of the dirty tactics to manipulate the appraising process and to falsify appraisal reports was to bribe appraisers with money or other illicit benefits. Forging fraudulent appraisals and assessments to defraud the state of its assets was a widespread illicit practice in the process of SOE ownership transformation and privatization. A case of negligence of duty and bribery concerning the formation and operation of a joint venture between Lanzhou Liancheng Aluminum Factory and an unscrupulous businessman in Guangdong province provides an elucidatory example of the extent and serious consequences of the scheme in the post-1992 era. In the early 1990s, Wei Guangqian, CEO of Lanzhou Liancheng Aluminum Factory in Gansu province in northwestern China, and the plant's executive team intended to use a 40-million-yuan bank loan designated for plant expansion to profiteer in land speculation in far-away Guangdong province in southern China. Without conducting necessary due diligence and credibility checks and also lacking basic

[70] http://t.2web.cn/wfdslsc/jdht/html/3151.html.

knowledge and information about land regulations and transactive procedures and processes in Guangdong, Wei's land purchaser Xu Guangming, a manager of the aluminum factory's subsidiary in Guangdong, was lured into a land deal of 200 mu at a cost of 36 million yuan; in return, Wei and Xu were offered 2.65 million yuan in kickback. It turned out later that the purchased land had not been granted land use right permits and certificates and could not therefore be resold to generate lucrative profit as planned. The land seller, Pan Zhixiong, then kicked off his second scheme to talk Wei and Xu into the formation of a joint venture to manufacture aluminum products and again offered them 3 million yuan in return for Wei's discretionary decision and facilitation for the partnership deal. Anxious to be freed from the trapped and embarrassing land deal and also motivated by the promised payoff, Wei pushed forward for the plant's decision on establishing a business partnership with Pan. To inflate the value of Pan's equity so that Pan's firm could reach the threshold of stake in the joint venture, Pan bought-off appraisers of a local accounting firm in Lanzhou and, in addition, offered the manager of the accounting firm a paid tour to Macau. As a result, Pan's equity was fraudulently appraised at 110 million yuan, seven times higher than what was worth in the market. After the partnership deal was inked, Wei turned the 3-million-yuan bribe from Pan into his investment in the joint venture with an agreed annual dividend payment of 25 percent. As Pan continued to make payoffs to Wei and his family members, Wei returned the favor by handing over the positions of president and legal representative of the joint venture to Pan, the minority shareholder of the partnership. Besides, as requested by Pan, Wei managed to revise the managerial contract of the joint venture to the benefit of Pan. The event, dubbed "the plant sellout and betrayal" by factory workers, marked the beginning of a series of Pan's elaborate deceptions to defraud Liancheng of its products and assets. Between 1994 and 1996, as directed by Wei, the plant continuously shipped aluminum ingots to Pan but had never received Pan's payments. When Wei was detained in 1996, the loss of SOE assets to Pan had accumulated to 279 million yuan in value, an equivalent of one-third Liancheng aluminum plant's total assets. Wei received life imprisonment in 2004, and Xu Guangming was sentenced to death in 1999.[71]

[71] http://t.2web.cn/wfdslsc/jdht/html/4469.html.

There were in general two main approaches to acquiring a SOE: acquisition by private business and acquisition by the SOE management team, and the latter had gradually become a common acquisition mode in the new reform era. Driven by incentives to minimize acquisition costs, as discussed earlier, SOE executives tended to utilize a variety of tactics to conceal SOE assets and revenues, inflate debts, manipulate asset appraisal, and illicitly transfer SOE assets to their own private companies that had been set up specifically for the purposes of misappropriation. Cases abounded in SOE privatization concerning concealed transfers of a SOE's assets to private firms controlled by SOE executives in a plot to privatize SOE assets piecemeal over time. A major SOE asset embezzlement case is quite explanatory of the worrisome tendency for the loss of state assets in recent decades. Zhang Xinhua, CEO of Baiyun Agricultural Industrial and Commercial Corporation in Guangzhou, deployed the intrigue to plunder state assets worth hundreds of millions of yuan when he assumed the top job of the company during 1998 and 2013. First of all, Zhang made his initial move to transfer Baiyun company's assets comprised of housing, factory buildings, orchards, and land to Guangtian Company, a subsidiary established in the name of safeguarding Baiyun's state assets and properties. Through his authority over the management and operation of Guangtian, Zhang had effectively put the to-be-misappropriated SOE assets under his control. In 2006, Zhang made his next move by setting up his own private firm, Guangzhou Xinyutian Real Estate Co., Ltd, and by amalgamating Guangtian Company, Zhang's Xinyutian proceeded to privatize the state assets owned by Guangtian. To facilitate his plundering, Zhang conspired to integrate some members of Guangtian's management team to Xinyutian by allocating them with Xinyutian shares. Zhang himself owned 25.4 percent of Xinyutian's total shares worth 72 million yuan. The value of the state lands and buildings peculated by Zhang was assessed at around 280 million yuan. In addition, by abusing his discretionary power over the transfer of the land use rights of the company-owned lands, Zhang took bribes worth over 97 million yuan (RMB). Zhang was sentenced to death in 2014.[72]

Bankruptcy constituted a frequently deployed illicit tactic to plunder the assets of a SOE in SOE privatization. Under this scheme, the SOE

[72] "Division-Level Corrupt Official Zhang Xinhua Who Embezzled 340 Million Yuan Was Sentenced to Death," *Nanfang Daily*, December 10, 2014. http://news.ifeng.com/a/20141210/42685782_0.shtml.

management colluded to bankrupt the enterprise so that the SOE could be acquired at a considerably depressed price. The CEO of Xinxiang Textile Plant in Henan province first of all purchased the operational rights of the plant's main equipment for the production of his own firm. In the meantime, he sold almost all the plant's assets and properties at very low prices, including inventories, weaving machines, buildings, and residential housing units, while transferring other assets to his own firm. Eventually the CEO bankrupted the state-owned plant under his management and dismissed half of its workforce. His last move was to transfer the remaining 800 workers along with their settlement funds to his own firm in an attempt to take over this state-owned plant worth nearly 100 million yuan at no cost.[73]

Still another illicit approach to looting state assets was to transfer superior SOE assets and profits from parent companies to their affiliated collective shareholding enterprises. For example, a SOE with a net profit of 140 million yuan transferred 160 million yuan to its newly established joint-stock cooperative, and thus brought the parent SOE to the brink of insolvency. Another case concerned the transfer of parent company's profit to its affiliated collective subsidiaries that had been set up to provide employment opportunities for retired SOE managers and staff's family members. Under such arrangements, SOEs were de facto transferring their profits to shareholders of these collective subsidiaries at the expense of the state. In this case, each shareholder of the affiliated collective shareholding enterprise received an annual payment of 70,000 yuan or an annual return of 3500 percent for his or her share contribution of 2000 yuan.[74] Loss of state assets thus incurred through the transfer of state profits to individuals via affiliated collective enterprises.

Besides, there were other predatory schemes to peculate public funds and state assets, and in whatever way, however, SOEs and their subsidiaries were often being treated like personal ATMs for funds misappropriation and squandering. In extreme cases, those who held paramount managerial and political power in a SOE could outright loot state funds and assets at will. The case of Xie Heting, CEO and Party boss of Guangdong Tianlong Group Corporation, attests to the recklessness and rampancy of the

[73] http://www.docin.com/p-882190852.html.

[74] "Ten Cases Regarding the Loss of State Assets," *China Economic News weekly*, 2003. http://business.sohu.com/88/26/article208662688.shtml (accessed April 1, 2020).

outright looting schemes. Xie utilized several illicit means and unsmart tricks to purloin public funds: (1) directing Tianlong's subsidiary in Hong Kong to take funds out of the SOE account and then using fake invoices and receipts to balance the accounts; (2) creating fictitious reasons and excuses to transfer corporate funds from the headquarters and subsidiaries to Hong Kong and then ripping off the funds from the Hong Kong account; (3) overtly and directly demanding funds and payments from subsidiaries for misappropriation purposes; and (4) borrowing funds from Tianlong's business partners and clients and then submitting IOUs in the name of Tianlong Group to transfer debts to corporate. Ultimately Xie's mismanagement, theft, and squandering, to a large extent, brought the Tianlong Group to the brink of bankruptcy; direct financial loss and loss of corporate assets and properties due to Xie's plundering and negligence of duty had piled up to over 200 million yuan and 400 million yuan, respectively. The company eventually became insolvent with net debt of over 43 million yuan.[75]

A notoriously high-profiled SOE executive corruption case revealed recently may shed light on the deterring effect as well as the endurability of Xi's anti-corruption drive. As recently as in 2018, five years after Xi's sweeping crackdown on official corruption, another "tiger" was ensnared in China's finance sector. Lai Xiaomin, president and Party secretary of China Huarong Asset Management Corporation (deputy ministerial level), a large central SOE in the finance sector, overtook Bai Enpei's national bribery record of nearly 250 million yuan and Wei Pengyuan's record of 230 million yuan in cash to become the most corrupted high-ranking official in the PRC history. The details of the massive financial corruption by Lai are truly jaw-dropping even by Chinese standards. Lai was detained in April 2018, and the subsequent search of his properties uncovered RMB and foreign currencies totaling 270 million yuan in cash (with foreign currencies converted into RMB). The pile of bank notes was reportedly in excess of three cubic meters and weighed approximately three tons. The details of the case were disclosed in a documentary series aired by state-owned broadcaster China Central Television (CCTV) in January 2020. The five-episode series showed a room filled with stacks of cash and a bank account of 300 million yuan under Lai's mother's name. Lai was also accused of living a decadent life, sheltering more than 100

[75] http://t.2web.cn/wfdslsc/jdht/html/3071.html; http://t.2web.cn/wfdslsc/jdht/html/?3079.html.

mistresses and lovers. But the stacks of 100-yuan bank notes were only part of Lai's illicit proceeds. He also received "gifts" of a large number of luxury vehicles, properties, gold items, and pieces of art. Lai Xiaomin was prosecuted in August 2020 for abuse of authority and extraction of ill-gotten wealth, including money and goods worth 1.79 billion yuan. He was also accused of colluding with others to embezzle public assets worth more than 25.13 million yuan.[76] More importantly, the loss of state assets resulted from Lai's power abuse and dereliction of duty could be many times more than what he had raked in through bribery and misappropriation.

What seemed to be shoring up Lai's decadent lifestyle were massive corporate governance defects at Huarong, according to observers. Huarong was established in 1999 by the central authorities with a mandate to take over and dispose nonperforming loans transferred from China's biggest commercial banks. Since Lai became the chairman and the Party chief in 2012, he turned the institution into a one-man piggy bank. Due to a dearth of supervision and oversight, Lai had abused his authority to such an extent over the years that he could arbitrarily grant credit worth billions of yuan to favored borrowers, and capriciously control and manipulate corporate affairs. As commented by an observer, "while Huarong may be an extreme case in China's financial industry, it is worth noting for those Chinese financial institutions that do not have proper internal governance, external oversight and a mechanism of checks and balances, the Lai corruption case is unlikely to be the last".[77]

[76] Pearl Liu, "Ex-Chairman of Hong Kong-Listed Bad Asset Manager Huarong Pleads Guilty to Accepting US$257.7 Million in Bribes," *South China Morning Post*, August 11, 2020. https://www.scmp.com/business/china-business/article/3096982/ex-chairman-hong-kong-listed-bad-asset-manager-huarong (accessed August 18, 2020).

[77] Zhou Xin, "Huarong Corruption Scandal Underscores Governance Failures at China's Financial Institutions," *South China Morning Post*, August 17, 2020. https://www.scmp.com/economy/china-economy/article/3097646/huarong-corruption-scandal-underscores-governance-failures (accessed August 18, 2020).

CHAPTER 5

Regulatory and Judicial Corruption

5.1 Regulatory Corruption

Governments provide public programs and services and also impose regulations and levy taxes. Similar to the utility of paying for an inside edge in public tenders, individuals and businesses have incentives to make payoffs to avoid costs. For example, businesses pay to get a favorable interpretation of the rule or regulation, or to reduce the regulatory load or obligation. "The loci of payoffs are remarkably similar throughout the world considering the large differences in culture, economic conditions, and political organization."[1] Similarly, government officials in socialist China are also incentivized to seek rents by bending rules. As discussed earlier, the changing dynamics of the reform phased out administrative powers in some sectors and shifted them to other spheres of the economy and society. For instance, after the government had retreated from the planned allocation and distribution of inputs and supplies, it took on new roles in the regulatory territory and mandated itself with an extended range of regulatory duties and enforcement responsibilities. The role shift and the new regulatory and enforcement powers similarly generated incentives among businesses to pay to avoid or reduce costs or to seek favors in arbitration and enforcement. As Yan Sun points out, "new government benefits stimulate incentives for obtaining exclusive access,

[1] Rose-Ackerman, 69.

F. C. Sun, *An Ineluctable Political Destiny*,
https://doi.org/10.1007/978-981-99-3146-0_5

while newly imposed costs generate incentives for favorable interpretation and enforcement of rules."[2] Costs in the context of reform China may include "regulatory barriers, tax burdens and delayed services". As presented below, irregularities and malfeasances prevailed in a broad range of spheres including tax, tariff, land and resources, licenses and permits, inspection, quality control, safety, environment assessment and enforcement, etc.

Land and Real Estate

Public lands and resources are generally hotbed of illicit payoffs and corruption in many developing countries. Unlawful businesses and venal officials engage in collusive corruption to seek illicit gains and to extract rents from government concessions that give private firms the right to exploit resources or to develop lands. In contrast to corruption in public programs and services where state funds and assets are misappropriated or prices are inflated for infrastructure and public procurements, corruption in concessions decreases the revenue streams to the state coffer in the form of intentionally lowered royalty rates. Like corruption in public programs and services, corruption in concessions not only causes immense loss to the state but also distorts production choices and the level of benefits and costs from exploitation and development.[3] Very often successful bidders pay to not only acquire concession contracts but also obtain connivance of authorities for violation of environmental protection codes or social obligations. In the context of reform China, for example, it had long been a problematic practice that developments of lands and resources were often undertaken at the expense of environment and the safety and wellbeing of the citizens. Unlawful enterprises also pay to assure official condonation and inaction for other corrupt and illegal acts such as breach of contracts, violation of concession terms and conditions, exceeding concession permits, evasion of customs duties and other taxes, etc. In contrast to strategies that are often employed to curb corruption in public programs and services by simply eliminating programs or services plagued

[2] Yan Sun, 54.

[3] Rose-Ackerman, 110–111.

by corruption, the best cure for corruption in concessions is not necessarily government exit from the resource sector, as that may simply leave the way open for unregulated profit-seeking.[4]

The real estate development boom since the 2000s had unleashed drastic demand for land, building materials, steel, and lumber and had either directly or indirectly stimulated the development and flourishing of the industries and sectors in its supply chain. However, there also arose widespread irregularities and corruption in land and development-related regulatory affairs. Land, along with SOE restructuring and infrastructure, were deemed the most corruption-riddled spheres in reform China. What underlay pervasive corruption in the real estate sector, to a large extent, was the partial reform of property rights of land. The Land Administration Law, enacted in 1986 and amended several times between 1988 and 2004, is a landmark event that has paved the way for incremental reform of land rights. The core element of the land reform is the incremental easing of the state's control over land use while leaving the ownership of state land unchanged. What is perceived as "singular legal breakthrough" is the separation of ownership rights from use rights, which, from a legal perspective, allows government to permit sale and transfer of land without altering the state ownership. In the meantime, a fee-based mechanism was established governing sale and transfer of land use rights in urban areas. The reformed land policy permits the auction, tender, and negotiation of land transfers. In the initial phase of the land reform, the vast majority of land transactions were conducted through secret negotiations rather than fair and transparent bidding and auction processes, which had unavoidably led to underpriced land sales at the expense of the state and widespread collusive corruption between developers and government officials. Aware of the high incidence of misdeed in land, the central authorities repeatedly enacted regulations between 1999 and 2002 to tighten rules on the transfer of land use rights, mandating that use rights for all state-owned land designated for development must be sold through auctions, bidding, or public notices. However, enforcement of the increasingly strict regulations and amendments proved to be problematic as local officials continued to seek lucrative rents from land transactions through faulty or fraudulent land-sale bidding and auction processes. Seemingly an innovative measure to separate use rights from ownership rights and thus

[4] Ibid., 113–114.

to create a market for land use, the partial reform of property rights of land may have created more dilemmas than solutions. "As long as the state owns the land and can determine the supply of land, a primary market for land use cannot exist. In addition, absent a real market for land transfer systems, cronyism and corruption are certain to be pervasive in a hybrid system in which political power set the price."[5]

The 1994 fiscal reform instituted a new revenue-sharing system between the central authorities and provinces, and the new arrangement granted local governments authority to tap into land sales to generate revenues to address local fiscal needs. A dramatic surge in the sale of land use rights in the post-1994 period reflected the growing dependence of local governments on land-sale revenues. While the new policy opened up a vast new revenue source—land sales—to fund local infrastructure and economic development, the land-based local fiscal system also generated new incentives for lucrative rent-seeking and collusive corruption. The regulatory framework and the land allocation mechanism were structured in such a way that were heavily tilted toward maximizing government control and official discretion. As stated above, before 2002, the vast majority of the land transactions were conducted through negotiations between governments and developers. In 2002, the central authorities ordered to implement a new land-sale process based on bidding, auctions, and public announcements; nevertheless, a large proportion of the land use rights deals had still been handled through the nontransparent and corruption-prone process of negotiation and nonpublic agreement until 2008.[6] In the early years of the land reform, as demonstrated in cases below, leading local officials, mostly party bosses, chose to directly involve or intervene in land-sale negotiations and transactions to help bribers to acquire the targeted land lots at bargain prices or to reduce or waive land transfer fees and taxes at the expense of the state. Even after the central authorities ordered the local governments to make collective rather than individual-directed decisions on major land-sale deals, leading officials continued to intervene in land transactions by manipulating the "collective decision-making process" in an attempt to continue to reap lucrative

[5] Pei, 50–53.

[6] Ibid., 54–57.

rents from land sales.[7] Revenue loss to the state coffer as a result of collusive corruption in land was immeasurable. For example, according to the National Audit Agency's audits of 11 provinces in 2009, a total of 38.1 billion yuan in land-sale revenue that should have been paid to the public coffer was foregone.[8]

With the land reform underway, cases of land corruption had surged since 2000. Statistics show that cases involving land corruption had increased from 6.43 percent of the total cases of corruption in 2000 to 29.14 percent in 2013. Land corruption in general causes more detrimental consequences than other patterns of corruption as it generally involves massive amount of illicit funds, multiple agencies and institutions, and a large number of corrupt actors. As mentioned above, although the central authorities have repeatedly directed local governments to conduct transactions of land use rights through public auctions and bidding, as revealed by the disclosed corruption cases, "the process of public auction and bidding is rigged to favor buyers who have bribed local officials."[9] Driven by incentive to capture high-rate illicit returns and rents, both government officials and SOE executives are involved in collusive corruption in land transactions and profiteering. For the latter, we quoted Li Yaoqi's case earlier, who colluded with family members and cronies to use shell companies and fraudulent land transactions to defraud Gang'ao Group and its subsidiary of 49 million yuan in state funds. What was more typical of land corruption in reform China was the involvement of high-ranking officials and leading local officials as well as officials in land administration in corrupt land deals, who joined forces to extract a share of the windfall profits generated from illegitimate land transactions. As pointed out earlier, most of the revealed major corruption cases were related to land and real estate corruption in one way or another. In a case cited previously concerning Cheng kejie, former Chairman of Guangxi Autonomous Region, it was Cheng's forceful intervention in a land deal that had resulted in his conviction and capital punishment. Cheng, in violation of state rules and land administrative procedures, pressured to have a government-owned land reallocated to a real estate developer at

[7] Liu Jian, *Thoughts and Enlightenment from Recent Major Land Corruption Cases* (in Chinese), *China Land* 4 (2004): 22–23.

[8] Pei, 58.

[9] Ibid., 57.

a discounted price. Cheng also wielded his authority to help the developer obtain a series of business loans from a state bank. In return, Cheng received cash bribes of over 17 million yuan (RMB) and 8 million Hong Kong dollars.

Arbitrary reduction and exemption in land transfer fees, levies, and taxes is another illicit means that corrupt officials employ to help developers increase profit margins in return for lucrative bribes. State fiscal loss resulted from this malpractice is immeasurable. Mu Suixin and Ma Xiangdong, the mayor and executive deputy mayor of Shenyang, the capital of Liaoning province, caused a huge loss in land transaction revenues between 1997 and 2000 by allocating municipal lands to developers and arbitrarily reducing or exempting land transfer fees and other related levies and taxes in favor of the bribers. During the three-year period, municipal land arbitrarily allocated by Mu and Ma accounted for 77 percent of the municipal construction land reserve. Ma, by abusing his discretionary power, managed to have a downtown lot of 24,000 square meters allocated to Liu Yong, a developer and also a mafia boss, free of charge. In return, Liu rendered Ma a cash bribe of $200,000 USD. The allocated prime lot in downtown Shenyang, as estimated by an independent appraiser, was worth 350 million yuan. Wang Huaizhong, deputy governor of Anhui province, was convicted of bribe-taking and possession of huge amount of unjustified assets and was sentenced to death in December 2003. Between 1994 and 1999, Wang raked in a large number of outsized bribes from real estate developers by helping them acquire land use rights for their developmental lots. Same as Ma and Mu, Wang either directed or intervened to have land transaction fees and development-related costs reduced to his bribers' advantage. Fees and costs of the sort included land transfer fee, urban construction supplement fee, fixed assets investment adjustment tax, etc. Wang's arbitrary reduction and exemption of the land transaction fees and developmental levies had costed the state tens of million yuan in fiscal loss.[10]

As land acquisition and real estate development generally entail approvals and permitting of multiple government departments and agencies, a collusive network, coordinated by scrupulous developers and participated by leading local Party-state officials and officials from functional departments, is often formed to facilitate the transaction of outsized

[10] Liu Jian, 21–22.

land deals and the development of real estate projects. What has bonded all corrupt players together in the conspiracy is the shared incentive for windfalls and lucrative rents. Developers need to buy off officials in the government hierarchy from top-level Party chiefs or mayors to officials in land administration and other regulatory agencies to assure smooth transition of their development projects through government red tape and the approval process. A well-publicized land corruption case in Dongfang City, Hainan province sheds some light on the nature, formation, and operation of such collusive networks. Zhang Yan'an, a real estate developer and profiteer, acquired over 1000 mu (1 mu = 0.16474 acre) of collective-owned farmland at an undercut price by bribing village officials. Zhang then colluded with another developer Liu, via whom they reached out to Tan Dengyao, the mayor of Dongfang City, requesting Tan to expropriate this parcel of land at a much higher price to the municipal construction land reserve. Tan then instructed the directors of the municipal departments of transport, land administration, construction, and urban investment as well as the deputy mayor to proceed to the planning and expropriation of the land. Zhang initially acquired the land at a price of 7000 yuan per mu and resold it to the city at 68,000 yuan per mu, generating a staggering profit of almost tenfold the original acquisition cost! While the lion's share went to the two developers, Tan received a kickback of 2.5 million yuan. Other municipal officials involved in the land deal each took a bribe of over 100,000 yuan. In total, 25 municipal and village officials were implicated in this land corruption case, and Tan was sentenced to 18 years in prison in 2011.[11]

Regulatory approvals and permits have always been a cradle of real estate corruption in reform China. Driven by motivation to earn high profit margins from real estate development, developers must not only acquire underpriced lands but also secure all required regulatory approvals, permits, and licenses to take their projects off the ground. Since a dozen of government departments and agencies have jurisdictions or regulatory approval authority over land use and development, officials in these agencies, therefore, were generally incentivized to extract rents from the application approval and permitting processes. As revealed by exposed cases, high-ranking officials who had helped bribers to obtain

[11] "Collective Corruption in Land led to the Fall of Mayor and Other Twenty-Five Officials in Dong Fang City Hai Nan Province," *Xinhua News*, February 14, 2011. https://news.qq.com/a/20110214/000423.htm (accessed April 25, 2020).

their targeted lands also assisted them to acquire approvals and permits for the development of the real estate projects. Tan Dengyao, mayor of Dongfang City, as cited in the case above, helped developer Liu to obtain municipal approvals for his scenic area development plan and other projects in exchange for a series of payoffs. Bai Enpei, former Party boss of Yunnan province, over his ten-year tenure as the highest Party official in the province, had amassed an astonishing fortune of over 246 million yuan through corruption. Bai was accused of abusing his power and influence to help businessmen acquire approvals and permits for mining, state land and land use rights, real estate development projects, etc.

In parallel with a surge in corruption in the Party-state officialdom, as discussed previously, corruption and embezzlement also pervaded in China's military. While selling and buying offices constituted the dominant pattern of malfeasance in the military officialdom, land, and real estate induced corruption was also pervasive, particularly in military logistics departments and institutions. Lieutenant General Gu Junshan, deputy minister of the General Logistics Department of the Central Military Commission (CMC), was the top official entrusted with military logistics operations. Gu had tremendous discretionary power over the leasing and transfer of military-owned lands as well as construction and maintenance of barracks and military housing projects. Gu had accumulated a massive fortune through bribery and kickbacks from unscrupulous developers and businessmen as well as embezzlement and misappropriation of military funds and assets. Over the years Gu had paved the way for his rapid rise in the Chinese army by bribing his superior, General Xu Caihou, Vice Chairman of the CMC, and part of his graft proceeds were used to fund his ascending to the top-level position. Gu was convicted on bribery, embezzlement, and abuse of authority, and was sentenced to suspended death penalty in August 2015.[12]

Also noteworthy is that collusive networks and reciprocal relationships did not necessarily end with the retirement of state regulatory officials. In many cases, retired officials set up consulting firms offering all sorts of development-related lobbying (or the so-called consultation) services. By taking advantage of their connections to the serving government officials (many of them may have been promoted to the executive positions under

12 "Gu Junshan," *bai du bai ke*, https://baike.baidu.com/item/谷俊山/6140962 (accessed April 6, 2020).

http://www.cnlawnn.com/jdht/html/?7308.html.

the influence of their patrons), those retired patrons continued to reap rents by helping developers clear obstacles in various regulatory spheres such as land use rights, developmental zoning, approval of building plans, construction permits, fire safety clearance, etc.

State Resources and Energy

Rapid development of China's manufacture and construction sectors and a booming energy industry had boosted demand for the exploration, mining and production of minerals, coal, and petroleum products in the reform era. To increase the overall production capacity of those important industrial materials and inputs, the Chinese government took measures to progressively decentralize control of mining without actually relinquishing its ownership rights in an effort to engage private sector investment and participation in mining in state-designated areas that may not be economically feasible for large and medium-sized state operations due to their limited mineral reserves and low mineral contents. Similar to reforms in land, while assuring legal ownership of mineral resources, the state opted to liberalize government control over mining on an incremental basis by formulating a legal and regulatory framework separating exploration, mining, and production rights from ownership rights. The Mineral Resources Law, enacted in 1986, encourages collective mines and individuals to explore and produce in a small scale in state-designated areas for their own use. In 1996, the central authorities further loosened its control over mining by permitting the transfer of mining rights, i.e., buying and selling mining rights, and the move was interpreted as a landmark event in mineral resource development in that it removed a significant constraint on mining rights transfers as stipulated in a previous legislation. In 1998, the central authorities further decentralized the administration of mineral resources by delegating approval authority to lower levels of government over the transfer of exploration and production rights. In addition, provinces were granted the authority over the approval of medium-sized and small mines in mining areas undesignated by the national government as well as certain exploration and production licenses for medium and small mines. Also in 1998, the State Council lifted the ban forbidding the sale of production rights. In the coal mining sector, approval authority over the transfer of production rights in coal mines was delegated to county-level governments.[13] While reforms in the regulatory realm had stimulated investment and rapid development in the mining sector, devolution of approval and licensing authority to local governments also triggered off rampant rent-seeking activities.

Escalated competition among competitors for limited mineral resources and the way mineral resources were allocated and distributed by state authority are perceived to be the underlying causes of widespread corruption in the mining sector. While new regulations allowed new players such as collectives, shareholding companies, and individuals to join forces with governments and TVEs to boost development in the mining sector, in the meantime, players, new or existing, were motivated to gain an advantage over their competitors by employing both licit and illicit means in the approval and permitting process. Opportunities for rent-seeking existed throughout various stages of mineral exploration, mining and production approval, and permitting processes, including project review and approval, mine construction, completion assessment, license issuance, evaluation of prices and fees, and supervision and enforcement. Take coal mining as an example; to qualify to be a licensed coal mining producer, an applicant must obtain six permits—the coal mining permit, the coal production permit, the production safety permit, the mine director qualification certificate, the mine director safety certificate, and the business license. The more the stages for approval and permitting and the more the discretionary power granted to presiding officials, the more rampant bribery and corruption in the approval and permitting process. Given the lengthy review and approval process and the amount of red tape involved, applicants often flocked to sideways or backdoors to buy off presiding officials for their discretionary decisions and speedy approvals of their applications. Some officials even went further by violating state rules and regulations to help their bribers forge applications and documents and to broker collusive connections between their bribers and other serving officials. Still others, in outright defiance of laws and regulations, illegally granted unqualified applicants the required business licenses and permits for mining operation and production in exchange for outsized bribes and kickbacks.

While the authorities had repeatedly directed local governments to marketize the transfer and transaction of mining rights through bidding,

[13] Pei, 60–65.

auction, and listing for sale, local officials, driven by largely venal incentives, still opted to transfer mining rights through negotiations and agreements to the advantage of the developers; or manipulate the bidding and auction process to the benefits of their bribers by secretly disclosing bidding information or fraudulently manipulating the evaluation and decision-making process in favor of their colluders. For example, the deputy director of Anhui provincial land department, Yang Xianjing, manipulated the screening and bidding processes for the transfer of iron ore exploration rights in such a way that his briber Ji licang and his firm were assessed and declared the only qualified bidder for the listed bidding. In return, Ji rendered Yang a cash bribe of over 10 million yuan. Similar to malpractices in land, arbitrary reductions and exemptions in royalties, mining rights fee, mining resource compensation fee, resource tax, etc. at the expense of the state were also widespread in the mining sector. In another example, Yang Xianjing, in sheer defiance of the bidding and auction rules and procedures, arbitrarily awarded the transfer of exploration rights for a state-owned iron ore reserve to Ji Licang at a cost of 150 million yuan, whereas the market value of the exploration rights was estimated at 810 million yuan.[14] In the coal-rich province of Shanxi, arbitrary reduction and exemption in mining rights fee was a widespread malpractice. In Linfen City, for example, such reductions amounted to 5.23 billion yuan in 2007; in the city of Luliang and Yangquan, the reductions were in the range of 3.4 billion yuan and 318 million yuan respectively in a two-year period.[15]

Rent-seeking took place in not only departments that had the authority over approval and permitting but also other government departments and agencies that had jurisdictions over the operation and production of mines. Take coal mines as an example; besides coal mine administration, government agencies mandated with coal mine safety supervision, environment protection, land administration, public safety, taxation, etc. all had decisive say regarding the mining and production of coal mines.

[14] Li Tian, "An Investigation into Corruption in Mineral Resources Extraction and Development," *zhong guo ji jian jian cha* No. 10 (2016). http://zgjjjc.ccdi.gov.cn/bqml/bqxx/201605/t20160519_79220.html (accessed April 28, 2020).

[15] "Investigation into Corruption in the Sector of Mineral Resources," *jian cha feng yun* No. 4 (2011). https://www.doc88.com/p-9893370627850.html (accessed April 29, 2020).

Disclosed corruption cases reveal that corrupt officials in those government agencies had rarely forgone opportunities to extract payoffs from mine owners and operators. Corrupt officials often plotted with owners and executives of mining companies to avoid enforcement, reduce penalties, and evade taxes and levies in exchange for personal gain. Corruption was overwhelmingly faulted as a major underlying cause of the astonishingly high coal mine accident and mortality rates as corrupt officials often acted to ignore coal mining safety rules, delay or avoid safety enforcement, and conspire to conceal mining accidents and miner fatalities to escape prosecution and penalties.

Cases of mineral resource corruption abound, and the majority of the most outsized bribery cases involve malfeasances in mineral resources and mining. Given the high illicit return of rent-seeking in the mining sector, both central and local officials were found to be involved in irregularities and corruption in mining. What is typical of abuse of approval authority and corruption at the ministry level is the case of Wei Pengyuan, deputy director of the coal department of the National Energy Bureau. Wei's tenure at the National Energy Bureau coincided with the rapid expansion of the coal industry in the mid-2000s. Wei shot up in notoriety in 2014 when a search of one of his condos in Beijing uncovered Chinese and foreign currencies of over 200-million yuan. Based on media reports, the quantities of bank notes stacked in the room were so large that the CCDI investigators had to call a bank to dispatch a team to help count all the paper bills. It took a dozen bank staff and 16 banknote counters 14 hours to get the job done. Four machines were burnt out as a result of the overload and the long operating hours. It was finally sorted out that Wei had stored in the residence 134.8 million yuan in RMB, 8.19 million euros, 3.82 million USD, 1.89 million Hong Kong dollars, and 16,000 British pounds, with a converted value equivalent to 230 million yuan in RMB. The event caught the authorities off guard and outraged the public as it was labled as the largest amount of cash that had ever been retrieved in a single case in the history of the PRC. Wei, a middle-level director at the state energy administration, was entrusted with approval authority over planning and control of coal production output, allocation of coal resource, coal mine planning, and coal mining development project review and approval. Over a fifteen-year period, a total of 228 enterprises and businesses including large SOEs and small private firms bribed Wei out of various motivations and purposes. Having the power of approval at his disposal, Wei also helped bribers obtain construction contracts from and sell equipment to his clients (mines and enterprises) in return for kickbacks. A private contractor, for example, with the assistance and facilitation of Wei, had successfully acquired a variety of contracts from Shenhua Ningxia Coal Mining Group, a large coal mining SOE in northwestern China, and made hundreds of million yuan in profit; in return, he rendered Wei several cash bribes and kickbacks totalling 67 million yuan. In another case, Wei helped the owner of an environmental engineering company to obtain water treatment contracts from several state-owned coal mines; to accommodate Wei's requests, those mines had to either alter or abolish project bidding procedures and process to allow Wei's crony to win the water treatment contracts. In return, Wei received three cash payments of 9 million yuan from the firm.[16] Wei was sentenced to suspended death penalty in 2016.[17]

At the local level, rent-seeking was also widespread and rampant, and cases of bribery and corruption were generally characterized by the involvement of local leading Party-state officials, sizeable bribes, reckless grafting, and extensive collusive networking. In the coal-rich province of Shanxi, coal-related corruption had escalated to such an extent that the malfeasance had even caused massive "collapse-style corruption" in many local officialdoms. Dong Hongyun, the Party chief of Xinzhou city, was charged in 2017 for bribe-taking and possession of large amount of assets that could not be legitimately justified and explained. Dong was once the mayor of Luliang city, a region that is well-known for its rich reserve of coal resource and also notoriously famous for rampant corruption in coal mining and marketing. Investigation revealed that by February 2015 Dong had been in possession of astonishingly large amount of assets worth 127 million yuan. Dong had extracted rents mainly through his authority over the approval and permitting of coal mining projects, land lease, coal mine operation and production, coal company share

16 "The Details of Wei Pengyuan Bribe-Extraction Case," *peng pai news*, February 16, 2017. http://news.sohu.com/20170216/n480880417.shtml (accessed May 7, 2020).

"Wei Pengyuan Confessed Bribe-Taking of 210 Million Yuan," *CCTV News*, October 20, 2016. https://news.qq.com/a/20161020/030163.htm (accessed May 8, 2020).

17 "The Details of Wei Pengyuan Bribe-Extraction Case," *peng pai news*, February 16, 2017. http://news.sohu.com/20170216/n480880417.shtml (accessed March 6, 2020).

"Wei Pengyuan confessed bribe-taking of 210 million yuan," *CCTV News*, October 20, 2016. https://news.qq.com/a/20161020/030163.htm (accessed March 15, 2020).

issuance and transfer, environment assessment, as well as selling offices and promotions.[18]

What had set the true record of bribe-taking in Shanxi province or even nationwide in terms of the sizes of individual bribes was the bribery case of Zhang Zhongsheng. Zhang, colleague of Dong Hongyun, was the deputy mayor of Luliang city and also the former magistrate of Zhongyang County. Zhang was prosecuted for bribe-taking in excess of 1 billion yuan and was sentenced to death in March 2018. Zhang, dubbed "the Godfather of Luliang", was the Party chief of Zhongyang County between 1997 and 2002. In 2003 he was promoted to deputy mayor of Luliang city and was put in charge of coal resources and the coal mining industry. Similar to Dong Hongyun, Zhang had also amassed an immense amount of assets through bribe-taking and extortion. With tremendous discretionary power and leeway over decisions on coal mine operation, mine closure, coal resource integration, and coal mine restructuring and reorganization, Zhang had allegedly become what was dubbed the "behind-the-scene boss" controlling most of the coal mines and enterprises in Zhongyang County. Among the eighteen bribes Zhang had extracted, two of them amounted to over 200-million yuan each. While the size of the bribes stunned the public, Zhang's downfall, however, was not a sheer surprise to the locals as almost all the top municipal Party and government officials such as Party secretaries, mayors, and deputy mayors in Luliang in the period had been investigated and convicted of bribery and corruption.[19]

As rampant and pervasive in mining was an abuse of power and corruption in energy. What was dubbed "collapsing-style corruption" in the state energy sector led to the investigation and detention of 19 high-ranking energy officials in 2013 and 2014, including Jiang Jiemin, director of State-Owned Assets Supervision and Administrative Commission (SASAC), Liu Tienan, director of the State Energy Bureau, and deputy director Xu Yongsheng, as well as directors of several departments in the State Energy Bureau and executives of state-owned energy corporations. Their downfalls were all related to abuse of administrative

[18] http://news.ifeng.com/a/20180415/57591701_0.shtml.

[19] http://news.ifeng.com/a/20180328/57135020_0.shtml. "Zhang Zhongsheng Who Took 1 Billion Yuan in Bribe Was Sentenced to Death Penalty," *peng pai news*, April 13, 2018. http://news.sina.com.cn/c/2018-04-13/doc-ifyuwqfa0218612.shtml (accessed March 27, 2020).

approval authority, bribery, and corruption. The State Energy Bureau is a subordinate agency of the State Development and Reform Commission and is delegated by the State Council to review, assess and approve capital investment proposals for energy development. As per the approval protocol, local governments and enterprises must submit their capital project proposals to the State Energy Bureau for review and preliminary approval to assure that the proposed investment and development were in line with the national energy development plan. This preliminary review and approval process was also an integral part of the energy investment risk management strategy aimed to minimize capital investment risks in the sector. Only upon the preliminary approval of the State Energy Bureau, a project was permitted to proceed to the stage of preparatory work such as land acquisition, environment assessment, power, and water supply, etc. Dubbed "route pass", this preliminary approval was deemed a critical milestone of the feasibility of the project, and state officials who presided over the project review and approval process often became the targets of illicit influence. To secure the issuance of the "route pass", local governments and energy corporations often dispatched liaison officials to Beijing to facilitate the proposal review process and also to curry favors with the presiding officials through illicit payoffs. As coal mining and electric power generation projects generally involved very high figures in capital investment, the departments of coal and electric power overseeing the review and approval of coal and electricity projects had become particularly prone to bribery and corruption. In 2014 alone, several directors (including former directors) of the electric power department were detained and investigated for irregularities and corruption.[20]

Although the central authorities have decentralized its control over mining, it still maintains tight grip on the exploration and production of petroleum and natural gas. However, this does not mean that the sector is immune to rent-seeking and collusive corruption. Well-connected businessmen, in particular those backed by the top elite, are still able to crack the tight lid to easily profiteer in these valuable resources. Take the case of Zhou Bin as an example; Zhou Bin is the son of Zhou Yongkang, the top Party chief of China's judiciary and police forces and the member of the Standing Committee of the CCP Politburo. Before entering the Politburo Standing Committee, Zhou had been the top executive of China's

[20] Li Fengtao, "The Route of Energy Corruption," *China Economic Weekly* No. 28, July 2014. http://www.ceweekly.cn/2014/0721/87612.shtml (accessed May 4, 2020).

state petroleum sector and later was appointed the Party chief of Sichuan province. Zhou's influence as well as his patron–client networks in the state petroleum sector and Sichuan province paved the way for his son to easily grab state resources for profiteering and to amass stunningly immense windfalls in no time. With the facilitation and intervention of his father's former subordinates and cronies (many of them were holding leading positions at the time) in the industry and localities, Zhou Bin profiteered in petroleum, hydropower, real estate, highway development, finance, and entertainment. Condoned and facilitated by the CEO of PetroChina, who was once the subordinate of Zhou Bin's father, Zhou Bin successfully acquired an oil plot in Shaanxi province at a cost of over 10 million yuan. He later sold the development permit for the oil reserve to a petroleum developer for 500 million yuan, raking in a staggering profit of 50-fold the original acquisition cost.

While analysis of corruption resulted from abuse of discretionary approval authority mainly focuses on economic impact, it is as important and crucial to examine its social consequences. The economic loss in many cases may seem to be finite, the social effect in the form of environmental degradation, casualties and loss of lives, etc. can be detrimental and long-lasting. Take collusive corruption in resources and mining as an example; widespread power abuse and corruption involving approval and issuance of production safety licenses are overwhelmingly faulted as the major contributing factor to the high incidence of mining accidents and disasters in China. In general, approval and issuance of mine production safety license entailed multiple review and approval processes starting at the village level till final approvals by provincial authorities. Instead of investing in equipment and training to meet the production safety standards, mine owners, in particular owners of small coal mines, often opted to bypass the formal procedure by bribing key officials at various review and approval stages to illegally acquire this essential certificate of coal mine operations. Driven by motivation for windfall fortune, unlawful mine owners and operators even risked potential heavy fines and jail term to open and operate coal mines without the mandatory mine production safety licenses. For example, in Shanxi province, there were around 4600 coal mines in operation in 2006, but only approximately 2000 mines were being operated legally with the mandatory safety certificates. Illegal mines of the sort tended to buy off mine safety inspectors and enforcement officials to remain in operation and to conceal mine accidents. Most of the coal mine accidents and casualties in the reform era were attributable to unlicensed mines and mines that may have acquired licenses through illicit payoffs but lacked the required equipment and capacity for safe production and operations. In 2005, a flooded mine accident at Xinjing Coal Mine in Zuoyun County, Shanxi province resulted in a loss of 56 miners. The disaster was the consequence of illegal cross-boundary mining and mining beyond capacity and safety measures. In the immediate aftermath of the accident, the owner of the Xinjing Mine plotted with township officials (one of them was his brother) to underreport the number of trapped miners and also took measures to conceal the severity of the accident. An investigation revealed that the mine had all the required licenses and permits for coal mining and production but some of the certificates such as the mine production safety license were obtained through bribery.[21]

Tax Evasion and Tax Fraud

Tax evasion and tax fraud are "black corruption" and criminal act across all polities and societies and can be particularly widespread and rampant in states that suffer from high level of corruption or have high nominal tax rates and high customs tariffs. While the poor seem to engage in "corruption without theft", i.e., extortion of bribes above and beyond official fees, the wealthy tend to involve in what is termed "corruption with theft"—tax evasion and avoidance of fees and fines. In terms of state tax revenue, the former may not have a direct impact on the intake to the state coffer, whereas the latter incurs a loss to the state treasure. Both malpractices represent a cost to the citizens; while the former increases individuals' financial burden on government benefits and services that they deserve for free or at a nominal fee, the latter leads to an overall cost that are born by taxpayers who have less connections, and by the general public in the form of reduced public services and higher nominal tax rates.[22]

Causes of tax evasion and customs tariffs avoidance are various. Some may be related to systemic factors such as a lack of institution and entrenched tradition for taxation and enforcement, others may originate from state taxation structures that are characterized by high nominal tax

[21] Zhao Chu, "Administrative Approval Related Corruption Is an Open Secret," *fa zhi zao bao*, July 9, 2006. http://news.sina.com.cn/c/2006-07-09/133710373633.shtml (accessed May 11, 2020).

[22] Rose-Ackerman, 76.

rates, high customs tariffs, and other related fees and levies. As validated in the case of post-Mao China, both scenarios prevailed in the reform era. In a high taxation environment, businesses and government officials are incentivized to collude to lower the sums channeled to the state treasure in exchange for rents and illicit gains for themselves. Tax evasion and corruption generally lead to a more regressive taxation system and also exacerbate inequality. In the worst scenario, high taxation and high tariff induce tax corruption and tariff evasion and fraud, "which lead to higher nominal rates, even more avoidance, and so forth in a vicious spiral."[23]

Tax evasion and fraud were widespread among private enterprises in the reform era, and it had been a common phenomenon that dishonest businessmen and corrupt taxation officials colluded to defraud the state of the due tax payments for their own illicit gains. While tax evasion and tax fraud had escalated in tandem with the rise of the private economy, the state-owned enterprises had also been a notorious player in the schemes in the early and mid-reform period. A statistical analysis by the National Statistics Bureau in the 1990s concluded that approximately 80 percent of private businesses, 50 percent of collective enterprises, and 40 percent of SOEs evaded taxes in one way or another. Given such rampant malfeasances of tax evasion and tax fraud in both the private and public sector, the loss of state tax revenue had been immeasurable. Between 1978 and 1992, the ratio of government budgetary revenues to GDP had dramatically decreased from 31 to 14.2 percent. While the decline of government tax revenues in the early reform years was partly attributable to decentralization and the ill-defined tax-sharing structure between the central authorities and local governments, it was also the grave consequences of widespread tax evasion in the economy and corruption in taxation authority. It was estimated that during 1985–1993 tax evasion-induced tax revenue loss incurred by governments was in the range of 100 billion yuan. As the figure was drawn from uncovered tax evasion cases, the true scope of tax evasion and the dollar figure implicated would be much graver and alarmingly high than those publicized. In tandem with the drop of government tax revenues was the skyrocketing of tax evasion cases. In the first quarter of 1995, for instance, over 1300 large tax

[23] Ibid., 76.

evasion cases were investigated, accounting for a 44 percent surge from the same quarter in the previous year.[24]

Corruption in taxation is manifested in various forms and patterns. First of all, corrupt tax officials colluded with unscrupulous businessmen to defraud the state of VAT tax rebates or cheat the state on VAT returns using fraudulent or fake VAT invoices. As discussed in Chapter 4, corrupt and fraudulent acts in VAT fraud were even encouraged and participated by local governments in an attempt to boost local GDP growth at the expense of the central authorities. Corrupt officials in taxation and other government agencies helped bribers to obtain the required documents, certificates, and invoices through various illicit means in exchange for payoffs. Prevalent corruption in VAT fraud had led to a tremendous fiscal loss to the state treasure. Second, tax corruption was also reflected in embezzlement and misappropriation of state tax revenues. This was considered probably the highest incidence in tax irregularities and corruption, and a range of major tax corruption cases revealed widespread collusive corruption among venal tax officials to graft or misappropriate tax dollars for various illicit purposes. Third, in violation of state rules and tax regulations, corrupt tax officials often used their discretionary taxation power to raise rates of levies and to inflate the scope of charges and fees. Arbitrary use of taxation authority was often employed to open up more opportunities for rent-seeking or generate additional tax revenue sources for misappropriation. Finally, "petty corruption" of tax extortion was particularly widespread and rampant among basic-level tax officials. Abuses of power, for example, were widely committed in areas of identifying would-be taxpayers, setting tax rates, and auditing tax-related cases. Tax officials plotted with businessmen to evade taxes or reduce tax payments to the state in return for their own gains. It had been a pervasive misdeed that lower-level tax officials even extorted small business owners in their taxation jurisdictions for free meals, free merchandises as well as other unpaid benefits. For example, a small retail shop owner in Chaoyang District, Beijing once complained that a taxation official, while visiting his store to review and set the annual business tax rate for his clothing retail store, extracted a "small gift" of 4 packs of cigarettes and a scarf from the store owner in exchange for a favorable assessment of the annual business tax rate; the official also demanded (extorted) another

[24] Ting Gong, "Forms and Characteristics of China's Corruption in the 1990s", 281–282.

scarf and a pair of gloves for his wife when he left the store. The store owner commented that the tax officer, who seemed to be a chain smoker, might have never paid for the cigarettes he had smoked.[25] If petty corruption of the sort was such commonplace in China's capital city, the malaise must have been much more widespread and worse in small cities and townships in less developed regions. Petty corruption was deemed a major contributing factor to the public outrage over government corruption as well as citizens' deteriorating confidence in the Party-state in reform China.

As VAT rebate and VAT invoice fraud and corruption have been reviewed in the previous chapter, below are several cases of tax corruption that manifest various patterns of irregularities and malfeasances in the state taxation system. Collusions between real estate developers and tax officials to evade due tax payments to the state were widespread, in particular in the real estate boom in the new century. A group corruption case involving 60 taxation officials in Nanyang city, Henan province, among whom were 26 directors and deputy directors of the municipal and county tax agencies, is typical of the depth and breadth of the tax-related collusive corruption in the real estate sector. Take tax corruption in Tanghe County as an example; motivated by the temptation for hefty bribes from real estate developers, tax and enforcement officials abused their discretionary taxation power to various extents to arbitrarily exempt or reduce property-related taxes, levies, and fees, which resulted in a loss of 44 million yuan in state taxes. A district tax audit agency director, after taking a bribe from a developer, made an illicit arrangement to exempt the outsized development-related taxes the briber had owed to the state for a nominal charge of late fee on the owed taxes.[26] Gao Xinyun, director of the municipal local taxation bureau, the highest-ranking official among the tax officials implicated in the group corruption case, was sentenced to eight years in prison in 2015 for taking bribes worth 1.7 million yuan.[27] Officials at a basic-level tax office in Chaoyang District, Beijing colluded with real estate brokers to arbitrarily evade or reduce due real estate transaction taxes and levies, which costed the state a loss of hundreds of million

[25] http://blog.sina.com.cn/s/blog_af5a1f0b01013u3t.html (accessed May 15, 2020).

[26] http://legal.people.com.cn/n/2015/0829/c188502-27530383.html (accessed May 13, 2020).

[27] http://news.cjn.cn/cjsp/gdzl/201510/t2728119.htm (accessed May 13, 2020).

yuan in tax revenue. In 2016, 26 officials of the tax office were investigated, among whom eleven were charged for bribery, tax evasion, and tax fraud.[28] In the aftermath of the burst of a real estate bubble in Hainan province, officials at Haikou local taxation bureau took advantage of the discretionary authority to handle "bad properties" resulted from the real estate bubble to illicitly exempt and reduce due taxes to the benefit of the developers in exchange for lucrative payoffs. An investigation concluded that illegally evaded deed tax and business tax in this case amounted to 300 million yuan and 880 million yuan respectively, and over 20 tax officials were investigated and charged for bribery and tax evasion.[29]

Many of the most notorious and well-publicized cases in reform China, more or less, involved tax evasion and tax fraud aided by corrupt tax and enforcement officials even though many major "crime scenes" were in non-taxation sectors. Take Lai Changxing smuggling case as an example; to profiteer in smuggled goods and automobiles, Lai must smuggle or transport those items out of the Xiamen tax-free zone to inland markets. Conspired with corrupt officials of the tax authority Lai was able to legitimize the smuggled goods for marketing in the mainland using fraudulent value-added tax receipts and documents. It was revealed that Lai falsely declared value-added taxes totaling 2.8 billion yuan, which had resulted in a loss of 357 million yuan in state tax. Using similar schemes, the bought-off officials at Xiamen commodity inspection agency and the police department also helped Lai to legitimize smuggled goods and vehicles by forging fake inspection and confiscation documents.

Customs and Inspection

Incidence of customs corruption escalated as smuggling activities grew rampant in the 1990s. Customs officials are entrusted with regulatory enforcement authority over import and export of goods and products and are generally targets of buyoffs of unlawful importers and organized smugglers. There exist mutual motives among smugglers and corrupt customs officials to engaging in collusive relationships to facilitate and

[28] "Collective Corruption in a Tax Office in Chaoyang District in Beijing," *wenku baidu*. https://wenku.baidu.com/view/74eb5ab80875f46527d3240c844769eae009a382.html (accessed May 13, 2020).

[29] http://www.china.com.cn/news/comment/2010-05/18/content_20062727.htm (accessed May 14, 2020).

conceal illicit dealings of tariff evasion and fraud in exchange for rents and illegal bonanzas. The surge in smuggling and the rise of corruption in customs in reform China was due partly to the soaring domestic demand for import vehicles, consumer and producer goods, and raw materials, and partly to the hefty profit margins resulted from the evasion of import duties and taxes. In addition, high customs tariffs and non-tariff barriers were also deemed decisive factors to the high level of customs corruption and rampancy of smuggling.

In the Chinese context, incentives for officials' involvement in tariff evasion and smuggling were more complicated and were beyond the typical scenario of collusive arrangements between smugglers and customs officials in pursuit of illegal profits and economic rents. Incentives may vary depending on the motives and purposes of the involvements of the participants. For example, local officials and customs agents may choose to help smugglers in return for payoffs or other personal gains; others were for the interests of the factions; still others simply for the promotion of economic growth of the localities. Although smuggling, as a category of official corruption and criminal act, was not so frequent in contrast to other forms of economic corruption, the motivations of the actors sometimes aroused controversies as they seemingly did not concern personal gains. This is what typifies organizational smuggling as a classical example of organizational corruption in the context of reform China. Due to its publicity, notoriety and detrimental impact on the economy, smuggling and smuggling cases involving organizational smuggling as a means to promote local economic growth are to be singled out as an independent category of bureaucratic corruption and economic crime that shall be detailed in the subsequent section of *smuggling*. In this section, we focus on a general review of corruption in customs, supplemented by several corruption cases to illustrate its manifestation, scope, and consequences.

Given the high tariffs the Chinese government imposed on certain import goods and products, particularly before China's accession to WTO in 2001, there always existed strong incentives for smuggling in pursuit of illegal windfalls. In the Chinese context, a career in customs and import and export merchandise inspection is generally regarded as a decent one with good pay and lucrative "grey" incomes. A Web search of the subject often results in discussions among job seekers on the potential income level that a customs official may earn, and most of his or her income, as asserted by some bloggers, may come from bribes and payoffs from smugglers. This is a manifestation of the high incidence and pervasiveness of the irregularities and malfeasances in customs and enforcement. Customs corruption presents the following patterns or manifests in the following areas. First of all, smugglers often conspire with customs officials, or even forge partnerships to jointly undertake smuggling activities and share illicit proceeds. This is a much worse and harmful scenario than simply "let-it-go" as the pattern generally entails collective collusion involving multiple customs and inspection officials throughout various stages of the inspection and approval process and often result in heavier loss of state tariff and tax revenues. The Yuanhua smuggling case, as shall be addressed in the section of *smuggling*, provides insight into various aspects of the scenario and illustrates its detrimental impact on the economy. Second, departments of a customs agency such as cargo management, shipping management, bonded, and investigation are usually hardest-hit departments by collusion and corruption as officials in these departments are entrusted with higher level of centralized and discretionary powers that are critical to the success of smuggling operations. Third, as revealed in various major smuggling cases, local leading officials such as Party chief, mayor, and deputy mayor tend to intervene in enforcement by pressuring the customs administration to condone smuggling activities or to step in to obstruct anti-smuggling investigations on smugglers' behalf. For example, a deputy mayor of Zhanjiang city, Guangdong province, was accused of talking (pressuring) the director of Zhanjiang customs agency into letting go of the smuggled shipments of canola oil and wheat to the benefit of the smugglers; in return, the customs director received a cash bribe of 2 million yuan from the smugglers. The Party boss of Xiamen city, Fujian province, after being bribed by smugglers, stepped in to intervene in or to obstruct three anti-smuggling investigations launched by the local customs bureau and enforcement agencies.[30] Fourth, dereliction of duty, irregularities, and corruption in law enforcement and judicial agencies such as police, port authority, commodity inspection agency, border patrol, etc. have, to a large extent, connived or encouraged the rise and pervasiveness of smuggling operations and activities throughout the reform era. Collusive corruption among customs and law enforcement was deemed a major contributing factor to spiraling regional smuggling

30 "Five characteristics of corruption in customs," *Jian Cha Daily*, October 14, 2003. https://www.chinacourt.org/article/detail/2003/10/id/85951.shtml (accessed May 19, 2020).

activities. Also included in the section of *smuggling* are cases of automobile and consumer goods smuggling in Zhanjiang, Dandong, and Rushan in the 1990s and also examples that showcase collusions across customs, local governments, and anti-smuggling and border patrol agencies that were forged to seize illegal payments or to take an illicit shortcut to promote local GDP growth. Last and most importantly, "collapsing-style corruption" (塌方式腐败), a vivid description of the extent and severity of corruption within the customs system, was generally deemed a fundamental cause of widespread smuggling in the post-1992 period. Corrupt customs directors often acted as bad role models for power abuse, rule-breaking, bribery, and corruption that had contributed to the formation and prevalence of an unethical and corrupt organizational culture that bred rampant rent-seeking, dereliction of duty, bribe extraction, and corruption. Take Xiamen Customs Bureau as an example; as revealed in the investigation of the Yuanhua smuggling case, the bureau and its five customs branches as well as three investigative and supervisory departments were all involved or implicated in "collapsing-style corruption" that had been attributable to power abuse and corrupt acts of the three leading officials of the bureau including the director, deputy director and the head of the discipline inspection department. According to the Procuratorate Daily, the official newspaper of the Supreme People's Procuratorate, during 1999 and 2001, a total of 410 corruption and criminal cases were filed and investigated, involving 812 customs officials including 25 officials at the bureau level and 139 officials at the division level. Among the 812 officials investigated, 162 were criminally prosecuted and 489 were administratively disciplined.[31]

The Party-state's efforts to crack down on corruption in customs, commodity inspection, and related law enforcement proved to be of limited success over the course of anti-smuggling campaigns. While the most notorious smuggling cases measured by scope and economic consequences occurred in the 1990s, the systemic environment in which rent-seeking and collusive corruption may breed and grow may have not been fundamentally eliminated or altered. The younger generations of customs and enforcement officials, though better educated and more qualified for the job, are still being plagued by the same ethical and moral dilemma that have haunted their predecessors, and they apparently face

[31] Ibid.

similar challenges to break away from the temptation of rent-seeking while carrying out their customs and enforcement duties. While major cases of similar scope and severity as the ones in the 1990s seem to be retreating, incidence of bribery and group corruption in customs and enforcement, as dubbed by the authorities, are still "frequent". In early 2014, an anti-smuggling raid on the office of Section Four of the Shatoujiao customs agency in Shenzhen seized cash bribes stuffed in envelopes totaling 1.08 million yuan. Smugglers of consumer goods, in collusion with the section chief and officials, had been smuggling baby formula, food, daily necessities, and other consumer goods from Hong Kong into the mainland. Consumer products from Hong Kong market were generally in great demand in the mainland as they were considered cheaper, safer, and higher quality alternatives. Investigation revealed that the smuggling operations were tightly organized and carefully executed, and cash bribes were distributed among participating section members in accordance with the level of risk each member might bear. For example, participating officials were divided into three groups and the head of each group would liaison with their partnering smugglers separately in an effort to minimize risks. The fee structure was also clearly sorted out and executed. For example, the price tags for a carload or a vanload of smuggled goods passing the customs checkpoint were set at 1200 yuan or 1500 yuan respectively, and the accumulated payoffs were settled every ten days. The section chief and officials divided up the rents and then allocated the remaining payoffs to a covert slush funds of the section. Similar collusions and corrupt acts were divulged at Huanggang Customs in Shenzhen and Beilun Customs in Ningbo, Zhejiang province, and customs officials were caught conniving at smuggling activities and aiding unlawful exporters to defraud the state of VAT rebates in exchange for illicit money.[32]

Environment Regulation and Enforcement

Over the past several decades industrial and economic development have become such a paramount priority in China that other needs and priorities including its ecology and environment have to give way to

[32] "Recurring Collective Corruption in Customs," *xiao xiang chen bao*, November 18, 2014. http://epaper.xxcb.cn/xxcba/html/2014-11/18/content_2816129.htm (accessed May 21, 2020).

economic growth. While contributing factors to China's polluted environment and deteriorating ecological system are various, its less sophisticated environment protection legislations and problematic environment law enforcement are faulted for the lack of fundamental progress in cleaning up its air and water and restoring its environment. Environment pollution has long been one of the top concerns of Chinese citizens, and corruption in environment law enforcement is therefore one of the most hated malfeasances in Chinese society. Both Chinese society and economy have been paying a hefty price for air pollution and the polluted environment resulted from rapid but reckless industrial development in the reform era. According to a study by the Chinese University of Hong Kong, air pollution from smog-inducing ozone and fine particles may cost China an estimated 267 billion yuan (US$38 billion) each year in the form of early deaths and lost food production. The estimate was derived by calculating the social costs of air pollution attributed to the impact on public health and reduced crop yields. The study found that pollutants in the air may cause an average 1.1 million premature deaths each year, and around 20 million tons of rice, wheat, maize, and soybean are also lost to exposure to ozone each year. Collectively, the economic costs from the public health damage—hospital and outpatient expenditures, absences from work, and the like—and crop losses amounted to 267 billion yuan, or about 0.66 percent of China's annual gross domestic product.[33]

As notorious as its air pollution is its polluted waterways. China has long been facing a shortage of water resources particularly in industrialized northern region; to make things worse, rapid industry development and lax environment regulation and enforcement have severely tainted its water supply across the country. For example, a widely published media story concerning the fishing out of more than 16,000 dead pigs from the Huangpu River, near Shanghai, and its tributaries is explanatory of the seriousness of the problem and the failure of the state environment protection. Outraged Chinese citizens have decried government negligence of the environment, flooding online forums with photos of riverbanks dotted with puce-colored carcasses. Preceded this story was a

[33] Ernest Kao, "Air Pollution Is Killing 1 Million People and Costing Chinese Economy 267 Billion a Year, Research from CUHK Shows," *South China Morning Post*, October 2, 2018. https://www.scmp.com/news/china/science/article/2166542/air-pollution-killing-1-million-people-and-costing-chinese (accessed July 23, 2020).

factory spill in Shanxi province that resulted in nine tons of the potential carcinogen aniline being dispersed into the Zhuozhang River. Factory officials waited five days to report the spill, forcing neighboring Handan city in Hebei province to temporarily cut off drinking water to a million people. These two episodes are but the latest in a long list of incidents that testify to China's growing water problem. "As much as 70 per cent of Chinese rivers and lakes are polluted from industrial facilities like chemical and textile plants. 'Cancer villages' have sprouted along waterways across the country, by-products of the ugly reality that 300 million Chinese in rural areas lack access to safe drinking water." A report by the China Geological Survey reveals an even more unnerving fact; it concludes that 90 percent of the Chinese cities may be tapped into polluted groundwater supplies, and groundwater in two-thirds of those cities is considered "severely polluted".[34]

Although the Chinese leadership has listed environment cleanup and protection as one of its top work priorities, the authorities, however, have been fighting an uphill battle to rein in environment pollution and to restore China's ecosystem. Despite the fact that the government has taken concrete measures to boost the status and authority as well as the budgetary capacity of the environment administration in recent years, the effectiveness and tangible results of its environment enhancement campaign are nevertheless limited. While contributing factors to the limited success in this regard are various, venal motivation and widespread rent-seeking in environment law and regulation enforcement are deemed the most important hurdle in bringing local heavy polluters under effective control. Incidences and cases of environment-related corruption have been trending upward in recent years. Between January 2012 and June 2013, 977 environment administrative and enforcement officials were investigated and were then either criminally prosecuted or administratively disciplined. While cases in 2012 increased by 30.2 percent in comparison to the 2008 figure, cases in 2013 surged by 60.4 percent from the 2012 level. In recent years, central allocation of funds for environment protection has been increasing year by year; for example, in 2013 the central authorities allocated 180 billion yuan in environment funding, whereas the fund allocation in 2014 was increased to 210.9

[34] Matthew Garland, "China's Deadly Water Problem," *South China Morning Post*, March 26, 2013. https://www.scmp.com/comment/insight-opinion/article/1199574/chinas-deadly-water-problem (accessed July 23, 2020).

billion yuan, representing a 17-percent increment on an annual basis.[35] While incremental increases in environment funding and funding support from local environment-designated special funds have contributed to the initial success of pollution control and ecosystem improvement, funds of the sort, on the other hand, have also generated new rent-seeking opportunities and induced incentives for embezzlement and funds misappropriation.

In addition to funding increase, the CCP top leadership also took structural reforms to consolidate the authority and influence of the environment protection administration in the Party-state apparatus and hierarchy to reinforce environment policy implementation and environment law enforcement. For example, in 2015 the central authorities established a new institution of environmental inspections, granting the environment ministry the authority to oversee provincial governments' performance of environment protection despite both are hierarchically at a parallel level in the Chinese bureaucracy. Modeled after China's regional anti-corruption task forces, the central environment inspection teams are granted discretionary power to conduct spot checks on environment-related work without notification, and to summon any local governments or company officials of any rank to address their work and performance of pollution control. Led by retired senior ministers, the inspection teams were dispatched to all provinces and regions, starting at the pollution hotspot of Hebei province, to inspect and assess how well China's environmental policies and standards were being upheld and enforced.[36]

In recent years China has been stepping up its supervision capabilities and has plugged thousands of factories into a real-time emissions monitoring system. However, a reality check indicates that the authorities have been in an arduous fight to acquire true real-time emission data and to enforce environment laws and regulations. China's lax local government officials and polluting companies are finding creative ways to fudge their environmental responsibilities and to outsmart Beijing's

[35] Yan Ming, "Who 'Polluted' Departments of Environmental Protection?" *China Discipline Inspection and Supervision*, April 23, 2014. http://www.scdjw.com.cn/portal.php?mod=view&aid=20398 (accessed May 26, 2020).

[36] "China Prepares for Next Round of Nationwide Inspections in 'War on Pollution'," *Reuters*, in *South China Morning Post*, June 27, 2019. https://www.scmp.com/news/china/politics/article/3016342/china-prepares-next-round-nationwide-inspections-war-pollution (accessed July 24, 2020).

pollution inspectors. It seems to be a common practice that central environment inspectors are frequently presented with fake data and fabricated documents, as local officials—sometimes working in league with companies—have devised multiple ways to cheat and cover up their inactions. For example, environmental officials in the city of Shizuishan, in the northwest region of Ningxia, tried to improve local air emission results in December 2017 by ordering sanitation workers to spray the building of the local environmental protection bureau with an anti-smog water cannon. The intention was to lower the amount of pollutant particles registered by the building's monitoring equipment. The scheme might have gone undetected if the weather had been warmer; the next day, however, a telltale layer of ice covering the whole building exposed the manipulative act, and, consequently, the chief and deputy chief of the environmental station in the district were disciplined for distorting monitoring results. Similar tactics were found to be deployed in Linfen, Shanxi province in March 2017 when the bureau chief and eleven officials were caught to alter air quality monitoring data during days of heavy pollution. The air quality monitoring machine was blocked and sprayed with water to improve air pollutant data. The bureau chief was accused of bribing someone to prevent the sabotage from being captured by the surveillance camera. According to the national environment ministry, six national observation stations in Linfen were found to have been distorted and compromised more than 100 times between April 2017 and March 2018. Collusions between local officials and businesses in obstructing inspections and manipulating emission results are also common and widespread. In 2019, for example, a ministerial notice on May 11 flagged collusion by local officials and businesses in Bozhou, Anhui province. It accused the local environment protection agency of illegally sending advance notices to local firms about upcoming environmental inspections, instructing the firms to forge fake contracts and to temporarily suspend production in a bid to deceive inspectors.[37] While officials misbehave to either protect the local interests or their own political achievements, the problem of fake data, however, could damage the government's credibility and also distort the central authorities' decisions about where to deploy resources.

[37] Echo Xie, "China's Green Efforts Hit by Fake Data and Corruption among the Grass Roots," *South China Morning Post*, May 19, 2019. https://www.scmp.com/news/china/politics/article/3010679/chinas-green-efforts-hit-fake-data-and-corruption-among-grass (accessed July 23, 2020).

While some officials try to gloss over their inertia, others are actively engaged in rent-seeking at the expense of local ecosystem and environment. Manifestations of corruption in environment administration and protection include bribery, embezzlement, misappropriation, dereliction of duty, etc., and malfeasances of the sort in general concentrate in environment assessment (EA), pollutants discharge monitoring, environment law enforcement, and penalty levying. Similar to EA protocol and procedures in developed nations, all industrial projects in China must undergo environmental impact assessments, including an assessment of their anti-pollution measures, before the proposed projects proceed to final review and approval. As environment impact assessments have become a vital prerequisite for the approval of development and construction projects, activities of rent-seeking and bribe extraction have been on the rise in the EA administration and approval process. Risk-assessment agencies with connections to local or central environmental authorities have been increasingly gaining favor among developers because their connections can help facilitate EA reviews and secure approvals. In an official directive issued in February 2015, the Central Commission for Discipline Inspection (CCDI) accused relatives and friends of some officials at the Ministry of Environmental Protection of "intervening" in EA reviews and profiteering by running environmental risk-assessment firms. Following the CCDI inspection report, the ministry took measures to ban or limit the work carried out by 63 EA firms and 22 assessors who were guilty of malpractice. Environment Minister Chen Jining pledged to cut links to eight EA agencies affiliated with the ministry by the end of the year, or to have their qualifications revoked.[38]

There are still others who take a more active approach to extracting rents from environmental administration and law enforcement. Environmental officials either bend rules to approve EA for unqualified projects in return for payoffs or extort qualified projects for payments by putting their EA approvals on hold. Rampant power-money exchanges in EA process erode the independence and impartiality of EA institutes and impair or destroy the quality and credibility of the EA reports, which in turn put the environment dimension of the proposed developmental

[38] Nectar Gan and Li Jing, "Crackdown on Corruption at Chinese Environmental Risk Assessment Agencies," *South China Morning Post*, April 29, 2015. https://www.scmp.com/news/china/policies-politics/article/1779975/crackdown-corruption-chinese-environmental-risk (accessed July 23, 2020).

and construction projects at risk. What seems preposterous, as mentioned above, is the malpractice that environment administrative officials "recommend" their affiliated EA agencies to project applicants for consideration of EA service. When an environment protection agency (also approver of the EA chapter of a developmental project) "recommends" its affiliated EA firm to an applicant, the applicant, who is usually in a cooperative mode to the request of the approver, would have no choice but to retain the service of the recommended EA firm. As pointed out earlier, many of these intermediaries are affiliated with government environment protection agencies in one way or another. According to the Ministry of Environmental Protection, as of 2011, 333 of the 1162 environment assessment firms were affiliated with local environment protection agencies and another 243 EA firms were classified as "non-profit government agencies". The remaining EA firms unaffiliated with government environmental agencies or other government entities were mainly owned by former officials of the local environmental protection bureaus.[39] There exists an obvious conflict of interest under such arrangements as the environmental administration officials are both approvers and EA brokers, and unfortunately such conflicts of interests are often intentionally ignored or tolerated so that rents can be extracted to benefit individuals or organizations. A publicized case of EA-related corruption provides insight into the manifestation and scope of the malpractice. Pan Jun was the director of an environment assessment institute affiliated with the municipal environment protection bureau in Hangzhou, Zhejiang province. During a three-year period, he had boosted his institute's EA business revenue by 600 percent by offering 30 percent kickbacks to municipal, district, and county environment protection departments and agencies as brokerage fees for EA contracts. Its commission payments, dubbed "EA collaboration fee", to those brokering government agencies amounted to 7.4 million yuan. Payments were made either in cash and bank transfers or in wages to its partnering agencies as benefits payments to their employees. Funds, deposited in covert slush funds, were generally distributed to members of the organization as benefits or were used to reimburse personal travel and entertainment expenses of the officials. In some cases, "EA collaboration fees" were simply partitioned and misappropriated by directors and deputy directors as "bonuses". For example, the director

[39] Minxin Pei, p. 238.

of Tonglu County Environment Protection Bureau split 455,000 yuan in EA kickback with two of his deputies in a three-year period.[40]

Administration of pollutant discharge and issuance of pollutant discharge permits is another area that has been haunted by high incidence of power abuse, bribery, and corruption. Corrupt officials violate state rules and regulations to grant heavy polluters permits that they may not be eligible for or abuse their discretionary power to arbitrarily reduce or exempt due pollutant discharge levies in exchange for payoffs. For example, the director of a municipal environment protection bureau in Guizhou province "negotiated" with local manufacturers and enterprises for reduced rates of sewage discharge fees in return for bribes. However, his gain was the loss of the state, and as a result the state incurred a loss of over 45 million yuan in due pollutant discharge levy.[41] Irregularities and corruption in environment law enforcement are also widespread, and the bought-off enforcers, who are supposed to be the stewards of clean air and water, often become the protectors of illegal polluters. This collusive relationship between polluters and enforcers is dubbed "cat-mouse family". By abusing their discretionary enforcement authority, corrupt enforcers either arbitrarily reduce or exempt penalties and fines charged to bribers for breach of pollutant discharge regulations or simply help cover up incidents of illegal discharge or over-discharge in exchange for kickbacks. In one extreme case, the manager of a municipal environment monitoring station in Pinghu, Zhejiang province had even gone so far to please and take care of the manufacturers and enterprises that had been reimbursing his personal consumption expenses for years. He would notify the factories of shutting down air outlets before the monitoring station began its air quality monitoring process; or choose a calm day to monitor dust pollution in the area; or place detectors as far as possible to monitor the level of noise pollution in the vicinity of the industrial operations. In his two-decade tenure as an environment enforcer, he had never

[40] "Hangzhou Thoroughly Investigates Corruption in Sector of Environmental Protection," *Economic Crimes News*, February 5, 2016. http://www.maxlaw.cn/l/20160205/841075947618.shtml (accessed May 28, 2020).

[41] Yan Ming, "Who 'Polluted' Departments of Environmental Protection?" http://www.scdjw.com.cn/portal.php?mod=view&aid=20398 (accessed May 29, 2020).

handed out a single ticket for illegal discharge of pollutants in his service area.[42]

Cases of embezzlement and misappropriation of pollution reduction and environment protection special funds are also on the rise in recent years as the central authorities increase its funding allocations to localities to help offset the costs that local enterprises have incurred to reduce pollutant emissions and to invest in more environment-friendly production facilities and equipment. According to a report by the National Audit Agency in 2009, between 2001 and 2007, over 400 million yuan in funds designated for river and lake pollution control were misappropriated by environment administrative officials. Besides, arbitrary reduction in due sewage discharge levies and misappropriation and interception of pollution treatment and control funds had amounted to a stunningly high figure of over 3.6 billion yuan.[43] An audit on the distribution of the central authorities allocated atmospheric pollution control funds between 2013 and 2015 revealed widespread funds misappropriation in recipient provinces and municipalities. For example, over 200-million yuan in the atmospheric pollution control funds were misappropriated in 10 recipient counties in Anhui province for non-designated uses such as staff bonus, operations, and office building maintenance and repairs.[44] In Shanxi province, 79 of the 97 municipalities and counties audited for the allocation and distribution of the environment-related special funds were found to have misappropriated the designated funds for other uses, and 56 municipal and county environment protection agencies were accused of violating rules to misallocate pollution control and treatment funds in an aggregate amount of over 34 million yuan (50 percent of the total funds designated for pollution control) to operations.[45] While

[42] Li Yunshu, Yang Xinyi, and Cai Xinping, "The Downfall of Meng Wei Led to Exposure of a Large Number Of Corrupt Officials," *China News Service*, April 12, 2019. http://news.sina.com.cn/c/2019-04-12/doc-ihvhiqax1913005.shtml (accessed May 29, 2020).

[43] "Corruption Affects China's Environmental Protection," *Xinhua News Agency*, November 13, 2009. https://oversea.huanqiu.com/article/9CaKrnJmEgh (accessed May 30, 2020).

[44] http://m.kdnet.net/share-12019625.html?from=timeline&isappinstalled=1 (accessed May 30, 2020).

[45] Liu Xiaoxiao, "Environmental Corruption: Eight Means to Make Illicit Payoffs," *fa zhi zao bao*, September 12, 2005. https://www.chinacourt.org/article/detail/2005/09/id/178204.shtml (accessed June 1, 2020).

irregularities of the sort are aimed mainly to benefit the staff of the organizations or subsidize the shortfall of operational funding, misappropriation in many other cases, however, involved conspiracy to embezzle and partition public funds. Official-business collusions in misappropriation of state pollution control funds abound; corrupt officials either use their discretionary power to directly allocate state funds to their cronies or indirectly broker funds allocations from superior departments in exchange for kickbacks from the recipient enterprises. Fraudulent means were often utilized in funds misappropriation and embezzlement. A group corruption case involving several directors and managers in the municipal and county environment protection agencies in Hangzhou is exemplifying of the nature, scope, and extent of power abuse and collusion to deceive state funds for illicit personal and business gains. In 2005, the City of Hangzhou set up a 200-million special funds to compensate for the costs of pollution reduction and treatment that local enterprises had incurred in their efforts to minimize pollution to the environment. Over a period of seven years, given a lack of supervisory and auditing mechanism, it is hardly surprising that the process of funding approval and allocation had been riddled with power abuse, political meddling, and manipulation. There were cases in which environment administrative officials plotted with dishonest businesses to file fraudulent pollution control projects that had never existed to defraud the municipality of the special funds. Once the ill-allocated funds were paid, recipient businesses and corrupt officials would divide the payments.[46]

A worrisome trend of environment corruption is the increasing involvement of high-ranking officials in power abuse, bribery, and funds misappropriation. A study found that approximately 40 percent of the leading officials of the environment protection agencies at various levels were involved or implicated in cases of corruption. Incidence of power abuse and corruption among directors and deputy directors of provincial environment protection departments are obviously on the rise, and cases of the sort in general involve outsized illicit funds and illegal payoffs. In as recent as past several years, high-ranking environment officials who have been brought down on corruption-related charges include Zhang Lijun, deputy minister of environment protection, Meng Wei, president

[46] "Hangzhou Thoroughly Investigates Corruption in Sector of Environmental Protection," *Economic Crimes News*, February 5, 2016. http://www.maxlaw.cn/l/20160205/841075947618.shtml.

of China Academy of Environmental Sciences, Liu Xiangdong, director of Shanxi provincial department of environment protection, Jiang Yimin, director of Hunan provincial department of environment protection, as well as deputy directors of provincial departments of environment protection in Hebei, Henan, Anhui, Fujian, Zhejiang, etc. Zhang Lijun, deputy minister of environment protection overseeing pollution control and enforcement, had obviously mistaken his authority and influence in the environment sector as opportunities for self-enrichment. For example, he opted to bend enforcement rules and distort procedures to allow polluting enterprises to continue to operate for the sake of illicit return, outright defying the enforcement protocol of production suspension or plant closure. Like others, project approvals, government procurements, and personnel promotions had also been exploited by Zhang as rent-generating opportunities. Zhang was charged and convicted for bribery in November 2016.[47] Equally alarming are the outsized bribes and misappropriated funds involved in corruption cases concerning high-ranking environment officials. For example, Li Bao, deputy director of Hebei provincial department of environment protection had raked in bribes worth 14 million yuan (RMB), and Liu Xiangdong, provincial environment director of Shanxi, had extracted a stunningly large illicit fortune of 68.81 million yuan (RMB), $3.78 million USD, 1.6 million Hong Kong dollars and 180,000 euros.[48]

Drug and Food Safety Administration

Parallel with people's concern of widespread official corruption is the growing concerns and grievances over food safety, inferior and fake drugs. Corrupt officials arbitrarily trade not only clean air and clean water, the essential elements of people's quality of life, but also the safety of food and drugs, a critical aspect of people's health and wellbeing, for illicit personal gains. As a sign of growing public grievances, the recent decades witnessed a series of nationwide public turmoil and protests catalyzed by scandals of

[47] "How Firms Colluded with Deputy Environmental Minister Zhang Lijun to Acquire Public Projects," *China Water Net*, December 12, 2016. http://www.h2o-china.com/news/250511.html (accessed June 4, 2020).

[48] Li Yunshu, Yang Xinyi, and Cai Xinping, "The Downfall of Meng Wei led to Exposure of a Large Number of Corrupt Officials," *China News Service*, April 12, 2019. http://news.sina.com.cn/c/2019-04-12/doc-ihvhiqax1913005.shtml.

toxic food products and fake drugs, and public concerns over food and drug safety frequently topped national polls and surveys. Cases of manufacturing and distribution of toxic food products and fake drugs as well as corruption involving food and drug regulatory and enforcement officials had multiplied. According to Chinese Supreme People's Procuratorate, in 2008, 3320 criminals were prosecuted for manufacturing and distribution of toxic food products and fake drugs, whereas by 2014 the figure had jumped to 16,428, a five-fold increase over six years. In 2011, 202 food and drug regulatory and enforcement officials were charged for bribery and negligence of duty; however, three years later, officials convicted of the offense increased to 2286.[49] One of the most publicized cases of food safety in recent history was the scandal of Sanlu infant formula in 2008, which had resulted in six deaths and caused health problems to more than 300,000 children. The tragedy was the consequences of greed and venality compounded by government coverups and dereliction of duty. While dairy farmers and milk agents, driven by greed for higher profit margin, illegally added melamine to milk in order to increase the level of protein in milk artificially, inspectors at the infant formula company Sanlu took bribes to intentionally overlook and let pass this dangerous scheme. As consumer complaints surfaced and started to deepen, Fonterra, a New Zealand firm owning 43 percent of Sanlu's stock, voted to issue a recall on the product, but was overruled by the majority of the Chinese shareholders. It was the New Zealand government's intervention in the matter by directly contacting Beijing that had finally pressured the board of Sanlu to take actions. According to media reports, it was the whitewash and inaction of Sanlu and the municipal government of Shijiazhuang, where Sanlu was located, that had aggravated the tragic consequences of the scandal and triggered furious public anger across the country. The exposure of the scandal led to inspection and testing of the quality of other infant formula brands, and the investigations revealed similar problems and malpractices employed by other major dairy product producers such as Mengniu, Yili, Yashili, Panda, etc. While the scandal had shattered people's confidence in the Chinese dairy industry, it also caused a backlash against Chinese infant formula products in foreign markets. In the wake of the Sanlu scandal, Chinese consumers flocked to Hong Kong and foreign markets or go online to shop for infant formula of foreign

[49] http://www.china.com.cn/legal/2015-03/17/content_35073814.htm (accessed June 5, 2020).

brands. The case concluded with Sanlu being fined over 49 million yuan and the chairman of the Sanlu group was sentenced to life imprisonment. Two milk farmers were executed, and nineteen others were sentenced to prison. Twenty-two companies in the industry were found guilty of using tainted milk in production. The Party chief, mayor, and deputy mayor of the City of Shijiazhuang were expelled from office, and the director of AQSIQ (General Administration of Quality Supervision, Inspection and Quarantine of People's Republic of China) resigned because of the scandal.[50]

While behavior and tactics of rent-seeking in the realm of food safety regulation and enforcement follow similar patterns and manifestations of corruption in other sectors such as rule-bending in return for personal gain, negligence of duty and local interest protection are also incentives that attribute to the spiral of the malpractice. Highly publicized cases concerning farming, processing, and marketing of clenbuterol-tainted pork and meat products are explanatory of the nature and magnitude of the malfeasance. The Chinese authorities prohibit the use of clenbuterol in hog feed due to its harmful effect on human health and safety. However, unscrupulous hog farmers and meat processing firms often violate rules to raise hogs using clenbuterol-tainted feeds as the substance produces a higher portion of lean meat. In 2006, based on media reports, clenbuterol-tainted pork, and pig livers and kidneys originated in Haiyan, Zhejiang caused several hundreds of consumers in Shanghai to fall sick and hospitalized. An investigation found that the processing, logistics, and marketing of the contaminated pork products in question were technically legitimate as the shipments had all the required animal quarantine and health certificates issued by the food and drug administration in the originating locality. In 2001, toxic pork tainted with clenbuterol made almost 500 people sick in Heyuan, Guangdong province, and the contamination was traced to hog feeds with clenbuterol ingredient. As authorities took measures to crack down on such offenses in the wake of the incident, it turned out that the clampdown had only limited deterring effects. Similar health hazards related to clenbuterol-contaminated pork occurred from time to time: in Suzhou in 2002; in Liaoyang in 2003; and in Foshan in 2004. In 2011, another scandal caught nationwide attention;

[50] Rose-Ackerman and Palifka, p. 73. https://baike.baidu.com/item/中国奶制品污染事件/86604?fromtitle=毒奶粉事件&fromid=11223275&fr=aladdin (accessed June 5, 2020).

it not only involved scrupulous pork farmers and vendors but also implicated the leading meat processing company in China, Shuanghui Industry Group in Henan province. Clenbuterol-tainted hogs raised in Henan were shipped to Nanjing with all the required quarantine documents and health certificates, where hogs were butchered, processed, and sold on market. As expected, power abuse, negligence of duty, and bribery were all attributable to the scandal. Local food and drug administration officials issued the quarantine and health certificates without conducting the mandatory on-site quarantine inspections. In the wake of the scandal, seventy-two hog farmers, processers, and vendors were detained and prosecuted for illegal farming and sale of clenbuterol-contaminated pork and 53 government officials were investigated for dereliction of duty and corruption. Shuanghui Group was accused of violating state regulations to procure clenbuterol-tainted hogs in pursuit of higher profit margin as the substance generally produces more lean meat. As the leading meat processor in the industry and one of the most recognized brands in the consumer market, the image and reputation of the Shuanghui Group were severely tainted by the scandal.[51]

As China has been continuously plagued by scandals and crises concerning food safety and inferior and fake drugs, one opinion contends that the state's overall record of public health safety and quality can be improved if its ruling class and elites source their foodstuffs or see doctors in the same way as ordinary people do. The political elites are criticized of enjoying a range of privileges and entitlements including special supply of organic foodstuffs from exclusive farms, known as "*tegong*", or seeing doctors at exclusive wings in public hospitals. The privilege of "tegong" is not limited only to top leaders. The canteens of local government officials, top executives of state-owned enterprises, and elite athletes all have access to "tegong". In sharp contrast to the privileged class, ordinary people are often in constant worry about hazardous food, such as meat laced with steroids or fish with hormones. It is argued that "unless the Chinese officials – 'servants of the people' – have skin in the game by abolishing

[51] Du Xiao and Gu Yandong, "Corruption and Dereliction of Duty Are Behind China's Food Safety Problems," *baidu wenku*. https://wenku.baidu.com/view/f50129d076a20029bd642d87.html (accessed June 11, 2020).

http://www.360doc.com/content/17/0202/15/24811_626008801.shtml (accessed June 11, 2020).

the *tegong* and *zhuangong* systems, their vows to improve the Chinese people's public health safety and welfare will always be found wanting."[52]

As notorious as the Sanlu scandal of toxic infant formula were the incidents of tainted vaccine products exposed in 2016 and 2018. Both scandals had caused widespread concerns and outrages among parents. The impact of the scandals is still being felt today as many mainland parents opt to have their children vaccinated in Hong Kong rather than at local health institutes. The 2018 scandal concerning manufacturing and distribution of inferior rabies vaccine and pertussis vaccine broke out in Changchun, the capital of Jilin province. The inferior vaccines at the center of the scandal were produced by Changchun Changsheng Biotechnology, a major Chinese vaccine maker listed on the Shenzhen Stock Exchange. The company had approval to release more than 250,000 DPT vaccines and had distributed them to Shandong province before sample testing in November 2017 revealed that the samples examined did not meet the designated levels of efficacy. An abrupt and unnotified official inspection at the vaccine manufacturer in July 2018 found that the company had forged data on the production, processing, and testing of the vaccines, a serious breach of the industry protocol and procedures. While the disclosure of the scandal caused widespread uproar across the country, it also shocked the top Chinese leadership. Premier Li Keqiang ordered a thorough investigation into the transgression. In July 2018, the provincial food and drug administration ordered the company to discontinue production of its rabies vaccines and canceled its pharmaceutical GMP certificate. In 2019, the company was delisted from the Shenzhen Stock Exchange. The national food and drug administration revoked Changsheng's pharmaceutical production license and also imposed a hefty fine of 9.1 billion yuan.[53] The president of Changsheng, Gao Junfang, and other 17 suspects were arrested in July 2018 and Gao was charged for

[52] Wang Xiangwei, "China's Bids to Improve Food Safety and Welfare for Its People Are Just Empty Words—Until Leadership Has Skin in the Game," *South China Morning Post*, March 23, 2019. https://www.scmp.com/week-asia/opinion/article/3002918/chinas-bids-improve-food-safety-and-welfare-its-people-are-just (accessed July 21, 2020).

[53] "The Changsheng Bio-Technology Vaccine Case 457 Days," *Tencent*, October 15, 2019.

https://new.qq.com/omn/20191015/20191015A07C5200.html (accessed June 14, 2020).

bribery and funds misappropriation in February 2019.[54] In the aftermath of the scandal, forty-eight government officials including six at provincial/ministerial level, 13 at prefecture/bureau level, and 23 at county/division level were either prosecuted or disciplined and removed from office, among whom including the deputy director of the CFDA, Wu Zhen.[55] These two vaccine scandals came to light after *Caixin*, a leading investigative publication, published a detailed report in 2013 chronicling the malpractices in production and sale of the vaccines that had caused deaths and injuries of children. The scandals have largely reinforced long-standing public concerns over the safety and efficacy of mainland food and medicine products. Millions of furious parents took to social media to express their anger and frustration over the wrongdoing. While some demanded a thorough investigation and called for tougher regulation and more severe punishment, others denounced the moral degradation of the society in reform China.

Graft and collusion are widely blamed for the rampancy and persistency of the malfeasances in the industry. As per industry insiders, lucrative voluntary patient-financed vaccination market offers incentives to drug regulators and disease control centers to be swayed on approvals. Court verdicts on China Judgments Online showed officials accepted anywhere from thousands of yuan to hundreds of thousands of yuan to approve a vaccine. For example, Yin Hongzhang, former department head of biological products registration at then China Food and Drug Administration (CFDA), extracted 3 million yuan in bribe from nine vaccine manufacturers to fast track their vaccine approvals without submission of the vaccine test data. Some officials at grassroots level CDCs took kickbacks to introduce specific vaccine products to parents. For example, the vaccination program manager at Yuhua district CDC in Shijiazhuang took 100,000 yuan in kickback from a company that was not certified to sell vaccines in return for procuring 1.57-million-yuan worth of voluntary chickenpox and influenza vaccines from the firm. Similar cases of CDC staff taking payoffs to procure from uncertified vaccine dealers

[54] "The 'Queen of Vaccine' Gao Junfang and Her Family Are Dismissed," *ifeng.com*, October 14, 2019. http://finance.ifeng.com/c/7qlzwf2dgEi (accessed June 14, 2020).

[55] "Offenders Involved in the Changsheng Bio-technology Vaccine Case Are Punished," *Xinhua News Agency*, February 2, 2019. http://www.xinhuanet.com/politics/2019-02/02/c_1124081062.htm (accessed June 14, 2020).

also occurred in Fujian, Inner Mongolia, and Hubei. As a countermeasure against the misdeed, grassroots level CDCs are now ordered to buy directly from provincial vaccine distributors to prevent bribe-taking and corruption.[56]

As in other regulatory spheres, the drug administration and enforcement realm is also troubled by systemic corruption. Entrusted with authority over various segments of the pharmaceutical manufacturing and distribution processes, regulatory officials have a decisive say about the approval and granting of pharmaceutical production and distribution licenses, pharmaceutical product quality supervision and control, product pricing, etc. At the state food and drug administration, the departments of drug registration and drug safety supervision appear to be the most powerful bodies overseeing approval and enforcement over almost all phases of pharmaceutical production, distribution, and drug use. Official discretions and decisions in those spheres generally affect or attribute to the survival and development of a pharmaceutical company, and officials who are in a position to make such crucial decisions often become the targets of buy-offs. Take drug batch number as an example. According to industry insiders, various known costs related to the review and approval of a drug batch number are normally in the range of over 2 million yuan and the review and approval process usually takes 2–3 years. Pharmaceutical enterprises, in general, have the incentives to have the drug batch numbers granted or to have the review and approval cycle shortened so that the proposed drugs could be brought to market ahead of schedule for greater financial gain. On the other hand, however, lowering the test standards of the biochemical and physic-chemical elements of a proposed drug in a shortened review and approval process often compromise the safety and efficacy of the drug.[57] For example, according to court verdict, also cited above, Yin Hongzhang, department head of biological products registration at the CFDA, extracted 3 million yuan in bribe from

[56] Zhuang Pinghui, "China's Vaccination System Has Been Tainted by Corruption, Weak Regulations and Staff Shortages," *South China Morning Post*, July 24, 2018. https://www.scmp.com/news/china/policies-politics/article/2156525/three-cancers-attacking-health-chinas-vaccine-system (accessed July 19, 2020).

[57] http://news.eastday.com/c/20100418/u1a5154829.html (accessed June 15, 2020).

nine vaccine manufacturers to fast track their vaccine approvals without submission of the vaccine test data.[58]

The most high-profile corruption case in drug administration and enforcement may be the prosecution and execution of China's top drug safety watchdog, the director of the State Drug Administration Bureau. As the top official bestowed with the paramount duty of administration and supervision of the Chinese pharmaceutical industry and drug manufacturing and research, Zheng Xiaoyu chose to compromise the quality and safety of manufactured drugs in return for venal interest. Zheng was accused of, together with his wife and son, extracting bribes valued at nearly 6.5 million yuan while presiding over the review, approval, and permitting of a variety of drugs and medical apparatus and instruments of eight pharmaceutical manufacturers between 1997 and 2006. He was also charged for violating regulations to arbitrarily lower relevant drug approval and certification standards, which had consequently led to the manufacturing and distribution of inferior and even fake drugs. Zheng's misconduct had caused grave consequences of drug-related injuries and even loss of lives. For instance, a bogus injection manufactured by Anhui Huayuan Biopharmaceutical Corporation was blamed for causing patient renal failure and the loss of ten lives in 2006. Zheng was convicted of bribery and neglect of duty and received death penalty in 2007. The unusual harsh sentence was tailored to hold Zheng accountable for his negligence and mismanagement of the drug safety portfolio, as well as citizens' eroded confidence in the capability of health management of the regime.[59]

Corruption in the Chinese food and drug administration is partly attributable to systemic factors such as overconcentration of approval authority, excess discretions over decision-making and enforcement, lack of supervision, etc. It would be difficult or even impossible to deter incentives for power abuse and corruption in drug administration and other sectors without addressing the structural and systemic elements that induce malfeasances. In the post-Zheng Xiaoyu era, the state food and

[58] Zhuang Pinghui, "China's Vaccination System Has Been Tainted by Corruption, Weak Regulations and Staff Shortages," *South China Morning Post*, July 24, 2018. https://www.scmp.com/news/china/policies-politics/article/2156525/three-cancers-attacking-health-chinas-vaccine-system (accessed July 19, 2020).

[59] "Zheng Xiaoyu" (in Chinese), *baidu baike*. https://baike.baidu.com/item/郑筱萸/10968065 (accessed June 15, 2020).

drug administration continues to be plagued by scandals of bribery and corruption. Following Zheng's detention, Zheng's two subordinates, the director of the medical devices department and the director of the drug registration department were also arrested and charged for bribery and corruption. In 2010, six officials in the drug registration department, the drug certification management center, and the national institute for control of pharmaceutical and biological products (all subordinate units of the state food and drug administration) were detained and charged for similar offenses. Five years later, another director of the medical device department and the deputy director of the drug evaluation center were arrested. In 2018, Wu Zhen, deputy director of the state food and drug administration was detained and investigated.[60] At local level, corruption in drug administration and enforcement is also widespread. According to media reports, 27 drug manufacturers, many of which are publicly traded firms, bribed Cai Ming, a division chief at Guangdong provincial food and drug administration for favors and discretions over decision-making and enforcement. Entrusted with authority over drug production license, GMP certificate, and supervision of pharmaceutical enterprises, Cai took payoffs worth approximately 14 million yuan from drug manufacturers in Guangdong province. Cai was convicted of bribery and power abuse and was sentenced to nine-year imprisonment in 2017.[61] Another group corruption case involving the deputy director of Hunan provincial food and drug administration Liu Guisheng and 25 venal officials in drug administration, health, price administration, and drug quality test and inspection demonstrates the breadth and depth of rent-seeking and collusive corruption in the provincial apparatus. Again, failure to tackle structural and systemic dimensions such as overconcentration of approval authority, lack of constraint on enforcement discretion, a faulty mechanism of public procurement, etc. is deemed attributable to the frequency

[60] http://news.eastday.com/c/20100418/u1a5154829.html.

"Three Family Members of FDA Official Yin Hongzhang Sentenced to Imprisonment" (in Chinese), *fa zhi wan bao*, January 3, 2017. https://finance.sina.com.cn/china/gncj/2017-01-03/doc-ifxzczsu6681612.shtml (accessed June 16, 2020).

Zhou Qunfeng, "The Abnormal Career Advancement of the 'Czar of Vaccine'" (in Chinese), *China News Weekly*, September 13, 2018. https://baijiahao.baidu.com/s?id=1611453454100451261&wfr=spider&for=pc (accessed June 16, 2020).

[61] "Arrest of FDA Director Reveals Corrupt Collusions Involving 27 Pharmaceutical Firms" (in Chinese), *Sina Finance*, October 29, 2018. http://finance.sina.com.cn/chanjing/gsnews/2018-10-29/doc-ifxeuwws9228643.shtml (accessed June 17, 2020).

and rampancy of malfeasances in drug administration and enforcement in Hunan.[62]

Similar to tax evasion and tax fraud, malpractices and criminal acts regarding inferior and fake drug manufacturing could be officially justified and backed by local governments under the banner of the promotion of regional economic development and economic growth. While problematic operations of the sort did create employment and generate wealth locally, other parts of the country, however, had to bear the resultant economic and social losses or even deadly consequences of human injury and mortality, let alone its distorting effects on regulations, ethics, and social norms. A well-publicized case in Henan province in early 1990s had preluded a nationwide surge in production and distribution of fake and inferior goods, food, and drugs in ensuing years. Zhoukou Prefectural No.1 Veterinary Drug Plant in Henan province, led by its executive Wang Zhiqiang, had rapidly risen from a small collective workshop with four staff to a well-known veterinary plant in the prefecture between 1986 and 1992 (the year Wang was detained) by recklessly engaging in manufacturing and distribution of fake veterinary drugs. The plant-manufactured tablets using starch and talcum powder mixed with a very limited amount of or even without medicinal ingredients. Similar illegal means were employed to produce injections simply made of pure distilled water. The plant was poorly equipped with insufficient technical and managerial capacity for the manufacturing of veterinary drugs; what was more ludicrous, however, was that the plant had even been engaged in the production of drugs for human use. Unsurprisingly, those fake drugs had either aggravated patients' conditions or caused death of livestock and poultry. Over a course of six years Wang had bought off his way throughout the fabricating process, including acquisition of business license and drug manufacturing permits, attaining arbitrary enforcement, as well as harboring and protection of the county government. Jin Guangyi, head of the veterinary division of Henan provincial livestock agriculture bureau and the principal watchdog and enforcer of government regulations in the industry, was bribed by Wang for intentional ignorance of the plant's illegal activities. Jin even went further by

[62] "Power-Money Exchanges in Food and Drug Administration in Hunan" (in Chinese), *Economic Information Daily*, October 18, 2013. http://www.chinanews.com/cj/2013/10-18/5394395.shtml (accessed June 17, 2020).

colluding with Wang and local officials to forge fake evidence to intervene in the investigation against Wang by the Ministry of Agriculture. Also bribed by Wang for political protection, tax evasion and facilitation of operations were the Party chief and the deputy magistrate of the county, as well as directors and deputy directors of the county government and state banks. Wang and his plant's rampant involvement in fake drug production and distribution set a bad role model for local entrepreneurs, causing a proliferation of counterfeit product manufacturers in Zhoukou Prefecture. With the disclosure of Wang's case, the reputation of the locality and the credibility of the local industries collapsed. Resultantly, local companies suffered from canceled contracts, declined payments, decrease in sales, production, and profits following Wang's investigation and prosecution. Wang's case had implicated a total of 55 Party and government officials at the provincial, prefectural, and county level, and Wang was sentenced to life imprisonment.[63]

Securities Corruption

The Chinese stock market is probably one of the most non-performing stock exchanges in the global capital market. Speculation, collusion, and corruption had once pushed the stock market to an unrealistic and unsustainable level before the bubble burst. In 2015, impacted by a variety of factors, the Chinese stock market made an effort to gain momentum but soon collapsed again. Since then, the Shanghai Composite Index has been sluggishly circling around the level of 3000. While lack of reform initiatives and slow economy growth are faulted as the underlying causes of the non-performing Chinese stock market, rent-seeking, collusion, and corruption involving power abuse, insider trading, market manipulation, accounting irregularities, and other fraudulent means are also imperative contributory factors. The Chinese and Western securities markets differ in various ways; the fundamental difference, however, lies in the system and mechanism of stock listing. Rather than letting market play

[63] Ibid.

Zhang Guo and Zhang Huijun, "The Zhoukou Fake Drug Case" (in Chinese), *shuku net*. http://www.shuku.net/novels/baogaowenxue/zgczfbjs/zgczfbjs46.html.

"Zhoukou No. 1 Veterinary Medicine Plant Manufacturing and Marketing Fake Drugs" (in Chinese), *Procuratorate Daily*, September 2, 2008. http://www.jcrb.com/zhuanti/fzzt/nwya/rwwz/200809/t20080902_68803.html (accessed June 30, 2020).

a dominant role in resource allocation, the Chinese authorities are in control of the review and approval of stock listing and IPO issuance. As raising capital through the stock market is critical to the expansion and innovation of a company, owners and executives of the firm, in general, are incentivized to deploy whatever tactics and means, licit or illicit, to achieve this goal. Besides its decisive role in regulatory affairs, the state also has tremendous influence over the stock market. Central financial institutions and local governments are prominent players of the Chinese securities market; they either directly or indirectly invest public funds in the securities market and are powerful market influencers due to the scale of the funds and the magnitude of the investments. Funds of the sort include social security funds, insurance funds, venture capital funds, etc. Similar to the pharmaceutical industry, overconcentration of government authority over approvals, stock listing, and enforcement, to a large extent, has predetermined the incidence, scope, and rampancy of rent-seeking, bribery and collusive corruption in the Chinese securities sector. Before addressing insider trading and corruption in top-level securities administration and state-owned brokerage institutions, we review stock-related corruption in SOEs and local governments that had been widespread and rampant throughout the reform era.

The opening of the Shanghai Stock Exchange in late 1990 was a landmark event for capital acquisition and restructuring of many Chinese enterprises including SOEs in the history of the PRC. As SOEs and shareholding companies rushed to go public to raise much-needed funds in stock market, corrupt SOE executives and managers quickly turned the event into an opportunity of appropriation. Cases of SOE stock irregularities and corruption abounded in the post-1992 era. The case we discussed previously involving the theft and plundering of SOE funds and assets by Li Yaoqi, president of Gang'ao International Group, is elucidatory of the rampancy and recklessness of the malfeasance among SOE executives and managers. The example below showcases another scheme of stock irregularity and corruption among SOE elite. In contrast to Li, who misappropriated public funds to purchase stock shares and then returned the "borrowed" funds through stock sale, executives of Dongguo Shareholding Group in Zigong, Sichuan province used the proceeds generated from the stock trades to pay for the cost of IPO shares only afterward. Similar to Li, however, the president, CEO, and two deputy CEOs of the Dongguo Group colluded to split 1.32 million shares of the IPOs among themselves and then sold them in the stock market for a hefty profit of 9 million yuan. Another case concerns the irregularity of using gift shares to buy off government officials for their condonation of stock corruption and tax evasion. The executives of Daqing Yanyi corporation in Daqing, Heilongjiang province allocated 2 million shares out of the 5 million shares reserved for staff as gift shares to influential government officials and agencies in the municipal government. In total, 941,500 shares of the company stock and nearly 11 million yuan in stock premium were distributed to the top-level municipal officials and directors of the state tax bureau. In return for the favor of the gift shares, the state tax bureau worked to help the company evade and delay tax payments to the state. High returns from stock irregularity and profiteering had enticed not only government officials but also judicial officials and law enforcers to the scheme. A prominent case concerns a top-level supreme judge's involvement in stock corruption. Xi Xiaoming, vice president of the Supreme Court, was prosecuted, along with bribe-taking and other offenses, for abusing his influence to help an investment firm to have its initial public offerings approved in the IPO review and approval process. As planned, the IPO of Tengxin company successfully went public in September 2014; in return, Tengxin president and CEO, Xu Wei, rendered Xi an oversized bribe of 39 million yuan in May 2015. Xi was sentenced to life imprisonment in 2017 for bribe-taking of 114 million yuan.[64]

While cases above were representative of stock irregularities and corruption in state-controlled shareholding companies and government agencies in the 1990s, malfeasances in securities take different patterns and manifestations in the new century. In comparison to the malpractices in the previous period, securities-related corruption in the new era exerts a more detrimental impact on the market and economy. For almost three decades, the Chinese capital market has been known for not only its heavy government influence but also for rampant insider trading and collusive corruption. According to an index of corruption for the finance sector compiled by China's central bank, the index rating of corruption in the securities sector reaches 7.26, far above the overall rating of 5.42 for the finance sector and 4.17 for the banking sector.[65] While family members

[64] Wang Heyan, "Supreme Court VP Xi Xiaoming Takes Bribes in 100 Million Yuan" (in Chinese), *Caixin*, January 12, 2017. https://news.qq.com/a/20170112/020334.htm (accessed July 5, 2020).

[65] https://wenku.baidu.com/view/9001533f294ac850ad02de80d4d8d15abf230035.html (accessed July 8, 2020).

and relatives of securities officials and executives of public traded companies capture immense illicit windfalls through insider trading and leak of inside information, they generally attain their gains at the expense of powerless and vulnerable retail investors, who account for approximately 80 percent of the Chinese securities investors. The twisted, corrupt, and unfair Chinese securities market was likened by Wu Jinglian, a prominent Chinese economist, to a casino two decades ago, "perhaps even worse than a casino". Unfortunately, the description is still apt to the disorder and corruptness of the Chinese stock market today.[66]

Irregularities and corruption in securities take various forms and are manifested in various genesis. First of all, as mentioned at the beginning of the section, as government holds the authority over IPO approval, companies, in particular those that are unqualified to go public, tend to buy their way into the stock market. Officials of China's securities watchdog—China Securities Regulatory Commission, who have the delegated authority over IPO approval, often become the targets of bribery and corruption. A crackdown on corruption in the securities sector in 2015 brought down several heavyweights including the vice chairman of China Securities Regulatory Commission (CSRC), Yao Gang, and the assistant chairman of the commission, Zhang Yujun. Yao Gang, dubbed "the King of IPO" due to his longstanding career and influence in leading China's IPO review and approval process, turned his regulatory and enforcement power into lucrative rent-seeking opportunities during his tenure at the commission. Yao amassed a huge sum of wealth by helping public companies attain illicit gains through mergers and acquisitions, share transfers, or by exempting them from administrative penalties. By abusing the privileges of his office and taking advantage of the sensitive information on enterprise reorganization and relisting, Yao also made illicit gains through insider trading. In September 2018, Yao was convicted of bribe-taking of over 69 million yuan and insider trading with an illicit gain of 2.1 million yuan and was sentenced to 18 years in prison.[67] Following in Yao's footsteps, in 2019, Liu Shiyu, Yao's successor to CSRC, was investigated for fast-tracking initial public

[66] Hu Shuli, "China Must Crack Down on Rampant Insider Trading," *South China Morning Post*, June 18, 2014. https://www.scmp.com/comment/article/1535460/china-must-crack-down-rampant-insider-trading (accessed July 8, 2020).

[67] "Yao Gang", *baidu baike*. https://baike.baidu.com/item/姚刚/10173 (accessed July 10, 2020).

offerings (IPO) of small banks in his home province of Jiangsu and also for helping family members obtain bonds at below-market prices from the banks that had been slated to go public.[68] Also brought down for investigations of bribery and power abuse in CSRC were middle-level directors and officials overseeing IPO approval and securities enforcement.[69]

Moreover, insider trading, stock manipulation, and other misconduct are widespread and rampant in China's securities sector. This is deemed a crucial factor that erodes retail investors' confidence in China's stock market and attributes to the sluggish market performance. China's securities watchdog has recently launched a crackdown on fraudulent disclosures and stock manipulation among publicly traded companies after a slew of recent cases in which companies were found to have tampered with balance sheets and colluded to misguide investors. These fraudulent practices and misdeed obviously weigh on an already shaky sentiment in the market amid slowing growth and the escalating trade war with the U.S. Accounting frauds, failure to reveal transactions with affiliates and changes of ownership, and misleading information were singled out by the regulator as major violations of corporate disclosures. According to media report, CSRC dealt with 170 cases linked to breaches of disclosure rules from 2016 to 2018, meting out fines totaling 201.6 million yuan (US$29.2 million) and slapping punishments on 1202 senior executives from listed companies. Nine cases were passed on to the police to face class-action lawsuits from small investors, and 80 people were banned from entering the stock market. Intermediary organizations were also targeted in the clampdown. In a period of three years, 10 brokerages, 17 auditing firms, four law firms, and six credit rating firms received administrative punishments with combined fines of 275 million yuan.[70]

[68] Jun Mai, "The Curious Corruption Case of China's Former Securities Chief Liu Shiyu and His Lenient Treatment," *South China Morning Post*, October 20, 2019. https://sg.news.yahoo.com/curious-corruption-case-china-former-105645689.html (accessed July 15, 2020).

[69] "The Power of IPO Approval Corrupts Securities Officials" (in Chinese), *Ifeng Securities*, April 22, 2017. http://www.yidianzixun.com/article/0GAOBwqo (accessed July 15, 2020).

[70] Zhang Shidong, "Insider Trading, Fake Disclosures Targeted in Crackdown by China's Stock Market Regulator," *South China Morning Post*, June 6, 2019. https://sg.news.yahoo.com/insider-trading-fake-disclosures-targeted-083922381.html (accessed July 16, 2020).

Of particularly hard hit to the public confidence in the stock market is the malfeasance of insider trading among various privileged groups such as state securities officials, executives of the state-owned brokerage firms, and publicly traded companies. Illegal insider trading activities are generally conducted by their family members and cronies and can be difficult or illusive to detect. Feng Xiaoshu, deputy director of Shenzhen Stock Exchange and a former member of the IPO assessment and approval committee, using stock accounts registered under the names of other individuals, made an illicit windfall profit of 248 million yuan through insider trading. The authorities confiscated all Feng's proceeds and also imposed a hefty fine of 251 million yuan. In addition, Feng was banned from entering the securities market in his lifetime.[71] As mentioned above, high-level CSRC officials such as vice chairman Yao Gang and several middle-level directors were also involved in insider trading. Other than central-level securities officials, high-ranking provincial and municipal officials were also caught in insider trading and leaking inside information. For example, Wang Xiaoguang, deputy governor of Guizhou province, was ensnared for insider trading in 2017. From August 2009 to February 2016, Wang used his office to obtain inside information that he and his relatives used to make illegal share transactions to the tune of 490 million yuan. While the magnitude of Wang Xiaoguang's insider trading caught the public attention, so too was his Mao-tai sideline. Wang had accumulated such a large quantity of the Chinese top-brand spirit "Mao-tai" through his official duties that he began considering selling them in retail. Wang managed to acquire liquor licenses for his relatives to run four liquor stores. Based on media report, Wang's wife had to pour away hundreds of expensive bottles of Mao-tai in a period of six months before anti-corruption agency closed in on her husband. Wang's counterpart in Anhui province, Chen Shulong, was also charged for bribe-taking, abuse of power and insider trading. Court documents show Chen's illegal gains from those trades totalled 137 million yuan. However, both Wang and Chen's dirty money from insider trading were soon dwarfed by those of Zhou Chunyu, another deputy governor of Anhui province. In October 2018, Zhou pleaded guilty to charges of bribery, abuse of

71 "The Power of IPO Approval Corrupts Securities Officials" (in Chinese), *Ifeng Securities*, April 22, 2017. http://www.yidianzixun.com/article/0GAOBwqo (accessed July 15, 2020).

power, concealing foreign deposits, and insider trading, with prosecutors rounding up his profits from illegal trades at 350 million yuan.[72] Zhou was sentenced to twenty-year imprisonment and was fined 361 million yuan. Chen received life imprisonment, and Wang was sentenced to twenty years in prison. Both men were fined 170 million yuan each. Corrupt acts of insider trading and leaking inside information also exist at the municipal level. For example, the mayor of Zhongshan, Guangdong province, Li Qihong, was investigated for her involvement in both insider trading of Zhongshan Public Utilities Group, a listed state-owned enterprise, and property speculation in 2010. More than 10 others were also detained besides Li, including the mayor's husband, her younger brother, younger sister, and younger sister-in-law. Li and her family members were prosecuted for illicit gain from insider trading totaling nearly 20 million yuan. Li was sentenced to 11 years in prison and was fined 20 million yuan.[73] Insider trading and leaking inside information are also common among state-owned brokerage firms. In 2015, senior executives of China's top state-owned securities broker CITIC Securities Co., Ltd. including its general manager and four other brokerage firms were detained and investigated for alleged insider trading and leaking inside information.[74]

Smuggling

With China's opening-up to the outside world in the 1980s, so arose organized smuggling activities. Incidence of smuggling escalated in the 1990s due partly to the soaring domestic demand for import vehicles, consumer and producer goods, and raw materials, and partly to the hefty profit margins resulted from evasion of import duties and taxes. Smuggling was and still is a major pattern of crime in the coastal region

[72] William Zheng, "Chinese Ex-official Admits to Making US$23 Million from Insider Trading," *South China Morning Post*, December 21, 2018. https://ph.news.yahoo.com/chinese-ex-official-admits-making-123112657.html (accessed July 17, 2020).

[73] http://www.csrc.gov.cn/pub/tianjin/tjfzyd/tjaljs/201211/t20121122_217185.htm (accessed July 17, 2020).

[74] http://finance.sina.com.cn/stock/y/20150917/095223273586.shtml (accessed July 19, 2020); "China Securities Executives under Probe for Insider Trading," *China Daily*, September 15, 2015. http://www.chinadaily.com.cn/bizchina/2015-09/15/content_21885442.htm (accessed July 19, 2020).

of China, and smuggled goods vary from time to time depending on the demand of domestic market and state tariffs on certain producer and consumer goods. While refined petroleum products, for instance, remain a popular smuggled goods in recent years, automobiles, electronic appliances, and cigarettes were the main smuggled items in the 1980s and 1990s. As pointed out previously, while the 1990s witnessed the rampancy and pervasiveness of official corruption across the state sector, the era was also marked by escalated smuggling activities and large-scale smuggling operations. Take import car smuggling in 1993 as an example. In the first four months of the year, the South Korea customs reportedly exported 26,688 cars to China whereas the Chinese customs recorded only 166 cars imported from South Korea for the same period. In the first half of 1993, a total of 6791 smuggled vehicles were reportedly seized along the coast of China.[75] This grave tendency was also validated by data from law enforcement and judiciary. In the first half of 1994, for instance, the procuratorial agencies in Fujan province filed and investigated a series of smuggling cases, each of which involved smuggled goods worth tens of millions of yuan.[76]

Incentives for officials' involvement in smuggling seem to be complicated and may not simply be elucidated as venal and for personal gain. While in most cases customs officials collude with smugglers in return for payments, others may pursue the scheme as an alternative to stimulate economic development and to generate economic growth. Collusion and corruption in this scenario often fall under the category of organizational smuggling, a classical example of organizational corruption in the context of reform China. Two cases shall be discussed here to illustrate the circumstances. The first case concerns cigarettes smuggling led by a municipal governmental agency. Liu Qishan, director of municipal commerce bureau of Rushan city, Shandong province, took on cigarettes smuggling as a shortcut to make quick and big bucks to the benefit of his organization and the local economy. Endorsed by the Party chief of the city and aided by the regional border patrol agency, Liu's team launched three cigarettes smuggling operations between December 1992 and June 1993, and smuggled in 13,800 boxes of cigarettes worth over 27 million

[75] http://blog.sina.com.cn/s/blog_98e199650101419i.html.

[76] Shentang Wen, "The Situation of Anti-corruption in 1994" (in Chinese), *The Blue Book of Anti-corruption* (1995), 140.

yuan. To facilitate further smuggling operations, Liu used public funds to buy off the chief and two managers of the regional border patrol agency. In return, the trio of the regional border patrol agency set up a scheme to help Liu to continue to smuggle import cigarettes in a seemingly legitimate way to evade customs duties.

In July 1993, Liu's team brought in another boatload of over 9900 boxes of cigarettes worth 22 million yuan. As planned, the border patrol agency dispatched an armed team to the high seas to escort the smuggling boat to the destination port. The municipal police force also played a certain role in the smuggling operations. After the revelation of the smuggling case, Wang Jianzhi, the municipal Party boss stepped in to obstruct the investigation of the smuggling activities. Liu Qishan and Fan Zhanwu, chief of the regional border patrol agency, were convicted of smuggling and bribery and were sentenced to death; Wang Jianzhi and other accomplices received sentences ranging from suspended death penalty to fixed-term imprisonment. The Rushan municipal commerce bureau, as a legal entity, was charged for smuggling and was fined 100,000 yuan. Liu Qishan appealed to the provincial high court on the ground that the organized smuggling operations had been intended to generate new revenue source to his organization rather than personal gains. The provincial high court, however, dismissed Liu's appeal and upheld the original sentence.[77]

Another case concerns large-scale automobile smuggling organized by the municipal government of Dandong, Liaoning province. While this case shares similarities with the Rushan smuggling case, the city government of Dandong had obviously played a more active role throughout various phases of the smuggling operations, including organization, coordination, facilitation, and execution. Dandong is a border city located on the west bank of the Yalu River, a waterway separating China from North Korea. Driven by similar motivation as that of Liu Qishan in Rushan, Wang Maorong, deputy director of Dandong municipal supply and marketing cooperatives, and Tian Zhaoliang, manager of Dandong municipal agricultural production inputs and supply company, colluded to smuggle South Korean automobiles to make quick and easy money for their SOEs. While being consulted for direction and decision on the scheme, Chang Yi, mayor of the City of Dandong, endorsed the proposed

[77] http://www.110.com/ziliao/article-55775.html.

smuggling plan as an alternative to revitalize the stagnate economy of the city. Chang instructed high-level municipal officials to coordinate relevant government agencies and law enforcement in the planning and execution of the scheme. In April 1993, in collaboration with the municipal shipping company (SOE) and the municipal foreign trade commission (government agency), Wang and Tian smuggled in the first batch of South Korean cars. To safeguard the operation, the chief of Dandong border guard detachment dispatched armed patrol boats to the high seas to guide and escort the smuggling ship to port for unloading. Upon learning the arrival of the shipment, the customs agency rushed to the port to seize the smuggled goods. Jiang Shantang, the secretary general of the municipal government, then stepped in to pressure the customs agency to back down from its attempted seizure. As planned, the smuggling SOE submitted fake documents for the smuggled goods and was instead fined 10,000 yuan per car by the border guard detachment. Upon release of the shipment, the company sold the smuggled import cars for a hefty profit. The city government had even gone this far to support smuggling by coordinating fundraising of 4 million yuan in loan from three state banks. Encouraged by the success of the initial smuggling operations, more SMEs followed suit. Coordinated by the City of Dandong, a protocol was even set up to dictate all other smuggling operations in the city. Within two months seven smuggling operations were launched, bringing in a total of 272 import vehicles worth over 41 million yuan. The smuggling activities resulted in a loss of import duties of over 44 million yuan to the state. Thirteen government officials including the mayor, the secretary general, the chief of the border guard detachment, as well as the managers of the smuggling SOEs were prosecuted for smuggling. What differed from the Rushan case is that, unlike corrupt officials in Rushan, none of the Dandong officials were involved in bribe-taking, and they therefore received lighter sentences ranging from 14 to 2 years imprisonment. Mayor Chang Yi was sentenced to 14 years in prison.[78]

The Dandong and Rushan cases were obviously organizational-oriented and were incentivized in the interest of the participating organizations and also as an alternative to revitalize local economies. They are categorized as organizational corruption in that the goals, motives,

[78] "The Dandong Automobile Smuggling Case" (in Chinese), *chinaacc.com*, March 11, 2003. http://www.chinaacc.com/new/253/264/2006/1/ad3822122635171600244444.htm (accessed July 25, 2020).

means, actors as well as potential beneficiaries of the illicit schemes were organizational in nature, and as illustrated in the Dandong case, it even did not entail direct illicit personal gains such as bribes or misappropriated public funds. The following two cases, major in scope and notorious in publicity, fall largely under the category of collective corruption in that they both involved collaboration and collusion between smugglers and law enforcement and government officials or among officials to collectively seek personal gains at the expense of the state. As pointed out earlier, given its scope, capacity, complexity, and technical requirements, a large-scale smuggling operation often involves close collaboration, assistance, coverup, and support of customs and police officials who hold various key positions and duties in law enforcement. Zhanjiang is a coastal city situated at the southwestern tip of Guangdong province. Surrounded by ocean and being a major port city in southern China, Zhanjiang has long been a hotspot for smuggling. In early 1993, as the authorities took actions to crack down on smuggling activities in eastern Guangdong, smugglers consequently repositioned their operations to the west of the province and thus triggered a surge of smuggling activities in Zhanjiang region. On the other hand, the local authorities' tolerance of smuggling was also attributable to the escalation of smuggling activities in the area. Like their counterparts in Dandong and Rushan, the leading municipal government officials not only viewed smuggling as a viable solution to the sluggish local economy, but also were involved in one way or another in smuggling activities for illicit personal and family gains. Most importantly, rampant corruption in law enforcement and government had to a large extent triggered an escalation of reckless smuggling operations in Zhanjiang in the 1990s.

There existed three organized groups of smugglers in Zhanjiang at the time, each dominating in its specialized category of smuggled goods. One group was heavily involved in smuggling of automobiles, auto parts, and steel. Using the ill-gotten proceeds, the smugglers bought off all key officials in customs, border patrol, commodity inspection, police, and the port authority. With their connivance and assistance, this group had even established a one-stop smuggling operations, encompassing smuggling, customs clearance of smuggled goods on behalf of other smugglers, and auction service to sell seized smuggled goods by law enforcement. The second group of smugglers specialized in the smuggling of refined petroleum products. The group had its own oil tankers and the leased docks for unloading and shipping. Like the first group, this group also had the integrated smuggling operations on refined petroleum products, comprising shipping, docking, warehousing, and marketing. Between January 1997 and September 1998, they smuggled in 974,160 tons of refined petroleum products (85 percent of the total smuggled refined petroleum in Zhanjiang in the same period) valued at 1.95 billion yuan, and evaded import duties and taxes totaling 444 million yuan.

The third group of smugglers was headed by Chen Lisheng, son of Chen Tongqing, the Party boss of Zhanjiang city. Using his influence and connections, Chen Tongqing, first of all, had managed to have his son dispatched to work in Hong Kong. After obtaining Hong Kong residency, Chen Lisheng returned to Zhanjiang as a Hong Kong businessman, and began to engage in automobile and oil smuggling under the guise of a seemingly legitimate joint venture. Between May 1996 and April 1998, Chen and his accomplices smuggled in 1905 vehicles and over 40,000 tons of diesel, and evaded state import duties and taxes of over 180 million yuan. His father, the most powerful man in Zhanjiang, had repeatedly abused his office to aid his son's smuggling operations or intervene in law enforcement against his son's illicit business. As mentioned earlier, Chen Tongqing once instructed three deputy mayors to issue a letter of guarantee in the name of the municipal government to help his son secure a business loan of 40 million Hong Kong dollars from a foreign bank, and the funds were later used by his son to fund smuggling operations on automobiles, copy machines, diesel, and import wine. When his son's smuggled car shipment was seized by a county police department, Chen stepped in to pressure the county Party chief and the director of the municipal police force (the superior of the county police chief) to order the seized automobiles to be released.

Led by a corrupt role model, there occurred "collapsing-style" corruption in the local officialdom and law enforcement. Senior municipal officials such as deputy mayors and directors including the one tasked with anti-smuggling jumped on the bandwagon to collude with smugglers in exchange for dirty payoffs. What seemed more shocking with respect to the Zhanjiang smuggling case was the number of law enforcement officials implicated in the smuggling activities. Over a course of several years the smugglers had bribed and conquered the directors of Zhanjiang and Maoming customs, the director and Party chief of the border patrol sub-bureau as well as almost all managers of the key posts in government, customs, border patrol, port authority, shipping agency, coast guard, and police. They functioned either as enablers and participants in smuggling operations or as protective umbrellas of smugglers. Among the over 200 law enforcement and government officials implicated, there were 132 customs officials or 19 percent of the customs' workforce. Given the extent and pervasiveness of official corruption in law enforcement in Zhanjiang, the regional anti-smuggling capacity had been severely compromised or completely collapsed. The port city of Zhanjiang had been turned into a de facto free passage for smuggled goods in the 1990s. Between early 1996 and September 1998, smugglers smuggled in automobiles, refined petroleum products, and steel worth 11 billion yuan, and resulted in a loss of 6.2 billion yuan in state duties and taxes. Over 130 smugglers and corrupt officials were detained, among whom 80 were prosecuted and convicted for smuggling and bribery. Four smuggling ring masterminds and the director of Zhanjiang customs agency were sentenced to death, and Chen Tongqing, along with other senior officials in government and law enforcement, received suspended death penalties. Over 200 officials were disciplined for their various involvements in the smuggling activities.[79]

In the meantime, an even larger scale of smuggling operation was taking place in Xiamen city, Fujian province. The disclosure of the smuggling scheme led to the panic flee of the ringleader Lai Changxing to Canada in 1999 and also set forth the prelude of a twelve-year legal and diplomatic battle to extradite Lai to China for justice. Lai, a poorly educated farmer, began to engage in casual and small-scale smuggling activities in the 1980s. In 1991 Lai obtained Hong Kong residency using fraudulent identity and set up his own company, Yuanhua International Limited, in Hong Kong. Upon returning to Xiamen as a Hong Kong businessman in 1994, Lai began to plan and prepare for large-scale smuggling operations along the Fujian and Guangdong coast. Lai, first of all, exploited various opportunities to build a network of government and law enforcement officials in key posts and important agencies. To conceal his own involvement in smuggling, Lai opted to partner with local SOEs with import and export licenses and permits to execute his smuggling plan. In collusion with Lai's firm, several large local SOEs began to involve in the smuggling of refined oil products, automobiles, cigarettes, vegetable oil,

[79] "The Zhanjiang Smuggling and Bribery Case" (in Chinese), ***baidu baike***. https://baike.baidu.com/item/%229898%22湛江特大走私受贿案/15117704?fr=aladdin (accessed July 20, 2020).

etc. Between 1996 and 1998, Lai smuggled in 26 shipments of import cigarettes worth over 2.2 billion yuan and evaded import duties and taxes of 1.65 billion yuan. Between May 1997 and June 1998, Lai conspired with Xiamen Kaiyuan International Trade Corporation to bring in over 26,000 tons of vegetable oil worth over 1.8 billion yuan and evaded duties and taxes estimated at over 1.2 billion yuan.

Lai utilized a variety of illicit means and tactics to facilitate the execution of his smuggling plan, and common schemes deployed included fraudulent entrepot trade, deceitful customs declarations, and even outright smuggling without customs declarations. However, execution and fulfillment of all those schemes and tactics called for collusion, collaboration, facilitation, and support of key officials and personnel in customs, port authority, border patrol, commodity inspection, and police, and failure at any link of the smuggling chain would lead to disastrous consequences for smugglers. With a bold plan on running large-scale smuggling operations and assuring protection from powerful government officials, Lai, with the assistance of his cronies, took actions to conquer influential officials in law enforcement and government. Take the Xiamen customs agency as an example; within three years Lai bribed over 160 customs officials or 13 percent of the agency's workforce, ranging from the director of the agency to officials of various key posts. In addition to monetary inducement, Lai also used other perks to captivate his targets. He would use young women to lure a womanizer and buy promotion for a power-seeker. To conquer the Xiamen customs director Yang Qianxian, Lai arranged a young woman to be Yang's mistress and, in the meantime, he rendered cash to fund the couple's extravagant way of life. In Lai's notorious building of entertainment in Xiamen, dubbed the "Red Mansion", Lai entertained his targeted officials with feasting, entertainment, and sexual service. Right in the Red Mansion, Lai managed to have corrupted officials in customs, port supervision, commodity inspection, port authority, border patrol, tax agency, state land administration, state banks, as well as SOEs entrusted with import and export rights and operations.

With collaboration, facilitation, assistance, and support of corrupt customs and law enforcement officials, Lai and his cronies had recklessly smuggled in import goods and automobiles worth over 50 billion yuan in the second half of the 1990s. They brought import cigarettes to warehouses at the tax-free port under the guise of entrepot trade, and then secretly removed cigarettes out of their package boxes. Subsequently they would ship and export the emptied packaging boxes in container to other Asian countries as per rules and regulations of entrepot trade. This seemingly absurd fraudulent scheme was made possible with the connivance and acquiescence of corrupt officials in customs and port authority. They brought in high-duty goods such as automobiles, and then plotted with corrupt customs officials to "randomly" inspect certain containers where import automobiles had been replaced with low-duty chemical materials as what had been originally declared. In this way Lai and his accomplices smuggled in 3588 vehicles in 1997 under the declaration of low-duty chemical inputs and evaded import duties of approximately 900 million yuan.

More frequently, however, with the help and condonation of the bought-off officials in customs, law enforcement, and port administration, Lai and his team simply smuggled in import goods by bypassing the mandatory customs declaration and inspection procedures and process. What seemed ironical was the fact that from the windows of a boardroom where government anti-smuggling meetings were often held, one could even see the arrival and unloading of Lai's smuggling tankers in the Xiamen port. Colluded with customs and port officials, Lai used this scheme to smuggle in over 4.5 million tons of refined oil products in three years. To profiteer in smuggled goods and automobiles, Lai must traffic those items out of the Xiamen tax-free zone to the inland market. Conspired with corrupt officials of the tax authority Lai was able to legitimize the smuggled goods for marketing in mainland using fraudulent value-added tax receipts and documents. It was revealed that Lai had falsely declared value-added taxes totaling 2.8 billion yuan, resulting in a loss of 357 million yuan in state tax. Using similar schemes, the bought-off officials at Xiamen commodity inspection agency and the police department also helped Lai to legitimize smuggled goods and vehicles by forging fake inspection and confiscation documents. To assist Lai to raise funds to fund his smuggling operations, the Xiamen branch of China Bank of Communications, in violation of state financial regulations and rules, issued a total of 25 letters of credits worth $38.41 million USD.

Following the formation of a powerful protective network made of central ministerial level officials down to local law enforcement and government officials, Lai began to engage in underground customs clearance business to expand his illicit revenue intakes. Aided by his established networks throughout the import and shipping operations, Lai was able to render smugglers and even SOEs paid customs clearance services to help them traffic illegal goods. Dubbed "the underground customs director", Lai extracted commissions ranging from 10 to 70 percent of the worth of the smuggled goods, and the illicit profits from his underground customs clearance services constituted for approximately half of his total illegal proceeds. With rapidly accumulated wealth, Lai frequently sent truckloads of banknotes to underground private banks in Jinjiang, Fujian province for money laundering so that the illicit proceeds could be timely transferred to his bank accounts in Hong Kong and overseas.

Lai was notoriously known for his generosity in bribing high-ranking or influential officials. For example, to curry favor and seek protection from Li Jizhou, deputy public security minister and also the leading state anti-smuggling official, Lai gifted Li's daughter $500,000 USD to fund her studies in the U.S. and rendered Li's wife 1 million yuan (RMB) to help her kickstart her business. Lai bribed Lan Fu, deputy mayor of Xiamen, $300,000 Australian dollars to fund Lan's house purchase for his son in Australia where he was attending university. To buy off Jie Peiyong, deputy customs director and head of the investigation bureau, Lai made the arrangement to bring Jie's mistress to work in his Yuanhua Company in Hong Kong and also spent nearly 10 million Hong Kong dollars to purchase residence for her. In return, those powerful officials often acted as Lai's enablers, facilitators, and protective umbrellas, either assisting or facilitating Lai's smuggling operations or stepping in to intervene in the investigation or enforcement against Lai's criminal offenses.

The Xiamen smuggling case—the largest smuggling operations and the most serious economic crime in the history of PRC—involved smuggling of 4.5 million tons of refined petroleum products, 450,000 tons of vegetable oil, over 3 million boxes of cigarettes, 3588 import vehicles, as well as large quantities of pharmaceutical and chemical inputs, textile raw materials, electronics, and machinery with a total value of 53 billion yuan. Lai's smuggling operations resulted in a loss of state import duties and taxes totaling 30 billion yuan and had exerted detrimental consequences in certain domestic industries. For example, millions of tons of smuggled refined petroleum products had significantly disrupted domestic oil production and supply and led to the shutdown of over 3000 oil wells and layoff of hundreds of thousands of workers in the industry. The direct economic loss attributable to Yuanhua's petroleum smuggling was in the range of 20 billion yuan.

Investigation led by the central authorities began in June 1999, followed by a coordinated effort to crack down on Lai's smuggling network. As the central investigation team secretly closed in on Lai, the deputy director of Fujian provincial public security department alerted Lai to flee. Between 1999 and 2000, over 600 smugglers and implicated officials were investigated and over 200 suspects on the run were captured and arrested. By the end of 2001, 213 officials had been prosecuted and sentenced, including deputy public security minister Li Jizhou, deputy mayors, and deputy Party secretaries of Xiamen city, as well as directors and senior officials in customs, police, and state banks. Among the convicted, eighteen were sentenced to death, one to suspended death, eighteen to life imprisonment, and 177 to long-term imprisonment. Following a long battle with the Canadian authorities over his refugee status and a series of negotiations between the Chinese government and the Canadian government, Lai was extradited to China in July 2011. Lai reportedly died of heart attack in a Chinese prison in September 2018.[80]

5.2 Judicial Corruption

Individuals and businesses make payoffs to not only obtain regulatory favors and avoid penalties and costs, but also distort decisions and judgements in judiciary. For example, people bribe police officers, court clerks, judges, and prison administrators to "avoid fines, tamper with evidence, shorten sentences, or get out of jail".[81] In other words, while dishonest individuals and unlawful businesses bribe to obtain unentitled benefits and services, they may also pay to violate regulations and break criminal laws. Illegal businesses and organized criminal groups cannot exist and flourish without collaboration and collusion with corrupt judicial and law enforcement officials. It is the intended pursuit and sharing of illegal profits and criminal proceeds that bond criminals and law enforcers in common interests.

Widespread judicial corruption is particularly damaging to the rule of law and the legitimacy of government "when the police accept bribes to overlook illegal acts - or when they use their power to extort bribes -

[80] http://news.cntv.cn/law/20110722/109501.shtml.
https://baijiahao.baidu.com/s?id=1553344309227332&wfr=spider&for=pc.
Yan Sun, 140.

[81] Rose-Ackerman, 79.

the rule of law is undermined". "And as the idea (bribery) spreads that any run-in with the law can be readily fixed by greasing a palm, people take the law less and less seriously. This is compounded when the judiciary system is also corrupt."[82] Besides, corruption in judiciary causes social injustice and class discrimination; while the poor complete their sentences, the rich may buy their way out. These malfeasances and their detrimental consequences, to a large extent, are identical across all polities and societies including China.

What exacerbates an inherently non-independent and weak judicial system in China is rampant corruption in judiciary and law enforcement. Incidence of corruption in law enforcement and judiciary has been on the rise steadily since the advent of the reform, and cases of judicial corruption in the early years of the reform, though limited in occurrence and benign in scope, reflected a troublesome tendency in a field that is endowed with the duty and responsibility to safeguard social justice. Following the patterns and trends of rent-seeking and corruption in the economic sphere, tempted by materialistic interests and hedonism, an increasing number of police officers, judges, and procurators opt to abuse their judicial and law enforcement powers in exchange for money and other illicit personal gains. There have been cases in which judges arbitrated commercial disputes or economic cases in favor of bribe payers; prison administrators and wardens were bribed to forge fabrications for commutation of sentence and parole; and police chiefs and officers were incented to provide paid services to mafias, smugglers, and criminals for distorted enforcement and protection. Bribery constitutes a major aspect of judicial corruption, and a surge in bribery cases involving high-ranking officials in police, courts, and procuratorates is particularly perturbing to the authorities and citizens alike. As pointed out by Manion, "when corruption is rampant in the judiciary, the entire anticorruption effort is at risk because ordinary citizens no longer believe in impartial justice, even where politics do not affect outcomes."[83] Although the CCP has made considerable efforts to upgrade the state's legislation and legal system in the post-Mao era, the outcome seems to be vague and conflicting. This is largely attributable to "the CCP's determination to maintain its monopoly of

[82] Ibid., 81.

[83] Manion, 106.

power, an objective that precludes a truly effective and independent judiciary."[84] Political control and widespread intervention in judicial affairs are faulted as the major determining factor to the politicization and corruption of China's judicial system.

High incidence of collusion and corruption occur in economic cases concerning business and contractual disputes and commercial litigations. Those cases have one thing in common: they generally involve high stakes in real estate, mining rights, land, and other valuable assets worth tens or hundreds of million yuan. Litigants of high-stake cases are in general highly incentivized to buy off corrupt judges in return for favorable legal outcomes. As cases of high monetary claims are generally tried in intermediate or high courts with several judges involved in the proceeding, litigants tend to bribe most or all of them to assure a favorable court ruling. This usually necessitates collusions and coordinated efforts among bribed judges in a joint effort to rule in the litigant's favor. However, what are up for sale in the Chinese judiciary are not limited to favorable court judgements only; in the field of enforcement, for example, judges and officials tasked with enforcement in intermediate and high courts may have better chance to capture more lucrative rents through collusion with auction houses by granting them the right to sell assets and properties seized by the court. Under many circumstances, enforcement of court rulings can be a difficult task for both law enforcement and litigants, and judges and enforcement officers therefore have incentives as well as opportunities to extract more lucrative payoffs by either enforcing favorable judgements or preventing enforcement of adverse judgements.[85]

The underlying institution of trial procedures and administrative hierarchies of China's legal system is deemed conducive to collusive corruption among judges and high-ranking court officials. "Unlike conventional courts of law, the Chinese judiciary functions as an instrument of rule for the CCP and is governed by a strict administrative hierarchy in which political status and administrative rank allow senior officials to exercise excessive influence over judicial proceedings and decisions". In the court system, as decisions of a presiding judge need to be vetted by the chief of the tribunal or the vice president overseeing the division, i.e., civil or criminal law, there occur the incentive and necessity for litigants to bribe or

[84] Pei, 217.

[85] Ibid., 223–227.

influence the presiding judge and his superiors. On the other hand, since the trial committee, which is comprised of the president, vice presidents, chief of tribunals, and senior judges, is authorized to decide on major cases and cases that collegial panels have failed to reach consensus, the arrangement often incentivizes litigants to buy off multiple members of the trial committee. Given their administrative power and excessive influence over judicial decisions, there exists a casual linkage between high incidence of corruption among high-ranking judges and judicial officials such as court presidents, vice presidents, and tribunal chiefs and the faulty and distorted trial arrangements and procedures.[86]

As in other corrupt polities, law enforcement in China had been fraught with rampant corruption and abuse of power in the new phase of the reform. Bribe-extraction and extortion in law enforcement were widespread and pervasive. The malfeasances were particularly acute in police forces at the county and township levels. Before discussing major or high-profile cases of corruption in law enforcement in recent years, we begin with several cases of police corruption in the early period of the reform that had received broad media coverage. Those early cases, though benign in scope and limited in bribe size, may shed light on the evolution and trend of irregularities and corruption in law enforcement over the past several decades. Guo Zhengmin, director of the public security department of Guizhou province and member of the provincial Party committee, an influential police chief in Guizhou, was detained in 1993 for acceptance and extortion of bribes from an unscrupulous overseas Chinese businessman. After the businessman provided 1 million yuan in funding to the hotel development project of the provincial public security department and bribed Guo with 30,000 yuan in cash, Guo rendered him two roundtrip Hong Kong and Macau travel passes—one for the businessman's wife and another for his business partner. What seemed preposterous was the businessman's request for an official rank and title of the provincial police force so that he could facilitate his business operations in Guizhou and other jurisdictions and also evade state taxes. Guo extorted 100,000 yuan from the businessman; in return, Guo, in outright violation of the state personnel rules and procedures, illicitly granted the businessman a police official title ranked at the division level.

[86] Ibid., 221–223.

In addition to its principal duties of maintaining social order and investigating criminal activities, Chinese public security agencies also have the functions and authority over traffic control, vehicle administration and registration, household registration, passport issuance, and immigration affairs, some of which offer lucrative rent-seeking opportunities. Hong Yonglin, director of Huizhou municipal public security bureau, Guangdong province, extracted large sizes of bribes between 1983 and 1991 by abusing his discretionary power to issue vehicle registrations to smuggled cars and to approve foreign travel applications and issue travel documents. Hong raked in 1.16 million Hong Kong dollars and RMB 570,000 yuan in bribe (a huge amount of money as per average income level at the time) by either directly approving or indirectly intervening in vehicle registrations of over 800 smuggled cars. In addition to the grafted amount, searches of his and his relatives' residences uncovered over $2 million Hong Kong dollar and RMB that Hong could not explain and justify its origin and legitimacy. Also uncovered were hundreds of bottles of top-brand liquor and vintage wine as well as luxury goods such as Rolex watches and gold jewelleries. Hong was convicted of bribery and was sentenced to death in 1993.[87]

Typical of corruption in local officialdom had been collusions between criminal gangs and corrupt police and officials, and the phenomenon dubbed "cat and mouse sleeping together" (officials and thieves in league) was particularly acute at lower levels. Gang-officials collusions were common at local level and corrupt police and local officials often acted as "protective umbrellas" for organized crime in return for payoffs. The campaign of anti-mafia and corruption since 2009 had had only limited deterring effect as organized crime and related official corruption had soon re-emerged and then escalated in the 2010s. Many village-level governments in rural China were allegedly dominated and controlled by organized criminal groups, and mafia-style criminal gangs often exploited legal loopholes and lax government controls to infiltrate the logistics and transport sector under the guise of legally registered companies and entities. Illegal gambling, underground banking, usury rendering, extortion and racketeering, fraudulent contract bidding, and illegal detention were

[87] Luo Jinhui, "The Hong Yonglin Bribe Extraction Case" (in Chinese), *Major and Important Anti-corruption Cases in the 1990s* (Beijing: Fangzheng Press, 1998). http://www.shuku.net/novels/baogaowenxue/zgczfbjs/zgczfbjs24.html (accessed August 18, 2020).

all evil practices that gang societies at grassroots level utilized to exploit citizens and to corrupt local administration and law enforcement. With the backing of their patrons in governments and law enforcement at higher levels, local mafias were often able to manipulate basic-level elections, suppress democracy, loot public assets and properties, and extort bribes and illicit gains from local businesses and residents.

Cases of the sort abounded in rural China, and a recent CCDI report singled out an organized crime and corruption case in a village in Luoning County, Henan province. Di Zhimin, the Party secretary and the director of the village committee, had been running the village government like a mafia for years. Between 1997 and 2017, condoned by corrupt officials in governments and law enforcement at higher levels, Di and his kinsmen and cronies colluded to sabotage village elections by means of violence, control and manipulate village administration, embezzle and misappropriate state funds designated for agricultural and poverty-relief projects, and extort villagers for illicit payoffs. A total of 56 government and law enforcement officials implicated in this case received Party and government disciplinary sanctions, and Di was expelled from the Party and was handed over to judiciary for criminal prosecution in 2018.[88]

Cases of mafia-police collusion generally involved officials in law enforcement at county and township levels. However, media reports in recent years also disclosed "protective umbrellas" at higher levels. In 2018, for example, a high-ranking law enforcement official in Hunan province was brought to justice following the detention of a ringleader in Changsha, capital of Hunan province. Wen Liehong and his mob had been involved in usurious loans, illegal gambling, extortion, fraudulent contract bidding, illegal detention, and other criminal activities since late 1990s, and had established well-organized criminal operations with illicit funding of hundreds of millions of yuan. To safeguard his growing illegal business operations, Wen had been seeking, by hook or by crook, to buy off powerful law enforcement and government officials for shielding and protection. Wen's major "protective umbrellas" included Zhou Fubo, executive deputy director of Hunan provincial public security department, Zhang Xiangtao, member of the standing committee of Changsha municipal CCP committee and director of the municipal propaganda department, and Li Zhengke, deputy secretary of Hunan provincial

[88] https://new.qq.com/cmsn/20181011A0718500.

discipline inspection commission. What seemed ludicrous was that Zhou Fubo, the provincial police chief, had been engaged in illegal gambling at Wen's underground casino when he was the deputy mayor of Shaoyang city. Zhou even borrowed gambling money from Wen at high-interest rates. When Zhou was promoted to the position of executive deputy director of the provincial police force, Wen exempted all the interest charges for Zhou's loaned gambling capital. In return, Zhou became Wen's protector of criminal operations. In 2015, when Changsha municipal police force planned to launch an investigation into Wen's illegal operations, Zhou intervened by directing the municipal police force to dismiss Wen's case. Zhou was charged for intervention and obstruction of justice, bribe-taking, buying and selling offices, and helping bribers to acquire construction contracts in return for kickbacks.[89]

Mafias and organized criminal gangs were able to buy not only harboring and protection for their illegal and criminal operations and activities but also commutation of sentences and paroles after their ringleaders were put behind bars. In September 2018, the public was stunned by a disclosed collective corruption case that had implicated over 90 law enforcement and government officials including high-ranking prison administrators and judicial officials in Shanxi province. Ren Aijun, one of the six most notorious ringleaders in Taiyuan, capital city of Shanxi province, was sentenced to life imprisonment in 2003 and was sent to Fenyang prison to serve his time. Ever since Ren's family and cronies, with the assistance and brokerage of their lawyer, had been making persistent efforts to buy off key prison officials and judges in order to get Ren out of jail. Given Ren's bad behavior and misconduct in Fenyang prison, as instructed by Wang Wei, Party chief and director of the provincial prison administration, the prison authority, in violation of judicial rules and procedures, transferred Ren from Fenyang prison to Jinzhong prison so that the latter was able to kickstart the process of commutation of Ren's sentence in a new setting. Colluded among wardens, prison officials, and guards, Fenyang prison fabricated documents that fraudulently verified Ren's good behavior and outstanding performance during his prison term for consideration of commutation. After Ren's case was handed over to Linfen Intermediate Court, pressured by officials at the higher level, the

[89] "Former Provincial Deputy Police Chief Was the 'Protective Umbrella' of the Mafia Boss in Changsha" (in Chinese), *peng pai news*, September 21, 2018. http://news.sina.com.cn/o/2018-09-21/doc-ifxeuwwr6760249.shtml (accessed August 22, 2020).

president of the intermediate court, the presiding judge, and the prosecutor teamed up to adjudicate three reductions of Ren's prison term from life imprisonment to fixed-term imprisonment. By June 2013, Ren had got out of prison as a free man. The case implicated over 90 law enforcement and judicial officials, including the director and deputy inspector of the provincial prison administration, the deputy inspector of the provincial people's procuratorate, and the president of the intermediate court, and twelve of them were subject to criminal prosecution and conviction. The remaining offenders all received disciplinary sanctions and penalties. Ren Aijun was rearrested in 2017 and was put behind bars again to continue to serve his term of life in prison.[90]

The case of Wen Qiang is probably the most publicized corruption case in law enforcement that had preceded the systemic clampdown on corruption in law enforcement and judiciary under Xi's rule. Led by the Party chief Bo Xilai, also a member of the CCP Politburo, the City of Chongqing preceded other jurisdictions to launch a fierce crackdown on organized crime and judicial corruption in July 2009. A landmark event of the anti-mafia campaign was the detention and prosecution of the director of the municipal justice department, Wen Qiang, and his subordinate police captains. The story received broad media coverage both at home and abroad, and had also prompted controversies over the nature, motivation, and political intervention of the campaign. Wen Qiang's case set the scene for Xi's crackdown on organized crime and corruption in judiciary and law enforcement, and may shed some light on the nature, rampancy, and severity of systemic police corruption in the Chinese urban centers. Wen Qiang, director of Chongqing municipal justice department and former executive deputy director of Chongqing municipal public security bureau, was the highest-ranking police chief ever executed for connivance and protection of mafias and corruption in the PRC history. During his sixteen-year tenure as the deputy director of the Chongqing police force, Wen had forged a network of external criminal elements and internal corrupt police captains and officers. Internally Wen sold offices and promotions to cronies in return for bribes, and externally he collected rents by being the "protective umbrella" of mafias and criminal gangs.

[90] Xu Menglong, "A Mafia Related Case Reveals Involvements of over 90 Public Officials" (in Chinese), *China Discipline Inspection and Supervision*, September 28, 2018. http://fanfu.people.com.cn/n1/2018/0928/c64371-30317795.html (accessed August 25, 2020).

Dubbed the "Godfather" of the corrupt network, Wen was in command of four powerful police captains and chiefs of the sub-bureaus of municipal police, through whom Wen allegedly rendered six mafias and criminal gangs protective services. In 2000, for instance, when a gambling operation was raided and shut down by local police, it was Wen who directed the local police authority to release the detainees and to return the seized gambling funds and vehicles to the gambling gang. Because of Wen's intervention, the criminal gang was able to resume its gambling operations two weeks after the police raid. Based on media reports, several dozens of nightclubs, underground brothels, and underground casinos in Chongqing were once under the sheltering and protection of Wen and his cronies in the municipal police force, and their condonation was deemed an imperative contributing factor to the rampancy and pervasiveness of prostitution and illegal gambling in the city. Wen Qiang's family members were also involved in or even leading illegal activities under Wen's influence. For example, Wen's sister-in-law Xie Caiping had once run the largest illegal gambling network in Chongqing. Connived by Wen, Wen's wife even became a stakeholder of Xie's gambling business. While aware of the family tie between Xie and Wen, local police often played deaf and dumb for Xie's illegal gambling operations.

The anti-organized-crime campaign in Chongqing, dubbed "anti-mafia storm", drew to a close with over 2000 members of the organized criminal groups being detained and investigated. Fifteen law enforcement and government officials were convicted of connivance and protection of mafias and bribery, among whom eight ranked at the bureau/prefecture level. In addition to Wen Qiang, other high-ranking officials convicted include the deputy chief of the municipal police force, the vice president of the municipal high people's court, and the deputy procurator general of the municipal high people's procuratorate. As revealed by the investigation, most of Wen Qiang's illicit fortune of over 26 million yuan were rendered or extorted from office buyers in the municipal police force, real estate developers, and businessmen. Wen Qiang was sentenced to death and executed in July 2010.[91]

[91] "Wen Qiang" (in Chinese), *baidu baike*. https://baike.baidu.com/item/文强/1445988.

"Chongqing Mafia Tends to Corrupt Officials at Deputy Departmental and Above Levels, Says Experts" (in Chinese), *fa zhi wan bao*, October 16, 2009. http://news.sina.com.cn/c/2009-10-16/132718844401.shtml (accessed August 25, 2020).

As indicated previously, corruption in law enforcement and judiciary in recent years is characterized by the increasing involvement of high-ranking officials and a surge in sizes of bribes and illicit funds. Listed in Table 3.7 are high-ranking judicial and law enforcement officials at the national and provincial levels who have been convicted/disciplined for bribe-taking and corruption. Although they differ in varying degrees in behavior, misconduct, impact, and locality, they share similarities in motivation, incentive as well as the detrimental consequences to the state judicial system and social justice. As cases and presentations so far suffice to attest the breadth and depth of official corruption in law enforcement and the judicial system, we'll use four well-publicized cases—the cases of Xi Xiaoming, Chen Xu, Li Huanan, and Wu Changshun, all high-ranking judicial officials representing police, the court of law, the prosecution, and the political and legal affairs commission—to conclude this section.

Xi Xiaoming, who was briefed on earlier, was a scholarly supreme court judge and the vice president of the supreme court. Xi holds a Ph.D. in economic law and a Master of civil and commercial law from prestigious Beijing University. Xi, given his tenure and experience of 33 years as a supreme court judge, presiding judge, and the vice president, was considered a respected expert of the Chinese civil and commercial law. He became the member of the judicial committee of the supreme court in 2000 and rose to vice president of the supreme court in 2004, overseeing the trial and adjudication of major civil and commercial cases. Since the 1980s Xi had published over 100 articles and complied and published three books on judicial work and cases of civil and commercial law. Xi was detained in 2015 for violation of state law and Party disciplines; his arrest consequently sent a shockwave across China's judicial system and the academic circle, and stunned many of Xi's colleagues and former university classmates. In 2017 Xi was prosecuted and convicted of bribe-taking and intervention in trials and judgements of commercial and economic cases. His son Xi Jiacheng, allegedly his major accomplice, acted as a broker of power-money swap, through whom Xi had raked in most of the illicit payoffs. Although Xi had extracted only a limited number of bribes, but the sizes of the payments sufficed to render him severe punishment. For instance, the CEO of the Founder Group in Beijing, Li You, had been bribing Xi for his favorable rulings and influence over the trial of several cases of commercial and financial disputes. Li made payoffs to Xi in the amount of approximately 50 million yuan. A billionaire in Shanxi province bribed Xi 30 million yuan for his favorable ruling over a major commercial dispute regarding the ownership of a coal mine in Shanxi. As mentioned earlier, Xi was also charged for abusing his influence to help an investment firm to have its IPO approved and issued in stock market. In return, Xi was awarded an immense bribe of 39 million yuan. Xi was sentenced to life imprisonment in 2017 for bribe-taking of 114 million yuan.[92]

Another case concerning a top prosecutor in Shanghai also received broad media coverage, and this case featured an extensive guanxi network the prosecutor had been cultivating for years and a large cohort of judicial and municipal government officials implicated in the case. Once dubbed the "law manipulator of Shanghai", Chen Xu was convicted in October 2018 for taking money and properties worth more than 74.2 million yuan (US$10.7 million) either personally or through family members between 2000 and 2015. The former chief prosecutor of Shanghai, who is serving life imprisonment for bribery, had implicated over 100 officials linked to his conviction. According to the *South China Morning Post*, Chen, who at the time was the deputy chief prosecutor in Shanghai's high court, was accused of intervention in the enforcement of a verdict to force the auction of a building owned by a Hong Kong developer to a company that had been allegedly controlled by members of his family for 200-million yuan—about a quarter of its true value. However, according to the article, Chen's conviction was solely on a charge of bribe-taking, and the court did not rule on accusations that he had exploited his office to help individuals and companies to win contracts or secure favorable court rulings.[93]

While the dominant patterns of judicial corruption in China continue to be bribery and abuse of power, similar to the trend in other sectors, the sums of bribes and illicit payoffs involved in cases revealed lately have increased dramatically. Li Huanan, who was the chief of the political and legal affairs commission of Shenzhen, was detained and charged in 2019 for bribe-taking, trading power for personal gains and sex, and indulging in gambling. His predecessor, Jiang Zunyu, was arrested in 2014 and

[92] Wang Heyan, "Supreme Court VP Xi Xiaoming Takes Bribes in 100 Million Yuan." https://news.qq.com/a/20170112/020334.htm.

[93] William Zheng, "Shanghai's Jailed Top Prosecutor 'Implicates 100 Other Officials in Corruption Case," *South China Morning Post*, November 12, 2018. https://www.scmp.com/news/china/politics/article/2172762/shanghais-jailed-top-prosecutor-implicates-100-other-officials (accessed August 17, 2020).

was later sentenced to life in prison for extracting more than 70 million yuan (US$10.4 million) in bribes. What had made Li's case a talk of the town was the amount of the bribes involved and the way Li conspired to have his dirty money laundered to foreign bank accounts. According to media report, Li allegedly offered up to half of his ill-gotten fortune—or more than US$70 million—to any underground banker who would be willing to move the money across the border to Hong Kong. Reportedly Li had extracted a lion's share of his windfalls through abuse of power and collusions with unlawful real estate developers when he was the Party chief of Guangming district in Shenzhen in previous years.[94]

The last case showcases the trajectory of Wu Changshun's rise and fall over the course of his long career in law enforcement and government in Tianjin. Wu, vice chairman of Tianjin municipal CPPCC (deputy ministerial/provincial level) and director of Tianjin municipal public security bureau, had been an influential figure in law enforcement and the political arena of the City of Tianjin for decades. Having worked in the municipal police force for 44 years and held the positions of deputy director and director of the bureau for 22 years, Wu, dubbed "Lord Wu" (武爷), had established a well-connected "guanxi" network comprising so many proteges and followers in the circle of law enforcement in Tianjin. Over the years Wu had abused his unconstrained discretionary power to extract rents and to amass illicit personal and family fortunes. Charges against Wu included embezzlement, bribery, misappropriation of public funds, selling offices, financial and accounting irregularities, etc. For instance, Wu was accused of embezzling over 400 million yuan and misappropriating over 100 million yuan in public funds and violating accounting rules and financial stipulations to manipulate and conceal the misappropriated funds. He was also accused of taking 84 million yuan in bribes through office selling and rendering bribes of over 10 million yuan in exchange for illicit family gains. Wu and his family owned and controlled over 70 firms and enterprises; to safeguard the clan's interests and to make inroads in local market, Wu was accused of abusing his law enforcement power to suppress and persecute competitors and rivals of his family businesses. In addition, he was also accused of living an extravagant life and fostering

[94] William Zheng, "Shenzhen Official Kicked Out of Chinese Communist Party for 'Trading Power for Personal Gain and Sex,'" *South China Morning Post*, April 10, 2019. https://www.scmp.com/news/china/politics/article/3005619/shenzhen-official-kicked-out-party-trading-power-personal-gain (accessed August 17, 2020).

mistresses including four policewomen. Wu received the suspended death penalty in May 2017.[95]

Given all the efforts the CCP had made to curb corruption in judiciary and law enforcement in recent decades, it appeared that only limited success had been achieved. The Xi regime saw a resolute and intensified fight against malfeasances and corruption in the field. In early 2018, the central authorities called for a nationwide crackdown on organized criminal gangs and their "protective umbrellas". In 2020, China's top law enforcement agency launched a campaign to purge "corrupt elements" from its ranks to create a so-called "ironclad army". The campaign was aimed to rid the country's justice system of "corrupt elements" and purge "two-faced" officials who only paid lip services to the Communist Party's rules and orders. The planned purge came after a three-year anti-vice crackdown on criminals and triad societies, as well as corrupt elements in law enforcement. By June 2020, according to official reports, some 67,190 law enforcement officers who acted as "protective umbrellas" for criminals had been investigated and prosecuted in the wake of the crackdown. The move was interpreted by observers as a sign that the top leadership "is increasingly relying on its security apparatus to control political risks and maintain social stability amid uncertainties ranging from the coronavirus pandemic to a shrinking economy". As a corrupt and abusive law enforcement system poses an existential threat to the legitimacy of the CCP, they argue, the Party-state tends to step up to the plate by cleansing its law enforcement system in an attempt to strengthen the Party's rule and legitimacy.[96] As commented by an American observer, "Xi Jinping has been fascinated by a vision of a highly controlled society", and he needs a powerful institution to materialize this vision. This may be the ultimate goal of Xi's "education and rectification" campaign.[97]

[95] https://new.qq.com/cmsn/20150402/20150402013122.
http://news.junminwang.com/2017/xinwen_pinglun_0527/222842.html.

[96] William Zheng, "China's Top Law Enforcement Body Unveils Campaign to Purge 'Corrupt Elements'," *South China Morning Post*, July 10, 2020. https://www.scmp.com/news/china/politics/article/3092559/chinas-top-law-enforcement-body-unveils-campaign-purge-corrupt (accessed August 10, 2020).

[97] Chris Buckley, "'Drive the Blade In': Xi Shakes Up China's Law-and-Order Forces," *New York Times*, August 21, 2020. https://cn.nytimes.com/china/20200821/china-xi-jinping communist-party/ (accessed September 1, 2020).

CHAPTER 6

Corruption Characteristic of Culture and Socialist Reform China

6.1 Corruption Induced by Culture and Tradition

Culture constitutes an important approach to the explanation of corruption. Traditional culture and norms, as suggested in *Introduction*, also generate corruption. "Culture is a collection of informal institutions (customs and taboos) that a group of people hold in common. These norms change over time and space, but change is usually slow, so many researchers take 'culture' as an exogenous, static variable".[1] The cultural approach holds that corruption is "shaped and conditioned by cultural attitudes and behavioral patterns that are defective".[2] In many traditional societies, "obligations to kin, tribe, religious sect, or local community significantly influence the behavior of public servants, leading them to corrupt practices in order to satisfy their client's demands".[3] In this sense, culture, rather than economics and politics, as argued by some scholars, is the primary determinant of corruption. In their view, as cultures differ, the definitions and perceptions of "corruption" as the misuse of public power for private gains differ across societies accordingly. In particular, as mentioned above, transactions that are labeled corrupt in developed

[1] Rose-Ackerman, 234.

[2] Hope, 132.

[3] Jabbra, "Bureaucratic Corruption in the Third World: Causes and remedy," 675.

F. C. Sun, *An Ineluctable Political Destiny*,
https://doi.org/10.1007/978-981-99-3146-0_6

economies and well-established democracies may be "perfectly acceptable and even normatively required" in developing nations. The problem seems to be much more vexing in traditional societies where "the line between market and family and between the public and the private sectors is often blurred, uncertain, and in flux".[4] In such an environment, it is not surprising that public interest is often sacrificed by public servants for the satisfaction of their family or parochial demands. In societies where such traditional norms prevail, "non-corrupt standards of public bureaucratic behavior have not been widely internalized, and administrative conduct continues to be determined by traditional, family and other parochial pressures".[5]

Certain cultural norms cause corruption, and deep historical and social norms shape present-day behavior and attitudes including perceptions of corruption. Culture and corruption can feed on each other; while culture can shape corruption, corruption can also affect culture. A corrupt culture breeds corruption, whereas a clean culture deters corruption. Under certain circumstances, expectations may be a decisive factor in the formation of people's behavior and norms. As expectations are generally derived from a shared culture, expectations of corruption help shape public attitudes that may lead to a higher level of corruption in a society. "Past experience of the efficacy of corruption helps to maintain it over time".[6]

In a society in which formal institutions are weak and impartial state action is not expected, an interpersonal trust may be all that is available. Such societies can fuel nepotism and cronyism as these informal institutions are often the response to the lack of formal state institutions in a society.[7] Even though some developing nations do have relatively sound state institutions in place, strong interpersonal trust and relationships, however, can still distort policy-making and state administration by favoring political and economic elites and those who are well-connected.

[4] Rose-Ackerman, 242.

[5] Jabbra, "Bureaucratic Corruption in the Third World: Causes and remedy," 676.

[6] Rose-Ackerman, 256.

[7] Ibid., 249–251.

Guanxi and Guanxixue

Guanxi literally means "connections" or "relations"; as commonly referred to in Chinese society, "it refers more narrowly to particularistic ties". These ties are based mainly on "ascribed or primordial" traits or connections such as kinship and principles of other social bonding including native-place, ethnicity, non-kin relations of equivalent status such as friends, colleagues, and schoolmates, as well as non-kin superior-subordinate relations. People may choose to "manufacture" guanxi networks if no prior basis exists. "While the bases for guanxi may naturally occurring or created, the important point is that guanxi must be consciously produced, cultivated, and maintained over time".[8]

While the phenomenon may not be unique to Chinese culture contemporarily or historically, what sets guanxi apart from a generalized notion of social capital is its special significance to interpersonal relations that turns guanxi into the "indigenous Chinese category". This view traces guanxi to "its enduring significance in traditional Chinese philosophy, in particular its stress on the centrality of social interaction in the formation of the individual's identity and sense of fulfillment as a 'person'".[9] Guanxi is based implicitly (rather than explicitly) on mutual interest and benefit, and favors and debt incurred, as mutually understood, are expected to be repaid without an explicitly set timeline. In this context, the notion of reciprocal obligation and indebtedness is central to the system of guanxi. In other words, guanxi is a system of gifts and favors in which obligation and indebtedness are manufactured, and its pervasiveness as a social fact in both traditional and modern-day China distinguishes itself from the general notion of social embeddedness and social connections in other contexts.[10]

The origin of guanxi can be traced to imperial times. For example, the practice of "reciprocity" (bao) had been inherited "as a continuous thread running from ancient to late imperial times". The personalistic relationship is also a core element of traditional Chinese culture and society, and

[8] Thomas Gold, Guthrie, Doug and Wank, David, *Social Connections in China: Institutions, Culture, and the Changing Role of Guanxi* (eds) (Cambridge, UK: Cambridge University Press, 2002), 6.

[9] Ibid., 10.

[10] Mayfair May-hui Yang, *Gifts, Favors and Banquets: the Art of Social Relationships in China* (Ithaca, NY: Cornell University Press, 1994), 149.

it could be based on kinship ties or other principles of social bonding.[11] Guanxi functions almost exclusively for instrumental purposes. Institutionalists hold that the system of guanxi is an outcome of the institutional structure of Chinese society, and the structure of Chinese society facilitates or encourages the reliance on networks to get things done. In the more recent era such as the pre-evolutionary "old society", for example, guanxi was essential and instrumental to accomplish things in virtually all spheres of social life. Gift-giving and banquets were widely practiced in order to curry favor and to create "renqing" (human sentiments) among job seekers and guanxi practitioners, as practically all jobs were the result of personal references by a friend or relative. The instrumentality of guanxi and "renqing" could even go as far as to get a person out of jail in the old days. Families and relatives of officials and professionals who had provided financial assistance to their education "considered the money given an investment and expected repayment in the form of positions". Refusal to comply with this unwritten custom was considered a breach of good faith.[12]

The art of manipulating and utilizing guanxi is guanxixue. "If we see guanxi as an established relationship, then guanxixue is the art of putting that relationship to use, of actualizing it".[13] "Guanxixue involves the exchange of gifts, favors, and banquets; the cultivation of personal relationships and networks of mutual dependence; and the manufacturing of obligation and indebtedness".[14] Family and kinship in general constitute the strongest kinship tie, followed by the extended family and consanguineous relations. In urban centers, non-kin relationships such as friends and neighbors may outweigh kinship bonds in terms of familiarity and mutual obligation due to proximity and connections. Besides, native-place (tongxiang) tie is another important network of relationships, and people who come from the same village, township, county, or province, or speak in the same dialect tend to have a natural tendency to count on each other to do a favor or to open a "back door". Another non-kin relationship in

[11] Ibid., 149–152.

[12] Ibid., 148–149.

[13] Ibid., 4.

[14] Ibid., 6.

cities is the relationship between teacher and student, master and apprentice in a factory, and work unit chief and subordinate.[15] In socialist China, "guanxixue evolved horizontally to bridge these rigid state boundaries and cut through the vertical links of administrative levels".[16]

Guanxi has both positive and negative connotations, with the latter being relevant to the theme of this book. In the context of reform China, what has made guanxixue so popular is its negative connotation and instrumentality to go through the back door to get things done, "though it undeniably performs a positive function as well, especially if there is no formal "front door" available". Critics of guanxixue blame it for fueling rampant corruption, faulting it for undermining China's modernization transformation based on the rule of law.[17] It is argued that the operation of guanxi networks poses as an "alternative system of relational ethics and social integration subverting and displacing state structures", and it neutralizes and even distorts state rules and regulations. Instead of respecting and complying with the rule of law, practitioners of guanxi tend to attain personal gains and benefits through "a process and an ethics that breaks up any unitary construction of the individual by stressing obligation, indebtedness, and interpersonal loyalty".[18]

The enduring persistence of guanxi in Chinese society reflects the complex interaction of culture, institutions, and informal politics. It has survived and even expanded even though conscious and conscientious efforts have been made by Communists and capitalists alike to eradicate it. "Given the Chinese Communists' relentless and sustained attacks on what they saw as such 'feudal' and backward traits as the reliance on particularistic guanxi-type rather than universalistic 'modern' orientations to the social world, and their efforts to build a set of institutions based on radically different principles, the stubborn persistence of guanxi in practice and in the popular mind require explanations".[19] As demonstrated in cases of corruption throughout this book, the persistence of guanxi and its expansion in the midst of a rapid institutional transformation in

[15] Ibid., 117–119.

[16] Ibid., 111–115.

[17] Gold, Guthrie and Wank, 3–6.

[18] Yang, Mayfair May-hui, 308–309.

[19] Gold, Guthrie and Wank, 4.

the reform era attest the enduring influence of the cultural traits and the complex interaction of tradition and modernization.

In contrast to the argument made by institutionalists that the practice of guanxi and guanxi influence would fade as China makes transition to a market economy and improves and consolidates its legal structure and state institutions, guanxixue instead persists and, to some extent, even has gained popularity in the reform era. It is true that the weight of renqing in the institution of guanxi began to diminish as the principles of market economy and monetary incentives started to pervade in Chinese society. For example, in the Mao era, favors and renqing were often converted into social capital in the form of indebtedness and obligations that were required to be paid back to the donor in an undefined timeline, whereas in the early years of the economic reform the paybacks instead were often made in petty cash. A surgeon, for instance, who had made extra efforts in the operation on a patient, may have been appreciated with a "hong bao" (red envelope) stuffed with cash from the patient family, rather than being treated with a banquet in an upscale restaurant or any other non-monetary favors in the pre-reform era. Direct monetary payments were preferred as it eliminated the elusive indebtedness and obligations in an unspecified form and timeframe and simplified the exchange of favors and transactions. On the other hand, practices of the sort and the evolving trend weaken the essentiality and importance of the art of guanxi in a traditional sense. Obviously, this form of settlement of guanxi interactions and transactions has quickly gained popularity and soon evolved into petty corruption that is widespread in all walks of life in contemporary China. Malpractice of cash-offering to buy off market inspectors, traffic police, highway inspectors, tax officers, vehicle safety inspectors, etc., for arbitrary administrative law enforcement and favorable treatment has been widespread and rampant in the reform era. The irregularities have also extended to hospitals and schools to buy doctors' special treatments for patients and teachers' favorable care of students. When questionable payoffs of the sort have become an accepted social norm, ignorance of the practice would incur negative consequences and punishments. For example, if parents do not offer appreciation in the form of a cash gift of several hundred yuan or more to school teachers, teachers may make their children's life difficult in school: placing the kids in the back of the classroom; excluding them from popular and favorable activities; unjustified or unreasonable criticism and embarrassment, etc. Petty corruption like these is faulted as one of the main determining factors to the increasingly toxic social sentiment and distrust among citizens in today's China.

However, the increasingly materialistic mentality and rampant petty corruption in Chinese society do not necessarily eradicate and even significantly weaken the existence and utility of guanxi networks. Several arguments justify this assertion. First of all, as Chinese society is basically a "renqing"-oriented society, there is always something beyond the reach of money, say, access to privileges, status, certain services, opportunities, etc. One needs connections to elite or certain guanxi networks to gain access to these opportunities or services. Money is needed to lubricate the connecting and interacting process and to further "renqing" and guanxi relationships among practitioners of guanxixue in the guanxi networks, but the role and utility of capital are by no means universal or imperative under this circumstance. It is deemed difficult for outsiders to knock the door open by direct and brusque bribe-offering to insiders. Second, some patron–client guanxi networks are largely built on special relationships such as native-place, university/college-classmates, military-comrades, former colleagues, friendship, etc., and patrons tend to select candidates from their own guanxi networks to trade well-sought opportunities such as public office, promotion, employment, and job transfer in return for payoffs. Again, money may not be an effective door cracker under these circumstances especially in the early phase of the reform. In the post-1992 period, although increasingly commercialized guanxi relationships resulted from marketization of the economy and society have led to widespread and rampant malfeasance of office-buying and selling, illicit power-money exchanges, however, take place largely within established patron–client networks that are built on trust, reciprocity, obligations, and favors. While the principle of impersonality derived from an increasingly institutionalized bureaucracy and the legal system is being introduced to government and businesses alike, it inevitably challenges the legitimacy of guanxixue and weakens the functionality and utility of the guanxi networks. Nevertheless, the art of guanxi is still playing a pivotal role in accomplishing goals in many circumstances in the midst of a radical transformation of the state and social institutions. Third, with guanxi networks and patron–client relationships being further commercialized as a result of the deepened reform, connections and the art of guanxi still remain crucial for gaining access to major infrastructure and government procurement contracts. Projects of the scale usually involve very large sums of public funds, and kickbacks based on implicit rules governing the rates of commissions in the industry tend to be large as well in dollar amount. High-ranking officials and powerful executives who have discretionary decision-making power over project awarding are normally risk-aversion; they generally rely on trusted cronies and insiders to negotiate and broker illicit deals with enterprises in an attempt to avoid or minimize the risks of being caught. This seems to be the paramount reason as to why the participation rate of family members, relatives, and cronies of corrupt high-ranking officials in collusive corruption has been so high in the advanced phase of the reform.

Family and Crony Corruption

As the closest dimension of kinship relationships, family members of corrupt officials have been playing a crucial role in colluding with husband/dad in seeking illicit riches. As discussed above, family corruption is deeply rooted in the traditional Chinese culture and norms. "Confucianism contains elements that vitiate corruption, but the same cultural norms can be used to justify practices that may be interpreted as corrupt".[20] The misdeed of seeking personal and family gains by exploiting or making illegitimate use of public power and political influence of prominent family members might have not been so intolerable in the traditional Chinese social and cultural context. As the popular Chinese sayings "夫荣妻贵" (As husbands rise in power and influence so do their wives' social status.) and "一人得道, 鸡犬升天" (As a man attains power and prominence, his family gains influence accordingly.) attest, it has long been a tradition that family members and relatives of powerful officials extract rents by simply exploiting and abusing the influence of their prominent family members. This manifests one of the facets of "grey corruption" in traditional Chinese political and social culture and has been largely tolerated in societies in ancient and even modern times. As in other traditional societies, the use of clientelistic networks such as guanxi networks to allocate public resources based on moral obligations and affective attachments has long been a malpractice in China. This culturally induced malfeasance often fuels a cycle of corruption in nations that are in transition from traditional societies to modern states. In Mao's era, as mentioned, practice of guanxi largely took the

[20] Rose-Ackerman, 247.

form of privilege-seeking and nepotism such as access to extra rationed goods and short supplies through "back door" or attaining employment in SOEs or enrollment in military for family members and relatives by utilizing one's "guanxi" networks or making unfair use of the dad's public office. As rent-seeking opportunities exploded in the new phase of the reform, so did the incentives and incidence of family-induced rent-seeking and corruption. Participation, collaboration, and collusion of family members in the looting game may have made the schemes more elusive, sophisticated, and profitable.

Family and clan-induced corruption is a pattern of collective corruption, and, like other forms of collective corruption, its ultimate goal is to attain personal gains at the state and citizens' expenses. The advanced phase of the reform saw an escalation of family and clan-oriented corruption. A regional survey conducted by a local Party discipline supervisory department concluded that corruption jointly committed by husband and wife constituted over 90 percent of all official corruption cases during the survey period.[21] In most cases, family-oriented corruption involves acceptance and extortion of bribes, seeking illicit business dealings, and acquiring land use rights and bank credits are among the common wrongdoing attributable to family collusion and corruption. It has been a growing and notorious tendency among political elites to covertly involve their family members and cronies in illicit dealings and collusions to broaden sources of economic rents and also to reduce the risk of detection for fathers. Many of the corruption cases cited before involve husband–wife or father–children collaboration and collusion. For example, in the Chu Shijian graft case, both Chu's daughter and wife acted as bribe-takers and extorters, and both were prosecuted and convicted of bribe extraction. Between 1991 and 1994, Zhang Deyuan, president and CEO of Hunan International Trust and Investment Corporation, colluded with his wife and adopted son to take bribes of 2.2 million yuan; in return, Zhang helped the bribers attain illicit profits at the expense of the state. Zhang received the death penalty while his adopted son and wife were sentenced to fixed-term imprisonment. Lin Guoti, director of Hunan provincial machinery administrative bureau, either acted alone or colluded with his son Lin Ruhai, took a total of 29 bribes worth 5.27 million yuan. Lin's wife also took part in the scheme. Lin and his son were sentenced

[21] Meng, Yan and Li, 21.

to death and life imprisonment, respectively. In Henan province, family corruption even threw the CEO of Henan Qinyang Aluminum Corporation and his nine family members into jail. Between 1993 and 1999, Qin Riqi, CEO of the corporation, in conspiration with his family members, raked in a series of bribes valued at 6.16 million yuan. Qin was sentenced to the suspended death penalty while his wife, son, three daughters, and four sons-in-law were all convicted of bribery, embezzlement, and other criminal offenses. The local media reported on the case by satirizing that "led by Qin Riqi, 10 members of the Qin family trooped into the state prison".[22]

What constitutes an alarming trend of collective corruption in reform China is a surge of collusive corruption cases involving top-level officials and their family members and mistresses. Generally speaking, corruption at the top-level entails various tactics or schemes such as conspiracy, collusion, collaboration, division of labor, planning, cover-up, and mutual protection. What distinguishes high-level corruption from lower-level plundering in the Chinese context are the astonishingly high-value bribes and huge sums of illicit funds involved as well as a large cohort of bribers and office-buyers. Su Rong, vice chairman of the CPPCC National Committee and former Party chief for three provinces, was a powerful figure with a seemingly unlimited discretionary power over a wide range of realms including official appointments, economic development, industry, finance, transportation, real estate, etc. Conspired and collaborated with his wife, son, son-in-law, and a dozen of relatives, Su and his gang of corrupters had amassed staggeringly high illicit wealth by selling offices, extracting bribes, and intervening in state land sales, development and construction projects, and public project bidding processes. With the participation and facilitation of his wife, dubbed "the underground director of the provincial organization department", and his son, Su "wholesaled" a significant number of positions to office-seekers in return for payoffs. As confessed by Su, over 40 high-ranking officials at the prefecture/bureau level had bribed him for promotion and personal gains. Su, guilty of abuse of authority and negligence, was also accused of causing loss of state assets worth billions of yuan in the SOE restructuring and privatization process in Jiangxi province. Su and his thirteen family members and relatives were charged and convicted of bribery, abuse

[22] Ibid., 21–22.

of authority, dereliction of duty, and the crime of possessing immense assets from unexplained and unjustified sources. Total illicit funds and assets involved in Su's case amounted to nearly 200 million yuan. Su was sentenced to life imprisonment in January 2017.[23]

As mentioned, it was a fairly common scheme that SOE executives and managers teamed up with their family members and relatives to defraud the state of SOE assets and public funds. Buying high for inputs, consumables, and equipment and selling low for finished products and services was a notorious scheme to loot SOE assets and properties. To facilitate the execution of the plot, corrupt SOE executives and state officials usually appointed their relatives and cronies to important internal positions such as middle-level managers, procurement officers, accountants, treasurers, etc., and then set up family- or crony-controlled companies as suppliers or agents to sell high to SOEs or buy low from SOEs for profiteering. With internal–external collusion, materials and supplies of low or even inferior quality were often procured by SOEs at above-market prices, whereas SOE products or services were often distributed to those companies at below-market prices to enable them to materialize windfall profits. This was one of the grave consequences of widespread nepotism in the state sector and also an outlet of loss of state assets in reform China. Cases abound concerning colluded embezzlement and looting of SOE funds and assets among family members and cronies. For instance, as mentioned previously, a VP overseeing the import and export portfolio at a SOE, colluded with his wife, the head of the finance department of the SOE, to plunder state funds and assets. The couple, first of all, let their two sons to set up two companies, and then helped their sons' firms to profiteer from business dealings with the SOE through selling high and buying low as well as other illicit and fraudulent schemes.

Most family corruption cases involving high-ranking officials and high-value illicit funds took place in areas of land deals, real estate, resource development, security irregularities, bank credits and loans, etc. There have been an increasing number of cases in which members of influential families colluded with unlawful developers and businessmen to share windfall profits through land and stock speculation, profiteering in real estate, public construction, and resource development. The Zhou Bin–Zhou Yongkang case cited earlier is explanatory of the nature and

[23] http://www.cnlawnn.com/jdht/html/8614.html.

scope of family corruption in energy, resource, and real estate development. This case serves as a typical manifestation of how a father–son team utilized their clientelistic network to misappropriate public resources under the illegitimate influence of moral obligations and affective attachments. Zhou Yongkang's influence as well as his patron–client networks in the state petroleum sector and Sichuan province paved the way for his son, Zhou Bin, to effortlessly grab state resources for profiteering. Zhou Bin, along with his wife and parent-in-law, profiteered in petroleum, hydropower, real estate, highway development, finance, and entertainment, and unsurprisingly, with the help, facilitation and intervention of his father's clients and cronies (many of them were holding leading positions at the time.), Zhou Bin had managed to amass an immense amount of illicit wealth in no time. As mentioned, with the facilitation and approval of the CEO of PetroChina, also Zhou Yongkang's former subordinate, Zhou Bin successfully acquired an oil plot in Shaanxi province at a cost of over 10 million yuan. He then flipped the oil plot development permit to a petroleum developer for 500 million yuan. Like Zhou Bin, his uncle, aunt-in-law, and cousin, as aided by Zhou Yongkang, were all involved in high-margin monopolistic business operations such as top-brand liquor wholesale, luxury car dealership, etc. According to court documents, the Zhou family's ill-gotten wealth had reached an inconceivable amount of 2.136 billion yuan![24]

As discussed at the beginning of the section, the interaction between guanxi networks and corruption appears to be illusive and complicated. Its evolution and development seem to be controversial among observers. As the state has loosened its grip on the economy, some argue, the role and influence of guanxi have actually expanded in Chinese society. According to this logic, "its role will continue to expand, leading to an economic system that is substantially different from the rational-legal systems that define Western market economies".[25] Others, mainly institutionalists, however, contend by predicting that as the institutions of the Chinese economy and society change, so too should the reliance on guanxi networks. The central notion is that there are specific structural and institutional conditions that have given rise to the reliance on guanxi to accomplish tasks in China's transforming economy. They

[24] http://www.cnlawnn.com/jdht/html/2923.html.

[25] Gold, Guthrie and Wank, 3–4.

argue that there was not much difference between socialist China and the socialist economies of Russia and Eastern European nations as they were all "shortage economies with weak legal infrastructures, so networking and trust become fundamental parts of economic transactions".[26] With the development of a market economy and the restructured mechanism of wealth distribution, the role and influence of guanxi will decline, and ultimately formal rational law will supplant the norms of the personal economy in Chinese society. As observed by the author, the current trend of social development in China seems to somewhat validate the institutionalist argument. As China's judicial system gradually improves and institutions and policies governing university/college enrollment, civil servant recruitment, public procurement bidding procedures, process, etc., are established and systemized, the trait of impersonality characterized by modern and Western administrative and management system begins to incrementally infiltrate the traditional value system and to erode the legitimacy and utility of guanxi. As indicated by noticeable changes in relevant regulations and institutions over the years, "back doors" for public employment have been replaced by the state's strict and impersonal civil service exams and public recruitment system, and access to government procurements, public lands, and public infrastructure and construction projects has been formalized with seemingly strictly administered and closely monitored project bidding and awarding processes. The utility and influence of guanxi seem to be diminishing in an environment that is being increasingly institutionalized. With an ever-expanding private economy, the private sector now plays a pivotal role in the hiring of university/college graduates and skilled workers. Hiring decisions are now based on candidates' qualifications, performance and potential rather than guanxi relations, social obligations, and indebtedness. However, the art of guanxi and guanxixue still play an elusive and important role in many aspects of the socioeconomic domain, where rule-based modes and procedures are institutionally weak or non-existent.

[26] Ibid., 13–14.

6.2 Malfeasances Characteristic of Socialism China

Collective and Organizational Corruption

Patterns, actors, and scope of corruption have been evolving and changing in accordance with the formulation and implementation of new reform policies and programs as well as the expansion of the Chinese economy in the post-1992 period. Instead of remaining individual, isolated, furtive, and secretive as manifested in the Mao era and the initial stage of the reform, corruption in the new phase of the reform has become more collectivized and organized and appears to be, under certain circumstances, less illegitimate and illicit as perceived by the general public. Group or collective corruption is "a form of corruption that occurs when a group of corrupt people conspire and collude to pursue individual interests at public expense". Generally, collective corruption can be divided into two categories: group corruption and organizational corruption. The former refers to corrupt behavior and acts committed by a group of officials in a work unit or organization, who collude to engage in rent-seeking activities in their respective interests. The latter generally pertains to "large" collective corruption, that is, the corrupt subject is the whole work unit, or as what the academic community refers to as "unit corruption" or "organizational corruption". Collective corruption is a more serious type of corruption relative to individual corruption. It is characterized by a large number of actors involved in a corrupt act, and accomplishment of the act often requires cooperation and collusion among members of the collective. As demonstrated in cases of collective corruption throughout the book, cases of the sort are generally complicated and difficult to investigate and prosecute.

Organizational corruption differs from collective corruption in that the former seeks monetary or material gains for a work unit or institution rather than individuals. Manifestations of organizational corruption are broad; in addition to the most explicit and known form of public bribery, patterns of organizational corruption also include malpractices in organizational decision-making, personnel, public expenditure, etc. When corruption has been institutionalized in an organization, it generally exhibits the following indicators or attributes: (1) corruption of the top leaders of the organization; (2) An organization does have well-established institution and system but corrupt behavior goes unimpeded in this organizational system; (3) Members of integrity within the organization are marginalized or even unable to survive, whereas the colluders and accomplices become the dominant players and also the beneficiary of the malpractice; and (4) institutionalized illegal or improper behavior and acts within the organization (such as slush funds, unit bribery, etc.).[27]

The main manifestations of collective corruption include collective embezzlement, collective bribery, collectively seeking personal gains, abuse of public power, welfare corruption, collective profligacy, and herd corruption. As discussed previously, organizational bribery, the most prominent pattern of organizational corruption, has gradually evolved into a worrisome trend that not only corrupts the Chinese bureaucracy but also erodes the norms and values of Chinese society. Actors of organizational corruption often offered illegitimate payoffs to government officials in the name of work unit or organization, and decisions on bribe-offering were usually discussed and approved at the executive meetings of the organization. The malpractice run particularly rampant in the traditional Chinese holiday seasons such as the Chinese New Year, and bribery of the sort often took the form of gift-giving aimed to cultivate or deepen guanxi networks and to curry favors with influential public officials. "Welfare corruption" was or may still be a common and widespread misdeed; monopolistic SOEs and public institutions provide resources and public services at their disposal to their employees free of charge or for a nominal fee in the name of "staff welfare and benefits". Collective squandering also falls under the category of organizational corruption. As mentioned, irregularities of the sort include feasting and entertainment at public expense, sightseeing tours funded by public funds, misuse or abuse of public vehicles such as over-standard configuration, private use of public vehicles, etc. In terms of administrative law enforcement, collective corruption often takes the form of arbitrary enforcement, inaction, and excessive red tape.[28]

Collective and organizational corruption in reform China is characterized by "innovative and sometimes extensive use of planning, collaboration, and other organizational means without ethical and legal

[27] Mao Zhaohui, "Organizational corruption: the most difficult corruption to control?" *lian zheng liao wang*, April 6, 2012. http://news.sohu.com/20120406/n339900562.shtml (accessed November 15, 2020).

[28] "Collective Corruption," *baidu baike*. https://baike.baidu.com/item/集体腐败/5513688.

boundaries".[29] Explanations of officials' pursuit of corruption in collaboration are various. One concerns the need for capacity, sophistication, and technical capability to carry out large-scale and complicated corrupt schemes as division of labor, coordination and collaboration are necessary prerequisites to warrant the successful execution of a plan and fulfillment of a corrupt transaction. Another consideration entails motivation and incentive to lower the risk of detection and to escape from or reduce potential punishment. This view holds that divided responsibilities among corrupt officials in collaboration leads to sharing of the risks, and more importantly engagement of officials at higher levels would create a protective mechanism against detection. In the case of bribery, by sharing bribes, either monetary or non-monetary benefits, with one's superiors, the corrupt official has actually made his boss a "bribe taker", thus lowering the risk of being caught as the boss, "compelled by the need for self-protection, would make an effort to protect him".[30] As China's central authorities stepped up its fight against corruption, collective corruption had become a seemingly viable alternative for corrupt officials and unlawful businessmen alike to collude with each other to seek personal gains at the expense of the state.

Most corruption cases in the new phase of the reform entailed bribery and embezzlement, and they were often being carried out in collective conspiracy in one way or another. Various major cases such as the Tai'an corruption case and the Changtu embezzlement case both involved collective corruption. Collective corruption in the post-1992 period was marked by several attributes. First, it in general involved a large number of actors and accomplices, both internal (officials and staff in government agencies and public enterprises and institutions) and external (dishonest businessmen and corrupt elements in the society), and in some cases, the corruption networks even involved high-ranking officials at the ministerial and provincial level. Second, the loci of the act varied depending on the nature, scope, capacity, technology, and sophistication of the schemes and operations. It may take place in a work unit or agency, or across several departments or sectors; in very large cases the corrupt networks may stretch out to other regions or provinces. The Cai Hangang case

[29] Ting Gong, "Dangerous Collusion: Corruption as a Collective Venture in Contemporary China," *Communist and Post-Communist Studies* No.35 (2002): 87.

[30] Ibid., 92–93.

is explanatory of the scope and gravity of collective corruption in the banking sector. Third, actors and cases were often interlinked to each other. This is what is termed "case in case" (案中案); the revelation of one case often leads to the disclosure of other cases, and the investigation of one corrupt official often results in the detention of other officials at higher levels as they are in general interlinked and bonded by bribery and other illicit interests. The Tai'an case and the Shenyang group corruption case are both illustrative in this regard. For example, the investigation of several officials and unscrupulous businessmen implicated in the Shenyang case had led to the revelation of "cases in cases" linked by bribery, and ultimately brought down a significant number of high-ranking municipal officials across the Party and government apparatus, judiciary, law enforcement, and economic administration, including the mayor, deputy mayor, the top judge, and the chief prosecutor of the city.

Buying and selling public office and promotion (买官卖官) also falls under this category as officials are connected through bribery, and detention and investigation of one client often leads to disclosure of his/her patron(s) at higher levels. In the meantime, the caught client may serve as other officials' patron, which naturally leads to the revelation of his/her clients at lower levels. Although selling and buying offices have become a common malfeasance in the officialdom, the phenomenon is particularly rampant in loci of economic stagnation as alternate means for self-enrichment tend to be limited in poor regions. There are more and more officials across ranks involving in the corrupt act of selling offices for money as the perceived logic holds that it in general would be a safer bet to accept bribes from one's subordinates. Given the scope, rampancy, and severity of the malfeasance, office-buying and office-selling shall be discussed in more detail in a separate section. Furthermore, as mentioned above, large-scale, sophisticated and technically oriented schemes often involve division of labor, leadership, collaboration, coordination, and structured operation. Large-scale smuggling operations and activities in Fujian and Guangdong in the 1990s, which were discussed in previous sections, testify to the formation and utilization of sophisticated networks for smuggling and organized crime. As demonstrated in the Lai Changxing smuggling case, divulgence of a major smuggling case could implicate up to hundreds of government officials from ministerial level to provincial and municipal level, and most of them would be subject to criminal prosecution and disciplinary sanctions. Lastly, collective and organized corruption could be carried out under the guise of local interest, which could seemingly legitimize illicit acts as they are often undertaken under the banner of economic development and employment creation. The previously cited Zhoukou fake drug manufacturing and marketing case attests to the manipulation and corruption in some localities as those criminal offenses were often overtly carried out by unlawful businessmen and endorsed and supported by local governments in the name of stimulating the local economy and job creation.

Organized corruption, particularly large-scale operations, often involves huge amount of illicit funds and can result in immeasurable losses to the state coffer. As indicated, the total value of smuggled automobiles involved in the Zhanjiang automobile smuggling case was in the range of 30 billion yuan and duties and taxes evaded amounted to over 10 billion yuan. The Xiamen smuggling case was even worse in terms of tax evasion and its impact on state economy. The total value of the smuggled goods involved in the Xiamen smuggling case was as high as 53 billion yuan with import duties evaded reaching over 30 billion yuan. Rampant smuggling of automobiles and petroleum products had also caused severe loss to the state economy and exerted a grave impact on the petrochemical industry. For example, the smuggling of refined oil via Xiamen in 1998 resulted in shutdown of over 3000 oil wells and layoff of over 300,000 workers in the industry. Direct economic loss attributable to the smuggling of refined oil products for the year was in the range of 20 billion yuan.[31]

The surge of organizational bribery in the new phase of the reform, as discussed previously, was largely attributable to the phase-out of the command economic system and the marketization of the state sector. The new reform framework abolished the mechanism of plan allocation of goods and finance and replaced it with the market allocation of resources and bank credits. Consequently, many SOEs lost their monopolistic power and status in market, and were left out in the marketplace to compete with a thriving private sector. Many SOEs, in particular SMEs in the non-strategic sectors, with phasing out of various privileges and advantages under the planned economy, were forced to compete with other SOEs and their private counterparts in the market for public developmental and infrastructure projects, land and real estate, bank credits and loans, governmental procurement, and marketing. In a bureaucracy

[31] Meng, Yan and Li, 24–27.

and economy that were permeated with corruption and faced with the dire fact that private enterprises in general deployed illicit means such as bribery to gain a competitive edge over rivals for the acquisition of projects, many SOEs or the reformed or transformed version—shareholding companies—were compelled to resort to bribery as well to compete with private firms for contracts and market shares. As pointed out in previous chapters, areas that had been hard hit by high occurrence of organizational bribery included major state projects and funds, infrastructure, construction, bank credits and loans, real estate transactions, IPO approvals, and land use rights approvals. In the post-1992 era, organizational or public bribery had even overtaken private bribery to become the dominant pattern of wrongdoing. A study of convicted bribery cases in the 2000s revealed that public bribery accounted for approximately 60 percent of all bribery cases, and public funds misappropriated for bribe-offering amounted to 65 percent of the total bribe money in the study period.[32]

Collective corruption attributes to "herd corruption" as it breeds a corrupt organizational culture in which public officials across the hierarchy are tacitly involved in rent-seeking and corrupt activities. The prevalence of collective and organizational corruption inevitably leads a society to a mode of governance of corruption. In this sense, organizational corruption would be more destructive than individual corruption, as it distorts organizational ethics and integrity, subverts social norms and values, erodes citizens' confidence in the Party and government, and causes more detrimental economic losses. However, organizational corruption and public bribery seem to be more tolerable than individual bribery in Chinese society in that they entail public or collective funds and seek to attain institutional gains and organizational benefits instead of individual ones. In many cases, both sides of the illicit transactions, the bribers and the bribe-takers, are public officials, and under certain circumstances what the public bribers seek are preferential or special policies for the localities. In contrast to individual or private bribery that tends to be conducted in secrecy, public bribery is often put on the meeting agenda for discussion and decision in executive or Party committee meetings. On the other hand, the costs of bribery are generally internalized and absorbed as business expenses for marketing and intermediary fees.

[32] Ibid., 23.

Given its various "public" attributes, organizational corruption and public bribery are often perceived to be semi-legitimate, and actors of the offense tend to feel less guilty of the behavior and acts. From the perspective of law enforcement and Party discipline, punishments for public bribery tend to be much less severe than penalties for individual bribery.

Buying and Selling Offices

A distinctive feature of bribery in the post-Mao era is its increasing instrumentality in facilitating the illicit trade of money for power. While office-buying and -selling (买官卖官) has evolved into an influential trend in the Chinese officialdom, bribery now has become an essential code for the acquisition of public office and promotion. As seen in many major cases, more and more high-ranking officials are found to be involved or implicated in office-selling, and payoffs rendered by office-buyers had even become the dominant source of illicit income for leaders of poor regions and generals of the Chinese military. In general, the bribers are lower-level officials who are paying their patrons for favors and discretionary personnel authority over promotion and career advancement.

While conventional bribery involves government officials and citizens, as bribery or corruption in a broader sense is defined and interpreted in Western societies, bribery with distinct Chinese characteristics involves public official patrons and public official clients. There are normally two circumstances entailing bribery among public officials. As discussed earlier, one involves organizational bribery targeting powerful officials at higher levels with an intent to gain access to and to win public investments and projects for localities or state enterprises. Under this circumstance, public funds in general become the source of the bribes but largely end up in the pockets of illicit officials. Another circumstance concerns the patron–client relationship among public officials. Clients or lower-level officials bribe patrons or higher-level officials for promotion, favor, and protection. Ill-gotten money, in general illicit gains from embezzlement, bribes or misappropriated funds, are used as bribe capital to patrons. While the former had become increasingly widespread since the mid-1990s, buying and selling offices, like regulated goods and short supplies for profiteering in the 1980s, has been gaining popularity among corrupt officials as an avenue to generate illegitimate wealth. "Selling official posts" (卖官) was not common in the Mao era, and the nature and scope were generally limited to "guanxi" and involved non-monetary materials such as gifts. As corruption grew in a broad range of political and social spheres, buying and selling offices, like the evolution of the gift economy, started to commercialize and have increasingly involved large cash transactions. The dynamics of buying and selling offices in recent years present two tendencies: an ever-increasing dollar amount implicated in the corrupt deals and exchanges, and an ever-increasing involvement of high-ranking officials in selling offices and influence in exchange for monetary rewards.

Incidence of buying and selling offices was relatively low and the sizes of bribes involved were also limited in the early years of the reform. The phenomenon had been more prevalent in poor inland regions than in relatively developed coastal regions and urban centers. With limited industrial and technological bases and capacities, economic opportunities and career potential in less developed regions tend to be finite. On the other hand, government power seems to be more discretionary, manipulative, and absolute in poor areas than in affluent regions where political and social consciousness and democratic norms tend to be more prevailing. In poor regions, public office may presumably offer more lucrative opportunities for rent-seeking and wealth accumulation than corporations. Several cases below involving buying and selling public offices occurred in less developed inland regions. The Party leader of Yongfeng county in Jiangxi province, Zheng Yuansheng, for example, extracted more than 300,000 yuan within three years by "selling official positions". Ironically, the Party leader of Fenxi county in Shanxi province, after receiving 26,000 yuan in bribes from a corrupt official, even recommended the briber to be promoted to the director position of the county anti-graft bureau.[33]

Since the early 1990s cases regarding senior officials' collective involvement in graft by selling public office and other illicit means had increased noticeably. The Tai'an collective corruption case, as mentioned earlier, also serves as a typical example of illicit office-selling and buying. What makes this case stand out among other bribery cases is the series of cases implicating so many top Party and municipal government leaders and influential officials as well as rampant illicit exchanges of public office for money. The Party leader Hu Jianxue collected 610,000 yuan from 42 bribers between 1990 and 1995, among whom many were office-buyers

[33] ZJTV news, 14 July 1996.

including the high-level officials in his inner circle. Services and favors rendered back as reciprocal returns to the bribes included promotions, job transfers, acquisition of stocks in short supply, public construction contracts, etc.[34]

With deepened reform and rapid economic development in the late 1990s and 2000s, official corruption grew widespread and rampant, and so did the malpractice of money-office swaps. Office-selling had become one of the most important and profitable rent-seeking opportunities for high-ranking Party chiefs and government officials to attain illicit windfalls. Following are a couple of examples to shed some light on the malpractice. Liu Zhuozhi, vice president of the Inner Mongolia Autonomous Region (deputy governor) traded public offices and promotions for money between 2003 and 2010 when he was the Party chief of Xilengrad League. Office-buyers included both government officials and businessmen seeking political status and titles. He collected bribes worth over 4.5 million yuan by "selling" 13 promotions and offices to his clients. After one of his "clients", a municipal Party chief, was arrested in November 2010, Liu's wrongdoing came to light. Liu's downfall disclosed a corrupt network made of corrupt office-buyers and businessmen.[35] In the previously cited cases of Wu Changshun, the police chief of Tianjin, and Cheng Kejie, the Party boss of Guangxi, both were accused of selling offices in exchange for illicit payoffs. Wu was charged for taking 84 million yuan in bribes through office-selling. Cheng was also accused of taking bribes from over a dozen of officials seeking his assistance and facilitation for promotion and job transfers. Statistically, almost all top-level leading officials convicted of corruption were involved in office-selling in one way or another. According to court documents, both state-level officials such as Zhou Yongkang, Su Rong, Ling Jihua, Guo Boxiong, and Xu Caihou, and provincial-level Party bosses including Chen Liangyu, Sun Zhengcai, Bai Enpei, Zhao Zhengyong, Wang Min, Wang Sanyun, etc., were accused of extracting bribes by selling offices and promotions. Although their cases are different in varying degrees in terms of scope, severity, and impact, one thing is in common—illicit proceeds from office-selling usually constituted a large portion of their

[34] FZRB, 12 July 1996.

[35] http://www.cnlawnn.com/jdht/html/6524.html.

ill-accumulated wealth. The leading Party officials' unconstrained discretionary power over personnel appointment and promotion enables them to extract rents from office-seekers, also their cronies, and taking money from clients, as indicated above, may presumably be a low-risk bet as both sides of the trade share the same motivation to keep the deal concealed. Office-selling, either through direct abuse of authority or indirect influence over personnel decisions to the benefit of office-seekers, has become an increasingly important source of illicit income for corrupt senior officials.

As discussed in the previous chapter, bribery and corruption have grown wild in the Chinese military. The main pattern of corruption in the army is office-selling and office-buying. For example, Guo Boxiong and Xu Caihou, both were vice chairman of the Central Military Commission, had accumulated their illicit bonanzas mainly through office-selling. We use the case of collusive corruption involving Xu Caihou and his subordinate, lieutenant general Gu Junshan, to demonstrate the pervasiveness and rampancy of office-selling and office-buying in China's officialdom in general and in its military in particular. The course of Xu's degeneration and corruption over the years can be highlighted by his relationship and illicit dealings with lieutenant general Gu Junshan, deputy minister of the general logistics department of the Central Military Commission. As the high-ranking official with authority over military logistics affairs, Gu had tremendous discretionary power over the leasing and transfer of military-owned lands as well as the construction and maintenance of barracks and military housing projects. Gu had accumulated a huge fortune through bribery and kickbacks from unscrupulous developers and businessmen as well as embezzlement and misappropriation of military funds and assets. Gu had allegedly been bribing Xu all the way from a field-grade officer in the regional military area command (MAC) to the rank of lieutenant general in the central headquarters in Beijing. As Xu's closest crony and accomplice, Gu's bribes to Xu included not only cash but also young women including a star singer in the Chinese military. As rumors regarding Gu's possible detention and investigation started to surface, Gu turned to Xu for rescue and protection, rendering Xu several cash bribes totaling over 40 million yuan. Consequently, the Central Military Commission's investigation against Gu could not proceed due to Xu's interference and obstruction of justice. It was the decision of Hu Jintao, Secretary General of the CCP and Chairman of the Central Military Commission, that had eventually brought down Gu on charges of bribery, embezzlement, and abuse of authority. Gu's arrest thus led to the investigation of Xu in March 2014. Gu was sentenced to the suspended death penalty in August 2015.[36] On his deathbed, Xu had reportedly confessed that almost all colonel generals except the Commissar of the General Logistics Department and the Commissar of the PLA National Defence University had bribed him for favor and consideration of promotion and high offices.

Squandering of Public Funds

Spending public money lavishly and illegitimately had long been a common malpractice since the early 1980s. A survey conducted by the State Council and the National Statistics Bureau in 1994 showed that official spending of public funds on feasting and entertainment was identified by survey respondents as the most serious corrupt phenomenon during the early period of the reform. Taking into account traditional Chinese culture and custom, squandering on feasting and dining and wining is thus considered a pattern of corruption with distinctive Chinese characteristics. There were two factors attributable to the pervasiveness of the illegitimate act. Feasts, first of all, were not necessarily held for the facilitation of business deals or public affairs. Officials often invented all kinds of justifications and excuses to dine and wine at public expense for the enjoyment of delicacies. Moreover, feasting at public expense tended to get more extravagant and its rampancy and pervasiveness had obviously grown out of control. Setup of slush funds or what dubbed "small treasury" (小金库) had rapidly gained popularity in governments, SOEs, and public institutions. Revenue sources for those off-book accounts were largely illegitimate funds collected through the "three arbitraries" (三乱) of illegitimate fines, charges, and levies or public funds secretly diverted or misappropriated from state funds designated for specific purposes. Accounting irregularities were in general committed to hide those funds from the books or to erase the physical traces of the transactions throughout the accounts. What distinguishes the nature and gravity of squandering from those of embezzlement are the violators, i.e., individuals vs. work units, and the intended usage of the misappropriated funds. While embezzlement concerns mainly individual predators or a small

[36] "Gu Junshan," *baidu baike*. https://baike.baidu.com/item/谷俊山/6140962. http://www.cnlawnn.com/jdht/html/?7308.html.

group of corrupt officials, squandering is carried out by mainly collective actors such as work units or organizations. Embezzlement of public funds is a criminal act intended for illicit personal gains, whereas squandering is largely treated as a disciplinary offense intended to benefit the members of an organization. While embezzlement is committed in secrecy, squandering can be carried out semi-overtly or even openly depending on the nature and beneficiaries of the wasteful spending. As a matter of fact, many corrupt officials rationally opted for squandering for the enjoyment of extravagance as this form of malpractice involved less risk and more lenient consequences than embezzlement. Officials of the personnel division in a provincial department in Anhui province, for example, were quite creative in inventing pretexts for feasting. In addition to receiving guests for government business, the division staff had treated themselves in various names with 163 banquets in 56 restaurants in Hefei, the capital of Anhui province, and the total cost incurred of dining and wining was in the range of 280,000 yuan, all paid out of the division's secretive slush funds account. The city of Heze in Shandong province was less developed in comparison to the coastal region of the province, whereas squandering of public funds at some public institutions seemed to be more "generous" than their counterparts in affluent regions. For example, staff of Heze Institute of Education, led by Li Xilin, the dean of the institute, had held dining and wining parties in almost all restaurants and eateries across the city, and the institute's annual budget on feasting and entertainment even exceeded 1.3 million yuan. By the time Li departed, the school's accounts payable for hospitality and entertainment had added up to a total of 43 pages. Yuan Jinjin, deputy director of Hexi District Labor Bureau in the city of Tianjin, had squandered 240,000 yuan in state funds on feasting and dining and wining in a period of over two months before he was detained, which averaged out at 3000 yuan per day. For one meal at an upscale restaurant, Yuan consumed delicacies that cost the state almost 10,000 yuan. During his 14-month tenure, Yuan had squandered half a million yuan in public funds on feasting, entertainment, and sightseeing. Yuan was sentenced to death with a two-year reprieve.[37] In some extreme cases, costs of feasting and entertainment charged to public accounts seemed to be absolutely preposterous. For example, the Municipal Tobacco Monopoly Administration in Shanwei,

[37] Meng, Yan and Li, p. 23.

a small city in southern Guangdong province, spent over 2 million yuan on hospitality and entertainment in a single month. It was suspected that embezzlement might be implicated through concealment of accounting irregularities.[38] Still another case involving a top executive of Sinopec, one of the largest state monopolies in China, might be one of the most stunned cases of bribery and squandering in the PRC history. Chen Tonghai, CEO of Sinopec, was convicted of bribe-taking of almost 200 million yuan between 1999 and 2007; what has made this case relevant to the topic of this section was Chen's lavish squandering of public funds. It was revealed that Chen's monthly expenditures including expenses of feasting, hospitality, and entertainment even exceeded 1.2 million yuan per month, or 40,000 yuan per day. Chen was sentenced to death with a two-year reprieve.[39]

It was estimated that there had been more than 120 government circulars since the 1960s and more than 30 circulars and regulations since 1979 that prohibited the officialdom from misappropriating public funds for drinking and feasting.[40] Unfortunately, despite considerable government efforts to curb the misdeed, the problem had in fact spiraled out of control in the post-Mao era. As what vividly satirized by a proverb of "eating bed legs and eating tires", countermeasures against the circulars and stipulations prohibiting publicly funded dining and wining varied from time to time. For example, feasting costs were often charged to public accounts in the name of hotel costs (eating bed legs) as costs of the sort were deemed legitimate and were eligible for reimbursement, whereas under other circumstances costs of dining and wining were fraudulently claimed as automobile repair and maintenance costs (eating tires) as costs of the sort usually involved high dollar figures. In addition to "eating bed legs and tires", other cost categories that had often been used to hide feasting costs include "training fees", "conference/meeting expenditures", and "office expenses". Negligence of duty and collusions between officials and accountants had often made those deceitful practices and claims more concealed in government agencies, public institutions, and state enterprises. Not only eating and drinking were paid for by public money but also entertainment or even pornographic services were

[38] http://news.163.com/14/0121/03/9J375JQ400014AED_mobile.html.

[39] http://finance.jrj.com.cn/people/2009/08/0514425701302.shtml.

[40] Xiping Tang, p. 8.

consumed at public expense. According to statistics, public money spent on banqueting in 1992 even reached a staggeringly high figure of 100 billion yuan.[41] Another source revealed a dramatic increase in squandering public funds on dining, wining, and entertainment between 1989 and 2002, and it listed the estimated annual expenditures by year: 37 billion yuan in 1989, 40 billion yuan in 1990, 80 billion yuan in 1992, and over 100 billion yuan in 1999. Since then, expenditures of the sort had shot up with annual spending quickly doubled to 200 billion yuan in 2002. To put into perspective, the total cost of public spending on feasting and entertainment in 2002 even equaled the development cost of the Three Gorges hydro project.[42] Ironically, free feasts often induced excessive and uncontrollable drinking, and there had been media reports on sudden deaths caused by excessive drinking paid for by public funds. Absurdly, some of the officials who lost their lives at banquet tables were even posthumously ratified as "revolutionary martyrs".[43] Feasting with public money had become so widespread throughout government, public institutions, and public enterprises that it had become a main source of revenue for large and medium-sized restaurants. According to statistics, 60–70 percent of the revenues of those restaurants nationwide in 1988 came from banquets paid by public money.[44] It was hardly surprising, therefore, that the business volume of high-end restaurants would drop dramatically whenever the Party-state took countermeasures to curb banqueting at public expense. Sales of liquor, particularly famous fine liquor such as Mao Tai (茅台) and Wu Liang Ye (五粮液) served as another effective indicator of the extent and severity of squandering in general and dining and wining in particular. State-funded consumption of Mao Tai, the finest and also the most expensive brand liquor on the market, normally accounted for 30 percent of the sales of the liquor; immediately after Xi's new administration launched its anti-corruption campaign and began to crack down on squandering of public funds in 2013, shares of Mao Tai as consumed in the public sector had dropped

[41] Ibid., 8.

[42] Yu Xueqiang, "An Analysis of Corruption of Dining and Wining at Public Expense," (in Chinese), *Journal of Guangzhou University (Social Science Edition)* Vol.10 (June 2011): 16.

[43] Xiping Tang, 8.

[44] Gong, *The Politics of Corruption in Contemporary China: An Analysis of Policy Outcomes*, 123.

from 30 percent to only 1 percent, immediately pushing the liquor company into economic downturn.[45]

What seemed more ludicrous was that some public officials even visited prostitutes at public expense. With a booming economy and softened state control over ideology and social life, luxurious restaurants and upscale entertainment operations such as private clubhouses, nightclubs, etc., began to rapidly gain popularity thanks to a surge in public consumption of feasting and entertainment. To stand out from fierce competition and to win customers of wealth and rank, some upscale clubhouses and restaurants started to render integrated one-stop entertainment services—dining, wining, entertainment, and bathing—and even escort services. Cases involving officials visiting prostitutes at home and even abroad at public expense had been on the rise. In January 2015, for example, a senior president of the Beijing branch of China Telecom Group, together with other executives, managers, and staff, held three extravagant feasting and entertainment parties in a hotel, costing the state corporation almost 80,000 yuan. Wang Haisheng, director of general office, ordered heterosexual massage and sexual services at the hotel, and those services, along with dining, wining, and entertainment with the main group, were all paid for by public funds from a secret slush funds account that the branch had previously set up with the hotel.[46] There are cases in which state officials even teamed up to go whoring. It was revealed that the director and the Party secretary of Chengdu municipal bureau of communication not only spent public money lavishly on banqueting and entertainment but also often visited prostitutes in company at the expense of the state.[47] Another case concerned 12 of the fourteen officials in a township governmental agency in Tongzhou, Jiangsu province. Over a period of three years, those officials had been collectively indulging in dining, wining, entertainment, and visiting prostitutes at public expense. In an extreme case, they even made more than twenty trips to ballrooms in Haimen in a single month. Illicit and reckless activities and consumptions of the sort had costed the state a total of 260,000 yuan. The irony was that over the same period

[45] http://news.ifeng.com/a/20161019/50125480_0.shtml?jhy.

[46] "Beijing Telecom official's feasting and call-girl service are paid for by public money" (in Chinese), *CCDI and Ministry of Supervision*, May 18, 2015. http://news.sina.com.cn/c/2015-05-18/115031845617.shtml (accessed December 5, 2020).

[47] DBCK No.11, 1996, 25–27.

the agency and its director were even honored with annual outstanding performance awards for three consecutive years.[48]

Aside from dining, drinking, and entertainment, a massive amount of public funds, in particular scarce foreign currencies, had also been spent on imported luxury automobiles and junkets in the name of inspection and observation. In the Chinese official and business circles incentive to own or to be equipped with a luxury import car is far beyond consideration of its basic function and utility of commute and convenience; it is more about the show-off of its owner or rider's political and social status or a symbol of wealth and rank. Given its symbolic implications in the context of reform China, the era had witnessed a dramatic surge in demand for import vehicles. As discussed, this ever-increasing demand had directly attributed to the rampancy and pervasiveness of smuggling of import cars throughout the 1980s and 1990s. Officials at various levels of governments sought to open up more revenue sources such as the "three arbitraries" or to divert, hold back or misappropriate funding appropriations from the upper levels of government to raise funds to purchase import cars. A report by the National Audit Bureau revealed that nearly one thousand counties and cities across the country had been found to have misappropriated poverty relief funds and funds designated for education to purchase automobiles.[49] As cited earlier, one county that had been in deficit for a prolonged period of time had its 84 county governmental agencies each equipped with two cars. One impoverished county in the northeastern region had even purchased over 700 cars by 1989, and while being allocated by the central government an annual poverty relief fund of 13.76 million yuan, the county ironically spent over 10 million yuan on gas and maintenance of the government fleet on an annual basis.

Also troublesome was the usage and maintenance of governmental vehicles. It was estimated that the annual average gas and maintenance cost of a government vehicle was in the range of 20,000–30,000 yuan, and in some cases, such expenditures had even eaten up 70 percent of the administrative budgets of some government departments and agencies. Statistics showed that nationwide public expenditures on gas and vehicle maintenance reached 11.4 billion yuan in 1992, and then quickly

[48] http://blog.sina.com.cn/s/blog_4d2fccf30100kd1b.html.

[49] Ibid., Jean-Louis Rocca, 410.

doubled to 20 billion yuan in the succeeding year.[50] In 2004, there were approximately 4 million state-owned vehicles, and total expenditures on automobile operation and maintenance were in the range of 400 billion yuan, accounting for 13 percent of the government revenue for the year.[51] What was more problematic was the usage of government or public-funded cars. As a saying goes, "one-third of a governmental car is used for the official's work, and another one-third for the official's family matters, with the remaining one-third used for the chauffeur's personal business". Rampant corruption and abuse in terms of purchase, usage, and maintenance of publicly funded vehicles in the reform era had largely catalyzed the reform of acquisition and management of governmental vehicles and fleets in the 2010s. With the rise of China and the rapid accumulation of public and private wealth since the 1990s, business jets and airplanes began to gain popularity in the circles of billionaires and movie stars, and also attracted the attention and aroused the interest of high-ranking public officials. Shangguan Yongqing, president and Party secretary of Shanxi Yongxin Investment Group, a large province-owned financial institution in Shanxi province, once took a lead role in coordinating fundraising of 390 million yuan among 12 enterprises that had business dealings with Yongxin Investment to purchase a business jet. The airplane was reportedly used at Shangguan's discretion for her own convenience as well as her VIP guests and clients. She was charged for bribe-taking, misappropriation of public funds and assets, squandering at public expense, nepotism, etc. Shangguan was expelled from the Party and office and was criminally convicted in 2016.[52]

Also noteworthy was the abuse of public-funded cellular phones at a time when the prices of cell phones stayed high. Research indicated that in the 1990s approximately 60 percent of all cell phones in use were not privately owned, among which 65 percent of them were purchased at public expense without proper authorization. "Examples abound of

[50] Yan Sun, *Corruption and Market in Contemporary China*, 102–103.

[51] Na Shu, "A probe into the issue of 'three-public-funds'" (in Chinese), *doc88.com,* December 15, 2014. http://www.doc88.com/p-9415766258648.html (accessed December 7, 2020).

[52] "Former Chairman of Shanxi Guoxin Investment Group Shangguan Yongqing is dismissed" (in Chinese), *peng pai news,* May 29, 2016. https://finance.sina.cn/china/gncj/2016-05-29/detail-ifxsqxxs7854152.d.html?sinawapsharesource=newsapp&wm=3200_0006 (accessed December 10, 2020).

situations where levies are exacted, taxes evaded, business losses ignored, loans misused, or subordinates coerced, all in an effort to finance what the public refers to as 'ear-side corruption'". Using cost data on public-funded cell phone purchases and phone bills in Hunan province in the mid-1990s as a proxy, which had a combined total cost of a bit over 1 billion yuan in a given year, it was estimated that total annual costs of public-funded cell phones nationwide would exceed 30 billion yuan, an equivalent of one-tenth of the national education budget in 1998.[53]

In addition to feasting and automobiles, public funds were also squandered on the construction of luxurious villas, office buildings, and residential units. In a residential community in Hepu County, Guangxi Autonomous Region, 18 luxurious villa-style residential buildings, dubbed "the Street of Corruption", had been built for the leading Party and government officials of the county. Those luxury villas each had a living area of 166 square meters (1786 square feet) and approximately 52 percent of the building cost of each villa had been paid for by state funds. Sixteen of the eighteen owners of the villas in the "Street of Corruption" were implicated in either economic crimes or disciplinary offenses with seven being detained and sixteen disciplined. As mentioned previously, the Ministry of Water Resources and its subordinate institutions, in a period of four years, had misappropriated 116 million yuan from special funds designated for water conservancy and irrigation, and the misappropriated funds were used mainly for the benefits and well-being of its staff such as building or purchasing office space and residential housing, investment and even speculating on stocks.[54] The executive deputy mayor of Beijing, Wang Baosen, through power abuse and financial irregularities, had not only purchased a luxury residence for himself but also built luxurious villas at public expense for himself and the mayor, Chen Xitong. As revealed in the media, those villas had costed the state approximately 100 million yuan for construction and renovation.[55] The Ministry of Light Industry spent a total of 1.16 billion yuan to build a

[53] Yan Sun, 103–104.

[54] Meng, Yan and Li, 23–24.

[55] TQSHWZB, August 1995.

luxury office complex with upscale imported interior decorating materials including gold and marble fronts. The construction was completed in 1988 at a cost that was fourfold of its original budget.[56]

A prosperous and open China had not only stimulated trade and commerce in economic affairs but also triggered a surge in communication and exchange in the scientific, cultural, educational, and academic domains at home and abroad. While conferences, inspections, and study and observation tours contributed to the dissemination of information, sharing of models and best practices, and inspiration of innovation, in the meantime, they were also subject to manipulation and abuse. It had long been a widely adopted informal practice nationwide to integrate sightseeing and leisure travel with conferences, business trips, inspection, and observation tours so that these sideline arrangements could also be funded by public funds. Sideline programs and even shopping sprees were in general paid by public funds through various accounting irregularities or, in the case of leading Party and government officials, were often sponsored by subordinate state enterprises or private businessmen who sought to cultivate reciprocal relationships with powerful officials. While low-level officials took on "business trips" or "observation tours" to visit domestic tourism attractions, middle- and high-ranking officials opted to go abroad, in particular Western nations, for observation and exchange. It is estimated that almost all Party and government leaders at or above the county level, including officials from many poor counties, have taken overseas observation tours at public expense.[57] In one extreme case, the bureau of meteorology in a poor city in Yunnan province had owed its employees several months' salaries on one hand, on the other hand, the bureau even decided to take a bank loan to finance its director's "observation" tour in Southeast Asia. Statistics indicated that state-funded overseas tours costed the state 2.5 billion yuan in 1992.[58] Since 2008, squandering on feasting, automobiles and sightseeing at public expense had once again triggered widespread public uproars across the country, compelling the authorities to take actions to crack down on public expenditure related corruption. Based on estimates by the academic circle, dining and wining,

[56] Yan Sun, 100.

[57] Fuhai Sun, "The Study of Today's Corruption and the Socialist Supervisory System" (in Chinese), *Beijing Social Science* No.2 (1995): 127.

[58] Yan Sun, 104.

public vehicles, and sightseeing at public expense each costed the state 300 billion yuan per annum.[59]

As the central authorities increasingly tightened up its scrutiny and control over state-funded overseas observation tours, there had emerged a variety of countermeasures and fraudulent means aimed to deceive funding approvals of these de facto overseas sightseeing and shopping trips. Illicit and fraudulent means and practices in this regard often encompassed the purchase of fake invitation letters via travel or intermediary agencies, falsely made-up itineraries to defraud approvals, altering tour routes and destinations or extending tour durations without authorization to accommodate sightseeing, double trip schedules or itineraries—one for the purpose of approval while the other for sightseeing and shopping, etc. Overseas "observation" tours were often financed by public funds misappropriated from other categories of the budget or covered by subordinate public enterprises or affiliated private firms. To circumvent the increasingly strict review and approval process, some officials even opted to go on the overseas trips using personal passports but managed to get reimbursed by their work units after returning home. Wang Haitao, CEO of the Qingdao Newspaper Media Group in Shandong province, oversaw the operation of the corporation as well as its advertising business, and hence had forged close ties and entrenched reciprocal relationships with enterprise customers. In the summer of 2014, Wang, accompanied by the executives of a real estate company in Qingdao, made a "business" trip to the U.S. to "inspect" a fabricated project, while the true destination of the trip was 2014 FIFA soccer games in Brazil as well as sightseeing in the U.S. To deceive the approval of the planned tour, Wang, in collusion with his business partner and a travel agency, submitted a fake invitation letter for project inspection along with a false itinerary specifically tailored for the "inspection" trip. The five-person group spent approximately 600,000 yuan on the soccer and sightseeing trip, and it was paid for by the sponsoring real estate firm. Wang was expelled from the Party and office in 2015.[60]

Accounting irregularities involving fraudulent use of invoices and receipts, dubbed "receipts corruption", to conceal squandering and misuse of public funds have been on the rise as the authorities took

[59] Xueqiang Yu, 16.

[60] http://baijiahao.baidu.com/s?id=1598971132458011539&wfr=spider&for=pc.

unprecedented measures to combat the "three squandering" (三公)—squandering on dining and wining, squandering on vehicles, and squandering on sightseeing—since 2013. As many types of squandering were either declared illegitimate or prohibited by the authorities, corruptors had to be creative to find ways to hide violations in the book as legitimate expenditures. Buying and selling fake or regular receipts have thus grown rampant to meet the surging demand of government agencies, public institutions, and state enterprises for book-cooking. Violations of state accounting rules and procedures to conceal illicit and wasteful spending are in general either committed through collusion between leading officials and accountants/cashiers or conducted by accountants as coerced by leading cadres. The administrative-related cost category that has seen the most abuses in recent years may be "office supplies and consumable materials". To attract public officials and to facilitate their book-cooking malpractice, some upscale restaurants and private clubs even provide customers with receipts of their shell companies that have been specifically set up for concealment, or genuine receipts purchased from office supplies and stationery stores. A weird phenomenon thus occurred—while spending on dining, wining, and entertainment had seemingly dropped thanks to the authorities' crackdown on squandering, the overall expenditures, however, had not decreased as costs of office supplies and consumable materials popped up accordingly. The malfeasance was so pervasive that in some extreme cases, a work unit of limited size could incur annual costs of "office supplies and consumable materials" up to over 1 million yuan. Given the increased demand and sizeable profits from illegal receipts trading, profiteers rushed to capitalize on this "business" opportunity. A criminal case involving over 30 receipt profiteers in Changsha, Hunan province, is exemplifying the extent and severity of "receipts corruption" in today's China. The profiteers, first of all, managed to acquire receipts from the staff of finance departments or store/supermarket cashiers by offering kickbacks, and then sold the receipts to their customers in governments, SOEs, and public institutions, charging 1.5–6 percent of the face value of the receipts; in return, the receipt vendors, i.e., the finance staff and cashiers, received kickbacks or commissions equaling 1–3.5 percent of the receipt value. The total value of the receipts transacted in a period of four years amounted to over 200 million yuan, and purchasers of those illicit receipts included large state banks, insurance companies, securities companies, real estate enterprises, government agencies, public institutions, and state-owned enterprises.

Items "sold" as printed on the receipts encompassed office supplies, computer consumables, work safety supplies, sporting goods, conference expenditures, dining invoices, etc. All the receipts were entered into the books to conceal de facto spending on bonuses, gifts, hospitality, public relations, client reception, etc.[61]

Moral Decadence and Official Corruption

Moral decadence and bourgeois lifestyle are what the CCP most faulted causal linkages to official corruption. Rather than focus on eradicating incentives and the underlying institutions, the CCP anti-corruption campaigns often declare war on personal ethics and immorality, endeavouring to correct ideological wrongs with so-called "revolutionary ideological education" and integrity education. Moral degeneration and decadence in the Chinese social and political context encompass a range of personal behavior, conduct, and lapses. These misconduct may be categorized into two groups: sexual oriented and moral and behavioral oriented. The latter includes disturbing public order, gambling, drug abuse, slandering and framing others, seeking promotion through fraud, domestic abuse, etc. The former encompasses divorcing or abandoning one's wife to marry a younger and/or educated woman, adultery, fostering mistresses or concubines, sexual harassment, soliciting prostitutes, pornography, etc.[62] While in Western societies some sexual-oriented behavior or misconduct may be perceived as personal lifestyle or scandals if a politician is involved or implicated, these same behavior and misconduct in contemporary China, as discussed before, are most likely defined and viewed as corruption by the authorities and the public alike. In the West, a politician's extramarital affair usually does not involve abuse of public power or misappropriation of public funds, whereas in the context of reform China there does exist an obvious and strong correlation between sexual hedonism and official corruption as corrupt officials often resort to power abuse to open up more income sources to foster mistresses or to indulge in sexual pleasures.

Under certain circumstances, it may not be illogical to simply assert that official corruption in reform China, to some extent, is sexually

[61] http://www.xinhuanet.com/legal/2016-04/12/c_1118598191.htm.

[62] Yan Sun, 33.

induced corruption as well, as per CCDI research and analysis, 95 percent of the corrupt officials investigated and convicted sheltered mistresses or had been involved in extramarital affairs. In many cases, the huge financial pressure to please those much younger and often insatiable mistresses often incentivizes or forces officials to engage in various venal wrongdoing. Another common offense that subjects pleasure seekers to corruption charges are sexual bribes and soliciting prostitutes at public expense as these offenses in general involve abuse of public power for illicit personal gains. As illustrated in cases, it had become a popular malpractice to visit special saunas and massage parlors and then claim for reimbursements from public accounts using fraudulent receipts and invoices or to patronize high-end escort services or accept sexual services at bribe-givers' expense. "Savvy private businessmen have also found such treats to be among the most effective forms of bribe".[63]

The exchange of power for sex, like the exchange of power for money, is a buyer–seller or business relationship. In general, three actors are involved in the trade: public officials (mainly males), sexual service providers (mainly women), and sexual service payers—in general unscrupulous businessmen who intend to curry favors or influence from public officials for illicit personal gains. The power-for-sex exchanges may be categorized into three types in terms of motives and purposes of sexual service providers or payers: power-for-money, power-for-public office or promotion, and power-for-other illicit interests and gains. The first category constitutes the most common type of power-for-sex exchanges, and many young and materialistic women opt to voluntarily engage in sexual relationships with officials in return for a better or luxurious way of life and material rewards such as housing, luxury cars, jewelry, high-end handbags, etc. In addition, being fostered by powerful government officials can also bring gains and benefits to mistresses' family members, which may include employment, job transfer, promotion, access to public project contracting or public procurement opportunities, etc. The intent and desire to keep up with their young mistresses' insatiable demand for material comforts and well-being are often deemed a primary drive for increasingly reckless graft in the officialdom of the reform era. For instance, Cao Jianliao, deputy mayor of Guangzhou and former Party boss of Zengcheng city, Guangdong province, had been engaging in

[63] Ibid.

sexual relationships with 11 women since 1988. In 1992, Cao began to foster a university student as his mistress and awarded her with condo and car purchases funded by his bribe money. When the relationship was ended several years later, as compensation, Cao managed to have her emigrated to Australia and also paid her 8 million Hong Kong dollars and RMB 9 million yuan, all paid out of the pockets of Cao's bribers.[64] Pang Jiayu, vice chairman of Shaanxi provincial CPPCC and former Party chief of Baoji city, sheltered 11 mistresses. To keep up with their material appetite and desire for money, Pang had repeatedly abused his power and influence to arbitrarily allocate contracts and sub-contracts of the municipal water supply pipeline and other construction projects to his mistresses, who then turned over shoddy and faulty work by cheating in labor and cutting down on materials. Deng Baoju, director of Shajing Credit Cooperative Bank in Shenzhen, Guangdong, embezzled and misappropriated over 230 million yuan in public funds in less than three years; Deng used part of the funds to foster 5 mistresses. During a period of two years Deng had spent lavishly on his fifth mistress, also his most beloved one, with a total expenditure of over 18 million yuan. While many were going for quantity, some were in pursuit of quality. For example, Zhang Zonghai, propaganda director of Chongqing municipal Party committee, was particularly fastidious about the qualitative attributes of his mistresses: good education with university undergraduate degree, good looking, and unmarried. There are notoriously extreme sexual scandals in which corrupt officials were involved in extramarital affairs with a large number of women. For example, Zhang Erjiang, Part secretary of Tianmen city in Hubei province, had engaged in or maintained sexual relationships with 107 women in 14 localities from 1989 to 2001. While on business travel, Zhang often directed his subordinates to "walk around and bring back pretty girls". Xu Qiyao, director of Jiansu provincial department of construction, had allegedly been the record-holder in this regard by sheltering over 140 mistresses. When his nurse mistress requested him to find an employment for her daughter, Xu took the opportunity to turn the young lady into his mistress as well.[65] Cases of the sort can go on and on.

[64] "How much does it cost for corrupt officials to break up with their mistresses?" (in Chinese), *Xin Jing Daily*, January 13, 2016. http://news.sohu.com/20160113/n434436636.shtml (accessed December 15, 2020).

[65] http://opinion.people.com.cn/GB/1036/9684956.html.

Instead of seeking monetary and material gains, another group of women incentivize themselves to acquire public offices or to seek promotions by engaging in sexual relationships with officials at higher levels. In most cases, mistresses or sexual service providers are generally public officials per se who are either subordinates of the corrupt officials or favor-seekers intending to advance their own careers in government. Zhang Xiuping, deputy secretary of the Shanxi provincial commission for discipline inspection, had been reportedly engaging in extramarital affairs with her two superiors, Jin Daoming and Jin Yinhuan, both being the leading officials of the provincial commission for discipline inspection. Zhang had once served as Jin Yinhuan's secretary before she was promoted to a middle-level director position and then to the position of a member of the standing committee of the provincial commission for discipline inspection in 2006. In 2013, Zhang was promoted again to be the deputy Party secretary of Jinzhong city until her detention in August 2014. Yang Xiaobo, mayor of Gaoping city, Shanxi province, served as another example in this regard. Yang was accused of seeking an illicit career path in government by engaging in sexual relationships with multiple high-ranking officials, including Shen Weichen, deputy minister of the central propaganda department and former mayor of the city of Taiyuan, capital of Shanxi province. Both Zhang Xiuping and Yang Xiaobo were prosecuted for bribe-taking in 2014. The downfall of Ji Jianye, mayor of Nanjing in Jiangsu province, in 2013, revealed the career path of Jin Qiufen, one of Ji's mistresses in Jiangsu. Jin's career in the provincial public service had been tied in with Ji's rise through the governmental ranks. Through Ji's arrangements, Jin was promoted to be the director of Yangzhou municipal environmental protection bureau before she was arrested in 2014. Reportedly among Ji's multiple mistresses two more others followed similar paths as Jin's. One rose from a typist for Ji to deputy director in Yangzhou municipal government, and another from a hotel attendant to the official of the tourism authority in Ji's jurisdiction. Jiang Yanping, VP of Hunan Construction Engineering Group, had been allegedly offering sexual bribes to multiple high-ranking officials in exchange for favors and promotions; as a result, Jiang transcended rapidly from a warehouse worker to a SOE executive within 13 years.[66] Lai Xiaomin, as cited previously, was also notoriously famous for his

[66] http://club.kdnet.net/dispbbs.asp?id=10536735&boardid=1.
https://www.shenchuang.com/firstpage/2013-10/18/content_3363937.htm.

deep involvement in power-sex swaps. Lai, as what the media described, had been in possession of "three over-100s", namely over 100 houses, over 100 power-for-money dealings, and over 100 mistresses, among whom nearly half were Lai's subordinates or employees of the Huarong Group. What had motivated those women to engage in sexual relationships with Lai was most likely their intentions of career advancement in a state-owned corporation led and controlled by Lai.[67]

While the behavior and misconduct of adultery, extramarital affairs and mistress fostering are classified as moral decadence and corruption, and are subject to Party and administrative sanctions, they are not necessarily criminal offenses. For officials who are in violation of "the socialism moral stipulations" but no acts of bribe-taking and misappropriation of public funds are involved, they are subject to internal Party and/ or administrative disciplinary penalties only. On the other hand, if the actors of an extramarital affairs, either the official or his mistresses or both, are involved or implicated in bribery and/or misappropriation of public funds, they are in general subject to criminal charges of graft. The majority of the official corruption cases involving women and mistresses, as mentioned, however, fall under the latter category.

[67] http://finance.jrj.com.cn/people/2018/10/17144625216183.shtml.

CHAPTER 7

How Does China Fare Amid Unprecedented Official Corruption?

There is a lack of informative and systemic research on the impact and consequences of corruption in reform China. As we all know, it is difficult or almost impossible to quantify the true impact of corruption in any society given the secretive nature of the offenses. The task is deemed even more unattainable in socialist China. Reasons and explanations are various with the politically centered being the major ones. The communist regime knowingly runs a tight-controlled and non-transparent government, which is notoriously tight-lipped for sensitive information, let alone information on scandals and corruption involving top-level CCP leaders. Even revelation of the true magnitude and severity of corruption within the Party is deemed an enduring embarrassment and political pain to the CCP. Equally relevant and important is the sensitivity of the subject per se as scholars tend to exercise greater caution not to step on the dangerous political land mine that may blow off their career and academic professions. Although the Chinese media has the motivation and capacity to expose and report on corruption cases, its primary intention and interest tend to be in major cases involving high-ranking offenders and hugeness of grafted funds. In addition, the media's sources of information are overwhelmingly from government anti-corruption agencies such as the DICs and procuratorates rather than its own stand-alone and independent investigations. This further compromises the quality of data and the

F. C. Sun, *An Ineluctable Political Destiny*,
https://doi.org/10.1007/978-981-99-3146-0_7

assessment of the true impact of corruption on the Chinese economy and society.

In the context of reform China there is a lack of consensus on the effects of corruption. While the Party-state perceives corruption as a political and moral evil that undermines its legitimacy as a ruling party, researchers of corruption, both internal and external, employ a multidisciplinary approach to the study of the phenomenon as well as its effects and origins. As early as the 1980s and 1990s, the CCP leadership had identified two major categories of negative impacts of corruption. They worried that corruption would impede the progress of the reform, harm the legitimacy of the Party, and further weaken the Party's ruling power. Hu Qili, then top Party official overseeing ideological work in the 1980s, warned that corruption "appeared with great impact and have spread very quickly .... have had an impact on reform work, and have confused the minds of some cadres and masses".[1] Jiang Zeming, the general secretary of the CCP from 1989 to 2002, warned the whole Party of the seriousness of official corruption, declaring that anti-corruption and maintaining the cleanness of the bureaucracy "is a crucial issue that is directly related to the survival of the Party".[2] Understandably, as a ruling party, what the CCP was concerned most was its legitimacy and monopoly because official corruption had caused "extremely serious harm to the Party's cause". This anxiety seemed justified when taking into account the results of some surveys conducted in the 1980s and 1990s. A nationwide survey by an influential journal in 1988 revealed that 78.15 percent of the respondents identified corruption as the issue concerning them the most. Several other polls carried out among various social groups such as the outstanding youths, prominent personages, etc. concluded with similar findings.[3] Recent surveys on social and economic issues as well as citizens' concerns, as discussed previously, share similar insights and conclusions. The persistent consistency of these survey results across various reform stages serves as an insightful indicator of the limitation and ineffectiveness of the CCP's anti-corruption strategies and actions.

[1] James T. Myers, "China: Modernization and 'Unhealthy Tendencies'," *Comparative Politics* (Jan. 1989): 199.

[2] Hongying Tang, 23.

[3] Yan Sun, "The Chinese Protests of 1989: the Issue of Corruption," *Asian Survey* Vol. XXXI, No.8 (August 1991): 768.

7.1 The Double-Edged Effect of Transactive Corruption

While the authorities and academics share consensus on the harmful effects of corruption on the society and economy, some scholars contend that the functionality of transactive corruption such as bribery may be fundamentally different from that of plunder such as graft. Transactive corruption is perceived to be more functional than plunder as "bribery is much more likely to involve profits making and economic activity that generates some amount of net growth".[4] Corruption, according to Nye and Bayley, helps promote economic development in the following ways: it facilitates capital formation; it helps reduce red tape; and it fosters entrepreneurialism.[5] This argument holds that, first of all, bureaucracies in developing nations, in general, are characterized by red tape and move at a "snail pace". Under such circumstances, bribery can function as a "direct incentive" to mobilize the government to involve in more proactive support for enterprise development and trade and to facilitate entrepreneurs' access to permits, licenses, credit, foreign exchange allocation, etc. Secondly, the bureaucratic systems of most developing nations are typified by "over-centralization" with vague lines of authority and low-quality personnel. These factors, to some extent, have inevitably reduced the capacity of the governments. Corruption, however, in the form of nepotism and bribery, may provide an alternative to enhance administrative capacity through informal connections and procedures. A government may achieve some of its goals through these nepotistic-oriented procedures rather than the formal ones. Thirdly, the potential opportunities for corruption may serve as an effective means of attracting (or keeping) talented people into (or in) governments of developing states where salary levels for public servants are significantly low. The prospect of spoils and the tangible rewards for the career attract able men into government and hence enhance the quality of public servants and the

[4] Wedeman, 122–123.

[5] David H. Bayley, "The Effects of Corruption in a Developing Nation," In Arnold J. Heidenheimer, Michael Johnston and Victor T. LeVine (eds), *Political Corruption: A Handbook* (New Brunswick [U.S.A.]: Transaction Publishers, 1989), 944-946.

J. S. Nye, "Corruption and Political Development: A Cost–Benefit Analysis," in Heidenheimer et al., 967–968.

capacity of bureaucracies.[6] Fourthly, entrepreneurship, another crucial factor for economic development, to some extent, can be promoted through corruption. Entrepreneurship of minority groups or those who have been excluded from the political system, by making use of graft, can overcome discrimination against them and buy themselves equal opportunities for the exhibition of their entrepreneurial talents. Lastly, corruption can also reduce uncertainty and enhance the rate of investment. Investment decisions are often marked by risks and uncertainties, which can be compounded in the economic and political environment of underdeveloped nations. In addition, investors also face a major political unknown—the behavior of the government, as well as its arbitrary and irrational style of decision-making and extensive intervention in the economy. Investors must have some assurance of predictable risks and manageable uncertainties over the course of investment decision-making and investment management. "By enabling entrepreneurs to control and render predictable and important influence on their environment, corruption can increase the rate of investment".[7]

Manifestations of corruption in reform China validate in varying degrees these arguments. While deferring our discussion of the costs and negative effects of corruption to the next section, we now look into various dimensions of the functionality of transactive corruption in the reform era. As argued, corruption functions to increase the rate of investment and enhance the efficiency and productivity of capital. In the context of China, "where the state-controlled assets are being used inefficiently, bribes that help move those assets from state control and onto the markets may have considerable long-term benefits, even if illicit transfers enable the first buyers to earn windfall profits and enrich dishonest and corrupt officials".[8] As presented, corruption also fosters entrepreneurship and helps access to governmental decision-making and reduces red tape. Some neoliberal Chinese scholars and local officials contend that corruption is a trade-off and part of the inevitable outcomes of the economic reform. They perceive corruption as a "lubricant" that helps "loosen up" the administrative command system and argue that

[6] Bayley, 121.

[7] Nathaniel H. Leff, "Economic Development Through Bureaucratic Corruption," *The American Behavioral Scientist* (Nov. 1964): 8–12.

[8] Wedeman, 122–123.

corruption contributes to efficiency and enables entrepreneurs to access government decisions and to facilitate market coordination. As observed by the author, entrepreneurs, including those who were profiled as undesired social elements from the perspective of prevailing orthodoxies in the Mao era and could otherwise be alienated or excluded from participation in business development, had managed to gain access to regulatory approvals and market, and some of them had even won out to become leading players in industries and localities. While contributing factors to their success may be various, one underlying circumstance seems to be common—bribery was widely deployed to facilitate acquisition of decisions, approvals, licenses and permits and to access essential production inputs, bank credits, foreign exchange allowance, land use rights, and market entry in the early and mid-reform era. It is a known fact that TVEs, also de facto private businesses, had used bribes and kickbacks to conquer government officials in an attempt to overcome systemic hurdles over the course of business development and growth. Nowadays as private economy has overtaken the state economy in terms of GDP contribution and job creation, the role and functionality of transactive corruption in the early days of the reform should be prudentially and objectively studied and assessed. Some libertarian economists hold that "corruption's destructiveness is positive in the Chinese context by helping to destroy the state economy". As quoted in Sun, an economist writes:" There are two ways to transfer or reallocate power: to seize it by compulsion (qiang duo) or by purchase (gou mai) .... Since officials do not easily give up their power and seizure is not possible, bribery—the exchange of money for power—becomes the only way to purchase power". They argue that corruption functions as necessary "toll payments" on the route to the market, and "likely a second-best strategy for development".[9]

While sharing consensus on the positive impact of transactive corruption or bribery as in the case of TVE development, some observers assess and compare the roles and effects of transactive corruption in different periods of the reform. Yan Sun, for instance, made observations on the market behavior and economic performance of several groups of players and actors such as TVEs, contractor managers of SOEs, self-employed, and speculators, and analyzes their corruptive behavior and acts in the early years of the reform. She concluded that "overall for the first

[9] Cited in Sun, 18–19.

period, bribery and the attendant speculative activities, while distorting the goals of the reform, did not result in overwhelming harms that strangled reform. While they entailed unfair access, hiked prices and led to income inequality, they also contributed to the flow of goods and information, an overall constructive role in a system just breaking away from its irrationality".[10] In the second period of the reform, however, the roles and effects of bribery became more negative as organizational corruption and collective bribery gradually became dominant. As discussed earlier, with the dismantlement of the command economy, SOEs, in particular state-owned SMEs, were thrusted into marketplace, fighting for survival and competing with the non-state sector for production inputs, supplies, bank credits and business loans as well as markets. Like their non-state counterparts, SOEs often resorted to collective bribe-giving in an attempt to reduce market entry and regulatory barriers. Given the magnitude of the public projects and investments as well as SOEs' organizational and financial capacity, organizational bribery tends to involve large amount of public funds and is manifested in multiple forms. Moreover, organizational bribery tends to have much larger outreaching impact across the economy and society and hence can exert greater harmful effects than non-state corruption and bribery. As pointed out by Sun, "while the bribery of TVEs and the self-employed contributed in part to clearing market barriers, SOEs bribery contributes to new market barriers". Instead of contributing to reform's goal of eliminating administrative command, organizational bribery helps aggravate administrative interventions. "Moreover, the behavior of public organizations exerts more legitimizing and exemplary effects on society than that of nonstate sector".[11]

The prospect of rent-seeking may have functioned to attract (or keep) talented people into (or in) government in the reform era. While there are a variety of contributing factors to China's economic success and prosperity, an increasingly educated public service as well as a modernized governance structure are deemed crucial determinants for the rise of its state power. Traditionally, the Chinese government pays mediocre remunerations to its employees, and poor pay was one of the major incentives that motivated government officials to "go to sea" (下海, setting up one's

[10] Yan Sun, 75–80.

[11] Ibid., 82.

own company to make money) and to pursue "job hopping" (跳槽) in the early years of the reform. Numerous ambitious and talented young government officials left their poorly paid government jobs in pursuit of business opportunities or to join the private sector for better remuneration and financial reward. However, this tendency came to a halt in the new phase of the reform partly due to the reform and transformation of the public service and, presumably, partly as a result of the burgeoning potential of rent-seeking in government. Although job stability and improved remunerations have made government jobs more attractive, equally attractive are the potential of rent-seeking in government. It is a known phenomenon that rapid development and sustained economic growth in many localities have been driven by large-scale capital investment and coordinated and efficient execution of the development plans led by talented and hardworking government officials. However, what have motivated political elites in pursuit of transformative developments and endured economic growth are not only job performance that is tied with one's career advancement but also officials' venal incentive to cut a slice of the developmental pie. As observed, when Xi launched his fierce crackdown on corruption, corruption has abated, and so have development and economic growth. Inertia and non-performance in governments in the middle of the sweeping anti-corruption campaign have become a worrisome trend that the authorities need to tackle and to reverse. This in part helps explain the causal linkage between rapid development and rampant official corruption in reform China.

The Economic Cost of Official Corruption

While the beneficial effects of corruption seem to be ambiguous, its adverse aspect is more obvious. Whatever forms and characters a corrupt act may have, it is harmful to the society in that it aims to achieve private gains at the expense of the common good or the public interest. It represents degeneration of moral standards, corrupts social values, exhausts government legitimacy, and sets the wrong direction for the future generations. There is overwhelming consensus on the negative impact of corruption in post-Mao China. The harmful effects of bureaucratic corruption can be grouped into four broad categories: economic, political, ideological, and social.

Corruption hinders rather than assists economic development. Capital accumulated through corruption may not be invested into economically desirable activities; rather, it may wind up in Swiss banks or diverted, as some existing evidence suggests, into less desirable or even wasteful pursuits such as consumption of luxurious goods. In the context of reform China, the economic consequences of corruption are manifested mainly as immeasurable loss of public funds and state properties as well as waste of social wealth. As mentioned above, it seems implausible to quantify the economic loss caused by official corruption in reform China. Literature research on the subject ended up with several rough estimates and figures, none of which, however, may be statistically sound and verified. One estimate put the total cost of corruption in a range between 4 and 17 percent of the Chinese GDP.[12] Another estimate puts the loss of public coffer due to corruption at approximately 4 percent of GDP annually at the end of the 1990s.[13] Still another estimates that direct economic losses and losses to consumers caused by corruption amounted to an annual average ranging from 987.5 billion yuan to 1.257 trillion yuan, or 13.2–16.8 percent of annual GDP in the latter half of the 1990s.[14] It was estimated that in 2009 public funds misappropriated and squandered amounted to 234.7 billion yuan and illicit transfers of grafted funds to foreign countries totaled 336 billion yuan, accounting for approximately 1.1 percent of China's GDP for the year. Capital flight of the sort and extent exert detrimental impact on China's reform and economic growth. In the period between 1982 and 1992, as estimated by the National Bureau of State Assets Management, total loss of state assets resulted from embezzlement, misappropriation and mismanagement exceeded 500 billion yuan, an equivalent of one-fifth of China's total fixed state assets of 2.6 trillion yuan in 1992 or 80 billion yuan more than the state's total revenues of 418.8 billion yuan for the same year.[15]

Corruption has diverted scarce resources from productive fields into consumption, and hence caused huge waste of social wealth. Squandering and wasteful uses of public funds on consumption such as feasting, gift-giving, domestic and international sightseeing, etc. constitute another category of direct loss of the public coffer, and as cited previously annual

[12] Minxin Pei, 12.

[13] Manion, P86.

[14] Hu Angang, cited in "Corruption wiped out 13–16 percent of China's GDP, researcher says," by Peter Wonacott, *Wall Street Journal*, March 8, 2001.

[15] Yan Sun, 115.

public expenditures on dining and wining even amounted to 200 billion yuan. According to data from the Ministry of Finance, the National Bureau of Statistics, and the National Development and Reform Commission, since 2005 public expenditures had been increasing by over 100 billion yuan on an annual basis, and between 2007 and 2012 consumptions in public funds had reached 900 billion yuan. Another widely quoted indicator is the share of public consumption in the sales of eateries and luxury goods. As mentioned, any major anti-corruption crackdowns in China could lead to a drop of up to 70 percent of the revenues of the luxury restaurants and fine liquor producers. The true consequences were likely graver than what the government had published as the Chinese government is inclined to report only what is good while concealing or downplaying what is bad. Aggregate data on total loss of state assets in the new phase of the reform is unknown; the loss, however, must be an immense figure. As cited previously, economic loss caused by rampant smuggling activities and collective corruption in government and law enforcement in Xiamen and Zhanjiang had even impacted the national economy. In 1997, smuggled petroleum products not only dominated the local oil supply in Zhanjiang but also constituted 10 percent of the imported oil supply in the domestic oil market. Lai Changxing's smuggling operations in Xiamen brought in huge quantity of petroleum products and rubber, causing turmoil to the supply of these products in the mainland market. Petroleum smuggling in Xiamen had caused direct economic loss of over 20 billion yuan and led to the closure of over 3000 oil wells and layoff of over 300,000 workers in the state petrochemical industry in 1998. The net loss of tariff and tax revenues as a result of organized smuggling in Xiamen was in the range of 30 billion yuan. In the aftermath of the crackdown on the two organized smuggling groups in Xiamen and Zhanjiang, the resulting tariff and tax revenue increase in 1999 were enough to enable the central authorities to give a raise to the nation's 80 million public servants.[16]

Corruption largely functions as a de facto and inefficient tax on business operations. Bribery, as a cost of doing business, is generally factored into overall production or operational costs, and is ultimately transferred to consumers in the final prices of the products and services. Corruption, in this sense, not only raises business cost and reduces profitability, but

[16] Yan Sun, 154.

also contributes to inflation and even triggers social unrest. According to Yan Sun, coal, as an essential industrial input, was heavily affected by cost increment at some middle-links. As a result of official speculation, its price increase sometimes reached as high as 500 percent in the period.[17] Rampant speculation and profiteering was a decisive impetus of inflation in the late 1980s. Among various contributing factors that had jointly led to the large-scale mass demonstrations in 1989, public concerns of rampant official corruption and surging inflation were deemed two crucial determinants. Given widespread malpractice of bribery in land transactions and real estate development, corruption, among other economic, political, and speculative factors, is partly faulted for the soaring and unaffordable housing prices as well as fueling public grievances and anger in this regard. The stubbornly and absurdly high housing prices and huge real estate bubbles in particularly in China's major urban centers are accused of having not only "kidnapped" citizens' consumptions on other necessities but also eroded China's real economy. In China's Tier 1 cities—Beijing, Shanghai, Guangzhou and Shenzhen, for example, many families are forced to squeeze out the savings of three generations (grandparents, parents and children) to make down payments to purchase residences for the young generation; on the other hand, expensive monthly installment payments often deprive the so-called "housing slaves" (房奴) of other consumptions and even necessities. The housing bubble resulted largely from the state policy failure and corruption has trapped the nation in an economic dilemma: on one hand, lucrative rents in real estate incentivize local officials to push for more developments, and on the other hand, high profit margins and red-hot speculation in real estate have induced industrialists and companies from other sectors to jump on the bandwagon of real estate in pursuit of windfall profits. This has in turn further pushed up the housing prices and abraded manufacturing and the real economy. More importantly, collusive corruption in bidding and competition of public construction projects distorts decision-making, drives up overall costs, depletes public investments, and give rise to inferior or shoddy projects that not only results in direct economic loss but also causes casualties and even loss of lives. The collapse of a bridge and the resultant loss of several dozens of lives in Qijiang, Chongqing in the 1990s as well as numerous public project failures and accidents across

[17] Yan Sun, "The Chinese Protests of 1989: The Issue of Corruption," 769.

the country manifest the gravity and consequences of power abuse and corruption in infrastructure and public investments.

The fundamental objective of China's economic reform is to establish a market economy based on the principles of fair trade and equal competition. However, corruption works to distort the purposes of the reform. Influence peddling, for example, disregards merits, efficacy, and equity, undermines fair competition, and defies reform policies. Corruption favors the most connected rather than the efficient and assists to form monopolistic dominance of the privileged by excluding the unconnected or unprivileged from market entry. As public players such as SOEs and local authorities joined forces to compete for large public investments and infrastructure projects using various illicit means and tactics such as organizational bribery in the post-1992 period, the market principle of fair competition had been further eroded. Corruption, to a large extent, has turned equal competition in market into "connection competition" and "power competition". Rampant collusive corruption in competition for public investment has largely distorted the decision-making process, resulted in reckless or redundant investments, driven up bidding costs of the competing localities and firms, and misallocated resources to poor-quality and even wasteful projects. Even though winning projects have generated tangible gains and benefits to the localities or the enterprises, this does not necessarily mean that the allocated resources have been put into the most efficient uses and have hence generated maximum economic gains and benefits. If state investments and public resources were allocated through more transparent and fairer competitions, higher level of efficiency and economic gains as well as more optimal social benefits would have been attained. A study indicates that among public investments and public projects involving bribery, only one-third of them were deemed efficient and profitable, and the remaining two-thirds were either struggling or uncompleted.[18] There have been a series of media exposures in recent years regarding the diversion and misappropriation of the state-designated poverty relief funds to city square construction, amenity development and other wasteful projects. Local authorities involved in irregularities of the sort have one thing in common: diverting centrally allocated special funds and resources to beef up their signature economic

[18] Chen Liang, "A Brief Analysis of the Harmful Effects of Corruption," *baidu wenku*, 2018. https://wenku.baidu.com/view/b4751b351fd9ad51f01dc281e53a580216fc50c7.html (accessed December 22, 2020).

or political achievements and to create impetus for the career advancement of local Party and government leaders. In many cases, these so-called "projects of political achievements" (政绩工程) were undertaken at the expense of impoverished rural families and poor villages, which were generally in dire need of the state poverty relief and farming aid funds and programs. By the same token, corruption and influence-peddled competition have also exerted detrimental impact on the state finance sector where distorted decision-making directs the flow of capital and bank credits to inefficient and unprofitable operations and is hence blamed for the worsening of a variety of problems in the banking industry such as wasteful undertakings, nonperforming loans, and bank insolvency. Understandably, what individuals or businesses offer to officials in exchange for their favors and arbitrary decision-making would be far less than what they could gain from the power-money swap as most bribers tend to conduct rational cost–benefit analysis or calculations for their venal dealings. In the case of Lai Xiaomin, for example, Lai had reportedly extracted huge bribes worth hundreds of millions of yuan in return for distorted decision-making that favored bribe-givers. However, the economic loss to the state resulted from Lai's venal acts is estimated to be dozens or even hundreds of times what Lai had raked in through corruption.

Corruption represents a net loss of public resources because looted public money flows out of the state treasury through either graft or public bribery into individuals' purses. If misappropriation of public funds is aimed to funnel gains and benefits to the members of the work unit, it may represent a partial loss to the public treasury as the act has at least helped to compensate the poorly paid public employees. With the deepening of the reform, the nature and scope of misappropriation had become more predatory. Looting of public funds and assets is more devastating to the economy as the stolen money, given its secretive nature and the looters' motivation for concealment, is less likely to be put into the domestic economy. Looting in this sense represents an absolute loss to an economy. In the Chinese context, capital flight of hundreds of billions of yuan each year destined for foreign bank accounts is deemed a one-way capital flow as much of the grafted money would never be directed back into China's economy or put into use for productive activities. As revealed in several major graft cases, instead of being covertly funneled to foreign accounts through money laundering, banknotes weighing several tons had been hidden in places and some bills had even become moldy and rotten.

Hidden illicit cash of the sort is most likely to be used for squandering or other wasteful consumptions and therefore has similar effects on the economy as capital flight.

The Political Cost of Official Corruption

Rampant corruption may cause detrimental consequences to a regime through political instability and even national disintegration. As pointed out by Nye and Caiden, corruption causes intense struggle for public power, ruins popular faith in government and creates a general mood of distrust. Under certain circumstances, widespread corruption may force the ruling group to sustain the political order by more repressive means[19]; or even cause the downfall of a regime by means of military takeover.[20]

In the context of reform China, widespread corruption has weakened people's beliefs in the Party and significantly hampered the prestige of the government. Public surveys in the early period of the reform indicated that some interviewees even compared corruption in the reform era with the corruptness of the KMT regime, declaring that today's corruption is at least as serious as that under the old regime. Some veteran cadres complain that the Party is no longer the same one as in the war times. The dramatic decline of the prestige of the Party and the government in recent years, as perceived by the public, is partly attributable to the seemingly uncontrollable cadre corruption. Corruption has become one of the top concerns and political dilemma of the CCP leadership as "it will collapse the regime if no actions taken to curb corruption; on the other hand, it will bring down the Party if relentless actions are taken to crack down on corruption". It implies that revelation of the true scope of official corruption will fundamentally endanger the CCP's legitimacy as a ruling party. Public opinion surveys conducted in recent years indicated that, for three consecutive years, interviewees had rated official corruption as the most damaging contributing factor that had harmed China's international image and reputation. It is argued that the aggregate GDP and the military power cannot make China a real power alone at the world

[19] Gerald E. Caiden, "Toward a General Theory of Official Corruption," *Asian Journal of Public Administration* Vol.10, No.1 (June 1988): 20.

[20] Nye, 971–972.

stage as a corrupt regime will be despised and alienated by the international community. Rampant official corruption in the long run will exert detrimental impact on the nation's economic growth and gradually deplete and weaken the capacity and influence of China. Widespread official corruption has severely undermined citizens' confidence and trust in the Party-state and is attributable to increasing social grievances and unrest. Petitions, demonstrations and even riots of various nature and in various scales have been breaking out in urban and rural China, and as a countermeasure the government has been investing heavily over the years to beef up security capacity to cope with sudden and unpredictable mass incidents.

Corruption enfeebles the regime by reducing the efficiency of the administration. The efficiency of Chinese bureaucracy has long been problematic, and rampant corruption in government has exacerbated the situation. Under the influence of the traditional "official-centered" norms, Chinese officials tend to regard their public offices as granted privileges and rent-extracting tools rather than obligations to serve citizens. In this sense, it is hardly surprising that corrupt officials often deliberately complicate procedures and processes or simply hold things up in anticipation for payoffs. Cases abound concerning long, complex and confusing procedures and process of approval and permitting; in extreme cases, it took project applicants months or even years to go around dozens of government departments and agencies for the acquisition of dozens of or even over 100 "official seals". Costs of payoffs of "greasing the palm" incurred in the processes often amounted to millions of yuan.

Corruption debilitates government capacity and jeopardizes its legitimacy. The competition within government for lucrative rents often leads to contradictions, disunion, and factionalism while the practice of nepotism and patronage damages the fairness in recruitment and promotion. As pointed out, the malpractice of office-selling and -buying pervades the officialdom and has even become one of the main avenues for high-ranking officials to capture rents. The vicious cycle tends to feed on itself—those who paid for their offices tend to make better use of their authority to not only get back their investment but also generate returns. Corruption in personnel administration acts to either keep able people out of public service or cause public servants to reduce their work efforts. Inertia and irrationality caused by corruption directly hinder the process of decision-making and the normal operation of bureaucratic machine. Widespread official corruption is seen to have undercut the public confidence in the evenhandedness of the government, and consequently endangers the legitimacy of the government. More importantly, political and bureaucratic corruption tends to have greater spillover effect. As mentioned, traditional Confucius orthodox profiles political elite as "parental officials" (父母官), and the morality and behavior of the "parental officials" often set standards and examples for citizens to follow. As demonstrated in this case study, led by a venal elite, political corruption has quickly spread to almost all walks of life in the reform era, causing widespread moral degeneration and corruption in Chinese society.

The Social Cost of Official Corruption

More serious are damages official corruption brings about to a society. The pursuit of self-interest by the whole society, both elites and non-elites, inevitably leads to social fragmentation, gives rise to endless political and social conflicts, and hence weakens national integration. Immorality and self-seeking in a society that have resulted from corruption may "cause widespread cynicism and social disunity, and thus reduce the willingness to make sacrifices for the society's economic development".[21] The social consequences of rampant corruption in reform China validate the aforementioned scholastic arguments and observations.

Corruption distorts the distribution of social wealth among various social groups and is deemed an important contributory factor to social instability. Income distribution is not only an important economic principle but also a crucial measure of social fairness. Fairness of social wealth distribution is deeply embedded in Chinese traditional culture and is deemed an important element of Chinese traditional social norms and values. Transitioned from the ideology and a remuneration system of equalitarianism in Mao's era, the Chinese society witnessed the shocking effect of escalated income inequality induced by a market-oriented remuneration mechanism and compounded by unprecedented corruption. SOE reform and large-scale SOE privatization in the 1980s and 1990s had made millions of SOE workers jobless. This has further aggregated the gap of income distribution between the rich and the poor. What is regarded the worst scenario was the large-scale illicit transfer of state

[21] Nathaniel H. Leff, "Economic Development through Bureaucratic Corruption," in Heidenheimer, 517.

wealth to the purses of the political and economic elites via the process of SOE ownership transformation and privatization. The change of the Gini coefficient of China's income distribution throughout the reform era elucidates the trend of rising income inequality in Chinese society. In 1978, the year China was about to launch rural economic reform, the Gini coefficient for income distribution in urban areas was just 0.15, virtually the lowest in the world for the year. It climbed to 0.19 in 1986, two years since the beginning of the urban reform in 1984. Income inequality increased dramatically ever since with Gini coefficient rising to 0.37 in 1994 and to 0.458 in 2001. The coefficient peaked at 0.491 in 2008 and then had slightly decreased ever since. Between 2004 and 2013, China's Gini coefficient averaged at 0.482 in contrast to EU's reading of 0.305, suggesting a much wider income distribution gap in Chinese society.[22] The actual coefficient is estimated to be higher as "black" and "gray" incomes of the upper income echelons were not reflected in the official figures. According to He, in 1998, the top 20 percent high income earners earned 9.6 times more than the bottom 20 percent low-income earners. While earners in the top 10 percent echelon earned 38.4 percent of the total income, their counterparts in the bottom 20 percent made only 5.5 percent of the total.[23] Again, the true figures underlaid by rents and illicit incomes resulted from graft and corruption should be higher than the officially released data. Widening social wealth gap causes public grievances and leads to social instability and unrest. Widespread official profiteering and corruption between 1985 and 1988, as discussed, along with other economic and social problems such as inflation, unfair distribution of social wealth, etc. had eventually triggered large-scale student and mass demonstrations in 1989. However, similar inducers or contributing factors still remain in effect today and this partly explains why mass protests and clashes continue to break out in the post-1989 period.

Widespread official corruption has also distorted the moral standards, degenerated social ethos, and caused damages in other social spheres. Corruption in law enforcement and judiciary tends to exert more detrimental impact on Chinese society as corruption undermines the integrity of judicial institutions that enforce laws and maintain rule and order in

[22] Qinglian He, 12.

Jin Han, Qingxia Zhao and Mengnan Zhang, "China's Income Inequality in the Global Context" (in Chinese), *Perspectives in Science* Vol.7 (March 2016): 27–29.

[23] Qinglian He, 12.

the marketplace. Once social justice, one of the most important and fundamental pillars of a society, is distorted, it carries powerful effects that distorts and destroys the morality, norms, and values of a society. The degeneration of moral standards in the reform era is unprecedentedly severe in the history of the PRC. Corruption, like a plague, has been rapidly raging across all spheres of the society. As demonstrated in pervious chapters, irregularities, malpractices, corruption and criminal acts in healthcare, education, food and drug safety, environment protection among others all attest to the extent and severity of immorality and corruption in society. Even religion is not immune from the harmful effects of corruption; stories and videos widely circulated in social media accuse monks of squandering of believers' donations or display temple elders driving luxury Rolls-Royce. Although the authorities have been making efforts to crack down on irregularities and malfeasances in the aforementioned sectors, but meaningful progresses have not been achieved. Public concerns and grievances over an over-commercialized healthcare, unaffordable housing, food and drug safety, environmental pollution among others, still exist and are even growing louder and graver.

Also noteworthy are the distortional effects of corruption on ideology and social ethos. What seems bewildering is that although everyone is indignant at or denounces corruption, one also feels that a minor misdeed of one's own should be acceptable. A survey conducted among urban youths elucidated this perception. Most respondents indicated that they would engage in bribery if their important personal needs or the interests of their organizations could be satisfied through provision of bribes.[24] This partly explains why some forms of minor misdeed are prevalent in today's China. As distorted social norms gradually gain legitimacy, abuse of power and bribery will become an accepted way and custom of doing business and attaining personal gains. The ultimate consequence would be the formation of a corrupt culture and society built upon monetary terms and venal interests.

In this sense, there seems to be reasonable grounds to argue that today's China is facing a crisis of integrity and trust—trust in the Party-state, the officialdom, the judiciary, the professional ethics and standards, social justice, and even the honesty and integrity of other members and groups of the society.

[24] *Reform Reference* No.8 (1996): 33.

7.2 Corruption Control Efforts and Countermeasures

The CCP leadership has made considerable efforts to curb corruption within the Party and government since 1978. In 1980, Deng, at a central politburo conference, criticized irregularities within the Party and attributed genesis of corruption to the existence of privileges; he pointed out that some cadres placed themselves in a status of the masters rather than civil servants of the citizens.[25] Beginning with Deng, the paramount Party leaders who have led through the reform era including Jiang Zeming, Hu Jintao and Xi Jinping have all launched anti-corruption campaigns since the beginning of the 1980s. While differing in emphasis, strategy, style, intensity and duration, these campaigns shared one common goal to stamp out rampant official corruption to safeguard the achievements of the reform and to maintain the legitimacy of the CCP ruling. This section begins with an overview of the mandates, functions and interactions of the Chinese anti-corruption institutions, followed by a presentation of the anti-corruption efforts and countermeasures in the regimes of Jiang and Hu, and concludes with a discussion of the seemingly unprecedented governmental crackdown on corruption launched by Xi since the 18th National Congress of the CCP in 2012.

Anti-Corruption Institutions—Mandate, Functions, and Interactions

The year 1978 is marked by the reinstatements of the Central Commission for Discipline Inspection (CCDI) and the Supreme People's Procuratorate. Also restored and reinstated were the discipline inspection commissions (DIC) and people's procuratorates at provincial, municipal, and county levels. These important anti-corruption institutions and mechanisms had been paralyzed or ceased to operate during the Cultural Revolution (1966–1976). The mandate and major functions of DICs are to enforce Party disciplines, combat malfeasances, and sanction offenders, and to lead and coordinate investigations among Party and governmental supervisory agencies and procuratorates. As part of the Party apparatus, DICs do not have judicial authority; in general, DICs forward cases and evidence that may be implicated in suspected criminal wrongdoing

[25] Wenbin Chen, 197–198.

and offenses to procuratorates for criminal investigation and prosecution. The CCDI is mandated with initiation, planning, organization, implementation, and overseeing nationwide anti-corruption campaigns. Another high-level anti-corruption institution is the Central Inspection Teams (CIT), mandated to coordinate anti-corruption tasks with provincial authorities and large state-owned enterprises and public institutions. CITs are dispatched by CCDI to provinces and organizations where the inspection teams would be stationed to carry out thorough audits into the conduct of high-ranking officials (the provincial/ministerial level and above) and also to look into possible irregularities and misdeed of the organizations. CTIs' audits and preliminary investigations serve as a prerequisite for CCDI formal investigative procedures and process entitled "双规" (administrative detention for investigation). The Supreme People's Procuratorate and its provincial and local branches are mandated with the supervision of law enforcement and investigation, as well as prosecution of economic crimes. Coordinated by DICs, procurators take over cases and evidence forwarded by DICs for formal criminal investigations and proceed to the prosecution and trial stage if warranted. The Ministry of Supervision and its counterparts at the provincial, municipal, and county levels were reinstated in 1987 and were tasked with similar mandates of the DICs to supervise the conduct of government officials and to enforce administrative disciplines in government. The Department of Supervision is under the command and coordination of the CCDI. In 1995, the Anti-Corruption Bureau and its counterparts at various levels were established. The bureau is an internal department of the Supreme People's Procuratorate and is mandated with investigation and prosecution of economic crimes encompassing embezzlement, bribery, misappropriation of public funds, theft of state assets and properties, possession of high-value assets that cannot be legitimately justified, etc. In 2007, a corruption preventive mechanism was initiated and added to the functions of the Chinese anti-corruption system, and the National Bureau of Corruption Prevention thus came into existence. The bureau, tasked with corruption prevention, is directly under the State Council and its director position was concurrently held by the Minister of Supervision. The arrangement was a manifestation of the authorities' long-term commitment to the reduction and prevention of corruption in the Party-state. Unlike the Ministry of Supervision, Procuratorate, or CCDI, the NCPB focuses on implementing preventive measures, monitoring the transfer of assets across organizations, facilitating information sharing among government agencies, and policing corrupt practices in the nongovernmental sector. Also noteworthy was the establishment of the National Supervisory Commission (NSC) in 2018. The NSC merges with CCDI and other anti-corruption agencies such as the Department of Supervision, the Anti-Corruption Bureau, and the Office Against Dereliction of Duty and is positioned as the state's leading anti-corruption agency. As a government agency, leading officials of the NSC are appointed by the National People's Congress. While the political institution and power structure remain unchanged, how effective the newly restructured anti-corruption system would respond to and cope with political interferences of varying degrees remain to be seen. This shall be discussed later in more detail.

CCP Efforts to CrackDown on Corruption Prior to the 18th CCP National Congress

There had been altogether four major anti-corruption campaigns in the post-Mao era. The first one began in 1982, the purpose of which was to crack down on rampant economic crimes such as smuggling, graft, bribery, speculation, etc. By September 1982, of 136,024 cases that had been investigated, more than 44,000 were brought to trial with 26,000 individuals sentenced.[26] The second was the 1983 Party rectification campaign, which had lasted for three years and was aimed to accomplish four tasks: "1) the achievement of ideological unity, or promoting general agreement with the reform line; 2) the rectification of the Party's style of work, or putting an end to unhealthy practices; 3) the strengthening of discipline; and 4) the purification of Party organization, or getting rid of those who by current standards had committed particularly egregious crimes in the past".[27] Corrupt and decadent elements within the Party had committed a variety of malpractices to such an extent that, as acclaimed by the Central Committee, the modernization programs would be "jeopardized", the CCP's public image "impaired", and "the public's confidence in the superiority of the socialist system undermined". Apart from anti-corruption, the CCP leadership also intended to purify the

[26] Zengke He, 101.

[27] McCormick, 166.

Party using other approaches—correcting the leftist and rightist tendencies, opposing paternalism, factionalism, anarchism, and liberalism, and combing out elements who had taken advantage of and benefitted from the Cultural Revolution. Unlike its counterparts in Mao's era, this rectification did not adopt Mao's conventional means of "mass line" but was more institutionally oriented. All Party members were subject to the re-registration of the Party membership at the final stage of the movement; those who were unable to meet the membership standards were expelled from the Party.[28] During the period of 1983–1986, a significant number of Party members were disciplined, among whom leading cadres at or above the county level numbered more than 35,000.[29] In the meantime, a series of directives and circulars were issued by the center, strictly prohibiting the Party and government agencies from appropriating public funds or loans to set up enterprises and disallowing the Party and government cadres including retired cadres to engage in commercial activities and official profiteering. To further push forward the campaign, in January 1986, the CCP leadership held an 8000-member plenary session and raised its grave concern that "corruption was endangering the Party's survival". To curb the impetus of corruption and calm down public resentment, the then Premier Zhao Ziyang put forward six measures prohibiting:

1. purchasing and exchanging of import cars among state and Party officials;
2. sending Party and government officials on unnecessary visits abroad;
3. publicly funded personal tours within the country;
4. offering luxurious and unnecessary gifts and entertainment to visitors;
5. officials from earning incomes in excess of what they received in official salaries and welfare payments;
6. officials, their spouses, and children from taking advantage of their status to earn money by running a business.[30]

[28] Ibid., 165–173.

[29] Zengke He, 101.

[30] Lo, 55–56.

In addition, the CCP leadership warned that all corrupt officials, including senior ones, and their offspring were subject to tough punishment including the death penalty if they were found guilty of serious offenses. Following the plenary session, actions were taken to crack down on corrupt officials including children of the old veterans at the top of the hierarchy. Though noticeable efforts had been made, irregularities were still not under control; rampant corruption, especially official profiteering, was still prevailing and had thus caused widespread discontent among citizens. The findings of several public opinion polls conducted between 1987 and 1989 put official corruption at the top of the list of serious social problems identified by the respondents. Under such circumstances, the CCP leadership "for the first time put the problem of corruption on its agenda" by holding a three-day politburo meeting in early June of 1988 to discuss the challenges. The meeting concluded with the resolution of launching another nationwide anti-corruption campaign aimed at improving the Party's legitimacy and public image, facilitating the progress of the reform and enhancing the cleanness and efficiency of the government.[31]

In collaboration, the Standing Committee of the National People's Congress, the State Council, ministries concerned, the Supreme People's Court, DICs, and some provinces either enacted laws and regulations or issued directives and circulars in a joint effort to curb specific corrupt practices and improper behavior. This period also witnessed "Deng Xiaoping's attack on several prominent state-run trading and investment conglomerates, including the one that had been affiliated with his eldest son".[32] A series of countermeasures against corruption were initiated and adopted by the authorities, among which several major ones are worth mentioning. First of all, as mentioned above, the establishment of the Ministry of Supervision and its counterparts at provincial, city, and county levels in 1987 institutionally strengthened the internal supervisory mechanism within the government. Another institutional measure was the establishment of Economic Crime Reporting Centers and Hotlines throughout the country, aimed to encourage citizens to report cases of corruption

[31] Gong, *The Politics of Corruption in Contemporary China: An Analysis of Policy Outcomes*, 135–136.

[32] Mark Findlay and Thomas Chiu Chor-Wing, "Sugar Coated Bullets: Corruption and the New Economic Order in China," *Contemporary Crisis* No.13 (1989): 151–153.

through various means and avenues. Those who had submitted important and valuable information would be rewarded. Secondly, efforts were made to curb inflation and rectify economic disorder caused by either unsophisticated reform policies or corruption. Countermeasures of the sort included price inspection and control as well as rectification of administrative corporations that were believed to be the key source of official profiteering. The crackdown on bureaucratic companies was intensified in the aftermath of the Tiananmen Movement mainly as a strategic manifestation of the authorities' determination to fight corruption so as to offset the negative impact of the event on public opinion. By the end of 1991, according to statistics, a total of 105,137 (35.2 percent) firms throughout the country had been ordered to close, and nearly 50,000 government officials, including retired officials who held posts in administrative companies, had resigned from their positions.[33]

Coupled with the process of rectifying companies were the tasks of investigation and rectification of the involvement of senior officials' children, retired cadres, and the army in illicit commercial activities and official profiteering. As a result, cadres holding concurrent positions in bureaucratic companies and retired cadres with residual powers were ordered to resign from any posts in state-run or foreign-funded enterprises, and military personnel were prohibited from engaging in commerce and trade.[34] Besides, measures were taken to curb the tendency of lavish spending of public funds. Government agencies and state-owned enterprises were ordered to control the convening of nationwide conferences and anniversary celebrations, the holding of press conferences, as well as banquets, gift-giving, etc. In the meantime, detailed stipulations regarding the duration and locality of conferences, dishes, wine, and even soft drinks served at conferences came into effect. For instance, national conferences were prohibited from holding in holiday resorts during holiday seasons, and conference meals were limited to five courses—four-dish-one-soup; some local governments began to impose taxes on lavish banquets. There were also strict restrictions on public consumption of luxurious goods, such as vehicles, rugs, color TVs,

[33] Wenbin Chen, 251.

[34] Lo, 61–62.

etc. A work unit was able to purchase the controlled luxury goods only with the approval of the authorized government agencies.[35]

While further reducing cadres' privileges and intensifying corruption crackdown, the authorities also beefed up propaganda to publicize major cases of corruption in the hope of "killing one to warn one hundred" corrupt elements. Several cases uncovered in the rectification of companies revealed that managers and officials of administrative corporations, by making use of their official status and social connections, had been involved in official profiteering in raw materials, graft, taking and extorting bribes, and cheating.[36] Another publicized case concerning five "high-profile" corporations, one of which was under the control of Deng's eldest son, revealed that these five corporations and their hundreds of subsidiaries "had been engaged in illicit activities such as tax evasion, speculation in productive materials, and black market transaction in foreign currencies".[37] A number of high-ranking officials at the provincial and ministerial level were disciplined or criminally charged for malpractices such as taking bribes, lavishly spending public funds, trading power for sexual favors, abusing power for illicit gains for their offspring and relatives, etc. Cases of this sort involved or implicated a deputy minister of railway transport, the governor of Jiangxi province, the governor of Hainan province, and the vice chairman of Xingjiang Autonomous Region.[38]

An important characteristic of the anti-corruption campaign in the late 1980s was the large-scale utilization of the strategy of "confession and accusation". On 15 August 1989, the Supreme People's Court and the Supreme People's Procuratorate issued an official announcement, calling for those who had committed corrupt acts and economic crimes to confess their wrongdoing by October 31, 1989, in exchange for lenient treatment. The announcement exerted considerable psychological pressure on suspects of corruption. During the stipulated period (78 days), more than 36,000 individuals "surrendered themselves", among whom included 742 cadres at the county or division level, 40 at the bureau

[35] Ibid., 63.

[36] Wenbin Chen, 254–255.

[37] Gong, 141–142.

[38] Wenbin Chen, 268–270.

level, and 1 at the ministerial level.[39] The immediate aftermath of the Tiananmen Movement in June 1989 marked the high tide of the third anti-corruption campaign. In 1989, according to official statistics, cases of graft and bribery handled by procuratorial agencies throughout the country numbered to 116,763, of which 58,926 cases were filed and investigated. The investigations had led to the arrest of 20,791 suspects and more than 400 million yuan grafted funds were eventually recovered. Between January and September 1990, cases of a similar nature had increased by 1.39 times as compared to the same period in the previous year, and 526 million yuan worth of grafted funds and items were recovered.

The fourth anti-corruption campaign began with the convening of the Second Plenary Session of the Central Commission for Discipline Inspection in August 1993 and had lasted throughout the 1990s. While Deng's southern tour in 1992 took economic reform to the center stage, a fiercer tide of "business fad" and rampant corruption spread across the nation. As mentioned earlier, although numerous regulations, directives, and stipulations with respect to corruption control and government integrity had been issued since the advent of the reform, the impetus of corruption had not yet been put under control. Injunctions and documents issued in the period were found to be similar or even contradictory to those in the previous years. To curb the surge of bureaucratic companies between 1992 and 1993, for example, two central directives were issued in June 1992 and June 1993 respectively to prohibit Party and government agencies at or above the county level from setting up their own companies and to disallow officials at or above the county level to engage in trade. The State Council issued four circulars or directives between December 1991 and October 1993 restressing the stipulations of prohibiting feasting and gift-giving at public expense as well as publicly funded domestic and overseas tours in the name of observation and inspection.[40] To combat the malpractice of the "three arbitraries" (三乱) and accounting irregularities, the authorities took measures to enforce financial regulations and accounting rules to curb the illicit tendency of administrative power abuse and misuse and squandering of extra-budgetary funds drawn from arbitrary fines, levies, and charges. In subsequent years, however, there

[39] Gong, 144.

[40] Wenbin Chen, 289–298.

had been other legal or quasi-legal moves for corruption control that are worth mentioning here. The institutional measure, as mentioned above, concerns the establishment of the Anti-Graft General Bureau under the jurisdiction of the Supreme People's Procuratorate in 1995 and its counterparts at the provincial and local levels in the subsequent year.[41] Other important measures include the establishment of the income declaration system for officials at or above the county or division level, and the enaction of provisional regulations governing the selection and appointment of leading cadres. In addition, other laws and regulations regarding corruption control and government uprightness were also in the preparatory process.[42]

Crackdown on "Tigers and Flies": Anti-Corruption Campaign in the Xi Regime

The 18th National Congress of the CCP in November 2012 marked the transition of the paramount state power from Hu Jintao to Xi Jinping, and the beginning of a new regime characterized by fierce crackdown on bureaucratic corruption and apparent deviation and retreat from the course of continued liberalization and development of the Chinese economy and society. The anti-corruption campaign, carried out under the aegis of Xi, is claimed to be the largest organized anti-graft effort in the history of the PRC. Upon being sworn into office, Xi vowed to take action to clamp down on "tigers and flies", namely, high-ranking officials and petty public servants alike. While following similar anti-corruption modes and strategies of the previous regimes, such as denunciations and slogans, heavy reliance on punitive measures, Party rectification and purge, ideological rectification and moral exhortations, and prominently displayed miscreants, Xi's strike on corruption differs from previous anti-corruption campaigns in various aspects. First of all, Xi has made more effective and frequent use of the institutional approach known as "central inspection teams" during his first term between 2012 and 2017. Commanded and coordinated by Xi's right-hand man, Wang Qishan, a member of the Politburo Standing Committee and the head of the CCDI, several rounds of central inspection teams had been dispatched to

[41] Xiping Tang, 94.

[42] Mingbo Liu, 8–9.

provinces and metropolises to collect local tip-offs and to undertake in-depth audits into the conduct of high-ranking officials and the disciplinary and legal compliances of the institutions. The first batch of the provinces for inspection included Jiangxi, Inner Mongolia, Hubei, Guizhou, and Chongqing, followed by the second round of inspection teams sent off in November 2013, touring the provinces of Shanxi, Jilin, Anhui, Yunnan, Hunan, and Guangdong, as well as the Xinhua News Agency, the Ministry of Commerce, and the SOE overseeing the construction of the Three Gorges Dam.[43] The third and fourth rounds of inspections encompassed the remaining provinces, major cities, and various central ministries, public institutions, and SOEs. In total, the central authorities had undertaken 12 rounds of nationwide inspections since the 18th National Congress of the CCP and had scrutinized almost all provinces and major public institutions and state-owned enterprises. There were cases in which the inspection teams unexpectedly swung around to pursue further investigations, often caught local authorities off guard. Meanwhile, the institutional model and practice of inspection teams have been widely adopted and followed by provincial authorities to inspect municipalities and public organizations in their jurisdictions. By April 2017, over 8300 localities, public institutions, and SOEs had been inspected and audited by provincial inspection teams. This approach proves to be effective in uncovering cases of corruption and economic crimes at a local level as central inspection teams are generally in an authoritative position to resist and curb local political interference and to encourage local whistleblowers to come forward for tip-off.

Secondly, the breadth and depth of Xi's anti-corruption campaign seem to be unprecedented in comparison to its counterparts in previous regimes and have thus produced encouraging results so far. As suggested above, the breadth of the inspection coverage as well as the frequency of inspection team dispatches were both unprecedented. According to statistics by the CCDI, during the period of 2012–2017, DICs and departments of supervision nationwide had filed and investigated 1.545 million cases and disciplinarily sanctioned 1.537 million officials for wrongdoing and corruption, among whom 58,000 cases/persons had been handed over to judicial organs for criminal investigation. Between January 2014 and August 2017, over 6100 Party branches and over 300 DICs nationwide

[43] "Anticorruption Campaign Under Xi Jinping," *Wikipedia*. https://en.wikipedia.org/wiki/Anticorruption_campaign_under_Xi_Jinping.

were investigated and held accountable for violation of Party stipulations and state regulations. A total of over 60,000 Party-leading officials nationwide were investigated and held accountable for improper and negligent acts and malpractices. Thirdly, as vowed by Xi to hunt down "tigers", Xi's anti-corruption campaign is featured by toppling of high-ranking Party-state officials, and it is record-setting as measured by both level/rank and absolute number. During the five-year period, over 70,000 officials at and above county level were investigated and punished, among whom included 440 high-ranking officials at the provincial/ministerial level (among them there were 43 Central Committee Members and Alternate Central Committee Members and 9 CCDI Members), 8900 officials at the prefecture/bureau level, and over 63,000 officials at the county/division level.[44] A record number of top-level leading officials were also rounded up for corruption, including members of the Politburo and the Central Military Commission as well as the vice chairman of the National CPPCC. (Refer to Chapter 3 for detail.) Of particular significance was the toppling of Zhou Yongkang, which made him the first member of the Politburo Standing Committee (PSC) ever charged and convicted of corruption since the end of the Cultural Revolution and had thus broken the implicit rule of "PSC criminal immunity" that had been the norm for over three decades. Also unprecedented is Xi's sweeping crackdown on corruption in the military, which has led to the downfall of approximately 90 generals. The vast majority of corruption cases involving high-ranking officials at or above the provincial/ministerial level were brought to light by Xi's "tiger" hunting campaign in 2012. Lastly, the authorities have been making efforts to undertake structural changes and reforms to further reduce rent-seeking loopholes and incentives by eliminating unnecessary requirements and procedures for administrative approvals at both central and local levels. For instance, between 2013 and August 2014, the State Council (Cabinet) either eliminated mandatory requirements or decentralized authority over administrative approval

[44] China Academy of Discipline Inspection and Supervision, "Comprehensively and strictly govern the Party," *baidu wenku*. https://wenku.baidu.com/view/c63343f051e2524de518964bcf84b9d528ea2c09.html (accessed January 3, 2021).

"Do you know how many problems have been revealed under the complete discipline inspection coverage of provincial and municipal Party committees since the 18th National Congress of the Communist Party of China?" (in Chinese), *CCDI and Ministry of Supervision*, June 9, 2017. http://www.ccdi.gov.cn/special/zyxszt/bjzl_zyxs/201706/t20170622_101538.html (accessed January 18, 2021).

of 632 items and projects. At the provincial level, similar reforms are also underway. Take Henan province as an example; between 2013 and 2014, the provincial authorities abolished and decentralized requirements and procedures for administrative approval of 85 and 66 items and projects respectively.[45] Changes of this sort are part of the Party-state's continued commitment and efforts to rein in governmental intervention in economic and social affairs in order to block or eliminate sources of bureaucratic corruption in the long run.

The CCDI, as the leading and coordinating agency for the nationwide anti-corruption campaigns, has undergone changes and reforms from both a structural and regulatory perspective under Xi's aegis. As observed by the state media and some observers within China, the CCDI started with measures and reforms to strengthen and consolidate its independence in the Party-state apparatus under the jurisdiction of the Hu-Wen administration and has continued to enact further reforms in the Xi regime with the aim of transforming itself into a "bona fide control and auditing organization governed by a sophisticated set of rules and regulations to ensure professionalism and procedural fairness". There is a widely held consensus that the CCDI has significantly extended its power and influence since Xi embarked upon his crackdown on corruption in late 2012 and is now better positioned to be able to carry out its own investigations that are much less likely to encounter local political resistance and interference.[46]

While Xi's fight against corruption has taken officials and observers alike by surprise in terms of its scope and intensity, as mentioned, there are contending views with respect to the true intent and the political and economic effects of Xi's anti-corruption drive. Some Western observers hold that the campaign is politically motivated and aimed at purging Xi's own political rivals, and they view corrupt allegations "as the latter-day weapon of choice in the winner-takes-all power struggles that the party has always suffered". Xi is criticized for relying on the Party's internal regulations rather than acting within the state legal framework in carrying out the "political purge". Others perceive Xi's anti-corruption campaign as a manifestation of factional struggle, as the campaign is suspected to

[45] https://wenku.baidu.com/view/db6129ad9f3143323968011ca300a6c30c22f13a.html.

[46] "Anticorruption Campaign under Xi Jinping," *Wikipedia*. https://en.wikipedia.org/wiki/Anticorruption_campaign_under_Xi_Jinping.

target members of the elite who are not part of the "princelings" (太子党), to which Xi, Wang Qishan and others belong. It is contended that between 2013 and 2015 almost all the high-ranking officials rounded up for corruption were from commoner backgrounds, mainly peasant origins. Still, another explanation argues that the campaign is aimed to extinguish vestiges of influence of Party "elders" who intend to intervene in state affairs and decision-making process in their retirement. Of the particular and also prominent example cited in this regard is the former paramount leader Jiang Zeming, who is criticized for the rise in patronage appointments in military and Party-government apparatus in his administration. Patron–client relationship and personal loyalty, rather than merit, had become the foremost factor for consideration of promotions. Jiang's refusal to relinquish his influence years after he had formally stepped down is said to have not only negatively impacted the ruling of his successor Hu Jintao but also affected the planning and implementation of the reform agenda at the time. While Xi's campaign is credited by some observers to be instrumental to stamp out patronage and factionalism in the Party-state, Xi's appointments of the members of his Zhejiang-Fujian clique to key leading posts in Beijing, Shanghai, and the central authority in recent years ironically contradicts with this argument. On the other hand, some scholars and observers in both China and abroad dismiss the hypothesis of political purge and factionalism cleanup, and credit Xi's campaign to having "the effect of truly curbing corrupt practices at all levels of government". Still others view the campaign to be part of a wider agenda of systemic reform, aimed to pursue "some much-needed 'clean-up' of entrenched and vested interests before pushing ahead with much larger structural reforms".[47]

[47] Ibid.

CHAPTER 8

What Are at Play and What Should Be Faulted For?

Why is corruption more rampant and widespread in underdeveloped states in comparison to Western democracies? Are politicians and public officials in developing nations more prone to corruption due to inherent human moral problems and degeneration as claimed by the moralists? Does corruption go side by side with the modernization process in countries like China as described by the revisionists? Do the culture and value systems of a traditional society play more important roles in the prevalence of corruption in society? Or do institutional factors such as political, economic, or organizational structures contribute more to corruption in these countries? Answers to these questions, however, represent various approaches to this issue, and each explains one dimension of its complex genesis. In the context of modern China, as mentioned in *Introduction*, there also exist various explanations for the formation of corruption. While Western scholars mainly take an institutional approach to probing its origin, the CCP tends to blame and denounce the ethical deficiency and moral degeneration of corrupt officials. Analysis of causes of corruption has important policy implications as the determination of geneses of corruption contributes to the formulation of anti-corruption strategies and preventive measures. As we all know, solutions derived from a biased and non-holistic approach will likely cause distortional consequences to socioeconomic development and the stability of the state in the long run. Before we proceed to discuss the genesis of corruption in reform China in

F. C. Sun, *An Ineluctable Political Destiny*,
https://doi.org/10.1007/978-981-99-3146-0_8

more detail, we begin with a general discussion of a variety of factors that are conducive to corruption in both developing and developed nations.

Over the past two decades, empirical studies of various scales have been undertaken to analyze and determine the causes and consequences of corruption. According to these studies, the main determining factors for corruption include (1) the size and structure of governments; (2) the democracy and the political system; (3) the quality of institutions; (4) economic freedom/ openness of economy; (5) salaries of civil service; (6) press freedom and judiciary; (7) cultural determinants; (8) percentage of women in the labor force and in parliament; (9) colonial heritage.[1] An empirical study on political institutions and accountability by Daniel Lederman et al. presents comparable observations and draws similar conclusions. For example, the study concludes that political institutions and political macrostructure—related to the political system, balance of powers, electoral competitiveness, and so on—are crucial determining factors to the incidence of corruption. Corruption tends to decrease systematically with democracy, parliamentary systems, democratic stability, and freedom of press.[2] The study points out that states of French and socialist legal tradition are more prone to corruption, since corruption is negatively associated with political competition and individual accountability. Besides, corruption is found to be directly related to public policy variables such as relative public wages and openness.[3] In a cross-national study on the causes of corruption in 2000, Daniel Treisman, while upholding to a large extent the aforementioned arguments, found the sizes of the effect may be different under various conditions. For example, he argues that democracy may not necessarily correlated to clean government, but the duration of the democracy is an important determining factor to the level of corruption in a state as "the regression estimates suggest a painfully slow process by which democracy undermines the foundation of corruption". In his empirical modeling, he found that countries with at least 40 years of consecutive democracy

[1] Dominik Enste and Christina Heldman, "Causes and Consequences of Corruption: An Overview of Empirical Results," *Cologne Institute for Economic Research, IW Report* (2017): 3.

[2] Daniel Lederman, Norman V. Loayza, and Rodrigo R. Soares, "Accountability and Corruption: Political Institutions Matter," *Economics & Politics* Vol. 17 (March 2005): 27.

[3] Ibid., 7.

behind them enjoyed a relatively lower level of corruption. His study also lends support to the argument that the process of economic development reduces corruption—"presumably through the rationalization of public and private roles and the spread of education"; however, corruption does not necessarily prevent economic growth while other factors are conducive. Treisman also points out that a state's cultural or institutional traditions can exert stronger influence than current state policies over the incidence and level of corruption, and federal states in general are more prone to corruption than unitary ones, controlling for the level of economic development.[4]

Wei's study in 2000 affirms some of the arguments and conclusions discussed above and emphasizes the importance of eliminating or reducing institutionalized opportunity of rent-seeking in government. "The more discretion government officials have over the operation of business or lives of citizenry, the more likely corruption would occur and flourish, other things being equal". Government over-regulation induces rent-seeking and corruption. Similarly, the size of government expenditures and the procedures of government funds allocation are positively correlated to the incidence and level of government corruption. Other systemic and institutional contributing factors to corruption include the lack of an independent and impartial judicial system, "democracy that serves the dual purpose of throwing corrupt officials out of power by the populace and protecting those individuals and organizations that dare to expose corrupt officials", and an independent and free press. Wei also echoes concerns about the recruitment and promotion of government officials as well as compensation for public servants, arguing that recruiting and promoting government officials on a merit basis and paying them a salary competitive to private sector alternative help to attract and retain high-quality, moral civil servants. Nepotism and patronage lead to corruption as the distorted success of career depends on advantages gained by connection and illicit payoffs rather than merit.[5]

Obviously, an atomistic or one-sided approach to the analysis of corruption like the one adopted by the CCP seems to be simplistic as

[4] Daniel Treisman, "The Causes of Corruption: A Cross-National Study," *Journal of Public Economics* 76 (2000): 438–441.

[5] Shang-jin Wei, "Corruption in Economic Development: Beneficial Grease, Minor Annoyance, or Major Obstacle?" 16–23. http://documents1.worldbank.org/curated/en/175291468765621959/pdf/multi-page.pdf (accessed February 8, 2021).

the genesis of corruption is a complicated process interwoven with multifaceted contributory factors and variables. According to Rose-Ackerman and Palifka, causes of corruption may be classified into three categories: structural (incentives), institutional, and personal ethics. "Corruption occurs at the intersection of situation-specific incentive, society-wide institutions, and personal ethics".[6] In this chapter, we begin our analytical work by reviewing and discussing the CCP's perceptions and diagnoses of the causes of the malfeasances, followed by a holistic approach to looking into structural factors such as discretion, monopolistic power, and lack of supervision and enforcement, and institutional factors such as political system, legal structure, the rule of law, as well as the Chinese tradition and culture at large. We suggest that the interactions of structural, institutional, sociocultural, and moral causal factors catalyzed by China's economic reform and modernization process have jointly attributed to the incidence and level of bureaucratic corruption in the post-Mao era. This holistic analytical approach has important policy implications as it presumably leads to a similarly holistic approach to formulating anti-corruption policies and corruption prevention measures that would help to deter and prevent bureaucratic corruption in the long run.

8.1 An Orthodox Approach and Theory of Corruption

As mentioned in *Introduction*, in the early years of the reform, the CCP leadership took a mainly ideological-oriented approach to trace the sources of official corruption. Chen Yun, first secretary of the Central DIC, viewed corruption as the inevitable consequences of the openness of the country to the West, and blamed "a bourgeois decadent ideology" for "seriously corrupting Party conduct and social conduct".[7] While the CCP's analyses of the causes of corruption have become more comprehensive and in-depth over the years, its early views of the malaise, however, seemed to be superficial and even simply denunciations rather than rational analyses. There are other official explanations that see corruption as personal moral problems of Party cadres or as

[6] Rose-Ackerman, 29.

[7] Stephen K. Ma, 41.

"manifestation of a serious impurity in party spirit".[8] This view attributes the genesis of corruption to officials' personal moral cultivations, inferior personal qualities, deteriorated ethics, and distorted values. According to this explanation, officials' displacement in value and money worship mentality in a new market economy often induces a strong impulse to corruption. Frequently cited motives and justifications for corruption in state media include compensation for low government remunerations, investment to generate desired financial returns, family financial needs, collective or organizational interests, hedonism, indulgence emulation, etc.

With the opening-up and transition to a market economy, a dramatic shift in mentality from political campaigns and ideological education to economic priorities had triggered an explosive social frenzy for money and material comforts. So had shifted the tone of official ideology and propaganda, which began to openly advocate citizens to enrich themselves but stop short of clarifying how to achieve this end in a legitimate way. This overemphasis on economic goals but neglect of appropriate legitimate, ethical, and legal means is blamed to cause moral confusions, ethical degeneration, and reckless corruption in the reform era. The increasingly diversified value system and people's strong desire to get rich quickly, as viewed by the CCP leadership, acted as strong inducements to rent-seeking and corruption in government. As the principle of exchange at equal values in the market economy was introduced to the political, social, and cultural realms, it was distorted and adopted for illicit practices such as influence peddling, power-money exchange, office buying and selling, etc. In this sense, introduction of and transition to a market economy are generally faulted for the distortion of Party conduct and social norms as well as degeneration of morality in government and society. Deng Xiaoping and Hu Qili called for Party cadres to be highly alert to "ushering in corrosive ideologies of capitalism and its values suggesting that money talks".[9] This view holds that the ideology of the exploiting class and egoism induce corruption as egoism incents people to harm others only to benefit themselves. This explanation seems to be the prevailing orthodox mainstream elucidation of corruption held by the Party leadership and leftist scholars within China. In his address to the Second Plenary

[8] Yan Sun, 775; Myers, 198.

[9] Ibid.

Session of CCDI in January 1998, Jiang Zeming faulted corruption for the ideology of exploitation, asserting that the phenomenon of corruption "is essentially the product of the exploitation system and exploiting class". It asserts that while China brings in trade, investment, and innovation, it has also brought in the decadent ideology and lifestyle of the bourgeoisie. What the orthodox view intends to convey is that in a capitalist world, everything can be traded for money; money is a symbol of success and a manifestation of happiness. This school of thought holds that Western values and money fetishism are the root causes of extreme individualism, extreme liberalism, and extreme egoism in Chinese society. In this sense, capitalism is blamed for the confusion of norms and values, the deterioration of morality, the crisis of ideal and faith, and more importantly, the genesis and prevalence of corruption.

Corruption, as a social malady, is much older than bourgeoisie, and abuse of official power had emerged in ancient China over three thousand years ago. It lacks reasonable grounds to simply assert corruption as capitalist wrongdoing. If so, how could one explain and justify the relative cleanness of Western bureaucracies and societies where the so-called "capitalism" underlies Western economies and political systems? On the other hand, Mao's new regime had crushed and ultimately eliminated the so-called exploration class since the 1950s, and the Party's official approaches therefore fail to explain why corruption in socialist China is still originated from the exploration system and its ideology that had been allegedly eradicated. Moreover, while a corrupt official's immorality and distorted ethics and values induce corruption, as criticized by the orthodox theory, many of them, however, held relatively high standards of morality and professional ethics when they were promoted by the CCP to important and leading positions. Overemphasis of an official's subjective and internal factors in tracing the sources of corruption can be misleading as it largely neglects the inducing effects and influence of objective and external factors, as well as the economic, political, and social contexts. The frequency of corruption has indeed increased with the introduction and progress of the economic reform programs, but it would not be impartial to simply fault the reform for the incidence and level of the malfeasance. Corruption, as Huntington points out, is a by-product of the modernization process of traditional societies. The economic reform in China, as in the cases of other developing societies that are embarking on modernization, opens up opportunities and loopholes for rent-seeking and corruption. In other words, the reform per se is not the crucial determinant of corruption, but rather, the external one that provides certain conditions in which the malaise breeds and grows. It is true that the incidence and graveness of corruption in the Mao era were of limited extent only due to the widespread use of ruthless political campaigns and Party rectification measures, but the approach of class struggle in Mao's time can no longer be utilized in the Post-Mao era due to its disastrous political and economic consequences, as witnessed in the Cultural Revolution, and its ideological collision with the democratic-oriented values as advocated by the reform per se. As a matter of fact, in the aftermath of the Cultural Revolution, many citizens and Party-state officials had obviously lost their faith in the communist ideology and government, and as a result, they switched instead to extreme egoism. The authorities' efforts of moral education for Party members and government officials were viewed by many as a total failure because the official ideology of "working hard but living simply" was increasingly deemed irrelevant to the daily life of the financially worse off public officials. As more and more people have enriched themselves through illegitimate and corrupt means, it has become more difficult for government officials to resist the temptation of rent-seeking through power abuse and corruption. Political morality education, in a sense, has had at best very limited effect on constraining the behavior and conduct of public officials. On the contrary, as illustrated in many cases in the previous chapters, structural and societal factors tend to have a much stronger influence over the behavior and conduct of Party-state officials. For example, the lack of business ethics and commercial morality in the transition phase of the reform induces corruption. While new market-oriented business norms and ethics are to be established, in the "vacuum" of such standards and practices, collusions between unscrupulous businessmen and venal officials and corruption prevail.[10]

[10] Zengke He, 254–255.

8.2 Structural Determinants and Incentives of Corruption

Now we proceed to explore the genesis of official corruption in the post-Mao era using a systemic and holistic approach in contrast to the CCP's one-sided perspective and overemphasis on ideology and personal immorality. As indicated in studies on the causes of corruption, apart from subjective contributory factors such as morality and personal ethics, there are objective factors that are conducive to corruption. In the context of socialist China, there exists a structural type of corruption described as "irregularity", "malpractice", "misconduct" or "disciplinary offense". This "gray" or "white" type of corruption is a distinctive feature of corruption or irregularities in the socialist and post-socialist states such as China and Russia among others. As evidenced in cases of corruption, state officials' unconstrained discretionary power over regulatory affairs and public investment provides them with ample and lucrative rent-seeking incentives and opportunities, whereas these seemingly unlimited discretions are largely originated from structural deficiencies, faulty institutions, as well as laxity in supervision and disciplinary enforcement. The dominant political system, the overwhelming public ownership of state assets and resources, the lack of an independent judiciary, as well as the absence of a mechanism of checks and balances are all crucial institutional factors that have inherently foreordained the nature, scope, patterns, and severity of bureaucratic corruption in post-Mao China. External factors such as the economic reform and the modernization process, in our view, have functioned largely as a powerful and influential catalyst that has helped to trigger and unleash widespread and rampant corruption in the reform era.

We begin by examining the structural causes, followed by institutional factors including culture as geneses of corruption in contemporary China. While certain patterns of corruption cause harmful effects and consequences, in the meantime, causes and consequences can work both ways, i.e., some consequences may also be the geneses of certain forms of corruption. For example, corruption causes inequality in wealth distribution; high inequality in wealth distribution, on the other hand, motivates state officials to rent public power in return for illicit payoffs in an attempt to compensate themselves for the poor remuneration of public office. Another example concerns the lack of trust in government as widespread official corruption erodes citizens' trust and confidence in state and public institutions. On the other hand, citizens' and businesses' widely held beliefs and expectations of a corruption-riddled government motivate them to pay to either avoid red tape or speed up the routine approval process.

8.3 Structural Defects Inherent in a Semi-Planned and Semi-Market Economy

Structural factors may be the most direct and important determinants that have attributed to widespread corruption in reform China. The unsound economic structure is deemed a key source of irregularities and malfeasances. The expanding role of government in economy often results in more government intervention in the socioeconomic spheres, which in turn expands the scope of government regulation over many microeconomic activities. Increasing bureaucratic control over the economy also provides bureaucrats with greater incentives and more opportunities for rent-seeking and corruption. The expansionary discretionary public power can serve as a "bargaining mechanism to induce the payments of bribes". This mechanism can even be exploited to the extent that "public officials would do nothing without bribes and payoffs".[11]

Excessive State Control and Intervention in Market Economy

In the pre-reform era, various aspects of the economy such as resource distribution, production, and marketing were under the tight control of the state planning system. In addition to economy, the state also placed various aspects of people's political and social life under its watch. Although the highly centralized state planning and distribution mechanism had worked to constrain and suppress the vitality and development of the economy, its rigid control and unitary means of resource distribution, on the other hand, had deterred the genesis and spread of corruption. Another major deterring force against corruption in Mao's era was the non-stop ideological cleansing and cruel political campaigns against the so-called enemies of proletariat and the ideology and behavior

[11] Hope, "Administrative Corruption and Administrative Reform in Developing States", 131.

of the exploiting and bourgeois class. The relative cleanness of the Party-state and the society in this era was obviously achieved and maintained at the cost of economic development as well as the expense of people's political rights and social freedoms.

As a reform, in particular urban economic reform, was phased in to revitalize the stagnant economy, the CCP leadership initiated a series of measures to promote the private economy in both rural and urban areas, granted local governments and enterprises more autonomy and decision-making power, and loosened price control over a wide range of products and materials. However, the leadership's emphasis on the role and functions of the market in Chinese economy did not imply that the command economy would completely give way to market economy. On the contrary, the state still controlled many key factors of production and raw materials, and still regulated and controlled many aspects of the operation of enterprises. Market competition and its mechanism of resource distribution were often overtaken and distorted by administrative power and irrational governmental interventions. In a distorted market economy businesses and enterprises tend to circumvent market competition in pursuit of shortcuts to maximize profits. The administrative forms of resource allocation such as governmental approvals, permits, licenses, and quotas are typical means and forms of arbitrary governmental intervention in a market economy and are generally well sought by businesses to win out over competitors for more gains. The politically powerful thus trade public power for money whereas the economic elite rent power for higher profits.

As pointed out, poor and unsophisticated regulations are conducive to official corruption. As evidenced in the reform era, codes, and regulations were often too broadly defined to be appropriate to specific situations, rendering middle and lower-level officials more flexibilities in dealing with concrete conditions and greater latitude for abuses of public duties.[12] The more the governmental interventions, the higher the rents, the stronger the rent-seeking motivations, and the more rampant the official corruption. This is a vicious cycle that prevails throughout China's reform journey. Even as the economic reforms had advanced to new stages, governmental control and intervention had diminished

[12] Zengke He, *The Political Cancer: The Issue of Corruption in Developing States* (in Chinese) (Beijing: The Central Publishing House of Translation and Editing, 1995), 29–30.

to only a limited extent. In the post-1992 period, with an expanding private sector and increasingly diversified ownership forms, the share of the state economy had shrunk to approximately 40 percent of the aggregate economy; however, the resources the state controlled and distributed still constituted over 70 percent of the Chinese economy.[13] This ratio is even presumably higher in recent years as the Xi-Li administration has apparently shifted away from the direction and course of the reform by placing higher priorities on and allocating more resources to large state monopolies and enterprises. This is an obvious move intended to enable China's mega SOEs to compete with the United States and other world powers on the economic and military fronts.

The Dual-Track Pricing System

The dual-track pricing system, a structural consequence of the co-existence of the planned and market economies in the reform era, was a prime cause of widespread corruption as it rendered plenty of incentives and opportunities for rent-seeking and corruption. The course of the economic reform between the late 1970s and 2000s was marked by three phases of the market reform in which planned and market economies for various goods co-existed in the interim and then the market economy gradually replaced the planned mechanism. The first phase saw the establishment of consumer goods market, which began in late 1970s and lasted until the mid-1980s. The second phase focused on market reform for producer goods, and the transition from the planned economy to a producer goods market completed in the early 1990s. The transition and establishment of a factor-production market characterized by a stock market, future market, real estate market, and capital market in Phase 3 began in the early 1990s and concluded in the 2000s. As discussed, the dual-track pricing system derived from the co-existence of the planned and market economies in each of the transitional processes had resulted in significant or even dramatic differentials between the planned (official) price and the market price of the same goods. It was estimated that in 1987 the aggregate rent resulted from price discrepancies, including the dual-track pricing systems in consumer and producer goods, credit rates,

[13] Yan Meng and Li, 107.

and exchange rates reached 200 billion yuan or 20 percent of the national income for the year.[14]

The dual-track pricing system first for short supplies and then for land, bank credits, and public contracts are classical examples that demonstrate the evolution, intensification, and consequences of official corruption brought about by the structurally defective political and economic arrangements. Due to the backwardness of the Chinese economy and some historical factors, the supply–demand imbalance for some important raw materials and commodities (as in the case of the 1980s) and factors of production such as capital (as in the case of the 1990s) had long been in existence. This imbalance had been further exacerbated by the mushrooming of private enterprises, rural industries, and collective firms. In general, the public resource distributive system and the state-controlled marketing system were mandated to serve the state-owned enterprises only when rationing important raw materials and short supplies. To guarantee production and gain market access for their products, rural industries, and private enterprises were often in desperate need to acquire scarce within-plan raw materials and sell their products by all means, both legit and illegal, mainly through bribery and kickbacks. In the capital market, loopholes resulted from unsophisticated and defective regulations were broadly exploited by corrupt state banks and government officials to generate rents and personal gains. Windfall profits in the transition process of the capital market also induced state financial institutions to either use their monopolistic power or to deploy the public resources they controlled to seek illegitimate gains for their organizations. Compared to the malfeasances in the previous two phases, corruption in Phase 3 had obviously caused more detrimental consequences marked by much larger sizes of illicit gains, as well as involvement of more public institutions and a larger number of senior officials in rent-seeking and misappropriation.

All in all, as discussed above, in the early years of the reform, rent-seeking and corruption concentrated mainly in sectors and industries in which dual-track pricing prevailed, whereas in the advanced phase of the reform, rent-seeking and corruption have shifted to public investments, land, and real estate, as well as banking and finance where staggeringly huge illicit payoffs can be captured through collusions between unlawful businessmen and corrupt state officials. This explains why the incidence

[14] Zengke He, 249–250.

of corruption in departments and agencies that control and manage materials in short supply, capital, construction projects, import and export permits, railway transport, etc., has been so high and even seemingly incurable. These widespread "power-renting" malpractices, therefore, have inevitably set off an escalation of illicit trade of power for money, and have exacerbated the decay of the politically powerful. Characterized by incrementality in the economic sphere and conservativity in the political realm, China's reform is seemingly destined for a prolonged period during which market mechanism and state control and intervention will continue to co-exist. This partly explains why the government-led anti-corruption campaigns have had only limited success over the course of the reform.

Unintended Policy Outcomes

Policy failures throughout the reform era are often faulted as contributing factors to bureaucratic corruption. There existed a steep learning curve for the Chinese leadership and government technocrats in leading the transition of the economy and in formulating reform policies and regulations, particularly in the early phases of the reform. Given the lack of vision, knowledge, expertise, and experience, errors in judgment and unsophistication in policy and regulation formulation often led to unintended policy consequences including corruption. For example, in the initial phase of the reform, the authorities continued to exercise direct administrative control to regulate and constrain the behavior and autonomy of economic actors, which had inevitably resulted in ineffective policy outcomes and economic inefficiency. As mentioned previously, while the role of government in the economy was being shifted from micro-management of enterprises to macro-management and regulation of the economy, it proved to be an unprecedented challenge and a steep experience curve for the Party elite and government technocrats. Loopholes, errors, and gaps abounded in the formulation and implementation of economic policies and programs, and legislations and regulations often lagged behind the changing dynamics of the economy and market conditions. Under such circumstances, the government has constantly been playing catchups in updating and revising regulations and policies to mend loopholes or launching campaign-style enforcements to fight corruption and economic crimes. Rampant speculation and profiteering, tax evasion, smuggling, reckless theft, and plunder of state assets in the process of SOE restructuring and privatization serve as explanatory examples in this regard.

The frenzy of bureaucratic business in the initial phase of the reform and the much-hated corrupt practice of the so-called "three arbitraries" are attributable to budget cuts and the irrational policy of "opening up revenue sources to supplement operations". Insufficient budget allocations once forced government agencies and public institutions to "make money" to supplement their inadequate operational budgets and to improve their staff's welfare. Government agencies and public institutions basically deployed their institutional power to arbitrarily impose fines and to charge administrative fees, or to engage in business activities via their satellite companies. Although the central authorities corrected this defective policy by making up for the budgetary deficiency for public institutions and resolutely purging bureaucratic firms, it turns out to be a much more arduous journey to stamp out the malpractice of the "three arbitraries". Many local governments simply disregarded the central directives and continued to cut or even terminate budgetary funding to their subordinate work units, compelling them to make up for their budgetary deficiencies and staff welfare through arbitrarily levied fees or imposed fines. In extreme cases, some local governments even demanded their subordinate work units to contribute a portion of their collections to the local public coffers.[15] Another unintended policy outcome is decentralization of decision-making power to SOEs and local governments. As evidenced, more discretionary power at the subsystem level had caused a surge in misappropriation of public funds for personal or small groups' advantages. The question to be raised here is why these apparently corrupt or at least improper acts can be perpetrated without or with little resistance. The answer may still lie in the power structure that is inherently derived from the political system and the vast public ownership of state assets and resources in socialist China.

The Double-Edged Effect of Decentralization

As mentioned, decentralization, while proving to be effective in unleashing initiatives and innovation of local governments and SOEs to promote economic and business development, was conducive to

[15] Zengke He, 252.

widespread corruption in the reform era. As addressed previously, since the reform a series of policies and initiatives had been formulated to "invigorate enterprises by relieving them of previous dependence upon the government", gradually loosen the central authorities' control over resource allocation, grant local governments "great autonomy ... to direct investment", and decentralize "its managerial power over enterprises". In short, all these decentralization reform policies and programs have jointly upgraded and consolidated local authorities and enterprises' discretionary power over finance, operation, and personnel at the expense of the center.[16] Enterprises and work units, by making use of retained profits and other financial sources, now have greater financial capability to render their employees more welfare and better benefits. Nonetheless, as Ting Gong points out, "whether all these can provide strong incentives for workers to work hard remains to be seen, but they do make workers too dependent upon their work units for more welfare and expand the resources at local managers' disposal".[17] Under such circumstances, it is hardly surprising that banqueting, gift-giving, bribery, extortion, nepotism, exchange of power for sexual favor, as well as other irregularities have become so pervasive since the reform. More discretionary powers at local level plus fewer worries about sanctions from the above, have thus exacerbated local corruption, and are also conducive to the occurrence of localism and decentralism.[18]

Inequality in Income Distribution

Inequality also leads to corruption. Dobel argues that "the corruption of a state results from the consequences of individual human nature interacting with systematic and enduring inequality in wealth, power and status".[19] As mentioned, high inequality in wealth can also be a consequence of corruption as corruption further exacerbates disparity between the rich and the poor. Deng's famous call—"let some get

[16] Ting Gong, "Corruption and Reform in China: An Analysis of Unintended Consequences," 316–317.

[17] Ibid.

[18] Wei Hu, "Fight Corruption by Treating Both its Root Causes and Symptoms," (in Chinese), *Probe and Debate* No.4 (1995): 10.

[19] J. Patrick Dobel, "The Corruption of a State," *American Political Science Review* Vol. 72 (1978): 961.

rich first"—emphasizes ends rather than means, and more importantly, lacks justification of why these people, not others, should enrich themselves first and how they should get rich. As a result, "the orientation encouraged therein is seen by some as overly materialistic and even vulgar, and is further faulted for deliberately turning people's attention to economic matters and away from other needs and rights".[20] The fact that a considerable cohort of poorly educated people and even undesired social elements as proclaimed in Mao's era have enriched themselves through illicit means had further exacerbated the psychological and income imbalances among various social groups. Inequity in income, on the other hand, also has the effect of diminishing officials' privileges and undermining their social status. While the income of Chinese employees of foreign-owned companies or joint ventures maintained at a relatively high level, salaries and benefits of managers and workers of state-owned enterprises had also outpaced remunerations of government officials since 1985. Simultaneously, high inflation in the 1980s and early 1990s further ate into the government cohort's disposal income. With the rising private entrepreneurs quickly amassing staggering wealth on one hand and compensation for bureaucrats increasing sluggishly on the other, the income gap between the two social groups had deepened to such an extent that the economically disadvantageous but politically powerful officials were impelled to "rent" public power for money in compensation for their economic loss in distribution of social wealth. Income disparity between the private sector and the public sector, as mentioned, also incentivized many work units and public institutions to open up illegitimate funding sources by exploiting their institutional power and resources in an attempt to improve their employees' welfare. Moreover, as suggested by Dobel, not only does inequality in wealth lead to corruption but so does inequality in the distribution of power. Junior officials often indulge in corruption just as a compensation for their deficiencies in power and social status. This is particularly true for middle and lower-level officials because all sorts of privileges possessed by senior officials can ensure themselves of a better life even after their retirement. Finally, still another psychological factor is the contrast in consumption between the economically rising group and those who rely upon fixed

[20] Feng Lin, "The Causes of Power Corruption and the Causative Anti-Corruption" (in Chinese), *China Science of Law* No.4 (1995): 12.

salaries.[21] As discussed, inflation has devaluated the disposable incomes of bureaucrats and thus has further widened the gap in consumption. In addition, over propagation of high-standard consumption by both media and government in the 1980s stimulated consumption emulation, which inevitably misled some officials to seek additional income through corruption so as to be able to keep up with the consumption fads.

Laxity in Supervision and Law Enforcement

Laxity in supervision and discipline enforcement constitutes another structural factor that attributes to surging corruption in the reform era. As mentioned earlier, the Party elite and some scholars attribute corruption to "the diminished stress during the 1980s on inculcating communist ideology and morals", i.e., the discontinuity of the mode of mass and political campaigns.[22] Outdated ideological and political education that had failed to adapt itself to the changing economic and social settings is faulted for the ineffectiveness of the Party's ideological education and control in the reform era. Political and power-oriented ideological education models and practices that had worked well under the planned economy had become non-persuasive and even irrelevant in a market economy that is being dominated by economic interests and rationale. The failure is believed to be partly attributable to escalated official corruption in the post-Mao era as the communist ideology and the Party code of conduct have failed to regulate corrupt officials' behavior and to deter bureaucratic corruption. A more detailed discussion on this topic is to follow when we extend our discussion to the institutional causes of corruption in the subsequent section.

8.4 Institutional Deficiencies Inherent in a Socialist and Authoritarian State

As fundamental as structural defects and imperfections are the defective design and faulty operations of its institutions. The more decisive causes of corruption in the case of China lie in the institutions of the state. These

[21] Yan Sun, 774.

[22] Ostergaard and Peterson, 93.

encompass its political system, legal structure, the rule of law, as well as its traditional culture and value system.

The Dominance of Public Ownership

First and foremost, the system of public ownership of means of production is a decisive institutional determinant of corruption. Unlike the capitalist system under which private ownership of means of production dominates and there exists a fully developed market mechanism in accordance with the ownership form, the public ownership system inherently predestines the ambiguity of demarcation between ownership and operation and creates an all-inclusive government and a state economic planning system. Under the circumstance of private ownership of means of production, definite and concrete relations of property rights and developed market mechanism, to a large extent, both protect and encourage fair competition and prevent the government from unnecessarily intervening in economy at the microeconomic level.[23] In other words, the market mechanism under the private ownership system, relatively speaking, is able to separate bureaucracy from microeconomic operations and thus works to minimize the occurrence and potential of "rent-seeking" in a capitalist economy and society. On the other hand, the availability and sum of rents under such a system are also limited given the limited roles and functions of government in business operations and economic affairs. In contrast, the public power system under the public ownership statehood is largely characteristic of comprehensiveness and totality. Its all-inclusive intervention in all dimensions of economic and social realms, especially its over-intervention in microeconomic affairs, tends to generate abundant rent-seeking incentives and opportunities.

In general, public enterprises in socialist states monopolize many important trades such as banking, energy, railway transportation, aviation, steel, cement, chemical industry, etc., and manipulate the market prices of these goods and services (as evidenced in the pre-reform China and the initial phase of the reform). In addition, state-owned enterprises are generally under the protection of state regulations and policies. In contrast to the public sector, however, government tends to impose various restrictions upon the behavior and economic activities of private

[23] Wei Hu, 10–11.

enterprises. The immensity of the state-owned assets and resources and the way the state economy is being operated and managed under the public ownership statehood is deemed a fertile ground for the genesis of corruption. In the case of China, moreover, given its population base and the enormity of its public institutions, the state may have the most public powers at its disposal in comparison to other nations in the world. Simply put, its vast troop of public servants in tens of millions are capable of unleashing huge potential for corruption if only a fraction of the officialdom chooses to abuse public power for personal gains. Most importantly, in an authoritarian state like China, an extremely high if not complete degree of control and regulation over public and private life makes the regime particularly prone to corruption. In the case of China, governmental behavior permeates almost every walk of life—politics, social, economic, culture, ideology, etc., and even intrudes into citizen's personal and family life. The functions and operation of a "work unit" (单位), the basic organizational module in socialist China, for instance, provide insight into how the regime once managed, controlled, and influenced various aspects of its citizens' behavior and conduct in both Mao's era and the initial phase of the reform. Work units (单位) are the basic component of Chinese society and economy. Work units in China, unlike their counterparts in the Western setting, discharge many social and family functions. Workers of state-owned enterprises not only earn monetary wages at the workplace but are also entitled to nonwage benefits such as pensions, housing, healthcare, child care, subsidizes, meal services, and even education and employment for workers' offspring.[24] In the pre-reform era, work units in China even intervened in their employees' social activities and personal affairs such as job transfers, going abroad, applying for marriage certificates, divorce, childbearing (compulsory requirement and forceful implementation of the "one-child" policy, for example), and even family disputes settling. Those all-inclusive interventions in and control over various dimensions of personal and family life have inevitably increased employees' social and economic dependency on their work units, political dependency on management, and personal

[24] David M. Lampton, "The Implementation Problem in Post-Mao China," In P.M. Lampton (eds), *Policy Implementation in Post-Mao China* (Berkeley: University of California Press, 1987), 15.

dependence on superiors.[25] These dependences, along with an inherently lack of transparency and democracy within the system, had made power supervision and checks and balances difficult and ineffective.

Dominant public ownership, as a crucial institutional factor, provides explanations of the origin of certain patterns of corruption in socialist states such as China and former Soviet-bloc countries. In contrast to private ownership, the structural and systemic defects and malfunction of public ownership make the whole system vulnerable to the agents' (public officials) exploitation and abuse. Understandably, it would be generally easier and more profitable for corrupt officials and unscrupulous businessmen to misappropriate public funds and assets than private ones. As evidenced in the SOE transformation and privatization, collusions between venal officials and unlawful businessmen, compounded by unsophisticated legislations, administrative loopholes, and lax supervision and law enforcement had led to immeasurable loss of state assets and property in the process. Loss of collective assets, however, is believed to be more profound as there had been more loopholes and laxer management and supervision in the sector. A survey by the Ministry of Agriculture in the late 1990s concerning 51,000 townships, 680,000 villages and 55,000 collective enterprises estimated that total collective assets, excluding collective-owned natural resources such as lands and forests, had amounted to 2.58 trillion yuan, accounting for 35.7 percent of the aggregate state assets in the period. This figure did not include the estimated value of collective assets in urban areas.[26] Similar to what had happened in SOE ownership reform and privatization, privatization of collective enterprises and businesses had also triggered rampant corruption and resulted in enormous loss of collective assets in the process. For example, akin to fraudulent schemes in the SOE restructuring and reform, one of the common ploys to steal and misappropriate was arbitrary assessment and appraisal of collective assets by collusions among managers, local officials, and third-party appraisers.[27] As the 15th National Congress of the Communist Party of China officially acknowledged the legitimacy of private economy in 1997, there came an era of decollectivizing

[25] Andrew G. Walder, *Communist Neo-Traditionalism: Work and Authority in Chinese Industry* (Berkeley: University of California Press, 1986), 12–22.

[26] Yan Meng and Li, 103–105.

[27] Ibid., 105.

collective enterprises in rural and urban areas. While transformation of the collective economy was obviously an important move toward the expansion and consolidation of the private economy, its positive results and effects, however, had been offset by abundant malpractices, illicit collusions, and misappropriations throughout the transition process.

A Faulty Political System

Overconcentration of government power and the lack of a corresponding mechanism of power countervailing outside government constitute another source of corruption in socialist states like China. The political structures of a socialist state usually take the form of single-party system. Rulers or political leaders of these regimes usually seize public power through revolution. The acquisition of power in these regimes is therefore irrelevant to citizens, and hence it multiplies possibilities of political corruption. These political structures are often characterized by a lack of countervailing force outside the network of the ruling parties. There do not exist "freely operating opposition political parties or independent judiciary system".[28] Legislatures are dependencies or ornaments of the ruling blocs, and the judiciary system lacks necessary independence. Laws and regulations have less influence on political leadership; rulers may ignore or even revise laws according to their own will or in their own interests.

As an authoritarian regime, the Chinese political system does not allow direct elections at the national level. Nominal and highly controlled and manipulated elections occur only at the local level. "The CCP tightly controls the nomination and election processes at every level in the people's congress system ... the tiered, indirect electoral mechanism in the People's Congress system ensures that deputies at the highest levels face no semblance of electoral accountability to the Chinese citizenry".[29] Under the Chinese political system, the General Secretary of the CCP holds ultimate power and authority over not only the Party but also the government and military. As most of the General Secretary's power stems from his paramount position of the CCP, the Party power prevails over

[28] Kempe Ronald Hope, "Administrative Corruption and Administrative Reform in Developing States," *Corruption and Reform* Vol. 2, No. 2 (1987): 132.

[29] https://en.wikipedia.org/wiki/politics_of_china.

state and military powers. As pointed out by Ian Johnson: "Run the party and you run China".[30] Similar to other socialist or autocratic states, there does not exist political opposition in a real sense nor do an independent judiciary and free press. All religious activities are controlled, dissent is suppressed, and civil rights are curtailed in socialist China.

What functions to incubate and grow bureaucratic corruption on the fertile ground of public ownership is China's political system and power structure. In contrast to the progress and achievements that China's market-oriented reforms have made so far, its political reform is obviously a laggard. As mentioned, the period since 2012 has witnessed not only the continued stagnation of political reform but also the trending reversal of reform momentum in economic spheres. The conflicts between the reformed economic module and a seemingly unfit political system are criticized for proliferating corruption. Parallel with the public ownership and the immensity of state-owned resources and assets are the dictatorial grip of the state power and the absolute Party supremacy and dominance over political, legal, economic, social, and cultural affairs. As the CCP doctrine propaganda goes: "All under the Party's command!" (一切听党指挥!), the state is structured in a way that every aspect of the society is de facto under the Party's dominance and control. Structurally, there are two sets of parallel institutions throughout the Party system and the government apparatus, and the Party organs command and override their government counterparts. For instance, the department of organization of the Party Committee oversees the personnel department in government; the Party's discipline inspection commission directs the department of supervision in government; the political and legal affairs committee of the Party Committee is in charge of judiciary and law enforcement; the list goes on. As mentioned above, the Party controls the state legislature—the National People's Congress, and the Chinese People's Political Consultative Conference (CPPCC), a consultation forum made of notabilities and prominent intellectuals from science and technology, higher education, industry, literature, arts, etc. The Party's control over government and legislature is derived from and also consolidated mainly by its authority over personnel appointment and agenda setting. All leading and important positions at various levels in government, People's Congress

[30] Lindsay Maizland and Eleanor Albert, "The Chinese Communist Party," *Council on Foreign Relations*, October 2, 2022. https://www.cfr.org/backgrounder/chinese-communist-party (accessed December 22, 2022).

and CPPCC must be nominated by the Party Committee and then only be nominally approved by People's Congress and CPPCC through corresponding approval procedures and processes. Under such arrangements, the NPC has neither independence nor authority to supervise and constrain political and administrative powers as its Western legislative counterparts do. The selection and composition of NPC deputies are also problematic. Rather than being elected through the People's Congress system, the departments of organization of the Party Committee are heavily involved in the selection and nomination of the deputies of the People's Congress at various levels. Dubbed "rubber stamp", NPC deputies are in general "yes-voters" because they are inclined to act in alignment with the authorities to render rapport, rather than pose challenges, for the proposition and adoption of NPC resolutions. Very often, the overwhelming political will of the Party leadership and overconcentration of state power makes it particularly challenging for the legislature and anti-corruption institutions to supervise leading Party officials and hold them accountable as top Party officials often concurrently hold top positions of the People's Congress in many localities.

Similar political arrangements apply to the judiciary and law enforcement as well. The Chinese judicial system does not have the necessary independence in tackling corruption or upholding social justice. Courts are under the control of the Party Committees and report to the People's Congress at the respective levels. Party Committees nominate and appoint presidents of People's Court, and structurally presidents of the courts are even ranked lower than police chiefs, i.e., directors of the public security bureau, in government hierarchy as many directors of the public security bureau concurrently hold the position of members of the Standing Committee of the Party Committee, the most powerful ruling group in a locality. Some of the police chiefs are concurrently deputy mayors overseeing law enforcement and judicial affairs. Under both circumstances, police chiefs are de facto superiors of court presidents. Courts in China are in general being treated as part of the government apparatus as both their staffing needs and operational funding are authorized and appropriated by the government. Under such arrangements, it is hardly surprising that political and administrative interventions in court judgments and law enforcement are prevalent in socialist China. In major cases that involve high-ranking officials or of a sensitive nature, the Party often steps in to dictate the outcome of cases in secrecy. Political will and Party decisions often overrule the rule of law and legal proceedings. Once the Party has made its decision, it dictates a court to deliver its ruling through court procedures. "As these cases have grown in number and importance, the role of the Party has also grown adding to the political intrigue, bargaining between rival factions of the Party, and the settling of old scores playing out behind the scenes in these cases in secretive Party proceedings".[31] In conflicts of interests or legal battles among localities, local courts are often required or even ordered by local Party and government leaders to rule in favor of local interests or stop executing court rulings against local enterprises and businesses.

Absence of an Independent Judiciary and the Presence of an Extrajudicial and Politicized System

An independent and constitutionally empowered judicial system is a fundamental and crucial prerequisite for clean government and social integrity. However, this is absent from China's political and legal institutions. The Party's control and intervention in judicial affairs and the outcomes of anti-corruption campaigns are mainly achieved through its CCDI's dominance over judicial organs and its manipulation of court procedures and processes. The Party Constitution and disciplinary provisions often override laws and legal procedures in the CCP's internal extrajudicial investigation and disciplinary process. The internal supervisory system within the Party Committee and government consists of the central and local Commission for Discipline Inspection, and the Ministry of Supervision and its local branches. The Central Commission for Discipline Inspection (CCDI) is the CCP's leading anti-corruption organ and is headed by a member of the Politburo Standing Committee. The CCDI is the Party's extrajudicial system of discipline and prosecution, wielding enormous power of investigation, detention, and determination of guilt and penalty. The CCDI is mandated to handle all major and high-profile corruption cases involving high-ranking officials at and above the provincial/ministerial level and is known for its secretive inner working process and proceedings. Operated largely outside the formal legal system, the Commission for Discipline Inspection at all levels is granted quasi-legal power to detain Party members accused of corruption and can hold them

[31] Daniel C.K. Chow, "How China's Crackdown on Corruption has Led to Less Transparency in the Enforcement of China's Anti-Bribery Laws." https://papers.ssrn.com/sol3/papers.cfm?abstract_id=2599448 (accessed May 30, 2021).

in undisclosed locations for investigation and interrogation. Under such arrangements, the accused are deprived of their constitutional protection during the CDI detention and investigation process, and their cases, if found guilty, would be handed over to the prosecutor for prosecution. The CDIs "effectively monopolize anti-corruption enforcement" and exert decisive influence over courts and procuratorates in terms of corruption investigation, prosecution, and outcomes of trials. According to Pei, "DICs occupy a uniquely powerful niche: only DICs are empowered to conduct the initial investigations, detain the accused, and determine guilt and punishment". In addition to their political status and formidable enforcement power, the DICs possess the potent weapon of "shuanggui", which allows the commission to detain the accused for an indefinite period of time to facilitate its interrogation, investigation, and deliberation. Once the accused are detained, they are locked in isolation to prevent them from either seeking help or leaking vital information. "Access to legal counsel is denied and DIC investigators frequently resort to torture and sleep deprivation to extract confessions from the accused".[32] Officials accused of corruption and economic crime are handed over to the procuratorate only after the DICs have completed their investigations and reached their own conclusions.

However, like the judicial system, the lack of independence and authority of the CCDI and its local branches is manifested in their incapability in exerting influence over leading figures, i.e., their political and administrative superiors, at the same level. This politicized design and arrangement of the CDI are viewed as the most serious flaw of China's anti-corruption institution and strategy. Both the internal supervisory agencies (DIC and Department of Supervision) and the judicial organs such as the Supreme and local Procurators and the Supreme and local Courts are under the command of the Politburo at the central level or of the local Party Committee to assure of absolute compliance with political decisions or in dealing with sensitive cases and issues. As mentioned above, the Party leadership is also in control of the appointment of leading officials of these agencies as well as the allocation of budgetary funding. In terms of cadre appointment/removal and reporting, directors of the DICs are nominated and appointed by the Party Committees and report directly to the Party boss. These political and personnel arrangements often put

[32] Minxin Pei, "How Not to Fight Corruption: Lessons from China," *Daedalus* Vol. 147, No. 3 (2018): 216–230.

directors of the DICs and departments of supervision in an awkward and powerless situation when cases concerning leading officials in a locality arise. “What puzzles casual observers is why the CCP has opted to further eviscerate the autonomy of its own in-house anti-corruption agency, the DIC, by denying this institution the requisite political status and independence needed to ensure its integrity, credibility, and effectiveness”.[33] In high-profile cases involving high-ranking officials at the ministerial/provincial level, for example, the CCDI must seek approval from the Standing Committee of the Politburo for initiation of investigations. This faulty institutional and procedural setup largely subjects the anti-corruption institutions and anti-corruption campaigns to political interference and manipulation. What a Western scholar commented referring to high-profile cases is insightful of the elusive nature of these cases; as disclosure of the details may cause embarrassment and a widening scandal to the Party, the Party leadership often steps in to “carefully orchestrate the outcome of these cases to avoid escalating the public embarrassment that accompanies any scandal involving high-ranking Party members”.[34] The utilization of patron–client networks as “protective umbrella” to shield corrupt senior officials from DIC investigation and sanction is another risk that impedes the independence and impartiality of anti-corruption institutions. Although the authorities have somewhat raised the rank of DIC directors in the hierarchy and upgraded the appointment and reporting structure and arrangements, the changes are deemed far short of what is required to consolidate the DICs’ requisite independence and impartiality in operation and investigation.

As mentioned, unsophistication in policy-making and regulation formulization is not only manifested in economic affairs but also reflected in anti-corruption laws and regulations. Ineffectiveness and failures to deter official corruption are also attributable to defects and problems associated with anti-corruption legislations, policies, and enforcement. The existing laws and regulations have often been enacted to cope with some emergent circumstances or incidents and hence lack comprehensiveness and universality. In addition, many of these laws and regulations are not

[33] Minxin Pei, “How Not to Fight Corruption: Lessons from China,” 222.

[34] Daniel C.K. Chow, “How China’s Crackdown on Corruption has Led to Less Transparency in the Enforcement of China’s Anti-Bribery Laws.”

legal in a real sense, but rather, anti-corruption and bureaucratic cleanness enforcement policies in the form of quasi-laws and regulations. These quasi-laws are characterized by ambiguity and non-rigorousness and even leave loopholes that can be easily exploited on behalf of the corrupt.[35] There are more prohibitory provisions to regulate the behavior of officials but stop short of addressing legal consequences for contravening these prohibitory stipulations. Similarly, with respect to terms and requirements specifying the implementation of certain preventive measures, there tend to be more provisions in principle rather than operability and implementing procedures. There are other drawbacks and problems concerning anti-corruption regulations and policies. For example, stipulations tend to be more elastic and discretionary than rigid and thus are more vulnerable to abuse and exploitation. There are more stipulations regulating the moral norms of the Party members but fewer for the code of conduct of government officials. Moreover, there is a lack of legal provisions governing administrative decision-making failures, which often result in economic losses that are generally far more serious than those caused by embezzlement and misappropriation. There are loopholes concerning the definition, scope, and penalty of the crime of possessing high-value assets of unknown or unidentified origins. These loopholes are often being exploited by corrupt officials to escape grave punishments that would otherwise be applicable in accordance with the amount of illicit funds grafted. Still another character of the system, as criticized by Western scholars, is its emphasis on penalties in the aftermath of exposure of corrupt acts but lacks corruption-preventive mechanism. Unsound and unsophisticated anti-corruption laws and regulations may actually induce more corruption rather than reduce or deter the malfeasances. Lack of expertise, experience, and professional training of China's anti-corruption agencies in dealing with technically sophisticated forms of corruption and economic crimes such as insider trading, manipulation of the stock market, money laundering, and cross-border corruption is deemed another factor that exacerbates the ineffectiveness of China's anti-corruption clampdown.

[35] Wandong Shen and Shaoren Wang, "On Causes of the Uncurbable Corruption and the Counter-measures" (in Chinese), *The Journal of Mudanjiang Teachers College* No. 3 (1991): 21–22.

Laxity in Enforcement

In parallel with the relatively unsophisticated anti-corruption laws and regulations is the lax and arbitrary enforcement of these laws, regulations, and stipulations. Lax and arbitrary enforcement is manifested in both disciplinary sanctions and criminal punishments. Party and administrative disciplinary sanctions are often applied as de facto protective measures to help reduce or even exempt due penalties for corrupt officials. Offenders, particularly those who are well-connected, are often harbored using a variety of tactics and measures such as substituting disciplinary sanctions or even fines for criminal prosecutions, arbitrarily reducing or altering the nature, scope, and consequences of the offenses, and even totally quashing the charges of the malfeasances, etc. In extreme cases, political will and faction interests may override the rule of law to shield clients from prosecution and conviction of corruption. As mentioned, for example, there arise louder criticisms in recent years at both home and abroad questioning the legitimacy and impartiality of Xi's anti-corruption campaign. It is asserted that Xi has been using what is dubbed "selective anti-corruption campaign" to clamp down on his political rivals while leaving his faction members and clients, say, the faction of princelings, untouched. "This raises the issue of whether the current anti-corruption gain is truly a crackdown on all corruption as opposed to a tool to settle political scores and to consolidate Xi's control".[36]

In the early years of the reform, local authorities often opted to ignore and tolerate the problematic and corrupt behavior and acts of the so-called able men who were able to bring or broker economic development projects or opportunities to localities. Corrupters and criminal economic schemers were often harbored under the assertion that "cleanness and integrity must make place for economy" (经济要上, 廉政要让). Some of the disciplinarily sanctioned officials were simply transferred to positions at the same levels in other localities or departments. Another indicator of ineffective enforcement is the low case filing rate. Between 1992 and 1997, for example, DICs and departments of supervision nationwide received 7.55 million complaints and tips, but only 731,000 persons/cases were filed for investigation, merely 9.7 percent of

[36] Daniel C.K. Chow, "How China's Crackdown on Corruption has Led to Less Transparency in the Enforcement of China's Anti-Bribery Laws."

the total reports received.[37] Difficulties and barriers in carrying out Party and administrative sanctions is another manifestation of the compromised anti-corruption law enforcement. Central and provincial surveys in late 1990s both revealed that a portion of the sanctions (3.5–11 percent), mainly demotions and salary reductions, were unable to be enforced due to various barriers and interferences in the bureaucracy. Laxity and unjustified leniency also exist in the criminal prosecution process. There has long been a tendency of applying lenient sentences to severe crimes and exemptions from punishment for less severe and minor offenses in the criminal prosecution and conviction process. According to the work reports of the Supreme People's Procuratorate and the Supreme People's Court, an average of 41.86 percent of the public-office-related crimes investigated during 1993–2001 were prosecuted and convicted, with the majority of the suspects investigated walking away free of charge. Another source indicates that only 6.6 percent of the officials investigated for corruption and economic crime were prosecuted and sentenced between 1993 and 1998. A noticeable tendency in corruption-related criminal prosecution in recent years is a dramatic drop in convictions of death penalties and the generous application of reprieve and suspended sentences. As presented in pervious chapters, in sharp contrast to convictions in the 1980s and 1990s, nowadays rarely corrupt officials received death sentences even though their cases often involved hundreds of millions of yuan in illicit funds. For those who have been convicted, they may have a better chance to stay out of prison as statistically a large cohort of the convicted tend to be put on probation or simply be exempted from punishment. In addition, application of economic sanctions and pecuniary penalty is also problematic and loopholes in this regard may help corrupt officials to alleviate the risk of economic and property losses. For those who have eventually been put behind bars, given their previous influence and political connections, imprisoned officials, particularly high-ranking ones, often receive better treatments, are assigned light work, and granted more flexibility and permissions to see visitors and even to host birthday parties in prison. More importantly, they have a better chance to be granted commutation, parole, medical parole, and serving a sentence outside jail. Imprisonment under such circumstances is by no means harsh punishment in a real sense and has failed to help

[37] Meng, Yan and Li, 156.

deter corruption in government.[38] With the improvement and consolidation of anti-corruption laws and regulations since 1998, laxity and reckless leniency in anti-corruption law enforcement have become a major contributing factors to a losing battle against corruption. Faulty enforcement has helped to shape what is dubbed the mentality of "low-cost and high-benefit corruption" in government and society and is blamed for the prevalence and rampancy of official corruption in post-Mao China.

Lack of Checks and Balances

Finally, the lack of checks and balances and a powerful internal and external power-constraining mechanism is the crucial structural defect that is conducive to corruption. The renewed calls for strengthened and consolidated Party leadership and the further retreat of civil society and freedom of speech in recent years have further weakened China's already fragile system of checks and balances. Unlike Western democracies, a powerful external power supervision and a constraining mechanism are absent in socialist China. While political competition helps keep the ruling party in check in a democracy, however, there are no political oppositions in a real sense in the communist regime; the so-called "democratic parties" are in reality appendages of the ruling CCP. As discussed above, legislation—the system of People's Congress, dubbed "rubber stamp"—is independent in name but subordinate to the CCP in reality. The judiciary system, as discussed earlier, is even more problematic; it is an internal mechanism rather than external and independent one in terms of both its vertical and horizontal relations with the Party and government. The political system grants Party leadership direct power to control the judiciary system, and leading officials are empowered to intervene or even manipulate judicial affairs and decisions through the political and legal affairs committee, an organ of the Party Committee that directly oversees police, courts, procuratorates, and justice institutions. The political and legal affairs committee and the Party Committee are authorized to review and decide on important cases submitted by the judicial system and to make important judgments and judicial decisions. This system may work when dealing with cases concerning middle- and lower-level officials, even though local leading cadres often stage interventions in the process of

[38] Ibid., 158–162.

investigation and disposal of major or sensitive cases. This institutional defect becomes more apparent when subjecting corrupt leading cadres, especially the top Party bosses of the localities, to the judicial system. Under such circumstances, the local judicial system often finds itself in an awkward situation when proceeding with an investigation and pressing for charges against local leaders. Very often cases of this sort cannot proceed without the intervention and support of higher authorities or even the state leaders. The Tai'an case in Shandong province is exemplifying in this regard. This was a case of collusion involving 24 municipal leading cadres and officials at the department/bureau level. The major suspect, the Party leader of the city Hu Jianxue, took full advantage of his political power and directly intervened in and obstructed the investigative process. Except for the municipal procuratorate, he had put the whole municipal judicial system including the municipal court and the police agency under his control and manipulated the system and even the Party committee to carry out counter-investigation against the procuratorate. The fierce struggle between power and law ended up with the victory of the justice, thanks to the direct involvement of the state supreme procurator general and the provincial Party and government leaders.[39] There exists a high probability that many sensitive cases and political scandals may have been simply covered up by both local judiciary and governments for unspecified considerations.

An independent and strong civil society of free press and NGOs is a powerful deterrent to government corruption. However, in today's China, anti-corruption campaign is part of the political will and arrangements that serve to maintain and strengthen the ruling Party's legitimacy to govern, and it is mainly a call of the top leadership. Although seemingly an integral part of the driving force of corruption crackdown, the news media and the public can play only a limited role. Civil society in China had been almost absent before 1978 and, since then has evolved and developed only gradually. The existence and development of civil society in today's China, to a large extent, rely on the "support and protection" of government at various levels.[40] Under Xi's rule, the civil society of NGOs, community groups, and social-advocacy organizations,

[39] SCGBDSB, August 29; September 5, 12, 19, 1996.

[40] Zengke He, 253–254.

which have made gradual progress in China's reform and modernization process over the past three decades, now faces increasing scrutiny of the Party-state.[41] Another source reveals that "after 2015, the whole of civil society began to collapse and become fragmented", and "an emergent independent media and academic freedoms have become all but destroyed".[42]

There is no independent press in China. Media in China "is better viewed as the publicity arm for the government rather than as a forum for free speech".[43] Media is always under the control of the Party Committee through the department of propaganda and is subject to censorship of the Party and government. According to a report by the US Council on Foreign Relations, China has one of the world's most restrictive media environments, and the regime relies on censorship to control information on both traditional and new media including social media. Since Chinese President Xi Jinping came to power in late 2012, censorship of all forms of media has been intensified. The Party-state has long kept tight reins on media to avoid potential subversion of its authority. Its surveillance and censorship mechanisms include a comprehensive monitoring system and the widely known Golden Shield Project, colloquially known as the Great Firewall, to block Chinese citizens' access to the United States and foreign websites. The regime is particularly keen on blocking reports of issues that could incite social unrest, like official corruption, the economy, health and environmental scandals, certain religious groups, and ethnic strife. Reportedly over two million workers employed by the state and media firms are constantly surveilling the internet and social media. In addition, the authorities employ a diverse range of methods to force journalists and media organizations to censor themselves, and offenders and opponents are subject to dismissals and demotions, libel lawsuits, fines, arrests, and forced televised confessions. As a result of the media clampdown, China's

[41] Echo Hui, "China's False War on Corruption," *The Walrus*, September 4, 2019. https://thewalrus.ca/corruption-chinas-false-war-on-corruption/ (accessed June 4, 2021).

[42] Author unknown, "How China's Civil Society Collapsed Under Xi," *AFP*, October 4, 2022. https://www.france24.com/en/live-news/20221004-how-china-s-civil-society-collapsed-under-xi (accessed December 20, 2022).

[43] Barbara N. Sands, "Decentralizing an Economy: The Role of Bureaucratic Corruption in China's Economic Reforms," *Public Choice* No. 65 (1990): 88.

ranking in international indexes of press freedom has dropped dramatically since Xi took office in 2012.[44] News media in China is not allowed to expose corruption or scandals without the permission of the Party, and media reports on cases of corruption, therefore, are usually made public prior to the conclusion of the official investigations.[45] Unsurprisingly, therefore, such a media would be inevitably weak and incapable of investigating and revealing malfeasances involving political elites.

8.5 Is Corruption Inherent in Chinese Norms and Culture?

Traditional culture and norms, as suggested in *Introduction*, also generate corruption. Corruption is "shaped and conditioned by cultural attitudes and behavioral patterns that are defective".[46] In many traditional societies, "obligations to kin, tribe, religious sect, or local community significantly influence the behavior of public servants, leading them to corrupt practices in order to satisfy their client's demands".[47] The behavior of taking advantage of public office for personal or sectional gains is at least acceptable in these societies if not praiseful. In such an environment, public interest is often sacrificed by public servants for the satisfaction of their family or parochial demands. In societies where such traditional norms prevail, "non-corrupt standards of public bureaucratic behavior have not been widely internalized, and administrative conduct continues to be determined by traditional, family and other parochial pressures".[48]

The Chinese orthodox approach also traces the sources of corruption "in the persistence of something old". It asserts that Chinese culture that had been formed throughout the long history of feudalism has lasting influence and causes a series of social maladies including corruption. The traditional value system exerts lasting influence over human behavior throughout different social systems regardless of any institutional changes.

[44] Beina Xu and Eleanor Albert, "Media Censorship in China." https://www.cfr.org/backgrounder/media-censorship-china (accessed June 29, 2021).

[45] Zengke He, 254.

[46] Hope, 132.

[47] Jabbra, "Bureaucratic Corruption in the Third World: Causes and remedy," 675.

[48] Ibid., 676.

This view holds that even very strong socialist states "have not been able to transform traditional culture radically".[49] Chinese culture is therefore faulted for its overemphasis on officialdom as well as its tolerance of the ideology of official privileges and arbitrary abuse of power. This approach argues that a wide range of corrupt practices is rooted in the traditional political culture; replacing the feudal official standard in Chinese culture with a new socialist value system and outlook of power can curb official corruption.

The cultural approach may be the least discussed perspective among both Western and Chinese scholars and observers in tracing genesis of corruption in post-Mao China. Culture is conducive to corruption mainly through interactions with formal institutions and social norms, both of which can differ across states and societies. By examining unique features and attributes of a specific culture, it helps generate insights into how sociocultural norms and values cause corruption in a society. Bureaucratic corruption in imperial China was so widespread that a famous Chinese scholar concluded that "the Twenty-Four Histories of China is in reality a history of graft".[50] Malfeasances such as nepotism, patron–client relationship, and bribery are deeply rooted in the traditional political culture. As discussed, several attributes of Chinese culture make Chinese polity and society particularly prone to power abuse and corruption. Even the CCP and its regime that are known for their radical philosophy and strong anti-feudalism and anti-tradition mentality and ideology is unable to free itself from the enduring influence of traditional Chinese norms over the morality and behavior of its modern-day officialdom. The core norms of Chinese culture, as mentioned, are largely derived from the influential Confucian philosophy and doctrines, and, as the traditional orthodoxy, it will most likely continue to clash with other doctrines and values, either the capitalist or the communist one, in the modern-day world. "Confucianism contains elements that vitiate corruption, but the same cultural norms can be used to justify practices that may be interpreted as corrupt".[51] In this sense, it would make a weak or even faulty argument

[49] Barrett L. McCormick, *Political Reform in Post-Mao China: Democracy and Bureaucracy in a Leninist State* (Berkeley: University of California Press, 1990), 71.

[50] The Twenty-Four Histories refers to the dynastic histories from remote antiquity till the Ming Dynasty. See Minglan Huang and Jing Fang, "The Causes of Official Corruption in Ancient China" (in Chinese), *Journal of Northwest University* No. 4 (1990): 40.

[51] Rose-Ackerman, 247.

to trace the geneses of corruption in reform China without addressing the deep causes of corruption that originally inhere in Chinese culture and norms.

Hofstede's cultural dimensions model constitutes another perspective in analyzing the causal linkages between Chinese culture and corruption in modern-day China. Four of Hofstede's six dimensions, i.e., power distance, individualism, masculinity, uncertainty avoidance, long-term orientation, and indulgence, are relevant to Chinese society's susceptibility to corruption. First of all, China scores 80 on the Power Distance ranking, which is well above the world average of 55. High ranking in this dimension indicates a high level of inequality of power and wealth within the society and the high inequalities are accepted by the society as their cultural heritage. Power distance is positively correlated with corruption. Second, China scores 20 on the dimension of Individualism, defined as the degree of interdependence a society maintains among its members. Such a low score attests to a highly collectivist Chinese culture, and in a collectivist culture, loyalty tends to be paramount. The high degree of interdependence in a social setting explains the prevalence of guanxi networks and practices in Chinese society. On the other hand, the mentality of in-group considerations underlies the pervasiveness of nepotism and cronyism in the political culture of both imperial and contemporary China. Third, China is assigned a low score of 30 on the dimension of Uncertainty Avoidance. As interpreted by Hofstede Insights, in such a society, members' "adherence to laws and rules may be flexible to suit the actual situation and pragmatism is a fact of life". In comparison to Uncertainty Avoidance, China obtains a high score of 87 in the category of Long-Term Orientation, which describes how every society has to maintain some links with its own past while dealing with the challenge of the present and future. Rated high on this dimension are cultures with a high degree of pragmatism. "In societies with a pragmatic orientation, people believe that truth depends very much on situation, context and time". In such a culture, the inclination of ambiguity and adaptability to circumvent rules and laws to fit situations make the society susceptible to corruption.[52]

In addition to the three attributes that characterize any other bureaucracies—absolute authority, hierarchical structures, and rigid operation,

[52] Hofstede Insights. https://www.hofstede-insights.com/country/china/ (accessed June 16, 2021).

the traditional Chinese bureaucracy is also marked by other features such as power integration, insecurity, and trade of power for wealth. Contrary to the Western democratic system, public office in imperial China was "more used to achieve wealth than wealth was used to achieve political office". Power had special meanings in the social life of ancient China because it could enrich an individual through "ways much faster than other avenues".[53] The social evolution of China is marked by a relatively direct shift from the feudal society to the socialist state without an intermediate social transition of capitalism, and hence there is little element of democracy in Chinese political culture. As Deng Xiaoping pointed out, "what the old China had left over to us is more tradition of the feudal dictatorship but less democracy and legality".[54] In ancient times, emperors held ultimate and absolute state power and the state bureaucracy was highly centralized and authoritative. An emperor ruled his dynasty by personal will rather than the rule of law and the emperor and high officials were generally regarded above the law. The traditional lack of demarcation of public and private spheres and a low level of respect for law in Chinese tradition subject Chinese polity and society to power abuse and corruption. "In such a society, establishing and maintaining political and economic orders relies on officials rather than legal systems. Therefore, it strengthens privileges and immunities of officials and opens up the potential for public corruption".[55] The tradition and the rule of "rule by the ruler" have been continuously carried over across dynasties and regimes in the long history of imperial China and the current CCP regime is no exception. This institutional weakness makes Chinese officialdom and society particularly vulnerable to nepotism, power abuse, and corruption.

Absolute rule, an important component of the traditional Chinese political culture, still exerts enduring influence in varying degrees over the mentality and behavior of government officials in today's China. In imperial China, under the absolute rule, rulers treated the state as their own private property and bureaucrats regarded public office as their personal

[53] Gong, 37–38.

[54] Wantong Li and Mingqing Li, "Causes of Corruption and the Restriction Measures" (in Chinese), *The Journal of Xinyang Teachers College* No. 4 (1990): 24.

[55] Winnie Tong, "Analysis of Corruption from Sociocultural Perspectives," *International Journal of Business and Social Science* Vol. 5, No. 11(1) (October 2014): 12.

privileges. Under such a rule, personal rule tends to override administrative power and the rule of law. In a polity and society governed by absolute rule and official standards culture, rulers and officials usually hold the highest social status and enjoy a wide range of privileges.[56] Official standards (guan ben wei) are important element of the traditional Chinese norms, which originated in the centralized bureaucratic hierarchy of the Qin Dynasty (221–206 BC) and had become a dominant norm of the Chinese political culture ever since. Official standards refer to "the cultural and political phenomenon that prioritizes state official rank as the primary measure of social status".[57] The social ethos of official standards (guan ben wei) and hierarchy in imperial China, for instance, have led to the formation and prevalence of "official supremacy" mentality in the present-day Chinese society. Traditional norms and values handed from generation to generation, such as "getting promoted and then becoming rich" (升官发财), "As a man attains power and prominence, his family gains influence accordingly". (一人得道, 鸡犬升天), and politically influential leaders and powerful officials can even "bring honor to their ancestors" (光宗耀祖), are still prevalent in Chinese politics and Chinese society. It is hardly surprising that cadres and their families often view their official status and the associated public power as their own personal privileges. Public office, in their mind, is not obligation of serving the people, but rather, an instrument of bestowing favors and attaining personal advantages. In a society that is dominated by the social ethos of official standards, high inequalities in power and wealth distribution are largely accepted as an inherent heritage. In such a social setting, the social stigma of corruption is generally low.

Particularism, another cultural element, contributes to nepotism and corruption. Observers of Chinese society conclude that Chinese culture is in its essence a personalistic, kinship-oriented one, and the reliance on social connections is fundamental in Chinese society. Particularistic practices such as guanxi networks, as pointed out previously, play an important role in the formation and evolution of various patterns of corruption such as nepotism, cronyism, bribery, selling and buying public office, etc. As a relationship-centered society that traditionally values interpersonal relationships and interactions, there is a lack of clear-cut demarcation between

[56] He, Zengke, 255.

[57] Winnie Tong, "Analysis of Corruption from Sociocultural Perspectives," 12.

gift-giving and bribery. "When defining corruption in China, it is best to consider corruption on a spectrum, since the difference between corruption and legitimate guanxi is often a matter of degree".[58] As discussed, guanxi is a system of gifts and favors in which obligation and indebtedness are manufactured, and its pervasiveness as a social fact in both traditional and modern-day China distinguishes itself from the general notion of social embeddedness and social connections in other contexts.[59] Citizens and public officials utilize networks of personal ties to seek either preferential treatments or promotions, respectively, and consequently, "guanxixue" has become an important means of favor-seeking in public life. In addition, the custom of reciprocity also fuels corruption. Practice of reciprocity, to a large extent, blurs the demarcation between public life and social life, and the malpractice has rapidly spilled over from the social setting to the public domain. Irregularities and malfeasances such as nepotism, gift-giving, and bribery under the guise of reciprocity can become seemingly legitimate and socially acceptable in society. As an alternative system of relational ethics, guanxi networks function to neutralize and even distort state rules and regulations. The enduring persistence of guanxi in Chinese society validates the complex interactions of culture, institutions, and informal politics, and also exemplifies the long-lasting influence of the cultural traits and the complex interaction of tradition and modernization. While acknowledging the affirmed causal linkage between guanxi networks and corruption, it seems "impractical to expect to eliminate its practice as a solution to corruption", given guanxi's ancient roots and prevalence in Chinese society.[60]

Gift-giving and bribery also have their deep roots in traditional Chinese culture and society. Gift-giving, bribery, and banqueting had been prevalent across feudal societies and were often utilized as lubricants to smooth and consolidate patron–client networks and to facilitate illicit exchanges of power-for-money and power-for-power in the officialdom. In imperial times, gift-giving and bribery were widespread in bureaucracy and bribes remained a major income source for high-ranking central officials as they

[58] Jacob Harding, "Corruption or Guanxi? Differentiating between the Legitimate, Unethical and Corrupt Activities of Chinese Government Officials," *Pacific Basin Law Journal (UCLA)* Vol. 31, No. 2 (2014): 129.

[59] Mayfair May-hui Yang, *Gifts, Favors and Banquets: the Art of Social Relationships in China*, 149.

[60] Harding, 131.

seldom had the opportunity to extract payoffs directly from local residents. It had long been a custom that bribes and gifts were implicitly requested when local officials visited central officials either on business or for personal matters. Bribes were sometimes openly solicited, and the sizes of the bribes were even clearly marked in accordance with the nature of the business or favors. In the more recent era such as the pre-evolutionary "old society", guanxi networks and bribes were essential and instrumental to get things done in virtually all walks of social life. The instrumentality and utility of guanxi and bribery could even go as far as to get a person out of jail in the old days.

Similarly, nepotism and sale of public office can also be traced back to the long imperial history of ancient China. In feudal times, the selection of officials, under certain circumstances, was not based on the candidates' merits and qualifications; rather, it was based on kinship, friendship, fellow townsmen, pupil–teacher relationship, and other personal interests. All sorts of interpersonal connections have special implications in the traditional political culture of China. To extract desirable resources and ensure political protection, it was necessary and crucial for feudal bureaucrats to cultivate their networks of social connections. It was "usually done by bringing more relatives, friends, and townspeople into the officialdom".[61] Both patrons and clients benefitted from those social networks because mutual aid and protection among the membership could facilitate corrupt exchanges and also reduce the risk of being exposed and punished. There was no lack of examples of nepotism in the feudal history of China. According to historical records, for example, in Han and Tang dynasties, powerful royal relatives and eunuchs orchestrated nepotism without scruples. They "promoted their trusted protégés in secrecy", and most of the important positions were occupied by their own people.[62] In Han Dynasty as well as the Wei and Jin Dynasties, candidates for official appointments were mainly from powerful families. Local officials tended to recommend and recruit candidates who either had family connections to them or had bribed them for the appointments.[63] Also noteworthy was the practice of the government-hosted sale of public office for money

[61] Gong, 40.

[62] Huang Minglan and Fang Jing, "On the Causes of Official Corruption in Ancient China" (in Chinese), *Journal of Northwest University* No. 4 (1990): 45.

[63] Xianqun Pu, *Corruption and Anti-corruption in the History of China* (in Chinese) (Lujiang Press, 2014), Chapter 1 (electronic version).

in ancient times; proceeds from office sales were either used to subside public treasury or simply embezzled by corrupt officials. The widespread malpractice of the sale of public office in imperial China was blamed for the erosion of the state capacity, the prevalence of official corruption, and the deterioration of the social norms and ethos.

Lastly, the modern-day public-funded squandering and extravagance are also deep-rooted in the imperial heritage of China. Extravagance and squandering were common characteristics of the lifestyle of many emperors in imperial dynasties, and hence had enduring influence over the lifestyle of the officialdom. Seeking and even competing with each other for luxury and extravagancy among feudal officials was an important contributing factor to rampant graft, extortion, and corruption in ancient times. In the Northern Song era, for example, banqueting at public expense was so prevalent that the royal court had to issue royal orders to limit the grade and level of the feasts. In Qing Dynasty, the annual funds appropriation earmarked for management and maintenance of the river systems was in the range of six million taels of silver; however, only about 10 percent of the appropriation was actually spent on river management and maintenance, and the remaining funds was either squandered on banquets and entertainment by river inspection officials or embezzled into personal purses.[64]

[64] Xiangjiang Xiong, "An Analysis of Bureaucratic Corruption in Ancient China" (in Chinese), *Journal of Nanning Polytechnic College* Vol. 9, No. 1 (2004): 79.

CHAPTER 9

Conclusion: The Dilemma of the CCP Anti-corruption Strategy—Systemic Corruption and the Trap of Partial Reform

9.1 Dilemmas Caused by the Partial Reform Trap

While the history of the Party-state is marked by political chaos, economic stagnation, and impoverishment in Mao's era, it is manifested by rapid economic growth and a surge in national power on the world stage in the post-Mao era. Few would deny the stunning strides the state has made over the past four decades; the very successes of the reform and opening-up, however, "have generated new and difficult problems that well demand a more thoroughgoing reconfiguration of political institutions and operations than the top leadership has yet been willing to undertake". For example, while the state has taken a series of bold economic measures to establish a market economy and boost economic growth, its progress and achievements in the sphere of social welfare—not to mention political and legal reforms—have to date been less impressive.[1] In the meantime, throughout the reform era, the state has been haunted by challenges in the economic and social sectors such as social unrest, environmental degradation, income disparity, growing public grievances in healthcare, education, food and drug safety, etc. In the political realm, topped the CCP agenda are the gruesome concerns about political stability, CCP legitimacy, and official corruption.

[1] Elizabeth J. Perry, "Growing Pains: Challenges for a Rising China," *Dædalus* Vol. 143, No. 2 (Spring 2014): 5–13.

F. C. Sun, *An Ineluctable Political Destiny*,
https://doi.org/10.1007/978-981-99-3146-0_9

The year 2021 marked the ninth year of Xi Jinping's presidency for the 2nd largest economy in the world, and a corruption crackdown characterized by intensive anti-corruption campaigns and political purge has been Xi's signature move since he came to power in late 2012. According to a report by the CCDI in June 2021, cases of corruption filed and investigated are in the range of 3.85 million, and over 4 million Party and government officials have been either criminally convicted or disciplinarily sanctioned.[2] While the number and achievement signify Xi's determination and the deterring effect of his sweeping clampdown on both "tigers and flies", the perceptions of both the outside world and Chinese citizens on the depth and breadth of China's corruption problem have barely changed over the past decade.

According to the latest Corruption Perceptions Index (CPI), the annual survey of the world's most and least corrupt countries carried out by Transparency International, China receives a score of 42 and ranks 78 out of 180 participating states, in parallel with Argentina, Bahrain, Kuwait, and Solomon Islands. The CPI is the widely cited index of corruption worldwide and is published annually by the nongovernmental organization Transparency International since 1995. China's corruption rankings in world surveys are self-explanatory with respect to the lack of overall confidence at both home and abroad about the effectiveness and long-term endurance of the state's anti-corruption campaign. Looking across China's rankings over the past decade, it's lowest to mid-range score of 42 in 2020 barely changed from 39 in 2012, the year Xi took the reins of the Party-state despite his intensive corruption clampdown and arrests and punishments of millions of corrupt Party and government officials. China's performance by CPI assessment and ranking suggests that the state has been chronically stuck at a level that is below the critical benchmark of 50, signifying that China and other lower-scored countries may have problems of systemic corruption to tackle. On the other hand, China also performs relatively poorly in comparison with countries in the Asia–Pacific region in terms of corruption control. China's CPI score of 42 in 2020 is lower than the average score of 45 for the 31 countries/territories assessed in the Asia–Pacific region. Eight years into Xi's iron-fisted rule and corruption eradication, however, according to

[2] "Xi Jinping's 8-Year Corruption Crackdown Led to Investigations and Punishments of over 4 Million Officials," *World Daily*, June 28, 2021. https://www.bcbay.com/news/2021/06/28/752097.html (accessed August 15, 2021).

the opinion surveys, as many as 62 percent of the citizens polled still regard government corruption is a big problem. To that end, 28 percent of citizens pay bribes for public services and 32 percent use personal connections to receive public services. These abstract percentage points translate into hundreds of millions of victims of government corruption in today's China. Transparency International suggests that "China needs to urgently and immediately put into place systems to reduce bribery within the public service sector".[3]

Given Xi's profoundly acclaimed move of a corruption crackdown, the most ferocious and prolonged in the history of the PRC, and the downfall of hundreds of high-ranking officials at the ministerial and provincial level, China's performance of anti-corruption, at least as judged by the Corruption Perceptions Index, however, has failed to impress. A logical question thus arises: is Xi's anti-corruption strategy simply not working or is the index not really measuring corruption at all? "It is both, but much more the former than the latter". Although the methodologies Transparency International adopts to measure corruption are facing contests and criticisms, nevertheless, "the Corruption Perceptions Index gives a broad idea of where problems and challenges lie, and where anti-corruption successes and failures are". While the task of measuring corruption seems "exceptionally difficult", the CPI still gets us "a feel for the direction in which countries are heading".[4]

What has gone wrong with Xi's decade-long corruption clampdown, which is intense in magnitude and unrelenting in nature? Why have the high-profile arrests of big "tigers" and sanctions of millions of corrupt government officials failed to impress outside observers and Chinese citizens alike? Is Xi's approach able to tackle the root causes that underpin the rampancy and persistence of China's corruption problem in the post-Mao era? What are the right remedies to curb and prevent corruption in the long run in the context of modern China? To begin with, we'll conduct an analysis to address the first three questions, and then discuss

[3] "CPI 2020: Asia Pacific," *Transparency International*, January 28, 2021. https://www.transparency.org/en/news/cpi-2020-asia-pacific (accessed August 14, 2021).

[4] Dan Hough, "China Still on an Anti-corruption Road to Nowhere, Despite Xi Jinping's Campaign?" *South China Morning Post*, January 25, 2020.

suggested changes and strategies that may effectively reduce and prevent corruption on a sustainable basis to conclude this study.

The failure of Xi's anti-corruption campaign to reshape people's view on the Party-state's fight against corruption is mainly attributable to the regime's failure to tackle the structural and institutional factors that cause tenaciously pervasive corruption in the reform era. Observers and citizens alike were first impressed with the breadth and depth of Xi's anti-corruption campaign and intensive enforcement measures that had led to the arrests and disciplinary sanctions of hundreds of thousands of corrupt officials when Xi took the top job in late 2012. People expected that more profound and fundamental changes and reforms would follow while ferocious crackdowns continue. Several years into the fight against corruption, however, the authorities' inaction to bring meaningful changes to a flawed political and legal system that underpin China's deep-rooted corruption problem began to stun and disappoint observers and citizens alike. The top leadership and their highly educated technocratic advisers are presumably well aware of various alternatives of reform plans and the corresponding effects and consequences, but instead, the political elite opt to intentionally eschew dramatic and systemic changes rather than continuously rely on high-handed enforcement to curb the momentum of official corruption. In the meantime, the traditional approach of moral and ideological education on integrity and communism ethics, like the one that had been widely utilized in the Mao era, was relaunched to complement the implementation of Xi's enforcement strategy. There are various explanations about the motives and the policy choice for the adoption of the enforcement-centered approach. One explanation holds that autocratic regimes such as China tend to opt for heavy reliance on enforcement-centered anti-corruption strategies rather than prevention-centered approaches as the former tends to generate immediate propaganda effects as well as greater political payoffs. Bringing dramatic and fundamental institutional changes to the system, however, risks to undermine the legitimacy of the CCP and to endanger the vested interests of the elite. As Pei puts it: "Policies and reforms designed to prevent corruption are almost certain to weaken the power of autocrats because the most widely applied instruments of prevention are those that deprive autocrats of discretion, undercut their ability to use patronage to maintain the support of their allies, and reduce their control over civil society and the media".[5]

Misconfiguration of Political Institution and Market Economy

Corruption in China is systemic in nature and corruption control and prevention, correspondingly, calls for a systemic approach to tackling the root causes of the malfeasance. The conflict between an increasingly liberated economy and a virtually untouched political system is manifested in not only the political arena such as abuse of public power and corruption but also the economic and social spheres such as the widening income inequality, environmental degradation, escalating social unrests, etc. China's success in the four-decade-long economic reform and a gradually liberated society warrant the reconfiguration of its political institutions and governance with its marketized economy to further economic growth and social transformation. However, this does not suggest a radical transformation of an authoritarian regime into Western-style democratization. As demonstrated over the developmental courses of other transitional economies, economic growth normally triggers changes to a nation's political institutions and governance. For example, as evidenced in the process of economic development and modernization in East Asia in the 1970s and 1980s, rapid economic growth led to social liberalization, and the expansion of the middle class and the growing awareness of political participation had to a large extent contributed to the formation of the trend of democratization in these states and regions. In contrast, China's reform and decades-long rapid economic growth have led to neither political reform in a real sense nor democratization, but rather, "only slightest movement toward democratic government".[6] In terms of institutional and legal reforms, China falls behind not only most of its east Asian neighbors but also most former Soviet-bloc countries.[7] As judged by the performance of the current regime, however, the top leadership's commitment to deepening reforms including institutional reform proves to be empty rhetoric as it has fallen short of delivering

[5] Minxin Pei, "How Not to Fight Corruption: Lessons from China," 217.

[6] Mary E. Gallagher, "'Reform and Openness': Why China's Economic Reforms Have Delayed Democracy," *World Politics*, 54 (April 2002): 338–339.

[7] Minxin Pei, "China Is Stagnating in Its 'Trapped Transition'," *Financial Times*, February 23, 2006.

its promised reform agenda. For example, after the CCP plenum in November 2013, the top leadership reaffirmed its commitment to deepening economic reform and also pushing forward with SOE reform amid the anti-corruption campaign. A study on the acclaimed SOE reform found that, while some minor adjustmental measures had been initiated, there was "no evidence" that the move was "designed to pave the way for genuine SOE reform". Corruption clampdown on powerful SOEs, rather than a tack to reform the state sector, is in reality "a power game at the top" to purge the political elite's rivals and to "distribute patronage and valuable resource among elite groups or factions to reap their loyalty and support".[8] "They may pledge reforms, but most such pledges are lip service or tactical adjustments aimed at maintaining the status quo".[9]

Explanations for the regime's lack of interest in and commitment to political reform and institutional overhaul are various, and one explanation holds that the CCP's stagnation on political reform is largely attributable to the dissipation of conditions and momentums that had jointly pushed for bold economic reforms since the 1980s. Economic growth and the success of some reform policies "stabilised elite politics", and as a result, "the party lost appetite for real democratic reforms".[10] Under the current regime, however, what the top elite is concerned about is the potential risks that changes to the political institutions and the legal system and process would pose to undermine its political monopoly and to threaten its own vested interests. Institutionally and structurally, China's one-party system is deemed inherently autocratic and susceptible to corruption. Inaction in bringing necessary changes to the political institutions and gradually loosening up its tight grip on freedom of speech and civil society is partly attributable to escalating public grievances and social unrests in recent years. In the domain of anti-corruption, as mentioned above, the lack of meaningful measures to tackle the institutional causes of the problem undermines the long-term prospect of corruption control and prevention. The argument holds true in this regard; the establishment of an effective corruption prevention mechanism demands corresponding changes to the political system and legal process, which poses potential

[8] Jun Zhang, Qi Zhang, and Zhikuo Liu, "The Political Logic of Partial Reform of China's State-Owned Enterprises," *Asian Survey* Vol. 57, No. 3 (May/June 2017): 414–415.

[9] Pei, "China Is Stagnating in Its 'Trapped Transition'."

[10] Ibid.

risks to the Party's dominance and monopoly in Chinese politics and judiciary. "For the CCP, embracing prevention-oriented reforms is equivalent to choosing a cure worse than the disease: doing so would almost certainly undermine the economic and political foundations of one-party rule".[11]

As reviewed and discussed in Chapter 8, multifaceted factors come into play in the geneses of official corruption in post-Mao China, both structural, institutional, cultural and ethical, and moral. Here we choose not to go over what has been summed up in the previous chapter, but to go directly to the essence of the subject of corruption control and prevention. Again, to effectively combat and prevent corruption in the long run, institutional and systemic reforms must be undertaken to minimize the Party-state's intervention in the economy, reduce discretions of government officials, uphold the rule of law and judicial independence, promote political competition, and place the Party and government under the watch of the citizenry. Although these are the cornerstones of a democratic polity and society, some of them are deemed irrelevant to or even against the constitution and guiding principles of the CCP. In this sense, it would be next to insurmountable for the CCP to initiate fundamental and comprehensive changes to its one-party rule and political system for the purposes of liberalization of Chinese society in general and prevention of bureaucratic corruption in specific. A quick scan into what has been done in various dimensions of Xi's anti-corruption strategy, however, helps facilitate our preliminary assessment of the performance of the anti-corruption campaign. These dimensions are deemed core components of a rational, balanced, and well-structured anti-corruption strategy that helps build an effective and sustainable mechanism of corruption prevention.

Public Sector Advances While Private Sector Retreats

As discussed in Chapter 8, public ownership and the role government plays in the economy are positively related to the breadth and depth of bureaucratic corruption. The current regime, while continuously engaging in empty rhetoric with respect to its commitment to supporting and strengthening an increasingly expanding private economy, has failed to live up to what it has committed to the private sector, the most vibrant

11 Minxin Pei, "How Not to Fight Corruption: Lessons from China," 226.

contributor to China's GDP growth and job creation. Entrepreneurs and private businesses in China have long been experiencing barriers and difficulties in accessing business loans from state-owned mega banks. State bank funds, as traditionally designated to finance the operations of SOEs under the planned economy, continue to be prioritized for state-owned enterprises. A recent study on China's state bank funds allocation reveals that there has been a dramatic shift of state bank credit away from the private sector in favor of state-owned enterprise since 2014. By 2016, while bank credit allocation to private enterprises had dropped to 11 percent, bank funds distributed to SOEs had surged from 35 percent in 2013 to 83 percent in 2016. As observed by the author of the study, "this tilt squeezed out the more productive private sector, contributing to the ongoing slowdown in China's growth".[12] Operations of the state-owned banks and financial institutions in China, to some extent, are against the free-market rules and principles, as a significant portion of the SOEs are operationally inefficient and even money-losing. This largely explains why the ratio of bad loans with the state banks is so high. According to Pei, "wrecked by politicisation and mismanagement, the state-owned banks have cost China nearly 30 percent of gross domestic product in loan write-offs and capital injections".[13] On the other hand, many private SMEs that are deemed efficient and innovative and are creating the vast majority of jobs in the Chinese economy are continuously deprived of the opportunities to access state bank credit for business expansion and innovation. More importantly, the Party-state's recognition and political endorsement of a dynamic private economy have recently become more muted, signaling a reversal of the most important policy designation of the reform era. The top elite's signature move in this regard was its recent crackdowns on Big Tech companies such as Alibaba, Tencent, Didi, etc. under the slogan of anti-competition, consumer data security, and so on, hinting a clear reminder to the economic elite of who their real boss is. By late summer 2021, the regime's anti-trust campaign against major internet platforms had led to a market rout, wiping $US1 trillion off the

[12] Nicolas R. Lardy, "State Sector Support in China is Accelerating," *China Economic Watch*, Peterson Institute for International Economics, October 28, 2019. https://www.piie.com/blogs/china-economic-watch/state-sector-support-china-accelerating (accessed March 21, 2023).

[13] Minxin Pei, "China Is Stagnating in Its 'Trapped Transition,'" *Financial Times*, February 23, 2006.

targeted Big Tech stocks. Encouraged by the progress and early results of the Big Tech clampdown, the top leadership recently called for strengthened Party "guidance" of private businesses.[14] In addition, the regime's recent crackdown on the off-campus tutoring industry, which used to employ 10 million people, dealt another blow to the private sector with stocks of the cohort in the industry crashing by losing 90 percent of their market values. With the closure and downsizing of those tutoring firms, millions of well-paid jobs have vanished overnight. The top leadership has repeatedly pressed for "all are under the CCP leadership" and "follow the Party forever", and their targets include all segments of the economy and society. After the 2021 Beidaihe retreat, Xi voiced his intent to promote "common prosperity" and demanded the rich to give back to the society. However, Xi continued to avoid detailing what conceptualize this policy and by what means he will accomplish this goal.

Moves like this, although rational in some respects and to some extent from a perspective of policy guidance and regulatory sanctions, attest the authorities' intention to further bring the private sector under its command. As mentioned above, while the true intention and the policy implications remain to be seen, the slogan inevitably stokes concerns and skepticism of the private sector about the direction and long-term prospect of China's reform and opening-up.

In the meantime, instead of downsizing the scale of the less efficient SOEs, the Xi-Li administration has taken a reversal course to politically and financially beef up monopolistic mega state-owned corporations. As discussed previously, the most radical and transformative reform of China's public sector took place under the leadership of the Jiang-Zhu administration. When the Hu-Wen administration took reins in 2002, the impetus of SOE reform and restructuring began to slow down and were even in slight reversal ever since. Dictated by the policy of "retain the large and release the small", many large state-owned corporations remained untouched and continued to have monopoly power over strategically important sectors and industries such as public utilities, telecommunication, transportation, extraction of oil and natural gas, and manufacturing of steal and cement, etc. What has changed for these state-owned behemoths are the names and appearances with their essences and public ownerships remained intact. For example, although a change in form

[14] Xinmei Shen, "Xi Jinping says Big Tech Crackdown Is Making Progress, Calls Communist Party to 'Guide' Companies", *South China Morning Post*, August 31, 2021.

turned an SOE from "the Party committee responsibility system" or "the manager responsibility system" into a shareholding company, the nature and the composition of the management have barely changed other than its title. Members of the Party committee are now members of the board of directors and are appointed by the Party and government. The former Party boss of an SOE now serves under the new title of "chairman of the Board". As what is dubbed "old wine in a new bottle", restructuring in form may not help turn an inefficient SOE around. What concerns entrepreneurs, liberal economists, and observers most is the current regime's policy orientation of "the state advances, the private sector retreats" (国进民退), a move aimed to financially and institutionally strengthen and consolidate the dominance, competitiveness, and monopoly of mega SOEs in strategic sectors on both domestic and international fronts. This is perceived to be a strategic move by the CCP to support and strengthen its ambition and influence over other developing countries and to better position itself to compete with the United States and its Western allies.

In comparison to previous administrations, there is less evidence to suggest that the current regime has taken any consequential measures to reduce governmental involvement in the economy. On the contrary, the Party-state has been playing a greater role in the economic and social affairs. While continuing to maintain public ownership of land and natural resources, the state sector, via SOEs and public institutions, has increasingly involved in the provision of goods and services such as infrastructure, utility, energy, transportation, telecommunication, etc. Although the government has been making efforts in recent years to look into various structural factors to reduce and constrain official discretions and to eliminate opportunities and incentives of rent-seeking (such as elimination of a range of programs and approval requirements, as well as streamlining of the approval process, as mentioned previously), progress and achievements seem to be limited to date. Today's China, amidst few regimes in the world, constitutes a rare case that showcases the widespread involvement and intervention of government in the economy and society. As the regime is determined to shy away from tackling the underlying institutional and systemic causes of official corruption, what has been brought under control by Xi's corruption clampdown remains to be symptoms rather than the root causes of the malady. As the intensity of Xi's anticorruption campaign begins to lessen, corruption, which is an inherently integral part of the flawed political system and governance, is surely to re-emerge with a vengeance.

A Non-independent Judiciary

The rule of law and judicial independence are the cornerstone of democracy and the centerpiece of corruption control and prevention institutions and mechanisms. As reviewed in Chapter 8, empirical studies indicate that the rule of law and judicial independence are negatively related to the level of corruption. While the current regime's high-handed corruption eradication continues to sustain, its inertia in reforming the state's legal framework and upholding the rule of law in a real sense has prohibited the state from institutionalizing an effective anti-corruption mechanism in the state's governance framework to enhance the prospect and sustainability of corruption control and prevention in the long run. As mentioned, the Party Committee controls the judiciary through its political and legal affairs committee, as well as appointments of the president of the people's court, chief procurator of the people's procuratorate, and police chief. The Central Committee for Discipline Inspection handles all major and sensitive cases involving or implicating high-ranking officials, and the affiliated court system is mandated to carry out the CCDI decisions through its seemingly "independent" trial and conviction procedures and process. This highly politicized judicial system is susceptible to political manipulation and can be distorted and abused by its political master to purge political rivals on charges of corruption and other accusations. In fact, both outside observers and Chinese critics have been expressing their growing skepticism and concerns over the mixed results of as well as response to the regime's anti-corruption campaign. Aided by the CCDI, the judiciary, and law enforcement, as the criticism goes, Xi has been using his "selective" corruption clampdown to consolidate power and to purge political opponents. As judged by recent moves and developments in the spheres of politics and the rule of law, the overall political ecology in China has deteriorated to the most extent in the post-Mao era.

The independence of the Chinese judiciary has been further weakened under Xi's watch, as the regime increasingly tightens up its grip on the Chinese judicial system to serve its purposes of suppressing economic and social freedoms in a move to safeguard the CCP's dominance and legitimacy. Through its control over the legislature, the People's Congress system—a rubber stamp for the CCP edicts, the Party continues to enact arbitrary laws and regulations, reinforced by forceful enforcement, to control and surveil social media, suppress press and public opinion, and subdue political dissent, which has provoked widespread public grievances and resentment among Netizens, bloggers, and intellectuals. Over the past several years, there have been dozens of high-profile dismissals, detentions, and prosecutions of well-known academics, political dissidents, and individuals who had been openly criticizing the autocratic regime and calling for Xi's resignation and the change of the regime. Whistleblowing is a dangerous practice in China, and leakage of sensitive information, depending on the nature and consequences of the acts, may result in dismissals, detention, and criminal convictions.

In conclusion, the independence and trustworthiness of the Chinese judicial system have further deteriorated under Xi's rule. The CCP inherently lacks interest in and commitment to the rule of law and the legal process because it does not derive its own legitimacy from the law. As demonstrated in countries that are consistently ranked high on the CPI, a functional judicial system built on independence, transparency, justice, and free of political intervention forms the foundation of checks and balances and underpins the functionality, effectiveness, and sustainability of a state's corruption control and prevention framework. Inaction and even reversal in reforming and upgrading the state's legal system undercut the efficacy and long-term prospect of the regime's anti-corruption campaign.

A Politicized Anti-corruption Institution

As pointed out in Chapter 8, the regime's institutional failures are manifested in not only a weak and non-independent judiciary but also the internal extralegal supervisory system—the Central Commission for Discipline Inspection—that is not independent of the Party Committee and functions as an instrument of the ruling CCP. Without the granted independence, mandate, and resource like those of the ICAC (Independent Commission Against Corruption) in Hong Kong, "it is simply not that case that the commission can investigate what and who it wants, when it wants".[15] As mentioned, it is the last thing that the CCP wants to do to enhance the efficacy of corruption control and prevention by granting the

[15] Dan Hough, "Why Reform of China's Anti-corruption Is Falling Short," *South China Morning Post*, January 11, 2017.

CCDI the political status and financial resource, because by doing so it would inevitably endanger the CCP's arbitrary exercise of the state power and put the vested interests of the top elite and their proteges at risk. During Xi's first term (2012–2017), however, some form of institutional restructuring took place in the midst of Xi's anti-corruption campaign. As mentioned in the previous chapter, the National Supervisory Commission (NSC) was established in 2018 with its functions and operations merged with the CCDI. Although the NSC ranks administratively in parallel with the Supreme People's Court and Supreme People's Procuratorate, it is by no means independent of the CCP's leading anti-corruption organ, the CCDI, and in this sense, the institutional change is deemed non-substantive. With its director sitting on the Standing Committee of the Politburo, the top decision-making body of the CCP, the CCDI has the overriding authority over all the anti-corruption institutions and agencies including the NSC. As Xi continues to expand and consolidate the Party's leading power at the expense of governmental authority and judicial independence, the move may further weaken the institutional capacity in the Party-state's fight against corruption. With the presence of a distorted and manipulated judicial system and the exclusion of free press and civil society, the CCP is in fact fighting with itself for enforcement and prevention of political corruption. Institutional arrangements like this do not make much logical sense as the self-correction mechanism tends to be circular. As mentioned earlier, Xi is being criticized for weaponizing his anti-corruption drive to bring down political rivals while shielding proteges and loyalists from exposure and punishment. As Dan Hough points out, "China's anti-corruption drive is nothing if not political, and attempts to uncover incidences of corruption that might lead to those at the top of the political pyramid get nowhere".[16] Additionally, what one should keep in mind is the deep politicization of the anti-corruption campaigns in communist China in general and in Xi's regime in particular. The Party bosses at all levels have "enormous discretion in picking the targets of these campaigns", and quite often these campaigns are utilized to bring down their adversaries and political threats. In a state bureaucracy in which at least 80 percent of the officeholders are presumably implicated in graft and corruption in one way or another, the practices of targeting seem to be in relatively high probability. If there is a political will

[16] Dan Hough, "Wayward Drive: China's Crackdown on Party Members Playing Golf Fails to Hit the Mark," *South China Morning Post*, November 4, 2015.

in this regard, the DICs are largely instrumental in assisting their political masters to fulfill these missions. At the highest level, the CCDI is seemingly functional and instrumental in general combat against corruption but prone to political interference and manipulation. Again, the regime's so-called reforms to date in the institution of corruption control and prevention are more propaganda-oriented and obviously lack substance. As commented by Pei, "what separates it is its ferocity and length, which are largely the result of Xi's political motivation of conducting a de facto and full-scale purge under the guise of an anti-corruption drive".[17] As long as the CCDI and the judiciary are under the absolute command of the Party leadership, the whole system remains to be manipulatable by the top elite to fulfill their concealed interests and agendas in the name of corruption crackdown.

Crackdown on Civil Society and Press

While the CCP leaders of the previous regimes were criticized for eschewing to engage the civil society in policy-making and anti-corruption, the current regime is known for its large-scale and ruthless crackdown on civil liberty and freedom of press. Models and empirical experience in clean states have taught us that the engagement of civil society and mass media in the fight against corruption is a critical component of a rational and effective anti-corruption strategy. Empowerment of civil society and citizen groups to join forces with the government to tackle corruption is a proven strategy for corruption control and prevention. Citizens, with the help of media and social media, can share their own stories and experience in dealing with bureaucrats, and collectively are able to place government agencies and officials under constant monitoring and surveillance for potential wrongdoing. This is what is dubbed "people power". Inherently and understandably the CCP is afraid of the so-called "people power" as the Party is constantly in fear of losing control over Chinese society while misleadingly self-acclaiming itself and its members as "people's servants". Since Xi took power in late 2012, the regime has taken unprecedented steps in the post-Mao era to restrict the freedoms of speech and assembly, forcing state- and non-state press to surveil bloggers, scrutinize contents, block reports and articles that may

[17] Minxin Pei, "How Not to Fight Corruption: Lessons from China."

endanger the legitimacy and ruling of the CCP, and blow the whistle on political dissidents and violators of the CCP rules. Under the current regime, independent media and citizen groups are now in the mode of extinction; with the official inlet and outlet of information and communication being entirely restricted and blocked, netizens turn to social media such as Weibo and WeChat to expose government corruption, exude grievances, and protest political and social injustice. As the top leadership continues to tighten up its grip on the private sector in general and Big Tech in particular, the regime is increasingly closing in on the liberal tendency in media and entertainment in a calculated move to rectify the "wrongs" in the ideological and cultural spheres. The drive started with the blocking of some of the biggest names in Chinese showbiz and the silencing of influential liberal bloggers by shutting down their Weibo and WeChat accounts.

Also noteworthy is the regime's increased utilization of high-tech such as A.I. in its monitoring and surveillance networks. China is leading the world in various areas of S&T and innovation, and one of the advances is in artificial intelligence (AI). While AI-based video surveillance enhances public security and law enforcement in an innovative and unprecedented way, it can also be used by authorities for other purposes. China's AI-powered facial recognition system now boasts the most technically advanced and sophisticated system in the world. Aided by over 500 million CCTV cameras on streets and in buildings, the authorities use facial recognition to track its vast population in smart cities but also use the technology for mass surveillance of minority populations that Beijing is long accused of oppressing.[18] To draw a conclusion, today's China has become one of the most controlled and suppressed societies in the world. Rapid deterioration of civil liberty and increased suppression of press under Xi's reins have further crippled the inherently weak checks and balances in socialist China and dimmed the long-term prospect of the regime's combat against corruption.

[18] Zack Whittaker, "A Huge Chinese Database of Faces and Vehicle License Plates Spilled Online," *TechCrunch*, August 30, 2022. https://techcrunch.com/2022/08/30/china-database-face-recognition/ (accessed February 28, 2023).

9.2 Concluding Remarks

The current regime is troubled by not only dilemmas in the political arena such as widespread corruption, but it also faces challenges in the economic and social spheres such as a slowing-down economy, environment pollution, worsening income inequality, growing popular grievances and social unrest, problems in minority ethnic regions such as Xinjiang, etc. According to data from Credit Suisse Research Institute, the wealthiest 1 percent of the Chinese population own nearly 31 percent of the wealth in the country, an almost 50 percent increase of the 2000 figure of 21 percent. Put it in perspective, the wealthiest 1 percent in the United States own 35 percent of the wealth in the country.[19] This is indicative of the mid-term and long-term trend of income disparity that has angered many middle- and low-income earners in today's China. More and more Chinese citizens, particularly the older generation, now yearn for the integrity of Mao Zedong in contrast to the corrupt elite nowadays, and they cherish the equal society characterized by low-income disparity and social equality in the Mao era. People intentionally opt for what was deemed good in the past in defiance of the bad in the present, such as the widening income gap, corruption, environmental pollution, and deteriorating morality and ethics in government and society, to name just a few. This explains why Xi has recently put forward the slogan of "common prosperity" and begun to take steps to pressure the rich to give back to the society, a move aimed to uphold the legitimacy of the Party. On the international front, the Party-state scrambles to deal with the escalating conflicts with the United States and its Western allies with respect to issues pertinent to the origin of COVID-19, Hong Kong, the South China Sea, Taiwan, India, etc. The CCP and the government are currently overwhelmed with more urgent and imminent issues and challenges at both home and abroad, and institutional restructuring and political reform are seemingly set low, if not entirely absent, on the political and economic agendas.

In an authoritarian regime like China, institutionally there exists a weak incentive for the ruling elite to undergo dramatic systemic changes to its institutions and power structure. By the same token, a dictator is not necessarily motivated to respect public opinion and to serve his own

[19] Chris Buckley, Ai Sha, and Cao li, "Warning of Income Gap, Xi Tells China's Tycoons to Share Wealth," *New York Times*, September 7, 2021.

people. The rationale is simple and straightforward: It all comes down to how and where their state powers are generated. In the case of the PRC, since the power and legitimacy of the CCP are not derived from the rule of law, the Party-state, therefore, is inherently less committed to upholding the independence of the Chinese judiciary and legal process. Moreover, since the CCP's governing status and authority are not granted and authorized through general elections, the Party-state is neither obligated nor committed to respect, serve, and fulfill the will and needs of Chinese citizens and to promote and safeguard their rights. Over the course of China's four-decade-long economic development, for example, with the rapid accumulation of national wealth, the Party-state has not made much effort and progress in transforming the social welfare system that encompasses healthcare, social security, education, etc. In sharp contrast to the state's ambition and rapid rise in national defense, space technology, infrastructure development, S&T, and innovation, a very large portion of Chinese population are still struggling to make ends meet with very limited disposable income. As the state opts to commercialize its healthcare system to shun the burden of the costly universal Medicare, sky-high treatment costs for cancer or ICU care often leave patients and their families with no other options except for liquidating their houses/apartment suites in a desperate move to save lives.[20]

In contrast to its low commitment to the social safety net, the government has been spending with little restraint to upgrade the state's security system. According to Creaders.net, the Party-state's expenditures on internal/domestic security in 2019 amounted to nearly 1.4 trillion yuan, excluding similar provincial and municipal budgetary expenditures in the same area. On an annual basis, total central and local budgets for security maintenance have reached over 3 trillion yuan since 2018.[21] Rather than investing this immense amount of state funds in healthcare and social welfare, the Party-state chooses to beef up the capacity of the police force and Internet surveillance apparatus to suppress political dissent and freedom of speech. As pointed out earlier, crackdowns on civil society and social media have intensified during Xi's 2nd term, and state expenditures on domestic security are now way above the national defense

[20] Liya Su, "'He's Going to Die Anyway': Woman in China Divorces 'Heartless' Husband Who Refuses to Sell Home to Save Gravely Ill Son," *South China Morning Post*, March 1, 2023.

[21] *Creaders.net*, February 14, 2022.

budget. This further validates the observation and assertion that the CCP is more fearful of the growing public grievances and internal conflicts, either political, economic, or social and ethnic than its external enemies.[22] Unlike democratic states in which state power and legitimacy to rule are granted and delegated to political parties and governments by citizens through general elections, Chinese citizens are constitutionally shut out of the state power derivation and delegation process. In this sense, it is therefore unsurprising that the CCP opts to outright ignore and defy its citizens' demand for better social welfare and basic human rights without concerning its regime continuation and political legitimacy.

Through analysis, it is not difficult to trace the origins of many problems to their deep roots—that is, the Party-state is currently stuck in a partial reform trap and is seemingly unable to set itself free without thoroughgoing systemic reform and institutional changes. As stated earlier, as the market economy evolves and develops, the incongruity in the basic makeup of the Chinese political economy becomes obvious with the Party's inaction in political and legal reforms. Throughout the course of the economic reform and opening-up for over four decades, increased economic interactions and activities in the international marketplace have inevitably brought about reformative changes in ideology, culture, and ethos in Chinese society. With the import of foreign goods, equipment, and technologies to the Chinese economy, so come with pluralism of ideologies, values, and concepts of Western democracy, clean government, liberty, freedom of speech, human rights, and social equality. Rapid and sustained economic growth, enhanced education level as well as a growing middle class logically call for incremental political liberalization and democratization. It is a natural and logical process to modernize governance and the rule of law, incrementally free up civil society and media, and undertake systemic reforms in state institutions in synchronization with the economic reform and marketization. It is unfeasible to simply shut the society down and reverse the societal ideology and values back to the Mao era while upholding the so-called economic prosperity of the twenty-first century. It seems incompatible and also unimaginable to operate a modern economy with per capita income reaching over $12,000 USD (2021) level while forcing the societal ideology, norms, and culture back to the pre-reform age. This line of reasoning is seemingly against the

[22] Roger Garside, "Regime Change in China Is Not only Possible, It Is Imperative," *Globe and Mail*, April 30, 2021.

laws of social and economic evolution and development and is deemed irrational.

The incongruity and conflict between a Leninist political institution and a marketized economy and an increasingly liberated society have become increasingly acute, and the clash between an old and rigid political system and a vibrant society had reached its apex in the middle of China's "zero-COVID" lockdown. Dubbed "the most stringent" pandemic policy in the world, the authorities had been forcefully and adamantly pursuing its "zero-COVID" strategy by using highly restrictive and suppressive means that had led to confinement of hundreds of millions of people and widespread public resentment and unrests. The blow to China's economy is serious: youth unemployment has reached a record 20 percent, numerous small firms have been forced out of business, corporate profits have slumped, and economic growth has fallen far short of target. Equally detrimental are the damages the policy failure has caused to the CCP's ruling capability and legitimacy. What happened in China's pandemic lockdown serves as an illustrative example that suffices to validate the argument over the incompatibility and misconfiguration of China's political institutions and its market economy. Under the current regime, the "partial reform" dilemma and the systemic incongruity are most likely to remain decisive obstacles to China's continued economic growth and social transformation.

The top leadership and their highly educated advisors may be well aware of the policy scenarios and the corresponding consequences, but they have decided to choose an unpopular and adverse path out of concerns over imminent political risks and threats to the CCP regime. As discussed, concerns over the CCP legitimacy, political stability, as well as the political elite's vested interests have prompted Party leaders in the post-Mao era to "preempt—or at least postpone—the need for a drastic political overhaul". As Elizabeth Perry points out, in a rapidly marketized China in the reform era, "the only thing that could be considered socialist about 'socialism with Chinese characteristics' was the continued rule of a ruthless Communist Party".[23] What concerns most to the top elite is the potential risks that political reform may trigger and catalyze, a scenario that the Party-state cannot afford to take as it may eventually undermine

[23] Perry, Elizabeth, 6.

the legitimacy of the CCP and topple its ruling. A sincere political overhaul requires the upholding of the rule of law and the independence of the judiciary, which will consequently override the CCDI protocol, process, and decisions and put the political elite and their proteges in imminent danger of prosecution and conviction of power abuse and corruption. This is a risk scenario that the political elite will fight tit-for-tat to circumvent. On the other hand, a liberalized civil society and free press will put the operations of government and the conduct of government officials under a microscope and expose malpractices and dirty deals, another scenario of risks that the Party-state cannot afford to accommodate. It is the concealment and cover-up in the operation of the government that have enabled political elites to graft, collude, and funnel privileges and lucrative benefits to their cronies and loyalists who may forgo their political commitments without the patronage and personal gains rendered. Transparency and accountability are deemed highly effective mechanisms to deter and prevent corruption, and these systemic changes, together with other necessary institutional reforms, will deprive high-ranking officials of discretions and significantly reduce and weaken opportunities and incentives for Party-state officials to engage in graft and illicit payoffs. However, while the qualitative nature of the CCP ruling remains unchanged, the only variance is the quantitative extent in various regimes. For example, the Deng and Jiang eras are deemed relatively enlightened regimes characterized by bold economic reform initiatives, political openness, ideological liberty, and a less controlled civil society and press. In contrast, the current regime sees reversals on almost all fronts—political, economic, legal, social, and ideological—with the most restricted freedoms of civil society and speech in the post-Mao era.

The Partial Reform Trap and the Paradox of Anti-corruption Policy

Xi's decade-long corruption crackdown is losing momentum and seems to be stuck in a partial reform trap as well—on one hand, heavy reliance on enforcement and disciplinary sanctions has indeed deterred the impetus of widespread official corruption, on the other hand, Xi's flawed anti-corruption strategy, which lacks the underpinning pillars of institutional and structural reforms, plus ruthless suppressions on press and civil society, raises serious questions about its long-term effectiveness and endurance. A decade into the fight against corruption, the regime has come under criticism for inaction in initiating fundamental institutional changes to tackle the root causes of corruption. As suggested by findings and conclusions of analysis and assessment of corruption in communist regimes like China, the Party itself is the root cause of corruption structurally and systemically. Under the flawed political arrangements, the CCP is basically supervising the CCP without the participation and involvement of the Chinese civil society and mass media, let alone a non-independent CCDI and a politically controlled and manipulated judiciary. Judged by the performance of the current regime, the Party's self-correction capability has been called into serious question in comparison to Deng's regime that was characterized by vision, innovation, openness, pragmatism, and a strong self-correction mechanism. In this sense, the CCP's anti-corruption campaign seems to be circular. While heavily relying on intensive and merciless crackdowns to curb the momentum of rampant corruption in the Chinese officialdom without addressing the underlying systemic and institutional causes that breed incentives for corruption, the high-intensity and high-cost of the current anti-corruption campaign, however, is unlikely to sustain in the long run. As observed, unintended consequences of Xi's corruption eradication have been manifested in the form of low morale, inertia, and non-performance in government, which in turn have partially resulted in a decline in investment and slower economic growth across regions and urban centers. With the easing of the scale and intensity of the anti-corruption campaign (as it will be inevitably sooner or later), corruption will again explode.

A balanced anti-corruption strategy, while aimed to curb and constrain the spread and rampancy of the malpractices through aggressive enforcement in the short term, is also designed to lay a systemic framework to structurally and ultimately prevent corruption by removing the breeding ground for the malady. As mentioned, the authorities have made efforts in recent years to take relevant measures to reduce and constrain discretions of government officials over program administration and regulatory affairs; in the meantime, structural changes in some form and to some extent have also been made to tackle the root causes of official corruption. For example, both the central and local authorities have axed a significant number of burdensome approval procedures and processes to cut government red tape and to relieve businesses of the corruption-riddled and time-consuming regulatory approval process. These measures, to a certain extent, have reduced rent-seeking opportunities and incentives in government. The Chinese government seems to be committed to continuing to look into program elimination and redesign to further reduce loopholes and incentives for rent-seeking and corruption.

As pointed up repeatedly, an obvious and viable solution to China's partial reform trap and the paradox of its anti-corruption strategy is to undergo fundamental and radical institutional reforms. As China's problem of corruption is systemic in nature, the corresponding changes must be systemic and substantive in scale and magnitude to reconfigure the system and governance to control and prevent incidence of corruption in a sustainable way. However, this reform must be an integral part of a set of broader systemic reforms encompassing political, legal, economic, and social reforms. However, since this scenario of drastic structural and institutional overhauls will inevitably confront the constitution and founding principles of the CCP and trigger transformative changes to China's political and legal setups, this avenue may be the least plausible for the political elite to explore and to consider. The logic is simple and straightforward: it will undoubtedly pose imminent risks to the interests and privileges of the political elite and endanger the CCP's political monopoly and dominance. It is in this context that the top leadership may have intentionally made their calculated move to divert from a trendy developmental course that had been destined for a more open economy and a more liberal society.

A less far-reaching scenario in which the CCP eschews drastic political overhaul to maintain its political monopoly can still exert a relatively strong deterring effect on rent-seeking and corruption. According to Ackerman, structural reform should be the first line of attack in an anti-corruption campaign.[24] Structural changes in this regard may include:

1. Eliminate public programs that are fraught with bribery and corruption. As illustrated by cases of embezzlement and bribery in previous chapters, a wide range of public funding programs are permeated with outright plunders and collusive dealings. The government has made progress in recent years in eliminating programs that had been experiencing widespread discretionary abuses, loopholes, embezzlement, and corruption. While tightening up program monitoring and supervision, comprehensive and in-depth program reviews and assessments must be conducted on a regular basis to terminate

[24] Ackerman, 160.

any ineffective and corruption-laden public programs. From the perspective of cost–benefit analysis, costs associated with running those programs, both direct and indirect (such as the monetary loss and negative social consequences resulting from corruption), may outweigh program benefits, and those programs no longer serve their predefined objectives. Under such circumstances, program elimination, therefore, is a simple and viable solution to the dilemma.

2. Reform and streamline public programs to eliminate or reduce officials' incentives and discretions that may induce corruption (for example, rule-based decision-making). Many public programs and services have strong rationale and justifications to exist, but loopholes and unrigid execution render officials with ample discretions for power abuse and extraction of illicit payoffs. Measures of simplifying and streamlining program design and administration include clear-cut program eligibility and requirements for approval to minimize discretionary interpretations and to reduce the layers of approval stages. The more the stages of procedural reviews and approvals, the more the opportunities and incentives a public program can generate for rent-seeking and corruption. The key to fix the dilemma is to reduce the magnitude of discretion by establishing a rule-based decision-making process. While some of the programs were poorly designed and executed due to a lack of capacity and expertise, others were intentionally set up in a loose way to afford administrators ample loopholes and discretions for rent-seeking and bribe extraction.
3. Undertake regulatory and tax reforms to streamline and simplify the processes to eliminate or reduce bureaucrats' discretions and incentives for corruption. High nominal tax rates and complicated regulations and tax laws motivate businesses and individuals to evade taxes or to circumvent regulations by making illicit payoffs to government officials at the expense of the state coffer. Reducing nominal rates may permit an escape from the trap where high rates lead to evasion, and evasion leads to higher nominal rates and even more evasion.[25] Poorly formulated and enacted regulations and loosely administrated enforcement processes are the root causes of

[25] Ibid., 135.

rampant tax evasions and widespread violations of laws and regulations in reform China. Again, streamlining regulation formulation and enforcement to minimize officials' discretions for interpretation of the regulation and establishing rule-based decision-making of enforcement help keep corruption at bay.

4. Establish an authoritative and well-resourced anti-corruption agency that is independent of the Party-state in carrying out its mandate, investigations, enforcement, and corruption prevention. Increased odds of detection and harsh punishments can keep off corruption by increasing the cost of corruption. Again, it is deemed unplausible for the initiative to be put in place under the current regime, but it is paramount to uphold the independence and authority of such an anti-corruption organization. As demonstrated by the success of the Singapore and Hong Kong models, an independent and authoritative anti-corruption agency staffed by highly qualified and well-trained professionals has the potential to bring corruption under control within a relatively short timeframe and to establish preventive mechanisms to limit the incidence of corruption in government. More importantly, a politically neutral anti-corruption institution will correct the wrong of weaponizing anti-corruption against political rivals and help boost citizens' trust and confidence in anti-corruption campaigns.
5. Further public service reform to establish a professional civil service. The general absence of "work ethic" in government can also be counted as a contributory factor to corruption. As Hope points out, "corruption is aided by the administrative laxity that results from the lack of a work ethic primarily derived from societal norms and poor training and education".[26] Public duties, as perceived by many government officials, are not obligations under which they need to provide citizens with public services, but rather, instruments that can be exploited for personal advantages. This is one of the dilemmas faced by the Chinese bureaucracy. An ethical and professional public service is the prerequisite of a clean government, and recruitment and promotion in public service must be based on merit and performance rather than nepotism and cronyism. Remunerate public servants with decent pay coupled with sufficient

[26] Hope, 130.

training to boost their commitment to and pride in their profession. However, merit recruitment and an ethical and professional cadre of civil servants are not possible unless remunerations are adequate. "A more professional, merit-based civil service that is paid and trained well and rewarded for competence is the bedrock on which any anti-corruption reforms must be built".[27] Singapore and Hong Kong offer models of success in this regard as highly paid government executives and officials have much less incentive to engage in corrupt acts and collusive deals. The rationale is sound—good remunerations increase the opportunity cost of losing out on a well-paying and respected job, and functions to reduce incentives for corruption.

6. Enhance the transparency of government operation and decision-making and strengthen accountability in proportion to officials' discretionary power. The Party-state has a long way to go to make its government more transparent. For example, the Open Budget Index (International Budget Partnership 2017) ranks the transparency of "central government budget transparency" on a 100-point scale; unsurprisingly, the index ranks New Zealand, Sweden, and Norway as the most open with scores of 89/100, 87/100 and 85/100 respectively, whereas China is rated as one of the least transparent, with a score of 13/100.[28] Allowing the press and civil society to play a role in monitoring government operations and its budget and expenditures constitutes an important step in enhancing government transparency and accountability. In addition, the government should also consider publicizing information on regulatory approvals, public tenders, and public project funding decisions to allow the public to monitor decision-making and public contract fulfillments and to help detect and expose collusions, corrupt deals, and illicit payoffs.
7. In general, corruption is often the consequence of a conflict of interest in governance. The government should enact laws and regulations to tackle widespread conflict of interest in the Chinese government. Under the influence of the traditional norms and values, as pointed out in Chapter 8, some forms of conflict of

[27] Ackerman, 174.

[28] Dominic Kwok, "An Investigation into Best Practices and Lessons Learnt with Respect to China's Crackdown on Corruption," *ScholarlyCommons*, University of Pennsylvania, 2018.

interest may not be deemed as what is explicitly defined as "corruption". Instead, the patterns and manifestations of the malpractices may look more like "gray" or "white" corruption as defined in the Western literature. The presence of widespread conflict of interest in state governance to a large extent explains why official wrongdoing and corruption are so prevalent and rampant in reform China. Provision of training and education on professional code of conduct and conflict of interest is needed in parallel with conflict-of-interest law enforcement and legal sanctions.

8. Reduce the privileges of high-level officials to curtail a major incentive for corruption in the CCP regime. The Party-state has long been criticized by both Chinese citizens and external observers for nurturing and promoting privileges for the political elite. Compounded by a culture that inherently tolerates various privileges and power abuses associated with the ruling elite, this political culture intrinsically breeds incentives for corruption. For example, according to the 2004 official data, the average funds received by each retired member of the Standing Committee of the Politburo for one year was in the range of RBM 27 million (US$ 4.4 million), excluding costs associated with free transportation, chartered flights, free use of vacation homes, as well as top-notch medical services they enjoy.[29] The extravagant way of life of the political elite funded by public funds sets a negative example for lower-level officials and the society at large to follow suit by exploiting ways to extract illicit gains at the expense of the state.

9.3 The Final Remarks

This book is not about democracy, but several core elements of democracy such as the rule of law, an independent judiciary, a free press, and an active civil society constitute the most effective institutions to deter and prevent political and bureaucratic corruption. As suggested, China does not have to pursue and adopt Western-style democracy to democratize its polity and society, but institutionalization of key democratic

[29] Zhou, X., "The High Expenditures of China's Leaders," Renminbao.com, November 6, 2011. http://www.renminbao.com/rmb/articles/2011/11/6/55579p.html. Cited in Shaomin Li (2017).

principles and elements in its overall governance structure is imperative to the long-term success of the state's efforts to eradicate and prevent corruption. However, as discussed, the current regime constitutes an all-inclusive reversal of the Party's decades-long collective and institutionalized rule established under Deng and characterized by openness, progressiveness, liberty, and tolerance. As commented by David Shambough, "Deng sought to institutionalize various procedures—collective leadership, mandatory retirement and fixed terms, no personality cults, meritocratic recruitment and promotion, intraparty 'democracy', etcetera—whereas Xi has violated every one of these procedures. Deng tolerated dissent and [allowed] considerable freedom of speech among intellectuals—Xi seems to have zero tolerance for intellectual freedom, diversity of opinion, and dissent". While Deng sought to remove the Party-state from the economy, Xi reversed this policy by strengthening the Party's control over the economy and "inserting the Party into the private sector".[30]

At the time I was about to bring an end to this case study, the Sixth Plenary Session of the 19th National Congress of the Communist Party of China had just concluded in Beijing. The Six Plenary Session is viewed as a landmark event for the CCP to transition from the five-year period of the 19th National Congress to the new five-year period of the 20th National Congress that is slated for late 2022. It is widely expected that Xi Jinping will be granted his 3rd term as the leader of the CCP at the 20th National Congress and continue to rule the CCP and the PRC for at least another five-year term. Granting a 3rd term as the Chairman of the PRC and the leader of the CCP is unprecedented in the post-Mao era as Xi's predecessors all stepped down from their paramount positions at the end of their second terms. However, what characterizes the CCP Sixth Plenary Session more as a historical event is its issuance of a resolution on history—the third such summation of history in the 100 years of the Communist Party of China—that anoints Xi one of the revered leaders of the CCP. The historical resolution sets Xi in the party's "firmament of epoch-defining leaders, alongside Mao Zedong and Deng Xiaoping". The resolution goes further to list Xi's achievements under his nine-year rule including corruption crackdown, pollution control, poverty alleviation, and clamp down of political oppositions but stops short to mention

[30] Daniel Kwan, "From Mao to Now: David Shambaugh Compares and Contrasts China's Leaders," *South China Morning Post*, October 10, 2021.

any missteps and policy failures during Xi's nine-year rule that may have attributed to the economic, social, political, and diplomatic challenges and difficulties that the state has been encountering since the commencement of Xi's 2nd term.[31]

The pass of the resolution and the elevation of Xi's status and influence to the new pitch at the Sixth Plenary Session have important implications for the prospect of China's democratization process and systemic political and social reforms. There are several explicit signals that the session and its resolution are set to convey to the outside world. First of all, Mao Zedong, the founding father of the PRC, is ultimately recognized in the resolution for his role in leading China to stand up against oppression while intentionally downplaying the disastrous consequences that China had gone through under Mao in the early years of the PRC. These include the Cultural Revolution, the great famine, endless political campaigns that had brought the economy to the brink of collapse, and extreme impoverishment. Revering Mao and legitimizing his legacy in the historical CCP document serve the purpose of enshrining Xi, a resolute Mao's follower, in the history of the CCP and legitimizing his ruling style of quasi-totalitarianism. Second, the resolution is the third in the history of the CCP and is therefore epoch-making in terms of strategic significance and historical influence as to how the CCP will rule the Party-state in the decades to come. While the resolution recognizes and endorses the ruling and the achievements/successes of Mao and Xi, it implicitly downplays the reform policies and practices of Deng and Jiang, which laid a solid foundation for China's rapid economic growth and integration into the global economy in the 1990s and 2000s. As mentioned previously, the eras of Deng and Jiang are marked by economic vitality, openness in ideology and culture, as well as a relatively liberated civil society. It is a fair and objective statement that where China stands now owes much more to Deng's epoch-making decisions to abolish China's planned economy system and to open the country to the world economy. However, this plain fact has been obviously distorted and downplayed for reasons that seem to be understandable in this particular juncture of the course of development of the Party-state. Due to its overwhelming influence over the formulation of the CCP policies in the future, the resolution has an obvious adverse effect on China's continued reform and

[31] Chris Buckley, "China's History Is Revised, to the Glory of Xi Jinping," *New York Times*, November 17, 2021.

systemic institutional changes that would contribute to the evolution of a more democratic polity and a cleaner government and officialdom. Third, the session conveys an obvious hint that Xi is most likely to be granted another five-year term at the CCP's Twentieth Congress. It may even anoint him with infinite terms of governance as the CCP leader and the President of the PRC. This is another scenario that may adversely affect the outcome of the state's political and social reforms in the foreseeable future.

A final note to the conclusion of this study is the recent release of the Central Commission for Discipline Inspection (CCDI)'s investigation report on the Sun Lijun case. Sun was the deputy minister of public security and was detained for an investigation on corruption in April 2020. Sun was dispelled from the CCP in September 2021 and was arrested for bribe-taking in November. Sun was accused of power abuse and corruption, a common accusation of wrongdoing for the vast majority of the convicted Party-state officials. What is uncommon for Sun's accusation is the allegation of Sun's "extremely expansionary political ambitions" and the cultivation of his own "political faction". Four of Sun's faction members were all high-ranking municipal and provincial police chiefs, and three of them concurrently held the positions of deputy mayor or deputy provincial governor (Shanghai, Chongqing, and Shanxi province). Wang Like, former police chief of Jiangsu province and Liaoning province, had been bribing Sun for patronage and promotion for years with a total amount of 90 million yuan in bribe funds. What makes this case relevant to the argument of this study is its validation for Xi's potential policy failure in this regard: most of the violations and corrupt acts committed by Sun and his clients took place in a period that is being hailed as the most unprecedented, sweeping and ruthless corruption crackdown in the PRC history. In his televised confession on the national TV network on January 15, 2022, Sun confessed: "I didn't stop (committing corrupt acts) even after the 18th and 19th (CCP) National Congress (Xi came to power at the 18th CCP National Congress in late 2012). I made a lot of mistakes and committed a lot of sins. Law enforcement is the defender of fairness and justice. I didn't expect that I would become a destroyer of the rule of law and fairness and justice".[32] Obviously, Sun is just one of the

[32] Tian Liang, "Seven Points of Interest in the Sun Lijun Case" (in Chinese), *Global People*, January 16, 2022. https://www.163.com/dy/article/GTQRGJ4J051283GO.html (accessed March 6, 2022).

unlucky corrupters who happened to get caught in the late stage of Xi's signature anti-corruption campaign, and, however, there are tens or even hundreds of thousands of "Sun Lijun"s who are still out there committing corruption because Xi's non-systemic approach and heavy reliance on high-handed campaigns and punishment are most likely to fail to cure the malady that is systemic and institutional in nature and scope.

Bibliography

"A Brief Analysis of the Four Clean-Ups Movement" (in Chinese). August 8, 2017. www.wenku.baidu.com.

"A Review of the Historical Background and the Great Significance of the Reform and Opening-Up in Contemporary China" (in Chinese). www.wenku.baidu.com/view

AFP (author unknown). "How China's Civil Society Collapsed Under Xi." *AFP.* October 4, 2022. https://www.france24.com/en/live-news/20221004-how-china-s-civil-society-collapsed-under-xi

"Anticorruption Campaign Under Xi Jinping." *Wikipedia.* https://en.wikipedia.org/wiki/Anticorruption_campaign_under_Xi_Jinping

"Arrest of FDA Director Reveals Corrupt Collusions Involving 27 Pharmaceutical Firms" (in Chinese). *sina finance.* October 29, 2018. http://finance.sina.com.cn/chanjing/gsnews/2018-10-29/doc-ifxeuwws9228643.shtml

Banfield, Edward C. *The Moral Basis of a Backward Society.* Chicago: The Free Press, 1958.

Baum, Richard. *Prelude to Revolution: Mao, the Party, and the Peasant Question.* New York: Columbia University Press, 1975.

Baum, Richard, and Frederick C. Teiwes. *Ssu-Ch'ing: The Socialist Education Movement of 1962–1966.* Berkeley, Calif.: Centre for Chinese Studies, 1968.

Bayley, David H. "The Effects of Corruption in a Developing Nation." In Arnold J. Heidenheimer, Michael Johnston and Victor T. LeVine (eds), *Political Corruption: A Handbook.* New Brunswick (U.S.A.): Transaction Publishers, 1989.

"Beijing Telecom Official's Feasting and Call-Girl Service are Paid for by Public Money" (in Chinese). *CCDI and Ministry of Supervision.* May 18, 2015.

F. C. Sun, *An Ineluctable Political Destiny*,
https://doi.org/10.1007/978-981-99-3146-0

Ben-Dor, Gabriel. "Corruption, Institutionalization, and Political Development: The Revisionist Theses Revisited." *Comparative Political Studies* Vol. 7, 1974, 63–83.

Brady, James P. *Justice and Politics in People's China: legal Order or Continuing Revolution?* New York: Academic Press, 1982.

Buckley, Chris. "'Drive the Blade In': Xi Shakes Up China's Law-and-Order Forces." *New York Times.* August 21, 2020. https://cn.nytimes.com/china/20200821/china-xi-jinping-communist-party/

———. "China's History is Revised, to the Glory of Xi Jinping." *New York Times.* November 17, 2021.

Buckley, Chris, Ai Sha, and Cao li. "Warning of Income Gap, Xi Tells China's Tycoons to Share Wealth." *New York Times.* September 7, 2021.

Caiden, Gerald E., "Toward a General Theory of Official Corruption." *Asian Journal of Public Administration* Vol. 10, No. 1, June 1988.

Caiden, Gerald E., and Naomi J. Caiden. "Administrative Corruption." *Public Administration Review.* May/June 1977.

Calhoun, Craig. "Protest in Beijing: the Conditions and Importance of the Chinese Student Movement of 1989." *Partisan Review* Vol. 56, No. 4, 1989.

CCDI. www.ccdi.gov.cn November 15, 2017.

CCP Central Committee (1963a) "The First Ten Points: Draft Resolution on Some Problems in Current Rural Work." In R. Baum and F.C. Teiwes, *Ssu-Ching: The Socialist Education Movement of 1962–1966.* Berkeley: Centre for Chinese Studies, 1968.

——— (1963b) "The Later Ten Points: Some Concrete Policy Formulations in the Rural Socialist Education Movement." In R. Baum and F.C. Teiwes, *Ssu-Ching: The Socialist Education Movement of 1962–1966.* Berkeley: Centre for Chinese Studies, 1968.

——— (1964) "Revised Later Ten Points: Some Concrete Policy Formulations in the Rural Socialist Education Movement." In R. Baum and F.C. Teiwes, *Ssu-Ching: The Socialist Education Movement of 1962–1966.* Berkeley: Centre for Chinese Studies, 1968.

——— (1965) "The Twenty-Three Articles: Some Problems Currently Arising in the Course of the Rural Socialist Education Movement." In R. Baum and F.C. Teiwes, *Ssu-Ching: The Socialist Education Movement of 1962–1966.* Berkeley: Centre for Chinese Studies, 1968.

———. "The Central Committee Directive on the Issue of Power Seizure During the Socialist Education Movement" (in Chinese). October 24, 1964. See www.news.qq.com July 5, 2009.

CCTV News. "Wei Pengyuan confessed bribe-taking of 210 million yuan." *CCTV News.* October 20, 2016.

Chang, Chungli. "Merit and Money." In *the Chinese Civil Service: Career Open to Talent?* edited by J.M. Menzel. Boston: D.C. Health and Company, 1963.

Chen, C.S. *Rural People's Communes in Lien-Chiang: Documents Concerning Communes in Lien-Chiang County, Fukien Province, 1962–1963*. Stanford: Stanford University Press, 1969.

Chen, Huaipeng and Ying Tian. "Further Promoting Party Conduct, Integrity and the Anti-Corruption Campaign" (in Chinese). *Qiu Shi* No. 4, 1999.

Chen, Liang. "A Brief Analysis of the Harmful Effects of Corruption". *Baidu Wenku*. 2018. https://wenku.baidu.com/view/b4751b351fd9ad51f01dc281e53a580216fc50c7.html

Chen, Lixiang. "The Philosophical Reflection on Bureaucratic Corruption in Ancient China" (in Chinese). *The Journal of Handan College* Vol. 20, No. 4, December 2010.

Chen, Wenbin. *The Anti-Corruption History of the CCP* (in Chinese). Beijing: Publishing House of the CCP's History, 1995.

Cheng, Yaowen and Lai Bojin. "The Bribery Case of Shenzhen Housing Administration Director Chen Bingeng." In *Major and Important Anti-Corruption Cases in the 1990s*. http://www.shuku.net/novels/baogaowenxue/zgczfbjs/zgczfbjs23.html

Chesneaux, Jean. *China: The People's Republic, 1949–1976*. Translated by Paul Auster and Lydia Davis. New York: Pantheon Books, 1979.

China Academy of Discipline Inspection and Supervision. "Comprehensively and Strictly Govern the Party." *baidu wenku*. https://wenku.baidu.com/view/c63343f051e2524de518964bcf84b9d528ea2c09.html

China News Service. "'Power broker' Ding Yuxin Sentenced to 20 Years in Prison." *China News Service*. December 16, 2014. http://www.chinanews.com/fz/2014/12-16/6880681.shtml

"China Prepares for Next Round of Nationwide Inspections in 'War on Pollution'." *Reuters*, in *South China Morning Post*. June 27, 2019. https://www.scmp.com/news/china/politics/article/3016342/china-prepares-next-round-nationwide-inspections-war-pollution

"China Securities Executives under Probe for Insider Trading." *China Daily*. September 15, 2015. http://www.chinadaily.com.cn/bizchina/2015-09/15/content_21885442.htm

"Chongqing Mafia Tends to Corrupt Officials at Deputy Departmental and Above Levels, Says Experts" (in Chinese). *fa zhi wan bao*. October 16, 2009. http://news.sina.com.cn/c/2009-10-16/132718844401.shtml

Chow, Daniel C.K. "How China's Crackdown on Corruption has Led to Less Transparency in the Enforcement of China's Anti-Bribery Laws." https://papers.ssrn.com/sol3/papers.cfm?abstract_id=2599448

Chung, Jae Ho. "The Politics of Prerogatives in Socialism: The Case of Taizidang in China." *Studies in Comparative Communism* Vol. XXIV, No. 1, March 1991.

"Collective Corruption." *baidu baike*. https://baike.baidu.com/item/集体腐败/5513688

Collective Corruption in a Tax Office in Chaoyang District in Beijing. https://wenku.baidu.com/view/74eb5ab80875f46527d3240c844769eae009a382.html

Coolidge, Jacqueline, and Susan Rose-Ackerman. "High-Level Rent Seeking and Corruption in African Regimes: Theory and Cases." *World Bank*, 1995.

"CPI 2020: Asia Pacific." *Transparency International*. January 28, 2021. https://www.transparency.org/en/news/cpi-2020-asia-pacific

Dai, Anlin. "Review of the Four Clean-Ups in Hunan" (in Chinese). *The CCP History Study and Teaching* No. 3, 2004.

Dittmer, Lowell. "China in 1980: Modernization and Its Discontents." *Asian Survey* Vol. XXI, No. 1, January 1981.

———. "China in 1988: the Continuing Dilemma of Socialist Reform." *Asian Survey* Vol. XXIX, No. 1, January 1989.

"Do You Know How Many Problems Have Been Revealed under the Complete Discipline Inspection Coverage of Provincial and Municipal Party Committees since the 18th National Congress of the Communist Party of China?" (in Chinese). *CCDI and Ministry of Supervision*. June 9, 2017. http://www.ccdi.gov.cn/special/zyxszt/bjzl_zyxs/201706/t20170622_101538.html

Dobel, J.P. "Corruption of a State." *American Political Science Review* Vol. 72, 1978.

Dong, Kechang, and Jingjie Guan. "On Jin Shizong's Anti-Corruption Measures and the Effects" (in Chinese). *Northern Forum* No. 5, 1995.

Dong, Keren. *Prevention and Warning of Public-Office Related Crimes*. Yinchuan, Ningxia: Ningxia People's Press, 2010.

Du, Xiao, and Gu Yandong. "Corruption and dereliction of duty are behind China's food safety problems." *baidu wenku*. https://wenku.baidu.com/view/f50129d076a20029bd642d87.html

Eckstein, Alexander. *China's Economic Revolution*. London: Cambridge University Press, 1977.

Enste, Dominik, and Christina Heldman. "Causes and Consequences of Corruption: An Overview of Empirical Results." *Cologne Institute for Economic Research*, *IW Report*, 2017.

Fairbank, John King. *The Great Chinese Revolution, 1800–1985*. New York: Harper & Row, 1986.

Fang, Jing. "The Relationship Between Official Corruption in Ancient China and the Institution" (in Chinese). *Journal of Peoples University of China* No. 5, 1993

Findlay, Mark, and Chor-Wing, Thomas Chiu. "Sugar Coated Bullets: Corruption and the New Economic Order in China." *Contemporary Crisis* Vol. 13, 1989.

Fisher, Max. "In a Race to Shape the Future, History is Under New Pressure." *New York Times.* January 7, 2022.

———. "Behind Kazakhstan Unrest, the 'Strongman's dilemma'." *New York Times.* January 10, 2022.

"Former Chairman of Shanxi Guoxin Investment Group Shangguan Yongqing is Dismissed" (in Chinese). *peng pai news.* May 29, 2016. https://finance.sina.cn/china/gncj/2016-05-29/detail-ifxsqxxs7854152.d.html?sinawapsharesource=newsapp&wm=3200_0006

Friedman, Edward. "Modernization and Democratization in Leninist States: The Case of China." *Studies in Comparative Communism* Vol. XXII, No. 2/3, Summer/Autumn 1989.

Friedrich, Carl. "Political Pathology." *Political Quarterly* Vol. 37, 1966.

Gallagher, Mary E. "'Reform and Openness': Why China's Economic Reforms Have Delayed Democracy." *World Politics* 54, April 2002.

Gan, Nectar, and Li Jing. "Crackdown on Corruption at Chinese Environmental Risk Assessment Agencies." *South China Morning Post.* April 29, 2015. https://www.scmp.com/news/china/policies-politics/article/1779975/crackdown-corruption-chinese-environmental-risk

"Gao Senxiang Corruption Case." *shuku net.* http://www.shuku.net/novels/baogaowenxue/zgczfbjs/zgczfbjs11.html

Gardner, J. "The Wu-fan Campaign in Shanghai: A Study in the Consolidation of Urban Control." In A.D. Barnett (ed.) *Chinese Communist Politics in Action.* Seattle: University of Washington Press, 1969.

Gardiner, John A. "Defining Corruption." *Corruption and Reform* Vol. 7, 1993.

Garland, Matthew. "China's deadly Water Problem." *South China Morning Post.* March 26, 2013. https://www.scmp.com/comment/insight-opinion/article/1199574/chinas-deadly-water-problem

Garside, Roger. "Regime Change in China is Not Only Possible, It is Imperative." *Globe and Mail.* April 30, 2021.

Gates, Hill. "Eating for Revenge: Consumption and Corruption Under Economic De-reform." *Dialectical Anthropology* Vol. 16, 1991.

Gerring, John, and Strom C. Thacker. "Political Institutions and Corruption: The Role of Unitarism and Parliamentarism." *British Journal of Political Science* Vol. 34, 2004. Cambridge University Press.

Gibbons, Kenneth M. "Toward an Attitudinal Definition of Corruption." In Arnold J. Heidenheimer, Michael Johnston and Victor T. LeVine (eds), *Political Corruption: A Handbook.* New Brunswick (U.S.A.): Transaction Publishers, 1989.

Gibbons, Kenneth M., and Donald C. Rowat (eds). *Political Corruption in Canada: Cases, Causes, and Cures*. Toronto: McClellend and Stewart Limited, 1976.

Global Times. "China Becomes Major Manufacturing and Cyber Power after Decades of achievements: MIIT." June 14, 2022. https://www.globaltimes.cn/page/202206/1268083.shtml

Gold, Thomas B. "Under Private Business and China's Reforms." In Richard Baum. (ed), *Reform and Reaction in Post-Mao China: The Road to Tiananmen.* New York: Routledge, Chapman and Hall, Inc., 1991.

Gold, Thomas, Doug Guthrie, and David Wank. *Social Connections in China: Institutions, Culture, and the Changing Role of Guanxi* (edited). Cambridge, UK: Cambridge University Press, 2002.

Gong, Ting. *The Politics of Corruption in Contemporary China: An Analysis of Policy Outcomes.* Westport: Praeger Publishers, 1994.

———. "Corruption and Reform in China: An Analysis of Unintended Consequences." *Crime, Law and Social Change* Vol. 19, 1993.

———. "Forms and Characteristics of China's Corruption in the 1990s: Changes with Continuity". *Communist and Post-Communist Studies* Vol. 30, No. 3, 1997.

———. "Dangerous Collusion: Corruption as a Collective Venture in Contemporary China." *Communist and Post-Communist Studies* No. 35, 2002.

Goodman, Margaret. "Does Political Corruption Really Help Economic Development?: Yucatan, Mexico." *Polity* Vol. VII, No. 2, 1974.

Graziosi, Graig. "Biden Says Chinese President Xi Jinping 'Doesn't Have a Democratic Bone' in his Body." *Independent.* March 25, 2021.

Guo, Dehong, and Xiaobo Lin. *The Records of the Four Clean-Ups Movement.* Hangzhou: Zhejiang People's Press, 2005.

Guo, Yong. "A Case Study on the Characteristics and Evolving Trend of Corruption in Transition China" (in Chinese). *Anti-Corruption Study* No. 8, 2009.

Guillermaz, J. *The Chinese Communist Party in Power 1949–1976.* Boulder: Westview Press, 1976.

Halpern, Nina P. "Economic Reform, Social Mobilization, and Democratization in Post-Mao China." In R. Baum (eds), *Reform and Reaction in Post-Mao China: the Road to Tiananmen.* New York: Routledge, Chapman and Hall Inc., 1991.

Han, Jin, Qingxia Zhao, and Mengnan Zhang. "China's Income Inequality in the Global Context" (in Chinese). *Perspectives in Science* Vol. 7, March 2016.

"Hangzhou Thoroughly Investigates Corruption in Sector of Environmental Protection." *Economic Crimes News.* February 5, 2016. http://www.maxlaw.cn/l/20160205/841075947618.shtml

Harding, Harry. *Organizing China: The Problem of Bureaucracy, 1949–1976.* Stanford: Stanford University Press, 1981.

———. *China's Second Revolution: Reform after Mao.* Washington, DC: The Brookings Institution, 1987.

Harding, Jacob. "Corruption or Guanxi? Differentiating between the Legitimate, Unethical and Corrupt Activities of Chinese Government Officials." *Pacific Basin Law Journal (UCLA)* Vol. 31, No. 2, 2014.
Harris, Peter. "Socialist Graft: The Soviet Union and the People's Republic of China—A Preliminary Survey." *Corruption and Reform* Vol. 1, 1986.
Harrison, James P. *The Long March to Power: A History of the Chinese Communist Party, 1921–1972.* New York: Praeger Publishers, 1972.
He, Huifeng. "Chinese Banker Who Embezzled US$108 Million Handed Suspended Death Sentence." *South China Morning Post.* December 27, 2019. https://www.scmp.com/economy/china-economy/article/3043714/death-sentence-corrupt-banker-china-gets-tough-lending-risks
He, Jiahong. "An Assessment of the Current Status of Corruption and Public-Office Related Crimes in China" (in Chinese). *Modern Law Science* No. 6, 2014.
He, Qinglian. "On Systemic Corruption in China and its Influence." 2011.
He, Yini. "China's Mobile Users Hit 1.3 Billion in 2015." *China Daily.* January 26, 2016.
He, Zengke. *The Political Cancer: The Issue of Corruption in Developing States* (in Chinese). Beijing: The Central Publishing House of Translation and Editing, 1995.
Heidenheimer, Arnold J. *Political Corruption: Readings in Comparative Analysis.* New York: Holt, Rinehart and Winston, Inc., 1970.
———. "Terms, Concepts, and Definitions: An Introduction." In Arnold J. Heidenheimer, Michael Johnston and Victor T. LeVine (eds), *Political Corruption: A Handbook.* New Brunswick (U.S.A.): Transaction Publishers, 1989.
———. "Perspective on the Perception of Corruption." In Arnold J. Heidenheimer, Michael Johnston and Victor T. LeVine (eds), *Political Corruption: A Handbook.* New Brunswick (U.S.A.): Transaction Publishers, 1989.
———. "The Evolution of Public Office Roles: An Introduction." In Arnold J. Heidenheimer, Michael Johnston and Victor T. LeVine (eds), *Political Corruption: A Handbook.* New Brunswick (U.S.A.): Transaction Publishers, 1989.
Hofstede Insights. https://www.hofstede-insights.com/country/china/
Holmes, Leslie. *The End of Communist Power: Anti-corruption Campaigns and Legitimation Crisis.* New York: Oxford University Press, 1993.
Hope, Kempe Ronald. "Administrative Corruption and Administrative Reform in Developing States." *Corruption and Reforms* Vol. 2. No. 2, 1987.
Hough, Dan. "China Still on an Anti-Corruption Road to Nowhere, Despite Xi Jinping's Campaign?". *South China Morning Post.* January 25, 2020.
———. "Why Reform of China's Anti-Corruption is Falling Short." *South China Morning Post.* January 11, 2017.

———. "Wayward Drive: China's Crackdown on Party Members playing Golf Fails to Hit the Mark." *South China Morning Post*. November 4, 2015.

"How Firms Colluded With Deputy Environmental Minister Zhang Lijun to Acquire Public Projects." *China water net*. December 12, 2016. http://www.h2o-china.com/news/250511.html

"How Much Does It Cost for Corrupt Officials to Break Up With Their Mistresses?" (in Chinese). *Xin Jing Daily*. January 13, 2016. http://news.sohu.com/20160113/n434436636.shtml

Hsu, Immanuel C.Y. *The Rise of Modern China*. New York: Oxford University Press, 1975.

Hu, Shuli. "Bureaucrats Must Not Be Allowed to Hold Back Reform of Approval Process." *South China Morning Post*. May 23, 2013.

———. "China Must Crack Down on Rampant Insider Trading." *South China Morning Post*. June 18, 2014. https://www.scmp.com/comment/article/1535460/china-must-crack-down-rampant-insider-trading

Hu, Wei. "Fight Corruption by Treating Both its Root Causes and Symptoms" (in Chinese). *Probe and Debate* No. 4, 1995.

Huang, Bailian. "The Comprehensive Causes of the Emergence of Corruption at the Present Stage" (in Chinese). *Qiou Suo* No. 4, 1995.

Huang, Jinxuan. "An Analysis of Corruption and Anti-Corruption in Ancient China" (in Chinese). December 2010. www.wenku.baidu.com.

Huang, Minglan. "The Relationship Between Official Corruption in Ancient China and Political Power" (in Chinese). *Beijing Social Sciences* No. 2, 1995.

Hui, Echo. "China's False War on Corruption." *The Walrus*. September 4, 2019. https://thewalrus.ca/corruption-chinas-false-war-on-corruption/

Hunag, Minglan, and Jing Fang. "On the Causes of Official Corruption in Ancient China" (in Chinese). *Journal of Northwest University* No. 4, 1990.

Huntington, Samuel P. *Political Order in Changing Societies*. New Haven, Conn.: Yale University Press, 1968.

iMarkets. February 24, 2017. www.finance.ifeng.com

Internet Live Stats. July 2016. www.InternetLiveStats.com

"Investigation into corruption in the sector of mineral resources." *jian cha feng yun* No. 4, 2011.

Jabbra, Joseph G. "Bureaucratic Corruption in the Third World: Causes and remedy." *The Indian Journal of Public Administration* Vol.XXII, 1976.

Jing, Si. "Mao Zedong and the Three-Anti and Five-Anti Campaign" (in Chinese). December 15, 2010. www.sina.com.cn

Jian Cha Daily. "Five characteristics of corruption in customs." *Jian Cha Daily*. October 14, 2003. https://www.chinacourt.org/article/detail/2003/10/id/85951.shtml

Johnston, Michael. "The Political Consequences of Corruption: A Reassessment." *Comparative Politics* Vol. 18, No. 1986, 459–477.

Kaiman, Jonathan. "China gets richer but more unequal." *The Guardian*. July 28, 2014.
Kao, Ernest. "Air Pollution is Killing 1 Million People and Costing Chinese Economy 267 Billion a Year, Research from CUHK Shows." *South China Morning Post*. October 2, 2018. https://www.scmp.com/news/china/science/article/2166542/air-pollution-killing-1-million-people-and-costing-chinese
Klaveren, Jacob van. "The Concept of Corruption." In Heidenheimer, Arnold J., Michael Johnston and Victor T. LeVine (eds), *Political Corruption: A Handbook*. New Brunswick (U.S.A.): Transaction Publishers, 1989.
Kwan, Daniel. "From Mao to Now: David Shambaugh Compares and Contrasts China's Leaders." *South China Morning Post*. October 10, 2021.
Kwok, Dominic. "An Investigation into Best Practices and Lessons Learnt with Respect to China's Crackdown on Corruption." *ScholarlyCommons*. University of Pennsylvania, 2018.
Kwong, Julia. *The Political Economy of Corruption in China*. M.E. Sharpe, Inc., 1997.
Laaksonen, Oiva. *Management in China: During and After Mao in Enterprises, Government and Party*. Berlin: Walter de Gruyter & Co., 1988.
Ladany, L. *The Communist Party of China and Marxism 1921–1985*. London: C. Hurst, 1988.
Lampton, David M. "The Implementation Problem in Post-Mao China." In P.M. Lampton (eds), *Policy Implementation in Post-Mao China*. Berkeley: University of California Press, 1987
Lan, Dongxing. "The Issue of Graft in the Middle and Late Ming Dynasty" (in Chinese). *The Journal of South-Western Normal University* No. 4, 1995.
Lardy, Nicolas R. "State Sector Support in China is Accelerating." *China Economic Watch*. Peterson Institute for International Economics. October 28, 2019. https://www.piie.com/blogs/china-economic-watch/state-sector-support-china-accelerating
Le, Wenhua, and Xiafei Yang. "The Causes of Official Corruption in the Late Northern Song Dynasty" (in Chinese). *Jiangxi Social Science* No. 8, 1995.
Lederman, Daniel, Norman V. Loayza, and Rodrigo R. Soares. "Accountability and Corruption: Political Institutions Matter." *Economics & Politics* Vol. 17, March 2005.
Lee, Peter Nan-shong. "Bureaucratic Corruption during the Deng Xiaoping Era." *Corruption and Reform* Vol. 5, 1990.
Lee, Wei-Chin. "Crimes of the Heart: Political Loyalty in Socialist China." *Studies in Comparative Communism* Vol. XXV, No. 3, September 1992.
Leff, Nathaniel H. "Economic Development Through Bureaucratic Corruption." *The American Behavioral Scientist*, November 1964.

Li, Fengtao. "The Route of Energy Corruption." *China Economic Weekly* No. 28. July 2014.
Li, Jing, and Wei Zhao. "The Origin of Corruption in Ancient China" (in Chinese). *The Journal of Guyuan Teachers College* No. 5, 1996.
Li, Nan. "The Relationship Between Corruption and Juan Na in Ancient China" (in Chinese). February 9, 2017. www.sohu.com
Li, Lixin. "What is Corruption?" *wenku.baidu.com*, 2016.
Li, Tian. "An Investigation into Corruption in Mineral Resources Extraction and Development." *zhong guo ji jian jian cha* No. 10, 2016.
Li, Wantong, and Mingqing Li. "Causes of Corruption and the Restriction Measures" (in Chinese). *The Journal of Xinyang Teachers College* No. 4, 1990.
Li, Yunshu, Yang Xinyi, and Cai Xinping. "The Downfall of Meng Wei Led to Exposure of a Large Number of Corrupt Officials." *China News Service*. April 12, 2019. http://news.sina.com.cn/c/2019-04-12/doc-ihvhiqax1913005.shtml
Lian, Jimin, and Cui Bo. "How an Attorney General Becomes a Prisoner" (in Chinese). *shuku net*. http://www.shuku.net/novels/baogaowenxue/zgczfbjs/zgczfbjs29.html
Lin, Feng. "The Causes of Power Corruption and the Causative Anti-Corruption" (in Chinese). *China Science of Law* No. 4, 1995.
Lin, Xiaobo. "The Origin of the Four Clean-Ups Movement" (in Chinese), *The CCP History Research and Teaching* No. 3, 2004.
Ling, Xiang. "The Bribery Case of Wei Shizhong Deputy Mayor of Yingtan City Jiangxi Province." In *Major and Important Anti-Corruption Cases in the 1990s*. http://www.shuku.net/novels/baogaowenxue/zgczfbjs/zgczfbjs25.html
Liu, Alan P.L. "The Politics of Corruption in the People's Republic of China." *The American Political Science Review* Vol. 77, March 1983.
Liu, Dejun. "Rethinking the Three-Anti and Five-Anti Campaigns" (in Chinese). *Tianfu New Forum* No. 3, 2009.
Liu, Jiancheng. "The State Enterprise Operator's Incentive and Restraint Mechanism Viewed from 'Dongfang Boiler' Stock Corruption Case" (MBA thesis). *University of Electronic Science and Technology of China*, 2001. http://www.docin.com/p-2045030094.html
Liu, Mingbo. "The Hunting of Several Big Tigers in the 1995 Anti-Corruption Campaign." *China Youth* No. 12, 1995.
Liu, Pearl. "Ex-Chairman of Hong Kong-Listed Bad Asset Manager Huarong Pleads Guilty to Accepting US$257.7 Million in Bribes." *South China Morning Post*. August 11, 2020. https://www.scmp.com/business/china-business/article/3096982/ex-chairman-hong-kong-listed-bad-asset-manager-huarong

Liu, Siyang, and Zheng Hongfan. "The Tragedy of the 'King of Tobacco'." *shuku.net*. http://www.shuku.net/novels/baogaowenxue/zgczfbjs/zgczfb js01.html

Liu, Xiaoxiao. "Environmental Corruption: Eight Means to Make Illicit Payoffs." *fa zhi zao bao*. September 12, 2005. https://www.chinacourt.org/article/det ail/2005/09/id/178204.shtml

Lo, T. Wing. *Corruption and Politics in Hong Kong and China*. Philadelphia: Open University Press, 1993.

Lu, Xiaobo. *Cadre and Corruption: The Organizational Involution of the Chinese Communist Party*. Redwood City, CA: Stanford University Press, 2000.

Luo, Jinhui. "The Hong Yonglin Bribe Extraction Case" (in Chinese). In *Major and Important Anti-Corruption Cases in the 1990s*. Beijing: Fangzheng Press, 1998. http://www.shuku.net/novels/baogaowenxue/zgczfbjs/zgczfb js24.html

Ma, Stephen K. "Reform Corruption: A Discussion on China's Current Development." *Pacific Affairs* Vol. 62, No. 1, Spring 1989.

Mai, Jun. "Corrupt Officials Holding Back China's Drive to Eliminate Poverty." *South China Morning Post*. August 29, 2017. https://www.scmp.com/news/ china/policies-politics/article/2108613/corrupt-officials-holding-back-chi nas-drive-eliminate

———. "The Curious Corruption Case of China's Former Securities Chief Liu Shiyu and His Lenient Treatment." *South China Morning Post*. October 20, 2019. https://sg.news.yahoo.com/curious-corruption-case-china-former-105 645689.html

———. "Shanghai Police Chief Under Investigation as Anti-Corruption Campaign Targets Security Services." *South China Morning Post*. August 18, 2020. https://www.scmp.com/news/china/politics/article/3097865/ shanghai-police-chief-under-investigation-anti-corruption

Maizland, Lindsay, and Eleanor Albert. "The Chinese Communist Party." *Council on Foreign Relations*. October 2, 2022. https://www.cfr.org/backgr ounder/chinese-communist-party

Major and Important Anti-Corruption Cases in the 1990s (in Chinese). Beijing: Fangzheng Press, 1998. http://www.shuku.net/novels/baogaowenxue/zgc zfbjs/zgczfbjs12.html

Manion, Melanie. *Corruption by Design: Building Clean Government in Mainland China and Hong Kong*. Cambridge, MA: Harvard University Press, 2004.

Mao, Zhaohui. "Organizational Corruption: The Most Difficult Corruption to Control?" *lian zheng liao wang*. April 6, 2012. http://news.sohu.com/201 20406/n339900562.shtml

Mason, T. David. "Modernization and Its Discontents Revisited: The Political Economy of Urban Unrest in the People's Republic of China." *The Journal of Politics* Vol. 56, No. 2, May 1994.

McMullan M. "Corruption in the Public Services of British Colonies and Ex-Colonies in West Africa." In Arnold J. Heidenheimer, Michael Johnston and Victor T. LeVine (eds), *Political Corruption: A Handbook*. New Brunswick (U.S.A.): Transaction Publishers, 1989.

Meaney, Connie Squires. "Market Reform in a Leninist System: Some Trends in the Distribution of Power, Status, and Money in Urban China." *Studies in Comparative Communism* Vol. XXII, No. 2/3, Summer/Autumn 1989.

"Media Reveals Embezzlements in Poverty-Relief Funds at Basic Level." *fa zhi zhou mo*. July 27, 2017. http://news.ifeng.com/a/20170727/51515987_0.shtml

Meng, Fanlin, Baolong Yan, and Junxia Li. *Study on Public-Office Related Crimes*. Lanzhou, Gansu: Gansu People's Press, 2013.

Minter, Adam. "Has China Reached Peak Urbanization?" *Bloomberg*. July 18, 2016.

MoCormick, Barrett L. *Political Reform in Post-Mao China: Democracy and Bureaucracy in a Leninist State*. Berkeley: University of California Press, 1990.

Moodie, Graeme C. "On Political Scandals and Corruption." *Government and Opposition* Vol. 15, No. 2, 1980.

Myers, James T. "China: Modernization and 'Unhealthy Tendencies'." *Comparative Politics*. January 1989.

Myrdal, Gunnar. "Corruption: Its Causes and Effects." In Heidenheimer, Arnold J. Michael Johnston and Victor T. LeVine (eds), *Political Corruption: A Handbook*. New Brunswick (U.S.A.): Transaction Publishers, 1989.

Na, Shu. "A Probe into the Issue of 'Three-Public-Funds'" (in Chinese). *doc88.com*. December 15, 2014. http://www.doc88.com/p-9415766258648.html

Nanfang Daily. "Division-Level Corrupt Official Zhang Xinhua Who Embezzled 340 Million Yuan was Sentenced to Death." *Nanfang Daily*. December 10, 2014. http://news.ifeng.com/a/20141210/42685782_0.shtml

"New Characteristics of Corruption in Banking Sector." *lian zheng liao wang* No. 3, 2006. http://news.sina.com.cn/c/2007-01-10/164712001355.shtml

Ni, Fangliu. "Unconventional Anti-Corruption Measures in Ancient China" (in Chinese). March 25, 2013. www.sohu.com

Nye, Joseph S. "Corruption and Political Development: A Cost-Benefit Analysis." In Heidenheimer, Arnold J. Michael Johnston and Victor T. LeVine (eds), *Political Corruption: A Handbook*. New Brunswick(U.S.A.): Transaction Publishers, 1989.

Oi, Jean C. "Market Reforms and Corruption in Rural China." *Studies in Comparative Communism* Vol. XXII, No. 2/3, 1989.

Ostergaard, Clemens Stubbe. "Explaining China's Recent Political Corruption: Patterns, Remedies and Counter-Strategies at the Local Level." *Corruption and Reform* Vol. 1, No. 3, 1986.

Ostergaard, Clemens Stubbe, and Christina Petersen. "Official Profiteering and the Tiananmen Square Demonstrations in China." *Corruption and Reform* Vol. 6, 1991.

Pei, Minxin. *China's Crony Capitalism: The Dynamics of Regime Decay.* Cambridge, MA: Harvard University Press, 2016.

———. "How Not to Fight Corruption: Lessons from China." *Daedalus* Vol. 147, No. 3, 2018.

———. "China is Stagnating in Its 'Trapped Transition.'" *Financial Times.* February 23, 2006.

peng pai news. "The Details of Wei Pengyuan Bribe-Extraction Case." *peng pai news.* February 16, 2017.

———. "Zhang Zhongsheng Who Took 1 Billion Yuan in Bribe was Sentenced to Death penaLty." *Peng pai news.* April 13, 2018.

———. "Former Provincial Deputy Police CHIEF was the 'Protective Umbrella' of the Mafia Boss in Changsha" (in Chinese). *peng pai news.* September 21, 2018. http://news.sina.com.cn/o/2018-09-21/doc-ifxeuwwr6760249.shtml

people.cn. "Seventeen Directors of Provincial Transport Bureaus Have Been Investigated in Nearly Two Decades." *people.cn.* October 17, 2014. http://politics.people.com.cn/n/2014/1017/c1001-25854895.html

Perry, Elizabeth J. "Growing Pains: Challenges for a Rising China." *Dædalus* Vol. 143, No. 2, Spring 2014.

Pildes, Richard. "Why So Many Democracies are Floundering." *New York Times.* December 30, 2021.

Pomeranz, Ken. "China Since the Square." *Dissent* Spring 1990.

"Power-Money Exchanges in Food and Drug Administration in Hunan" (in Chinese). *Economic Information Daily.* October 18, 2013. http://www.chinanews.com/cj/2013/10-18/5394395.shtml

Prybyla, Jan. "Adjustment and Reform of the Chines Economy." In Franz Micheal (ed), *China and the Crisis of Marxism-Leninism.*

Pu, Xianqun. *Corruption and Anti-corruption in the History of China* (Electronic Version in Chinese). Lujiang Press, 2014.

Qian, Gengwen, and Mingbo Liu. "A Brief Analysis of the Anti-Corruption System in Ancient China" (in Chinese). *Academic Monthly* No. 4, 1994.

Qin, Tiezheng. "Determining Anti-Corruption Measures in the Context of the Causes of Bureaucratic Corruption in Ancient China" (in Chinese). *The Science of Leadership,* January 2009.

Qu, Chaoli. "The Historical Inspiration of the Anti-Corruption Institutions in Ancient China" (in Chinese). April 2017. www.rmlt.com.cn

Quah, Jon S.T. "Bureaucratic Corruption in the ASEAN Countries: A Comparative Analysis of their Anti-corruption Strategies." *Journal of Southeast Asian Studies* Vol. XIII, No. 1, 1982.

Ramzy, Austin. "How Hong Kong's 'Patriots Only' Elections Bolster Beijing's Grip." *New York Times*. December 20, 2021.

Reform Reference No. 8, 1996.

Ren, Dan. "China's Financial Sector Crackdown Aimed at Laying Groundwork for Overhaul, Says Analyst." *South China Morning Post*. November 15, 2015. https://www.scmp.com/news/china/policies-politics/article/1878925/chinas-financial-sector-crackdown-aimed-laying

Research Division of Hainan Provincial People's Court and Research Division of Haikou Municipal Intermediate People's Court. "The Embezzlement Case that Involves the Largest Amount of State Funds Since the Founding of the PRC" (in Chinese). In *Major and Important Anti-Corruption Cases in the 1990s*. Beijing: Fangzheng Press, 1998.

Rocca, Jean-Louis. "Corruption and its Shadow: An Anthropological View of Corruption in China." *The China Quarterly* No. 130, 1990.

Rose-Ackerman, Susan, and Bonnie J. Palifka. *Corruption and Government: Causes, Consequences, and Reform* (2nd edition). Cambridge, UK: Cambridge University Press, 2016.

"Rural and Urban Socialist Education Movement and the Evolution of the Leftism Tendency" (in Chinese). June 3, 2014. www.theory.people.com.cn

Sands, Barbara N. "Decentralizing an Economy: The Role of Bureaucratic Corruption in China's Economic Reforms." *Public Choice* Vol. 65, 1990.

Schenone, Osvaldo H. "An Economic Approach to Corruption." Universidad de San Andres, 2002.

Scott, James C. "The Analysis of Corruption in Developing Nations." *Comparative Studies in Society and History* Vol. 11, 1969.

———. *Comparative Political Corruption*. Englewood Cliffs, N.J.: Prentice-Hall, 1972.

Shaanxi Provincial Commission for Discipline Inspection. "Provincial Deputy Director Yang Feng Misappropriated Over 4.4 Million Yuan in Public Funds." In *Major and Important Anti-Corruption Cases in the 1990s*. http://www.shuku.net/novels/baogaowenxue/zgczfbjs/zgczfbjs42.html

Shao, Daosheng. "The Sociological Thinking of 'Chain Case' and 'Lair Case'" (in Chinese). *Public Opinion* No. 3, 1996.

Shen, Wandong, and Shaoren Wang. "On Causes of the Uncurbable Corruption and the Counter-Measures" (in Chinese). *The Journal of Mudanjiang Teachers College* No. 3, 1991.

Shen, Xinmei. "Xi Jinping Says Big Tech Crackdown is Making Progress, Calls Communist Party to 'Guide' Companies." *South China Morning Post*. August 31, 2021.

Shi, Jiangtao. "Xi Jinping Puts China's Mafia in Cross Hairs, But Fears of Judicial Abuse Remain." *South China Morning Post*. January 26, 2018. https://www.scmp.com/news/china/policies-politics/article/2130629/xi-puts-chinas-mafia-cross-hairs-fears-judicial-abuse

Solinger, Dorothy J. "Urban Reform and Relational Contracting in Post-Mao China: An interpretation of the Transition from Plan to Market." *Studies in Comparative Communism* Vol. XXII, No. 2/3, Summer/Autumn 1989.

Statista. 2016. www.statista.com

Stavis, Benedict. "The Political Economy of Inflation in China." *Studies in Comparative Communism* Vol. XXII, No. 2/3, Summer/Autumn 1989.

Su, Liya. "'He's Going to Die Anyway': Woman in China Divorces 'Heartless' Husband Who Refuses to Sell Home to Save Gravely Ill son." *South China Morning Post*. March 1, 2023.

Sun, Fuhai. "The Study of Today's Corruption and the Socialist Supervisory System" (in Chinese). *Beijing Social Science* No. 2, 1995.

Sun, Yan. *Corruption and Market in Contemporary China*. Ithaca, NY: Cornell University Press, 2004

———. "The Chinese Protests of 1989: The Issue of Corruption." *Asian Survey* Vol. XXXI, No. 8, August 1991.

"The Changsheng Bio-technology vaccine case 457 days." *Tencent*. October 15, 2019. https://new.qq.com/omn/20191015/20191015A07C5200.html

"The Dandong Automobile Smuggling Case" (in Chinese). *chinaacc.com*. March 11, 2003. http://www.chinaacc.com/new/253/264/2006/1/ad382212263517160024444.htm

"The Historical Background of the Reform and Opening-Up" (in Chinese). September 17, 2017. www.wenku.baidu.com/view

"The No. 1 Case of Tax Fraud in China." *CCTV*. January 12, 2002. http://news.sina.com.cn/c/2002-02-01/465118.html

"The Power of IPO Approval Corrupts Securities Officials" (in Chinese). *ifeng securities*. April 22, 2017. http://www.yidianzixun.com/article/0GAOBwqo

The Publishing House of Economic Management. *Brandishing the sword: Reports on Anti-Corruption and Purging Graft in China* (in Chinese). Beijing, 1993.

The 'Queen of Vaccine' Gao Junfang and Her Family Are Dismissed." *ifeng.com*. October 14, 2019. http://finance.ifeng.com/c/7qlzwf2dgEi

The Supreme People's Procuratorate Work Report 1993–2016. www.spp.gov.cn

The Supreme People's Procuratorate Annual Work Report (1997). http://www.spp.gov.cn/spp/gzbg/200602/t20060222_16400.shtml

The Supreme People's Procuratorate Annual Work Report (1984). http://www.spp.gov.cn/spp/gzbg/201208/t20120820_2488.shtml

Tan, Xueshu. "Anti-corruption in Song Dynasty." *The Social Sciences* (in Chinese) No. 4, 1996.
Tang, Hongying. "The Anti-Corruption Struggle and its Characteristics in the History of the CCP." *Research of Social Sciences* No. 4, 1991.
Tang, Keliang. "On Officials' Engagement in Business in the Northern Song Dynasty" (in Chinese). *Probe* No. 6, 1993.
Tang, Xiping. "An Overview of 1995 Anti-Corruption and Purging graft in China" (in Chinese). *The Kaifang Monthly* No. 3, 1996.
Teiwes, Frederich. *Politics and Purges in China*. New York: M.E. Sharpe, Inc., 1979.
"Ten Cases Regarding the Loss of State Assets." *China Economic News weekly*, 2003. http://business.sohu.com/88/26/article208662688.shtml
The World Bank. 2017. www.data.worldbank.org
Theobald, Robin. *Corruption, Development and Underdevelopment*. Durham: Duke University Press, 1990.
"Three Family Members of FDA Official Yin Hongzhang Sentenced to Imprisonment" (in Chinese). *fa zhi wan bao*. January 3, 2017. https://finance.sina.com.cn/china/gncj/2017-01-03/doc-ifxzczsu6681612.shtml
Tian, Guoqiang. "A Review and Outlook on China's Reform and Opening-Up over the Three Decade" (in Chinese). www.wenku.baidu.com/view
Tian, Liang. "Seven Points of Interest in the Sun Lijun case" (in Chinese). *Global People*. January 16, 2022. https://www.163.com/dy/article/GTQRGJ4J051283GO.html
Tilman, Robert O. "Emergence of Black-Market Bureaucracy: Administration, Development, and Corruption in the New States." *Public Administration Review* Vol. 28, 1968.
Tong, Winnie. "Analysis of Corruption from Sociocultural Perspectives." *International Journal of Business and Social Science* Vol. 5, No. 11(1), October 2014.
Transparency International. "Corruption Perceptions Index 2016." www.transparency.org/news/feature/corruption_perceptions_index_2016
Treisman, Daniel. "The Causes of Corruption: A Cross-National Study." *Journal of Public Economics* Vol. 76, 2000.
Veugelers, Veinhilde. "China is the World's New Science and Technology Powerhouse." *Bruegel*. December 21, 2017. https://www.bruegel.org/comment/china-worlds-new-science-and-technology-powerhouse
Walder, Andrew G. *Communist Neo-Traditionalism: Work and Authority in Chinese Industry*. Berkeley: University of California Press, 1986.
———. "Workers, Managers and the State: The Reform Era and the Political Crisis of 1989." *The China Quarterly* No. 127, September 1991.
Wang, Chunjie. "An Analysis of the Four Clean-Ups Movement's Impact on the Cultural Revolution" (in Chinese). *Academia* No. 2, 1996.

Wang, Chunyu. "Revealing the Effective Anti-Corruption Measures in Ancient China: Opinion Freedom" (in Chinese). July 2014. www.ifeng.com

Wang, Heyan. "Supreme Court VP Xi Xiaoming Takes Bribes in 100 Million Yuan" (in Chinese). *Caixin*. January 12, 2017. https://news.qq.com/a/20170112/020334.htm

Wang, Liansheng, and Binlan Zhang. "The Gain and Loss of the Socialist Education Movement in the 1960s" (in Chinese). *Nandu Academic Forum* No. 1, 1995.

Wang, Peijun. "The System and Corruption: An Interrelated Analysis" (in Chinese). *The Journal of Academy* No. 4. 1994.

Wang, Shanzhong. "A Review of the Three-Anti and Five-Anti Campaigns in the Early Years of the New China" (in Chinese). August 23, 2015. www.360doc.com

Wang, Xianjin. "The Three-Anti and Five-Anti Campaign" (in Chinese). January 2015. www.hexun.com

Wang, Xiangwei. "China's Bids to Improve FOOD safety and Welfare for Its People are Just Empty Words – Until Leadership has Skin in the Game." *South China Morning Post*. March 23, 2019. https://www.scmp.com/week-asia/opinion/article/3002918/chinas-bids-improve-food-safety-and-welfare-its-people-are-just

Wedeman, Andrew. *Double Paradox: Rapid Growth and Rising Corruption in China*. Ithaca, NY: Cornell University Press, 2012.

Wei, Shang-jin. "Corruption in Economic Development: Beneficial Grease, Minor Annoyance, or Major Obstacle?" http://documents1.worldbank.org/curated/en/175291468765621959/pdf/multi-page.pdf

Wei, Yunheng. "Anti-Corruption: Where does the Difficult Point lie?" (in Chinese). *Ban Yue Tan* No. 2, 1996.

"Wen Qiang" (in Chinese). *baidu baike*. https://baike.baidu.com/item/文强/1445988

Whittaker, Zack. "A Huge Chinese Database of Faces and Vehicle License Plates Spilled Online." *TechCrunch*. August 30, 2022. https://techcrunch.com/2022/08/30/china-database-face-recognition/

Wu, Xiaobo. *The Surging Thirty Years: Chinese Enterprises 1978–2008* (in Chinese). Shanghai: Zhongxing Press, 2008. http://www.dubaocankao.com/html/news/shgc/2015/0611/6116.html

Xia, Fei. "Mao Zedong and the Socialist Education Movement" (in Chinese). September 14, 2015. www.people.com.cn

Xiao, Dan. "Study of Anti-Corruption from the Perspective of the Institution of the Imperial Itinerant Inspectors in Ancient China" (in Chinese). May 2015. www.wenku.baidu.com

xiao xiang chen bao. "Recurring Collective Corruption in Customs." *xiao xiang chen bao.* November 18, 2014. http://epaper.xxcb.cn/xxcba/html/2014-11/18/content_2816129.htm

Xie, Baogui. "The Function of the Chinese Procuratorial Organ in the Combat Against Corruption." *Asian Journal of Public Administration* Vol. 10, No. 1, June 1988.

Xie, Echo. "China's Green Efforts Hit by Fake Data and Corruption Among the Grass Roots." *South China Morning Post.* May 19, 2019. https://www.scmp.com/news/china/politics/article/3010679/chinas-green-efforts-hit-fake-data-and-corruption-among-grass

"Xi Jinping's 8-Year Corruption Crackdown Led to Investigations and Punishments of Over 4 Million Officials." *World Daily.* June 28, 2021. https://www.bcbay.com/news/2021/06/28/752097.html

Xing, Hang. "The Chinese Traditional Official Culture and Official Corruption" (in Chinese). July 12, 2013. www.cul.qq.com

Xinhua News Agency. "Factbox: China's High-tech Achievements in 13th Five-Year Plan Period." *XINHUA NET*. July 19, 2022. http://www.news.cn/english/2021-11/02/c_1310286160.htm

Xinhua News Agency. "Collective Corruption in Land Led to the Fall of Mayor and Other Twenty-five Officials in Dong Fang City Hai Nan Province." *Xinhua News.* February 14, 2011. https://news.qq.com/a/20110214/000423.htm

Xinhua News Agency. "Principal Offender for the $4-Billion Case of Bank of China in Kaiping Extradited." *Xinhua News Agency.* September 24, 2015. http://m.jrj.com.cn/news/finance/2015/09/24163419861559.shtml

Xinhua News Agency. "Corruption affects China's Environmental Protection." *Xinhua News Agency.* November 13, 2009. https://oversea.huanqiu.com/article/9CaKrnJmEgh

Xinhua News Agency. "Offenders Involved in the Changsheng Bio-Technology Vaccine Case are Punished." *Xinhua News Agency.* February 2, 2019. http://www.xinhuanet.com/politics/2019-02/02/c_1124081062.htm

Xinhua News Agency. "Zhou Bing, Son of Zhou Yongkang, Sentenced to 18 Years in Prison and Also Fined Over 300 Million Yuan." *Xinhua News Agency.* June 15, 2016. https://finance.ifeng.com/a/20160615/14491336_0.shtml

Xiong, Xiangjiang. "An Analysis of Bureaucratic Corruption in Ancient China" (in Chinese). *Journal of Nanning Polytechnic College* Vol. 9, No. 1, 2004.

Xu, Beina, and Eleanor Albert. "Media Censorship in China." https://www.cfr.org/backgrounder/media-censorship-china

Xu, Ligang. "The Historical Lessons of the 'Leftism' Mistakes from the Three-Anti and Five-Anti Campaign: The Case of Jiangsu Region" (in Chinese). August 1, 2012. www.sina.com.cn

Xu, Menglong. "A Mafia Related Case Reveals Involvements of Over 90 Public Officials" (in Chinese). *China Discipline Inspection and Supervision*. September 28, 2018. http://fanfu.people.com.cn/n1/2018/0928/c64371-30317795.html

Yan, Ming. "Who 'Polluted' Departments of Environmental Protection?" *China Discipline Inspection and Supervision*. April 23, 2014. http://www.scdjw.com.cn/portal.php?mod=view&aid=20398

Yang, Dali L. *Remaking the Chinese Leviathan: Market Transition and the Politics of Governance in China*. Stanford: Stanford University Press, 2004.

Yang, Mayfair May-hui. *Gifts, Favors and Banquets: The Art of Social Relationships in China*. Ithaca, NY: Cornell University Press, 1994.

Yang, Qixuan. "The Implicit Rules between Emperors and Courtiers with Regard to Anti-Corruption in Ancient China" (in Chinese). October 13, 2016. www.views.news.qq.com

"Yao Gang". *baidu baike*. https://baike.baidu.com/item/姚刚/10173

Ye, Josh. "Big Banks on Notice That They're Losing Ground to China's Fintech Giants." *CNBC*. August 10, 2017. www.cnbc.com

Yu, Jianying. "A Study of the Four Clean-Ups Movement in Shanghai (1963–1966)" (in Chinese). October 18, 2014. www.doc88.com

Yu, Xueqiang. "An Analysis of Corruption of Dining and Wining at Public Expense" in Chinese). *Journal of Guangzhou University (Social Science Edition)* Vol. 10, June 2011.

Yue, Hongge. "The Liu Huimin Embezzlement Case." *shuku net*. http://www.shuku.net/novels/baogaowenxue/zgczfbjs/zgczfbjs37.html

Zafanolli, Wojtek. "A Brief Outline of China's Second Economy." *Asian Survey* Vol. XXV, No. 7, July 1985.

Zhang, Guo and Zhang Huijun. "The Zhoukou Fake Drug Case" (in Chinese). *shuku net*. http://www.shuku.net/novels/baogaowenxue/zgczfbjs/zgczfbjs46.html

Zhang, Hongjie. "The Dilemma of the Ancient Dynasties" (in Chinese). *Tianjin Daily*. December 30, 2016.

———. "The Institutional Corruption in the History of China" (in Chinese). September 22, 2015. www.hexun.com

Zhang, Jun, Qi Zhang, and Zhikuo Liu. "The Political Logic of Partial Reform of China's State-Owned Enterprises." *Asian Survey*. Vol. 57, No. 3, June 2017.

Zhang, Liping, and Zhumei Chen. "The Causes of Corruption and the Remedy" (in Chinese). *Liaoning Economy* No. 2, 1995.

Zhang, Ming. "The Moral Dilemma of Governing and the Approaches to Breakthrough: An Analysis of the Three-Anti and Five-Anti Campaign" (in Chinese). *Twenty-First Century* No. 12, 2005.

Zhang, Ri. "The Surprising 'Kong Shou Dao': An Analysis of the Behavior of Rent-Seeking in China in the 1990s" (in Chinese). *Ban Yue Tan* No. 5, 1996.

Zhang, Shidong. "Insider Trading, Fake Disclosures Targeted in Crack-down by China's Stock Market Regulator." *South China Morning Post*. June 6, 2019. https://sg.news.yahoo.com/insider-trading-fake-disclosures-targeted-083922381.html

Zhang, Xule. "The Private Finance Industry in Shanghai and the Three and Five Anti Campaign" (in Chinese). *Study on the Contemporary History of China* No. 6, 2005.

"The Zhanjiang Smuggling and Bribery Case" (in Chinese). *baidu baike*. https://baike.baidu.com/item/%229898%22湛江特大走私受贿案/15117704?fr=aladdin

Zhao, Chu. "Administrative Approval Related Corruption is an Open Secret." *fa zhi zao bao*. July 9, 2006. http://news.sina.com.cn/c/2006-07-09/133710373633.shtml

Zhao, Danyang. "The Eight Major Causes of Graft and Corruption in the Society of Ancient China" (in Chinese). www.360doc.com (accessed August 7, 2016).

Zhao, Dongling, and Wuyue Zhang. "Thinking About the Construction of an Honest Administration in Ancient China" (in Chinese). *Journal of Xinyang Teachers College* (Philos. & Soc. Sci. Edit.) Vol. 14, No. 2, June 1994.

Zheng, Qian. "The Process of the Socialist Education Movement and An Institutional Analysis of the Campaign" (in Chinese). *The CCP History Study* No. 2, 2006.

Zheng, William. "Chinese Ex-Official Admits to Making US$23 Million from Insider Trading." *South China Morning Post*. December 21, 2018. https://ph.news.yahoo.com/chinese-ex-official-admits-making-123112657.html

———. "Shanghai's Jailed Top Prosecutor 'Implicates 100 Other Officials in Corruption Case." *South China Morning Post*. November 12, 2018. https://www.scmp.com/news/china/politics/article/2172762/shanghais-jailed-top-prosecutor-implicates-100-other-officials

———. "Shenzhen Official Kicked Out of Chinese Communist Party for 'Trading Power for Personal Gain and Sex'." *South China Morning Post*. April 10, 2019. https://www.scmp.com/news/china/politics/article/3005619/shenzhen-official-kicked-out-party-trading-power-personal-gain

———. "China's Top Law Enforcement Body Unveils Campaign to Purge 'Corrupt Elements'." *South China Morning Post*. July 10, 2020. https://www.scmp.com/news/china/politics/article/3092559/chinas-top-law-enforcement-body-unveils-campaign-purge-corrupt

"Zheng Xiaoyu" (in Chinese). *baidu baike*. https://baike.baidu.com/item/郑筱萸/10968065

Zheng, Yongnian. *The Three Stages of China's Reform*. East Press, 2012.

Zhong, Jianying. "A Review of the Socialist Education Movement in Rural Fujian" (in Chinese). December 6, 2010. www.lunwentianxia.com.

Zhou, Anbo. "The Ideological Sources of the Phenomenon of Corruption: An Analysis of Privilege Thinking" (in Chinese). *Jiangsu Social Science* No. 2, 1995.

"Zhoukou No. 1 Veterinary Medicine Plant Manufacturing and Marketing Fake Drugs" (in Chinese). *Procuratorate Daily.* September 2, 2008. http://www.jcrb.com/zhuanti/fzzt/nwya/rwwz/200809/t20080902_68803.html

Zhou, Qunfeng. "The Abnormal Career Advancement of the 'Czar of Vaccine'" (in Chinese). *China News Weekly.* September 13, 2018. https://baijiahao.baidu.com/s?id=1611453454100451261&wfr=spider&for=pc

Zhou, X. "The High Expenditures of China's Leaders." *Renminbao.com.* November 6, 2011. http://www.renminbao.com/rmb/articles/2011/11/6/55579p.html

Zhou Xin. "Huarong Corruption Scandal Underscores Governance Failures at China's Financial Institutions." *South China Morning Post.* August 17, 2020.

Zhu, Jiangnan. *Officials' Promotion Likelihood and Regional Variation of Corruption in China.* a Ph.D dissertation, Northwestern University. December 2008.

Zhuang, Pinghui, Wendy Wu and Emily Tsang. "Vaccine Scandal – China Detains 37 Suspects as Senior Officials Admit to Problems in Drug System." *South China Morning Post.* March 23, 2016. https://www.scmp.com/news/china/society/article/1929384/vaccine-scandal-china-detains-37-suspects-senior-official-admits

Zhuang Pinghui, "China's vaccination System has Been Tainted by Corruption, Weak Regulations and Staff Shortages." *South China Morning Post.* July 24, 2018. https://www.scmp.com/news/china/policies-politics/article/2156525/three-cancers-attacking-health-chinas-vaccine-system

Index

F. C. Sun, *An Ineluctable Political Destiny*,
https://doi.org/10.1007/978-981-99-3146-0

FSC
www.fsc.org
MIX
Papier | Fördert gute Waldnutzung
FSC® C083411

Kolibri 360 GmbH
Ferdinand-Jühlke-Straße 7
99095 Erfurt, Deutschland
produktsicherheit@kolibri360.de